In *Everything's Good,* Toni Chapman shares a treasure trove of brand-new recipes (and some viral favorites) with tips and tricks to set you up for success. Toni's dishes are soulful and cozy. Several recipes have been passed down from her family, like The Perfect Pollo Guisado (Puerto Rican chicken stew); some are inspired by the Southern staples she grew up eating, such as Honey Butter Corn Bread; and others are Toni's takes on the classics, like Creamy White Chicken Enchiladas with Salsa Verde.

For Toni, food is a source of joy and solace. *Everything's Good* is a reminder that no matter what life throws your way, you can find comfort in preparing and sharing a delicious meal.

"I absolutely love Toni Chapman, and I have no doubt her new cookbook, *Everything's Good*, will become a staple in your kitchen. These are the kind of recipes you'll find yourself coming back to day after day."

—Gina Homolka, *New York Times* bestselling author and founder of Skinnytaste

"*Everything's Good* is a joyful, flavor-packed love letter to comfort food, heritage, and hustle. With every page, Toni invites you into her world—vibrant, playful, and unapologetically delicious. The recipes are bold, craveable, and easy to love, with photos that make you want to lick the page and a design that feels like you're walking into the best party buffet ever—everything looks so good that you won't know where to begin. (Spoiler: Start with the Pizza Supreme Dip. It literally made me drool.)"

—Rick Martínez, chef and author of *Mi Cocina* and *Salsa Daddy*

"Toni Chapman's *Everything's Good* is exactly the kind of cookbook that refuses to just sit pretty on a shelf—it's meant to live and breathe in your kitchen, with worn pages splashed with sauce. It's packed with soulful family faves like her pernil and the drive-thru hits you crave (but made a thousand times better at home). This isn't just another collection of recipes. It's healing and pure joy you can taste. Trust ya girl—when Toni says everything's good, she means it and delivers."

—Jocelyn Delk Adams, television host and award-winning cookbook author of *Grandbaby Cakes* and *Everyday Grand*

"*Everything's Good* is that cozy classic you'll keep coming back to—today, tomorrow, forever. Toni Chapman brings you recipes that hit home every time: full of flavor, love, and that extra touch that makes people stop and say, 'Who made this?' This book isn't just for the kitchen—it's your go-to move when you want to show out and show love. Trust me. You're gonna want this one on your shelf."

—JJ Johnson, chef and restaurateur

"Toni's recipes are famous for being drippy, gooey, cheesy, and awe-inducing. The vibrant and beautiful pages of *Everything's Good* transport you to her kitchen and allow you to re-create delicious dishes like The Perfect Pollo Guisado, Rum and Cola Wings, and more, making it a must-buy!"

—Adrianna Adarme, author of *The Year of Cozy* and founder of *A Cozy Kitchen*

Everything's Good

Everything's Good

**Cozy Classics
You'll Cook
Always & Forever**

Clarkson Potter
New York

Toni Chapman

Photographs by Brittany Conerly

For Dad, the real MVP.

We did it, Dad. Can you believe it? Your sacrifices, your love, and your unwavering belief in me built the foundation for all of this. Because of you, I get to tell our family's stories, share our recipes, and carry our legacy forward. Everything good I am, and everything that's good in this book, started with you.

Your daughter

Introduction 9
Food for Everyone 10
The OG Girl Dad 12
My Path to Food 13

It's All About the Recipes 15
How to Become a Better Cook 16
Flavor Blending 16
The Six Elements of Great Cooking 17

1
Start with Something Special

Honey Butter Hawaiian Rolls	24
Pizza Supreme Dip	27
Hot Honey Fried Shrimp	28
Mussels with Champagne Sauce	31
Crunchy Garlic Toast	31
Juicy Red Sofrito Chicken Empanadas	32
Cheesy Chicken Alfredo Bread	35
Buffalo Chicken Taquitos	36
Spinach, Crab, and Artichoke–Stuffed Shrimp	39
Creamy Roasted Garlic Dip with Italian Sausage	40
Rum and Cola Wings	43
Cajun Crab-Stuffed Oysters	44
Chopped Cheese Sliders	47

2
Soulful Soups

Spicy Lasagna Soup	51
Abuelita's Chicken Soup (aka Kick the Cold Soup)	52
The Very Best Pozole Verde	55
Creamy Chicken and Dumplings	56
Marry Me Chicken Soup	59
Island Pasta Soup	60
The Ultimate Loaded Baked Potato Soup	63
Parmesan Garlic Breadsticks	64

5
What's for Dinner?

Cheesy Chipotle Chicken Quesadillas	129
Seared Salmon with Creamy Lemon Orzo and Spinach	130
The Perfect Pollo Guisado	133
Classic Chili	134
Puerto Rican Pepper Steak	137
Creamy Shrimp and Crab–Stuffed Shells	138
How to Make Rice 101	140
Garlic Parmesan Chicken Thighs and Potatoes	143
Cola-Braised Short Ribs	144
Habichuelas Guisadas (Puerto Rican Beans)	147
Tuscan Chicken Meatballs with Sun-Dried Tomatoes and Spinach	148
GAH DAMN Gumbo	151
Cajun-Spiced Potatoes	154
Secret Ingredient Chicken Parmesan	157
Hooked-Up Hamburger Pasta	158
One-Pot Dirty Rice with Chicken and Sausage	161
Blackened Fish and Grits	162

6
Family Style

Pernil (Puerto Rican Roast Pork)	166
Coquito	169
Arroz con Gandules	170
Pastelón	175
Cajun Butter Turkey	177
Creamy Mac and Cheese	181
Honey Butter Corn Bread	182
Collard Greens with Smoked Turkey	185
Candied Yams	186
Mofongo con Camarones de Ajillo	190
Real-Deal Fried Chicken	195
New Year's Black-Eyed Peas	197
Southern-Fried Cabbage with Brussels	198
Louisiana Red Beans and Rice	201
Sausage and Gravy Biscuit Bake	202
Down South–Style Fried Fish	205

Equipment and Tools 18
Cooking Glossary 19
Six Steps to Joy in the Kitchen 20

Acknowledgments 251
Index 252

3

On a Lighter Note (Bright and Easy)

Goes-with-Everything Salad	68
Mango House Margarita	71
Cajun Lemon Pepper Corn	72
Shrimp and Mango Ceviche	75
Good Vibes Rum Punch	76
Lemon-Butter Cod	79
Caribbean-Style Jerk Chicken	80
Papi's Seafood Pasta Salad	83
Plantain and Cream Cheese–Stuffed Pork Chops with Guava Sauce	84
Crunchy Beef Tacos	87
Pico de Gallo	88
Sip Slow Sangria	91

4

Takeout Classics

Pork Fried Rice	95
Shrimp Egg Rolls	96
General Tso's Chicken	99
New York City–Style Chicken Wings (aka Chinese Takeout Wings)	102
Copycat Panda Chow Mein	105
Char Siu Pork	106
Halal Cart Chicken and Rice Bowls with Tzatziki Sauce	109
Jamaican-Style Oxtail with Rice and Peas	110
Garlic Parmesan French Fries	115
Straight-Fire Smash Burgers	116
Drive-Thru Chicken Nuggets	119
Freezer Door Breakfast Sandos	120
Indian-Style Chicken	123
Creamy White Chicken Enchiladas with Salsa Verde	124

7

Life Is Sweet

Strawberries and Cream Croissant Bake	208
Classic New York–Style Cheesecake	211
Brioche Bread Pudding	212
Brown Butter Chocolate Chip Cookies	215
Biscuit-Top Peach Cobbler	216
Cookies and Cream Tres Leches	219
The Very Best Flan	220
Crème Brûlée Sweet Potato Pie	223
Backyard Banana Pudding	224
Key Lime Pie	227
On-Point Pancakes with Brown Butter Syrup	228

8

Sauces

The Perfect Sauce for Everything	232
Abuela's Green Sofrito	233
My Famous Red Sofrito	236
Salsa Verde	238
Jerk Marinade	239
The Real MVP Ranch Dressing	241
Peruvian Ají Verde Sauce	242
Traditional Chimichurri Sauce	244
Easy Peasy Pesto	245
All-in-One Teriyaki Sauce	247
Bold and Smoky BBQ Sauce	248
Duck Sauce	249

Introduction

♥

This cookbook is meant for you. Although I may not know your background or your story, if you have this book in your hands, I know that you share my passion for incredible, memorable comfort food.

The food in this book is all about the dishes that feel nostalgic, homey, and familiar, like you're cozied up in a warm sweater. What you crave during Sunday Scaries, Thirsty Thursdays, and everything in between. The favorites that both you and I grew up loving. These recipes are worthy of your get-togethers with your friends and family with really high standards who will never let you forget showing up with dry mac and cheese, so you *must* come correct. You will be able to walk into any party with your head held high—whether you're carrying my stunning Spinach, Crab, and Artichoke–Stuffed Shrimp (page 39), Cheesy Chicken Alfredo Bread (page 35), Brioche Bread Pudding (page 212), or any number of other dishes—excited for everyone to devour the masterpiece you made because *everything's good*.

These recipes will set you up for a lifetime of comforting, impressing, partying, and finding solace during tough times. As you nail one after the other, you'll see why the title of this book is about so much more than just incredible food. It's also about how a joyful attitude can empower you through any challenge thrown your way—in and out of the kitchen. In these pages, you'll find the pollo guisado that I grew up with, the creamy shrimp and crab–stuffed shells that my guests raved about for weeks, and the chicken and dumplings that always feels like a big warm hug.

Before I became @themoodyfoody on social media, with a five-million-plus fan base who love my viral recipes, I was just the girl next door facing a lot of challenges on this journey called life. Raised by a single father in the inner city, I experienced a lot of adversity. But no matter what, I always remained positive. During tough times when I couldn't afford gifts for people I loved, I turned to cooking, finding that a bottle of homemade Coquito (page 169) or a plate of fried chicken was worth more than any present. When my career in finance came to an abrupt end, I started a small business serving beautifully prepared lunches from my home, which eventually grew into a successful family business. And in my career as a recipe developer, I always focused on making everything better, which sometimes meant turning mistakes into masterpieces or tweaking a recipe thirty times before it was worthy enough to share with my fans. I always did my best—in the kitchen and in life.

In my many moments of pain but also happiness, food has always brought me healing, peace, and purpose, and I wrote this cookbook to help you experience the same.

Food for Everyone

I could never imagine being boxed into making just one kind of cuisine, so in this cookbook, you will see food from all over the globe. I like a little bit of everything because I grew up around a little bit of everything. My cooking style mixes my Afro-Latina heritage with so many other influences: I Americanize Puerto Rican dishes; I add adobo to mac and cheese, and Sazón to fried chicken. This all comes naturally to me because I grew up in one of the world's great multicultural communities, Jersey City, New Jersey, right across the Hudson River from Manhattan.

One of my first memories of food is bright green sofrito, the aromatic base of the most delicious dishes that my dad's mom, my abuelita Edie, made. You could smell its heavenly aroma of herbs and garlic through the plastic containers that Edie, a home medical aide, brought to her patients. She was born in a small Puerto Rican town, the second-oldest of eighteen children. Edie was descended from the indigenous Taíno people and married four times, all to African American men. She often told us to never forget we were descendants of indigenous people and slaves. "You remember who you are," she would say.

For the first part of my childhood, it was Edie, my dad, and me. I was born when my dad was nineteen, and my mom fell victim to addiction soon after that. While we didn't have much money, we ate very well. When I came home from school, Edie would serve me a "snack"—a pork chop, rice, and a lot of beans. A few hours later, she would serve me more rice and beans, which I ate alone in my room.

While my family would sometimes gather for extended meals for holidays and special occasions, I ate most everyday dinners by myself. That is, unless I went to my friend Amy's house, where no one ate dinner until everyone was home. We would wait patiently for her dad and brother to come home from work, then we would all sit on pillows on the floor and feast on her mom's Senegalese whole fish and rice, and more sauces than I had ever seen at one meal. We ate with our hands, and it was there that I saw how food could be about connecting with people, not just about eating.

My biological half-sister, Amber, lived right down the street. After our mother left our lives, Amber was adopted by a Filipino family who could not have loved her more. And I loved diving into her family's meals. Filipino staples like lumpia were a favorite, but when they knew I was coming to visit, they would order Chinese takeout from the local hole-in-the-wall as a special treat, too. Those foods would become my lifelong cravings and to this day I still dream about egg foo young, egg rolls dunked in lots of duck sauce, and pork fried rice.

And then there was Shenice, who I am still very close with. Her family was from Trinidad, and going to her house taught me the meaning of splurge. They generously served me things my family could never have afforded and enjoyed the finer things. I owe the origins of my What's for Dinner? chapter to Shenice, who generously taught me that every meal—no matter how simple or cheap—should taste and look special.

The OG Girl Dad

My dad also played a huge part in shaping my worldview, culinary and otherwise. I would never have had the drive to write this book if my dad had not started talking to me about success when I was very young. We'd drive to Liberty State Park with a bag of sunflower seeds, walk around, and chat about life. We'd get ice cream at Crown Fried Chicken. He was always drilling into me the importance of trying my best, seeing to every little detail, knowing that I should never lose when I could win.

When I was seven, my dad had saved up enough for us to get our own place. He was able to move us out of Abuelita Edie's house and into our own apartment a few blocks away. And that was when the parties started.

My dad was never happier than when in front of a grill, flipping chicken wings and shrimp, surrounded by dozens of his closest friends. The Super Bowl. A big fight night. A fantasy football draft. He loved any excuse to celebrate. It wasn't unusual for me to wander out of my room on a Friday night and find our apartment crowded with a diverse group of friends of all ages—neighbors, co-workers, childhood friends, and often friends of theirs that we had never met before. They were from all over—Jamaican, Filipino, Chinese. My dad's friend brought Haitian djon djon, other friends made Dominican rice, while my aunt's Filipino boyfriend brought pancit noodles. It was a little bit of everything—and everything was good.

As a result, I constantly see so much beauty in the intersectionality of food and family. I learned so much from these people surrounding me, and from the purpose and meaning my dad found in these gatherings. Teaching people about new foods, as my dad had always done, would become my life's mission, too.

My Path to Food

In order to pay my way through college, I started working as a bank teller. When my bosses saw my people skills in action, they promoted me to a role that had me working directly with customers opening credit card accounts, and soon I was outperforming longtime employees. I got fantastic training in sales and relationships that help me to this day: I became a person who could finesse my way into any room, any opportunity. When used with integrity, to empower and educate people, this is one of the skills that I am the most proud of.

I decided to pour my pent-up creativity into the lunches I was packing for Mike, my boyfriend at the time. No sad sandwich or salad for him: I sent him in with neat packages of salmon, shrimp fried rice, or jerk chicken.

Once Mike started taking my lunches to work, he became a celebrity. Soon I was making lunch for a bunch of his co-workers, too, and posting pictures of everything online. Inevitably, my finance job ended, and I posted this on Twitter that night in 2017: "LOL, guys, I just got fired from my job. I've been making these lunches. Does anybody want to buy them so I don't end up broke and poor on the street?"

It was a joke. But when I woke up, my mouth dropped open: I had tens of thousands of retweets and inquiries. One of them was from the director Ava DuVernay's team. Ava posted my food on her Instagram, and suddenly I had more customers than I knew what to do with.

That very night, I put up a website and a logo, and Toni Cooks was born. We instantly had so much demand for our healthy, delicious prepared meals. All of the colorful, flavorful lunches that I once packed for a few guys are, to this day, being served to thousands every day—schoolkids and sports teams and corporate employees and even celebrities.

While I enjoyed being the head of my own company, the more smiles I saw on the faces of our customers, the more I realized my mission in life. It was in the kitchen, creating and teaching. I wanted to do more than just feed people; I wanted them to feel liberated and confident while feeding themselves. So I began focusing my attention on creating recipes and videos for my online platform—and I'm so glad I did.

It's All About the Recipes

I'll tell you a secret. When I first started developing all of the recipes that later went viral and made me famous, I was just messing around. But I channeled the drive from my dad and abuelita and my training to finesse my way into any room. I combined that with my a-little-bit-of-everything brain and my intense passion for the smallest details that can make or break a dish—details that other recipes often leave out. Maybe it's resting the meat for ten minutes before serving. Maybe it's freezing the chicken before tossing it into that stir-fry so that it can be sliced thin and still stay super moist. This book details a lot of these, not just in the instructions but also in the Little Detail, BIG Impact and Chef's Kiss tips. (*Do not ignore these instructions!* They may seem a little fussy, but I want to set you up for success.) And I am absolutely fearless about seeking out these little cooking tricks. You may find me shouting questions into the kitchen of my local Chinese restaurant, searching Reddit for the secrets behind a Cheesecake Factory pasta, or packing in every trick to make the most moist roast turkey. Every day, I'm working with my right-hand woman, recipe developer Tara Hall, cooking the same dishes over and over, to make the best food we can.

I know what it's like to have little time and little money and not want to waste either. My abuelita Edie would have one of her fits if I made you waste your time and effort! But more important, I know how nailing a dish can bring meaning to your life outside the kitchen.

For years, I have wondered how Edie made her arroz con gandules (rice with pigeon peas). It always came out right on the first try and became the centerpiece of my family gatherings. While it seems simple, so many things can go wrong: It can be too mushy, or too dry; there can be not enough flavor or too much salt. Now that we, the next generation, are in charge of a beloved dish for our families, it's a lot of pressure! And if your family is anything like mine, they will never let you forget that you screwed it up. I began hearing from more and more of my readers that we, the next generation, were now in charge of this monumental dish but that we had no idea how to cook it, and when we didn't get it right, it felt so shameful.

Well, I finally figured it out. I cooked this dish nearly three dozen times to make sure that when you turn to that page, you will soon be cooking just like my grandmother.

This book will help you discover so many other reasons to celebrate the good in your life, too: the mussels with garlic butter sauce that you can make with part of the bottle of bubbly you popped to celebrate a promotion; a big biscuits-and-gravy pan that you can easily throw together Christmas Day. And of course, my viral Cajun butter turkey that so many of you made for your own Thanksgiving. I want this cookbook to show you how the kitchen is truly a place where everything can be okay. Even if something doesn't come out exactly how you want it to. (Plus, not only have my recipes been thoroughly tested, they're also filled with enough butter and cheese that even if you mess up a step, it's still going to be good.)

Food is at the center of everything: family, community, empowerment. And empowering *you* to make the best food you possibly can has kept me going all of these years: It reminds me that no matter what, *everything's good*.

How to Become a Better Cook

People are constantly asking me: How did you learn to cook? It's the number one question I get. This section is the start of my answer to this question. A huge part of being a great home cook is nailing flavor, equipment, tools, and basic techniques. I've listed my most important lessons for you here. Use them to build out your skill set and make sure you're prepared in the kitchen, or as a reference when you're confused.

I hope that over time, you may find that people will start asking *you*: How did *you* learn to cook?

Building Flavor
Want to know what gives my food such a wow factor? I lay a foundation of flavor using aromatics, then build from there with spices and seasonings. Here's why my dishes are so flavorful and balanced.

The Foundation: Aromatics
You gotta have these first: They lay the groundwork upon which you can build everything else. While I can't live without the basics—onions, garlic, ginger, bell peppers—my favorite aromatics are fresh herbs. Parsley. Cilantro (and its feisty little cousin, culantro). Rosemary. Basil. I promise that you will never regret buying fresh herbs—they are an inexpensive way to boost your flavor. Toss any leftovers in a bag in the freezer and make stock later.

Keep Building
Spices will give you an essential layer of flavor. Cayenne, paprika, and chili powder add warm heat. Cinnamon, turmeric, and nutmeg give many of my dishes their toasty warmth. Oregano and thyme give herbal undertones. Sazón, adobo, and cumin lend that Latin edge. Allspice, ground ginger, and thyme give special Caribbean flavors.

Flavor Blending

1
Biscuit-Top Peach Cobbler (page 216)
= Salty + Sweet

2
Brioche Bread Pudding (page 212)
= Creamy + Sweet + Salty

3
Mofongo con Camarones de Ajillo (page 190)
= Salty + Creamy + Acidic

4
Indian-Style Chicken (page 123)
= Salty + Spicy + Creamy

5
The Very Best Pozole Verde (page 55)
= Salty + Creamy + Spicy + Acidic

The Six Elements of Great Cooking

Each dish has at least two of these elements, and many have more. These are the important ways in which my recipes will pack flavor, texture, and that depth that I know you're looking for. Including multiple elements is what will make your cooking flavorful and balanced. Let's explore.

1 Creamy
You know when you eat something and instantly feel safe, warm, and comforted? A creamy texture is often involved, and not just heavy cream: I create creamy textures with heavy cream plus butter, cream cheese, or Cheddar. There are so many ways to create that nostalgic feeling of warmth.

Craving creamy? Try Creamy Mac and Cheese (page 181), Cheesy Chicken Alfredo Bread (page 35), Hooked-Up Hamburger Pasta (page 158), or Seared Salmon with Creamy Lemon Orzo and Spinach (page 130).

2 Crunchy
Crunch adds texture and balance to a dish—it's the bite that wakes up your palate. In cooking, it's not just about flavor; it's about the experience, and crunch contrasts with softer elements, making each bite more dynamic.

Craving crunchy? Try Buffalo Chicken Taquitos (page 36), New York City–Style Chicken Wings (page 102), Brown Butter Chocolate Chip Cookies (page 215), or Secret Ingredient Chicken Parmesan (page 157).

3 Spicy/Heat
Having a kick is nice, especially in Caribbean and Latin cooking. I am definitely a little bit spicy in nature, and so is my food. My dishes don't approach spice too forcefully though: I like to add a nice undercurrent of heat. People's enjoyment of heat is all over the place. You can experiment with how much heat best suits your palate by adjusting the amount of hot peppers and red pepper flakes.

Craving spicy? Try The Very Best Pozole Verde (page 55), Jamaican-Style Oxtail with Rice and Peas (page 110), or Blackened Fish and Grits (page 162).

4 Salty
You gotta have seasoning. I salt 1 teaspoon at a time, which is generally enough to season a dish without oversalting it. I am definitely a kosher salt person and often think about how my abuelita Edie kept it in a little bowl by the stove. She taught me that it's always easy to add more salt, but it can be difficult to take it away. So when in doubt, add less. All of the recipes in this book were tested with Diamond Crystal kosher salt, though if Badia is available in your area, I highly recommend that brand as well.

Craving salty? Try New York City–Style Chicken Wings (page 102), Creamy Shrimp and Crab–Stuffed Shells (page 138), or Garlic Parmesan French Fries (page 115).

5 Sweet
I love sugar, all different types, and find that it's not only important for dessert but also to create balance in savory dishes. I use sugar or even burnt sugar in recipes like teriyaki sauce and sausage; it also adds a special dimension to savory stews and brings out the natural sweetness of tomatoes.

Craving sweets? Try Strawberries and Cream Croissant Bake (page 208), Brown Butter Chocolate Chip Cookies (page 215), or All-in-One Teriyaki Sauce (page 247).

6 Acidic
Acid is an important part of my cooking: It cuts richness, balances flavors, and livens up your meal. I love fresh lime juice in so many dishes, especially Caribbean and Latin foods, and I find that fresh orange juice adds a milder acid.

Craving acid? Try Abuelita's Chicken Soup (page 52), Cilantro-Lime Rice (page 140), Seared Salmon with Creamy Lemon Orzo and Spinach (page 130), or The Perfect Sauce for Everything (page 232).

Equipment and Tools

Baking dish (9 × 13-inch)—You can go cheap here! Target has great 9 × 13-inch baking dishes for $12 to $15. Just make sure it's broilerproof. My favorite is ceramic, and it makes a stunning way to present mac and cheese and bread pudding right from the oven to the table.

Box grater—We will be grating a lot of cheese. A LOT. Always hand-grate cheese. Never buy that preshredded stuff, because not only is it more expensive, it contains additives that prevent the cheese from melting well.

Caldero—This is a traditional cooking pot that is mandatory for Caribbean and Hispanic cooking, but so useful for everything beyond, too. It allows the heat to circulate within the pot, so the food comes out really moist. If I used anything else to cook a pollo guisado, my abuelita would not be pleased.

Cast-iron skillet (12- or 13-inch)—Yeah, a big one, just because this best-in-class skillet is so versatile: You can fry, sear, or bake in it, making it perfect for everything from pot pies to corn bread and fried chicken.

Chef's knife—The best, safest way to improve your cooking is to use a really good, sharp, versatile knife, like a chef's knife. You do not want to butcher your beautiful vegetables: You want to get the nicest, most symmetrical cuts possible. You are going to be cutting *everything*, and you do not want to cut yourself in the process. It's an investment in being a better home cook.
 My absolute favorite knife is the Hedley & Bennett 8-inch chef's knife, which retails for a very reasonable $115. Whatever brand you choose, make sure you keep it nice and sharp.

Cutting board (wooden)—Plastic cutting boards are no good: They slip all over the place, they're not durable, and they don't protect your knives nearly as well as wood. A proper wooden cutting board will be another one of those beautiful investments that will make you feel like a serious home cook.

Dutch oven (5-quart)—The absolute best investment you can make in your cooking, and crucial for so many of these recipes. You can fry in it, bake in it, braise in it, stew in it. I'm a Staub Dutch oven girl: Not only do I love their nonstick cast-iron pots, but I've also worked with the brand, and I admire their work with communities of color. You can also find inexpensive versions of Dutch ovens at T.J. Maxx (my favorite place to find bargains on cooking equipment) and Amazon.

Fine-mesh sieve—Indispensable for rinsing rice and sprinkling powdered sugar over desserts.

Pilón (small, wooden)—This is a type of mortar and pestle that I recommend over all others for crushing and mashing ingredients. It's crucial that it be wood, which is super strong.

Sheet pan (13 × 18-inch) and wire rack—Also known as a "half-sheet pan," this is the perfect large size for home ovens. A wire rack that fits on top is crucial: It can be used to cool everything from cookies to fried chicken.

Spider strainer—We do a lot of frying in this cookbook, and this wire skimmer/strainer is the fastest and neatest way to transfer food in and out of hot oil. It's something that my family personally never used much, but I find it makes everything much easier. A 5-inch size is the most versatile.

Spoons (wooden)—The best protection for your beautiful pots and pans. We need to treat those investments well, and avoid any chips or scratches on those babies. Using a wooden spoon to stir will help you with that!

Thermometers (yes, more than one)—In my world, you need both an instant-read thermometer (for testing meat) and a candy/deep-fry thermometer (for ensuring that frying oil is at the right temperature).

Cooking Glossary

These are the most important, most-used terms and techniques in my kitchen.

Al dente
An important term for cooking noodles and rice, *al dente* means "to the tooth." Often in the first step of a recipe you want to undercook pasta or rice just a bit, because you will be continuing the cooking process in the next step and don't want them to overcook.

Broil
When you want to get a gorgeous golden glow with a crisp top, you use the broiler setting in the oven, which blasts the food with high heat (often up to 500°F).

Deglaze
This is what you do after you've browned something in a pot or pan and then add some kind of liquid (like broth or wine) and scrape up all of that wonderful flavor off the bottom. I do this a ton, especially in rice, stews, and gumbo. Deglazing is essential to building flavor from the ground up.

Fry (deep and shallow)
When you deep-fry, it's a heavy fry: Whatever you're frying is fully submerged in oil, usually 4 to 6 cups of oil in a deep pot. When you shallow-fry, you use about 1 inch of oil to get some color and crunch.

Marinate
Soaking meat and other ingredients in seasoned liquid allows the flavor to seep in. I mostly do this in the refrigerator, but sometimes you just need 15 minutes on the countertop to build potent flavor.

Reduce
Reducing a sauce or soup means that you cook it out a little, evaporating some of the water, which allows the ingredients to meld together and intensify in flavor. This is particularly important to my cooking, because I include so much alcohol. For example, reducing the sauce for my Seared Salmon with Creamy Lemon Orzo and Spinach (page 130) cooks out the bitterness of the white wine while allowing the acidity of the lemon to come through.

Roux
This is a classic, centuries-old technique for thickening a stew, soup, or sauce. It involves stirring flour into fat and cooking it. It gives the dish so much depth, whether it's a blonde roux or a dark roux. While combining flour and fat may sound simple, so many things can go wrong. Many people burn their roux or don't properly incorporate it, resulting in floury-tasting food. It's important to start over low heat. You don't have to worry about the measurements; my recipes have those covered. Relax and focus on taking your time.

Sauté
This is cooking in just a bit of oil or fat, without liquid, over medium-low to medium-high heat, and stirring the ingredients most of the time. We often do this with vegetables or small pieces of meat to release their flavors.

Sear
Cooking something on high heat, without moving it, for a short period of time, is known as searing. It creates more flavor, color, and texture all at once.

Simmer
Simmering, or cooking a liquid, such as soup, over low heat, allows the flavors to blend together beautifully.

Six Steps to Joy in the Kitchen

Follow the Recipe

I never include any details that aren't absolutely crucial to making a dish you will love. I never put anything into a recipe that doesn't matter. I use different ingredients to get the texture and flavor I know you want in a recipe. I use different techniques—some easy, some more involved—because they lead to the best result possible. We are not trying to be good. We are trying to be great!

Buy the Best You Can Afford

This doesn't mean that you have to spend a lot. It just means that you should spend as much as you can on high-quality ingredients, which will pay off big time in your finished dish. This may mean you spend a few more dollars to get a higher-quality cheese or butter. Or maybe you upgrade to seafood or steak whenever you have the funds to do so.

In general, most of the food in this cookbook is budget-friendly, and I am very mindful of keeping costs as low as possible. Some recipes include possible substitutions, too.

Presentation Matters

Take a few seconds to make your dish look beautiful. Sliced fruit, a sprinkle of powdered sugar, a sprig of mint—all of these details transform a meal into a memory. Guests will be snapping photos for social or just for personal memories, and you want that "ooh and aah" reaction from the get. Including fresh garnishes, colorful platters, and aromatics takes things to the next level, and you'll soon earn the title "host of the year."

Take Your Time

In a world where everyone is always rushing, I want to get all of you back in the kitchen again. I grew up in a very erratic environment, and taking my time not only improved my cooking, it slowed down everything else in my life, too. It was like therapy, meditation, and alchemy all in one: Even when life was going fast, I could use cooking to relax, shut down the nonstop thinking running through my brain, and just focus on making my dish the best it could be.

So yes, you should braise the meat for hours. Yes, you should thaw the turkey the way I instruct! Yes, simmering that stew for as long as I call for will not only result in incredible flavor, it will also send a wonderful aroma throughout your house. Allow time to do all of this and it will make all the difference.

Respect Tradition

Many of my cooking techniques go back generations, and I pay them proper respect here. Why do my black-eyed peas use ham hock AND bacon AND turkey? Because the combination adds flavor and smoke and heat. And this is not something I invented. In our history, enslaved Black and Brown people were often given the scraps of the pig, which they then used to create classic dishes.

These techniques have lasted as long as they have for a reason!

Remember, Everything's Good

Take it easy! Cooking is supposed to be fun. One time, I ran a cooking hotline on Thanksgiving and had to spend a lot of time calming people down. People were crying, people were cursing their husbands. I always just told them the one thing I love most about cooking: You can finesse your way out of anything. Some of my best recipes come from a time that I screwed something up or forgot to buy an ingredient. If I can turn burned cookies into a viral ice cream topping, you can finesse your way out of anything, too. Remember: Food is a way for us to get to where we should be, which is at the table with our family. The fact that you've tried and put your best effort into it is really all that matters.

1
Start with Something Special

Growing up, my dad was the glue that kept everyone together. He loved to host, be it a barbecue, fight night, or a birthday party, and it always seemed like we were having people over. From a young age, I watched my dad invest in these gatherings, even when money was tight, because he took pride in being the host of his family and his friend group. So our house became the place where everyone came to drink, party, and, most important, eat.

I learned lots of important tips from him, like not cutting corners when it comes to quality—always buy the best ingredients you can afford. Dad would also always say, "Stay ready so you don't have to get ready," because prep was very important. I remember staying up with him into the wee hours of the morning pre-party, marinating the wings that would go on the grill, cleaning out and prepping coolers to keep drinks, and getting his side dishes together. He took so much pride in feeding others and wanted everyone to have fun—including himself!

As an adult, I naturally followed in his footsteps and became the self-proclaimed hostess with the mostest. My love of entertaining blossomed in college, and it was *my* house that became the spot for pre-gaming and after-hours. I cooked for my classmates while we laughed and bonded.

There's something sacred about cooking for others—be it for potlucks, parties, or just bringing a dish to help out someone else's party. And when someone makes one of *my* recipes to share with their closest people? That gives me so much purpose and fills me with excitement!

In this chapter, I celebrate the food that kicked off the party—the recipes that often serve as the first bite for all your special moments in life. I love making the Pizza Supreme Dip (page 27), Rum and Cola Wings (page 43), and Chopped Cheese Sliders (page 47) on game day (to watch the Yankees win, of course!). The Spinach, Crab, and Artichoke–Stuffed Shrimp (page 39) is ideal for a romantic date night because it's sexy and memorable. When it's girls' night and we're clinking wine glasses all night long and laughing until we cry, I make my Cajun Crab-Stuffed Oysters (page 44), one of my favorites. And for holidays and big gatherings, I'd honestly make every recipe in this chapter because there's no such thing as doing too much—I promise! Regardless of the moment, big or small, you can rely on these recipes to start it off special.

Honey Butter Hawaiian Rolls

Makes **15** Rolls

Making bread at home isn't as tough as you might think, and these copycat King's Hawaiian rolls are the real deal. They get topped with a honey butter and flaky salt, but the pillowy, fluffy texture is what will make the prep time worth it. I love using these for sliders, or lathering them up with a ton of butter as a savory snack, or using the leftovers for my famous Brioche Bread Pudding (page 212). This recipe guarantees the fluffiest, sweetest, warmest, most delicious buns you'll ever taste.

Hawaiian Slider Rolls

¾ cup whole milk
1 packet instant yeast (2¼ teaspoons)
½ cup sugar
4¼ cups all-purpose flour, plus more for kneading
2 tablespoons freshly squeezed lemon juice
2 tablespoons honey
1 teaspoon kosher salt
3 large eggs, at room temperature
2 sticks (8 ounces) unsalted butter, at room temperature, cut into 1-tablespoon slices
Softened butter, for the baking dish
Egg wash: 1 large egg (at room temperature) beaten with 1 tablespoon heavy cream or whole milk

Honey Butter

4 tablespoons (½ stick/2 ounces) unsalted butter
2 tablespoons honey
Flaky sea salt

Make the Hawaiian slider rolls: In a heatproof liquid measuring cup, microwave the milk until warm but not hot; it should be 110° to 115°F. Add the yeast and a pinch of the sugar and stir to combine. Set aside for 5 minutes to allow the yeast to bloom.

In a large bowl, combine the flour, the remaining sugar, the lemon juice, honey, and kosher salt. Mix until combined, then add the milk mixture. Stir for 5 to 10 minutes, until the dough comes together and is relatively smooth.

Stir in the eggs, one at a time, waiting until each is fully incorporated before adding the next. Stir in the butter, 1 to 2 tablespoons at a time, once again waiting until each bit is fully incorporated before adding the next. Lightly flour your hands and knead the dough for about 10 minutes, or until it's glossy and smooth. Tilt the dough onto the counter and shape into a neat ball. Return the ball to the bowl, cover with plastic wrap or a damp cloth, and set in a warm place to proof until it's about doubled in size, 1½ to 2 hours.

Butter a 9 × 13-inch baking dish. Once proofed, cut the dough into 15 equal portions (if possible, weigh the portions: they should be about 78g each). Roll each portion into a ball and place evenly spaced in the prepared baking dish.

Allow the dough balls to proof again, uncovered, until roughly doubled in size and touching each other, 1 to 1½ hours. (An instant-read thermometer poked into the center of the middle roll should read between 70° and 75°F.)

With 20 minutes left in the proofing time, preheat the oven to 350°F.

Meanwhile, make the egg wash, whisking until smooth.

When the dough is ready to bake, brush each dough ball with the egg wash.

Transfer to the oven and bake for 25 to 30 minutes, until puffed up, deeply browned, and cooked through, and an instant-read thermometer poked into the center of the middle roll reads 190°F.

Meanwhile, make the honey butter: In a small saucepan, combine the butter, honey, and a pinch of kosher salt and heat over medium-low heat until the butter is melted, 2 to 3 minutes.

When the rolls are done, immediately brush them generously with the honey butter and sprinkle with more flaky salt. Let sit in the pan for 15 minutes, then enjoy warm!

Everything's Good

Pizza Supreme Dip

Serves 6

This pizza dip is all the best parts of a loaded slice turned into a dip—and let me tell you, it's a whole vibe. Layers of marinara, creamy cream cheese, spicy Italian sausage, and plenty of pepperoni, all topped with a ridiculous amount of melted mozzarella. It's cheesy, it's meaty, and it's straight-up addictive.

This is the dip you bring to the party knowing it's gonna be the first thing gone. Serve it with garlic toast, chips, bread, or honestly just let people scoop it with their hands—it's that good. A little spicy, extra cheesy, and impossible to stop eating, this dip is the real MVP of any spread.

6 slices bacon, chopped
1 pound sweet Italian sausage, casings removed (or hot Italian sausage for a spicy kick)
16 ounces cream cheese (2 blocks), at room temperature
½ cup sour cream
1 teaspoon garlic powder
1 teaspoon chopped fresh basil
⅔ cup marinara sauce
8 ounces mozzarella cheese, freshly shredded (2 cups)
1 cup pepperoni slices
Crunchy Garlic Toast (page 31), for serving

Preheat the oven to 375°F.

Cook the bacon: Line a plate with paper towels. In a large skillet, sauté the bacon over medium heat, stirring occasionally, for about 5 minutes, or until crispy. Use a slotted spoon to remove the bacon from the fat and transfer to the paper towels. Drain the fat from the pan.

Cook the sausage: In the same skillet, cook the sausage over medium heat for 8 to 10 minutes, breaking it apart with a spoon and stirring occasionally, until browned and cooked through. Use a slotted spoon to remove the sausage from the fat and transfer to the plate with the bacon.

Assemble the dip: In a large bowl, mix together the cream cheese, sour cream, garlic powder, and basil until fully combined. Transfer to a 9-inch pie dish and use a spatula to spread the mixture over the bottom of the dish. Evenly spread the marinara sauce on top, then sprinkle with the mozzarella. Layer the bacon, sausage, and pepperoni on top.

Bake the dip: Transfer to the oven and bake for about 20 minutes, or until the dip is warm and the cheese is bubbling.

Serve warm with garlic toast.

Hot Honey Fried Shrimp

Serves 6

Anything fried, sweet, and crunchy is my *thing*. This fried shrimp tossed in a homemade hot honey sauce comes together fast, is super crowd-friendly, and honestly, pretty easy to make. You can really taste the difference when you make your own hot honey sauce—it makes the whole dish brighter and more flavorful. Believe me, you'll be licking the sauce off your fingers and going back for seconds... maybe even thirds. If deep-frying is intimidating to you, shrimp are a great way to start because they don't need as much oil (cheaper!) and they cook quickly (done!). Once you get the hang of it, you'll be making this all the time and not just for a starter—to make it a meal, it goes perfectly with Cilantro-Lime Rice (page 140).

Hot Honey Sauce

2 tablespoons (1 ounce) unsalted butter
½ cup packed dark brown sugar
2 tablespoons ground ginger
4 garlic cloves, minced (about 4 teaspoons)
1 teaspoon smoked paprika
½ cup hot sauce (I use Crystal)
½ cup honey

Fried Shrimp

Vegetable oil, for deep-frying
2 cups buttermilk
1 large egg
3 teaspoons smoked paprika
1 cup all-purpose flour
1 cup finely ground yellow cornmeal
¼ cup cornstarch
2 tablespoons kosher salt
1 teaspoon ground ginger
2 pounds shrimp (21/25 count), peeled and deveined, tails on

Lemon wedges, for serving

Make the hot honey sauce: In a small saucepan, melt the butter over medium heat. Add the brown sugar, ginger, garlic, and smoked paprika. Slowly pour in the hot sauce, then add the honey and whisk until fully combined. Reduce the heat to low and simmer for 2 to 3 minutes, until the sauce is thickened, like honey. Set aside to cool slightly.

Fry the shrimp: Pour enough oil into a large, deep pot or Dutch oven to come up halfway. Clip a candy/deep-fry thermometer to the side and heat the oil over medium-high until it reaches 350°F.

In a medium bowl, whisk together the buttermilk, egg, and 1 teaspoon of the smoked paprika until smooth and well combined. In another medium bowl, whisk together the flour, cornmeal, cornstarch, salt, ginger, and remaining 2 teaspoons smoked paprika.

Dredge the shrimp, one at a time, in the buttermilk mixture, then in the flour mixture, dusting off any excess flour.

Working in batches to avoid overcrowding, use tongs to carefully drop the shrimp into the oil and fry for 4 to 6 minutes, until golden brown. Use a slotted spoon or tongs to remove the shrimp and transfer them to a large bowl.

Glaze the shrimp: Pour the cooled hot honey sauce onto the hot shrimp and toss to evenly coat (you can also save some extra for dipping on the side). Serve hot with lemon wedges for squeezing.

Chef's Kiss: Don't we love a dish that's versatile? These shrimp are so good in tacos with shredded green cabbage, or over a salad when I'm trying to get my greens.

Mussels with Champagne Sauce

Serves 6

I've always loved flavorful mussels—restaurant-style, where the sauce is just as important, if not more, than the mussels themselves. You know, the kind where you're soaking up all that juice with some crusty bread? But honestly, finding places that do them right has become a struggle, which is why I started making them at home. And let me tell you, mussels aren't intimidating at all. The key? Get them cleaned at the store (saves time), toss any that are open before cooking, and make sure they don't overcook—easy tips, right? If you follow these and nail this bomb sauce (I know you got this), you'll be making these mussels on repeat. Trust me, once you've had them like this, there's no going back!

8 tablespoons (1 stick/4 ounces) unsalted butter
1 tablespoon extra-virgin olive oil
3 tablespoons finely chopped shallot
6 garlic cloves, minced (about 2 tablespoons)
1 tablespoon Better Than Bouillon chicken base
½ cup chicken broth
¼ cup champagne or other sparkling wine
2 tablespoons heavy cream
½ teaspoon red pepper flakes
2 pounds mussels, scrubbed
Finely chopped fresh parsley, for serving
Crunchy Garlic Toast (below), for serving

Make the champagne sauce: In a large nonstick skillet, melt 5 tablespoons of the butter and the oil over medium heat. When the butter is melted, add the shallot and garlic and sauté, stirring frequently, for 2 to 3 minutes, until fragrant. Stir in the bouillon base and cook for 2 minutes to let the flavors meld. Pour in the chicken broth and champagne and cook for 2 to 3 minutes, until reduced in volume by half. Stir in the cream and season with the pepper flakes.

Cook the mussels: Add the mussels to the pan and stir to coat in the sauce. Cover and cook for 4 to 5 minutes, until the mussels open. After 5 minutes, discard any mussels that haven't opened.

Transfer the mussels to a large bowl and use a ladle to pour the cooking liquid over them. Garnish with parsley and serve with garlic toast on the side for soaking up the sauce.

Crunchy Garlic Toast

Serves 6

This toast goes with just about everything. It's the perfect quick and easy side for all the dips and sauces in this book and especially alongside soups. It takes less than five minutes to make, and it's got that perfect crunchy, buttery vibe that you can't get enough of.

4 tablespoons (½ stick/2 ounces) unsalted butter
1 loaf Italian bread, cut into 2-inch slices
3 garlic cloves, peeled but whole

In a large skillet, melt the butter over medium heat. Add the bread to the pan, cut-side down, and cook for 2 to 3 minutes on each side, until lightly golden brown and toasted. Remove the bread from the pan and while the bread is still hot, rub a clove of garlic over the bread on both sides until fragrant. Serve warm.

Juicy Red Sofrito Chicken Empanadas

Makes **12** empanadas

At nearly every corner in Jersey City, Brooklyn, or the Bronx, you'll find those classic Hispanic spots selling hot, crispy empanadas displayed under a heat lamp. Beef, chicken, or guava and cheese; they've always been there, usually for just a buck. They aren't always bursting with filling, but they are packed with flavor, reminding me that sometimes simplicity is enough.

But when it comes to my own empanadas, I like to take it up a notch. I pack them tight with slow-cooked shredded chicken thighs (because thighs stay juicy), Sazón, cilantro, and tomato sauce. So when you bite into one, the juices practically ooze out—each bite loaded with richness and flavor. These empanadas strike a perfect balance between tradition and something a little extra. By slow-cooking the chicken in Sazón and sofrito, I create a juicy sauce that complements the crunchiness. They're still easy, though—we use store-bought dough to keep things simple. It's my way of honoring those flavors I grew up with, but with a little more punch and even more love.

Chicken Filling

2 pounds boneless, skinless chicken thighs
6 sprigs cilantro
⅔ cup canned tomato sauce
¼ cup My Famous Red Sofrito (page 236)
1½ teaspoons Goya Sazón (culantro y achiote)
1 teaspoon dried oregano
1 teaspoon ground cumin
1 teaspoon kosher salt
Juice of ½ lime

Empanadas

Vegetable oil, for deep-frying
12 (7-inch) frozen empanada dough rounds, thawed

Preheat the oven to 350°F.

Bake the chicken filling: Arrange the chicken thighs in a 9 × 13-inch baking dish. Add the cilantro, tomato sauce, red sofrito, ¼ cup water, Sazón, oregano, cumin, salt, and lime juice. Mix well until everything is fully incorporated. Cover with aluminum foil.

Transfer to the oven and bake for about 50 minutes, or until the juices run clear and an instant-read thermometer inserted into the thighs reads 165°F. Remove from the oven and immediately shred the chicken with 2 forks. Drain off some excess liquid, but keep the chicken saucy.

Assemble and fry the empanadas: Pour enough oil into a large, deep pot or Dutch oven to come up halfway. Clip a candy/deep-fry thermometer to the side and heat the oil over medium-high until it reaches 350°F. Line a plate with paper towels and have near the stove.

Lay out the empanada rounds. Add 2 tablespoons of the chicken filling to the middle of each empanada round. Fold the dough over and seal them shut by pressing the edges with a fork.

Working in batches to avoid overcrowding, fry the empanadas for 4 to 6 minutes, until golden brown. Use tongs to transfer the empanadas to the paper towels to drain. Serve warm.

Cheesy Chicken Alfredo Bread

Serves 2 to 4

I've always loved Alfredo sauce, how rich, creamy, and comforting it is. Since we've all seen a lot of chicken Alfredo recipes (a dish that's done often but not always done well), I wanted to pay homage to the classic but with a Toni twist. So I combined chicken Alfredo with another cozy classic, garlic bread, and created this ultimate app that's a guaranteed head turner. It's gorgeous with so much cheese pull, and family-friendly, too. (Who wouldn't like cheese, chicken, and bread?) I love making this on a weeknight and pairing it with my Sip Slow Sangria (page 91) and Creamy Shrimp and Crab–Stuffed Shells (page 138).

Garlic Bread

- 8 tablespoons (1 stick/4 ounces) unsalted butter, at room temperature
- 1 tablespoon finely chopped fresh rosemary (from about 1 sprig)
- 1 tablespoon finely chopped fresh thyme (from about 3 sprigs)
- 3 garlic cloves, minced (about 1 tablespoon)
- 1 loaf Italian bread

Chicken

- 1 pound boneless, skinless chicken breasts, cut into 1-inch cubes
- 1 teaspoon kosher salt
- 1 teaspoon garlic powder
- 1 teaspoon onion powder
- 1 teaspoon smoked paprika
- 1 teaspoon Italian seasoning
- 1 tablespoon plus 1 teaspoon extra-virgin olive oil or vegetable oil

Alfredo Sauce

- 2 cups heavy cream
- 4 tablespoons (½ stick/2 ounces) unsalted butter
- 4 ounces mozzarella cheese, freshly shredded (1 cup)
- 1 teaspoon garlic powder
- ½ teaspoon kosher salt

Assembly

- 4 ounces mozzarella cheese, freshly shredded (1 cup)
- 1 ounce Parmesan cheese, freshly grated (about ¼ cup)
- Chopped fresh basil and flat-leaf parsley, for serving

Preheat the oven to 425°F.

Bake the garlic bread: In a large bowl, combine the butter, rosemary, thyme, and garlic. Use a fork to mash and mix it up, until the butter is smooth and the herbs are well distributed.

Slice the bread in half lengthwise and place on a baking sheet. Spread the seasoned butter evenly on both halves of the bread. Bake for 10 minutes, or until a little toasted and browned at the edges. Remove from the oven and set aside. (Keep the oven on.)

Meanwhile, cook the chicken: In a medium bowl, combine the chicken, salt, garlic powder, onion powder, smoked paprika, Italian seasoning, and the 1 teaspoon olive oil. Toss to evenly coat the chicken.

In a medium skillet, heat the remaining 1 tablespoon oil over medium-high heat until hot and shimmering. Add the chicken and cook, stirring occasionally, for 7 minutes, or until golden brown and cooked through. Remove from the heat and set aside.

Make the Alfredo sauce: In a small saucepan, combine the cream and butter and warm slowly over medium-low heat, stirring occasionally, for about 5 minutes (it should come to a bare simmer—don't let the cream boil over!). Add the mozzarella, garlic powder, and salt. Stir until nice and creamy.

Assemble and bake: Spread some of the Alfredo sauce over both halves of the toasted bread (like you would sauce a pizza, so don't drown it). Then sprinkle ½ cup of the mozzarella and all the Parmesan over the Alfredo sauce. Top each half with cooked chicken. Finish with the remaining ½ cup mozzarella.

Bake for about 10 minutes, or until the cheese is bubbling and browning. Garnish with chopped basil and parsley, and more Alfredo sauce (optional, but highly recommended), and serve.

Chef's Kiss: Want to use your favorite frozen garlic bread, or store-bought Alfredo sauce? Shrimp instead of chicken? Go right ahead!

Start with Something Special

Buffalo Chicken Taquitos

Makes
12
taquitos

When considering the perfect appetizer, I like to think about a few things: 1. Is it crowd-friendly? 2. Is it easy to make? and 3. Can it be made ahead? These crunchy, juicy, flavor-packed taquitos made in under 30 minutes check all the boxes, making them one of my go-tos for large gatherings. I first made them for a Super Bowl back when Beyoncé took the stage—and Bey and these taquitos killed it. Now, more than a decade later, her performance and these taquitos live rent-free in my head. What makes this recipe *that* memorable is the homemade Buffalo sauce that gets mixed into the tender chicken filling.

Shredded Chicken

2 pounds boneless, skinless chicken breasts
1 tablespoon hot sauce (I like Crystal)
1 tablespoon vegetable oil
1 tablespoon smoked paprika
1 tablespoon onion powder
1 tablespoon garlic powder
2 teaspoons kosher salt

Buffalo Sauce

8 tablespoons (1 stick/4 ounces) unsalted butter
1 cup hot sauce (Crystal if you have it)
2 teaspoons Worcestershire sauce
2 teaspoons smoked paprika

Taquitos

Vegetable oil, for deep-frying
1 cup plus 2 tablespoons freshly shredded mozzarella cheese
4 ounces cream cheese (½ block), at room temperature
12 (6-inch) corn tortillas, preferably white corn

Chopped fresh cilantro, for serving
The Real MVP Ranch Dressing (page 241) or blue cheese dressing, for serving

Preheat the oven to 350°F.

Make the shredded chicken: Arrange the chicken in a 9 × 13-inch baking dish and rub all over with the hot sauce, then the oil. Season with the smoked paprika, onion powder, garlic powder, and salt, rubbing in evenly. Add 4 cups water and cover with foil, crimping around the edges.

Transfer to the oven and bake for 45 to 50 minutes, until the chicken is cooked through and an instant-read thermometer inserted into the thickest part reads 165°F. Set aside to cool for 5 minutes.

Meanwhile, make the Buffalo sauce: In a small saucepan, melt the butter over medium-low heat. Once the butter is melted, whisk in the hot sauce, Worcestershire sauce, and smoked paprika. Remove from the heat and pour into a heatproof medium bowl.

Assemble and fry the taquitos: Pour enough oil into a large, deep pot or Dutch oven to come up halfway. Clip a candy/deep-fry thermometer to the side and heat the oil over medium-high until it reaches 350°F. Line a cutting board or baking sheet with paper towels and have near the stove.

While the oil warms up, shred the cooked chicken into a large bowl. Add the mozzarella, cream cheese, and ½ cup of the Buffalo sauce and mix until combined.

Place about ¼ cup of the shredded chicken mixture on the bottom half of a tortilla and tightly roll up to prevent the filling from leaking out. Turn it seam-side down and fasten with 3 to 4 toothpicks so the taquito stays closed. Repeat with the remaining chicken filling and tortillas.

Working in batches to avoid overcrowding, fry the taquitos for 3 to 4 minutes, until golden brown. Use tongs to remove the taquitos from the oil and transfer to the paper towels to drain. Carefully remove the toothpicks.

Arrange the taquitos on a platter, sprinkle with cilantro, and serve hot with the remaining Buffalo sauce and ranch dressing on the side.

Little Detail, BIG Impact: Wrap the tortillas in a damp paper towel and microwave flat for 20 seconds to help them roll without breaking.

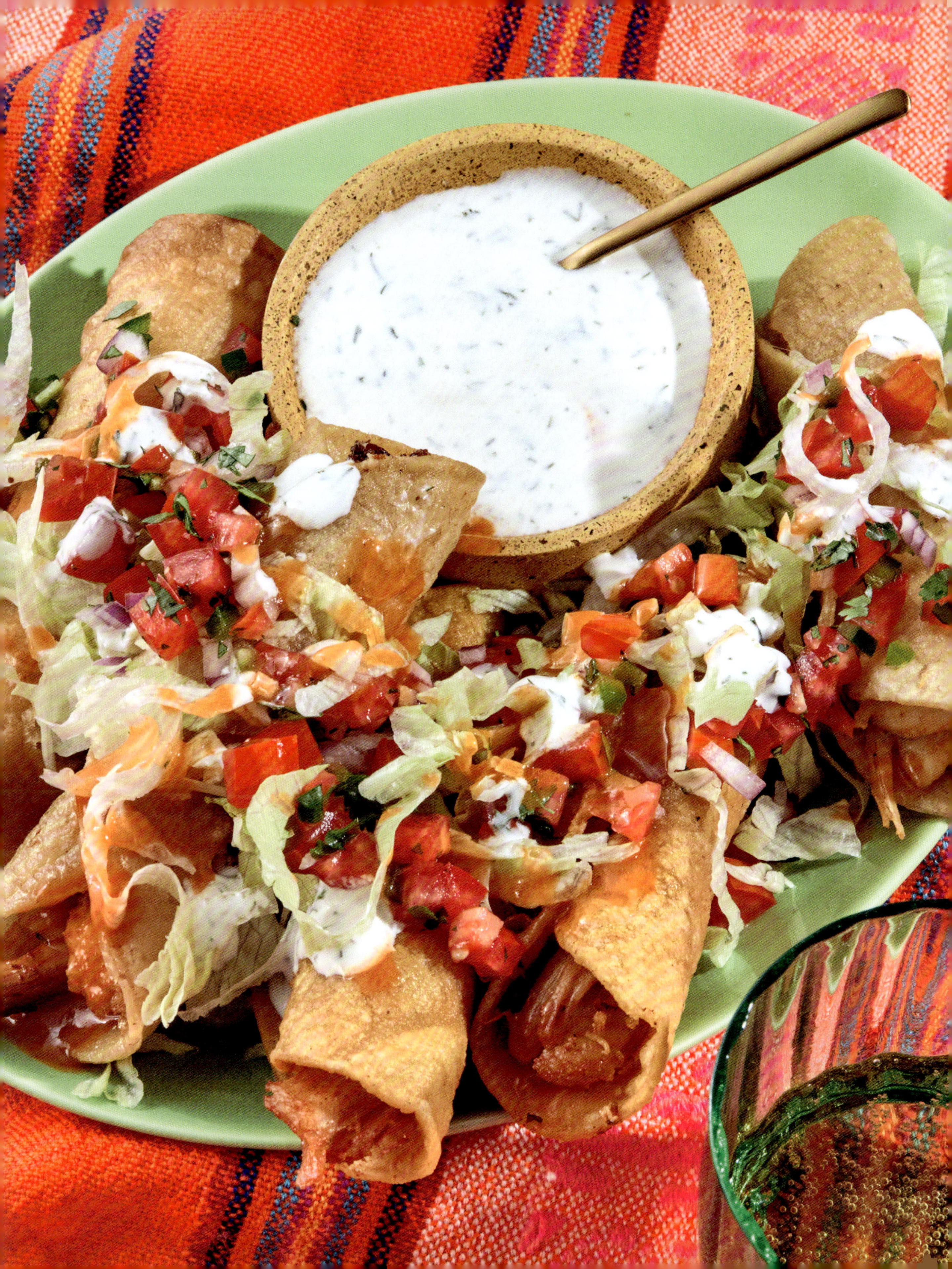

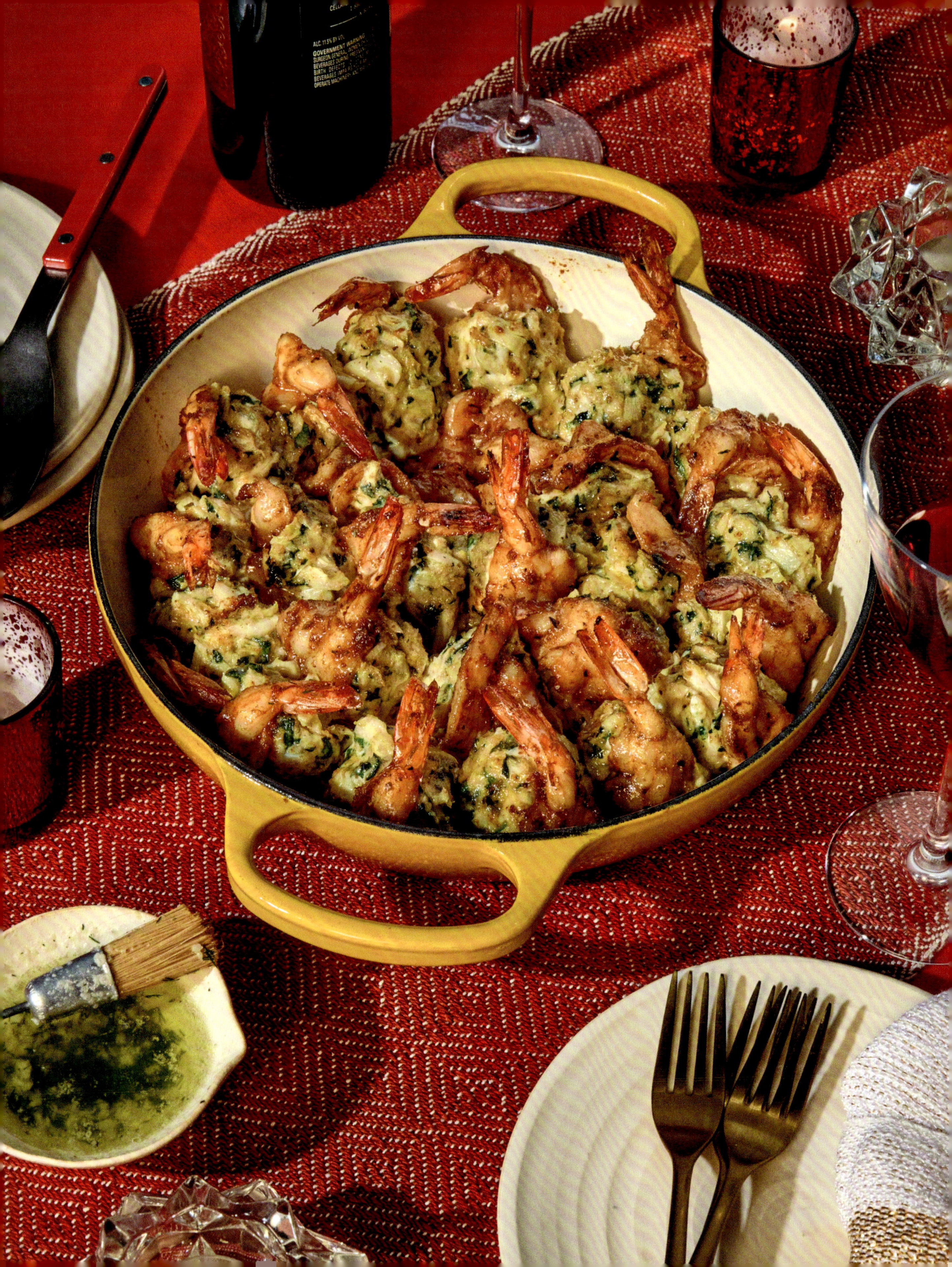
ALC 11.5% BY VOL
GOVERNMENT WARNING

Spinach, Crab, and Artichoke–Stuffed Shrimp

Serves 8

This is my all-time favorite appetizer and my signature holiday recipe. It's a crowd favorite and arguably the most popular stuffed shrimp recipe online. Stuffing a shrimp is easy, so don't worry, and the filling is my favorite part. It has crabmeat, Parmesan cheese, and artichokes—ingredients that definitely make the dish feel luxurious and restaurant-worthy.

I love bringing these shrimp to gatherings because I can prep everything ahead of time, and it tastes incredible and leaves a lasting impression on everyone who gets to try it!

Shrimp

- 2 pounds shrimp (21/25 count), peeled and deveined, tails on, butterflied (see tip)
- 1 tablespoon extra-virgin olive oil
- 2 teaspoons smoked paprika
- 1 teaspoon Old Bay seasoning
- 1 teaspoon garlic powder
- 1 teaspoon onion powder
- ½ teaspoon Italian seasoning
- ½ teaspoon freshly ground black pepper

Spinach-Artichoke Stuffing

- 8 ounces lump or claw crabmeat, picked over for shells
- 1 cup cooked baby spinach, squeezed dry and finely chopped
- 1 cup unseasoned canned artichokes, drained and finely chopped
- 1 cup mayonnaise, sour cream, or cream cheese
- 8 ounces cheese (I use half mozzarella and half pepper Jack), freshly shredded (2 cups)
- ½ cup fine dried bread crumbs
- 3 garlic cloves, minced (about 1 tablespoon)
- 1 teaspoon garlic powder
- 1 teaspoon Italian seasoning
- 1 teaspoon garlic salt
- Grated zest of 1 lemon
- 1 tablespoon freshly squeezed lemon juice

Garlic-Dill Butter

- 4 tablespoons (½ stick/2 ounces) unsalted butter
- 3 garlic cloves, minced (about 1 tablespoon)
- 1 teaspoon chopped fresh dill

Preheat the oven to 350°F. Line a baking sheet with parchment paper or foil.

Prepare the shrimp: In a large bowl, toss the shrimp with the olive oil, smoked paprika, Old Bay, garlic powder, onion powder, Italian seasoning, and pepper until well coated. Lay the shrimp with the split side down across the prepared pan without overlapping.

Make the spinach-artichoke stuffing: In a separate large bowl, mix together the crabmeat, spinach, artichokes, mayonnaise, cheese, bread crumbs, minced garlic, garlic powder, Italian seasoning, garlic salt, lemon zest, and lemon juice until evenly combined.

Assemble and bake: Take a large spoonful of the filling (about 1 tablespoon) and add it to the top of the shrimp, to create a "C" shape with the split side down and the tail resting on top. Press the tail of the shrimp down over the filling to help hold it in place. Repeat with the remaining shrimp.

Line a 12-inch cast-iron skillet with the stuffed shrimp, arranging them in a circular shape with the tails standing upright to create a ring. Bake for about 25 minutes, or until the shrimp are cooked through (they'll look opaque) and the stuffing is golden and bubbling.

Meanwhile, make the garlic-dill butter: In a medium saucepan, melt the butter with the minced garlic over medium-low heat. Stir in the dill.

Baste the warm shrimp with the garlic butter and serve.

Little Detail, BIG Impact: To butterfly shrimp, gently run a sharp paring knife from tip to end along the back of the shrimp (along the line where the vein used to be) and slice the shrimp *nearly* in half (but not all the way), so it fans out like a butterfly. Now it's ready for stuffing.

Creamy Roasted Garlic Dip with Italian Sausage

Serves 8

There's nothing like a really good dip—the kind that everybody digs into at a party and can't get enough of. You want a dip that holds up to all kinds of dippers: potato chips, celery sticks, nachos, carrots—whatever you've got. This one right here? It's that dip. You've got roasted garlic, sausage, and aromatic onions and peppers, but then of course we take it up a notch—because you know how we do—with heavy cream, mozzarella, *and* Parmesan. Go hard or go home. This dip is perfect for game days, or hearty enough to hold everyone over until the main course but still gets them excited for what's next.

1 head garlic
1 tablespoon extra-virgin olive oil
1 pound mild Italian sausage, casings removed (or hot Italian sausage for a spicy kick)
1 small white onion, finely diced (about 1 cup)
½ small red bell pepper, finely diced (about ½ cup)
12 ounces mozzarella cheese, freshly shredded (1½ cups)
4 ounces freshly grated Parmesan cheese (1 cup)
8 ounces cream cheese (1 block), at room temperature
½ cup sour cream
2 teaspoons Italian seasoning
2 teaspoons ground white pepper
2 teaspoons sweet paprika
1 teaspoon onion powder
1 teaspoon kosher salt
¼ cup heavy cream
Crunchy Garlic Toast (page 31), for serving

Preheat the oven to 400°F.

Roast the garlic: Slice off about ¼ inch from the top of the head of garlic to expose the cloves. Drizzle the olive oil over the exposed cloves, wrap the head tightly in foil, and roast in the oven for about 1 hour 10 minutes, or until the cloves are soft and caramelized. Let it cool slightly, then squeeze out the roasted garlic cloves into a small bowl and set aside. Reduce the oven temperature to 375°F.

Meanwhile, cook the sausage and vegetables: In a large skillet, cook the Italian sausage over medium heat for 8 to 10 minutes, breaking it apart with a spoon and stirring frequently, until browned and cooked through. Drain the excess fat.

Add the onion and bell pepper to the skillet and sauté, stirring frequently, for 5 to 6 minutes, until softened.

Assemble and bake the dip: In a large bowl, stir together half the mozzarella, half the Parmesan, the cream cheese, sour cream, Italian seasoning, white pepper, paprika, onion powder, and salt until fully combined. Stir in the cooked sausage, peppers, and onions. Use a fork to mash the roasted garlic cloves into the mixture until well combined. Add the heavy cream and stir until combined.

Evenly spread the dip mixture into the bottom of a 9 × 13-inch baking dish. Sprinkle the remaining mozzarella and Parmesan on top.

Bake for 15 minutes, or until the cheese is melted, bubbling, and golden brown. Serve hot with garlic toast for dipping.

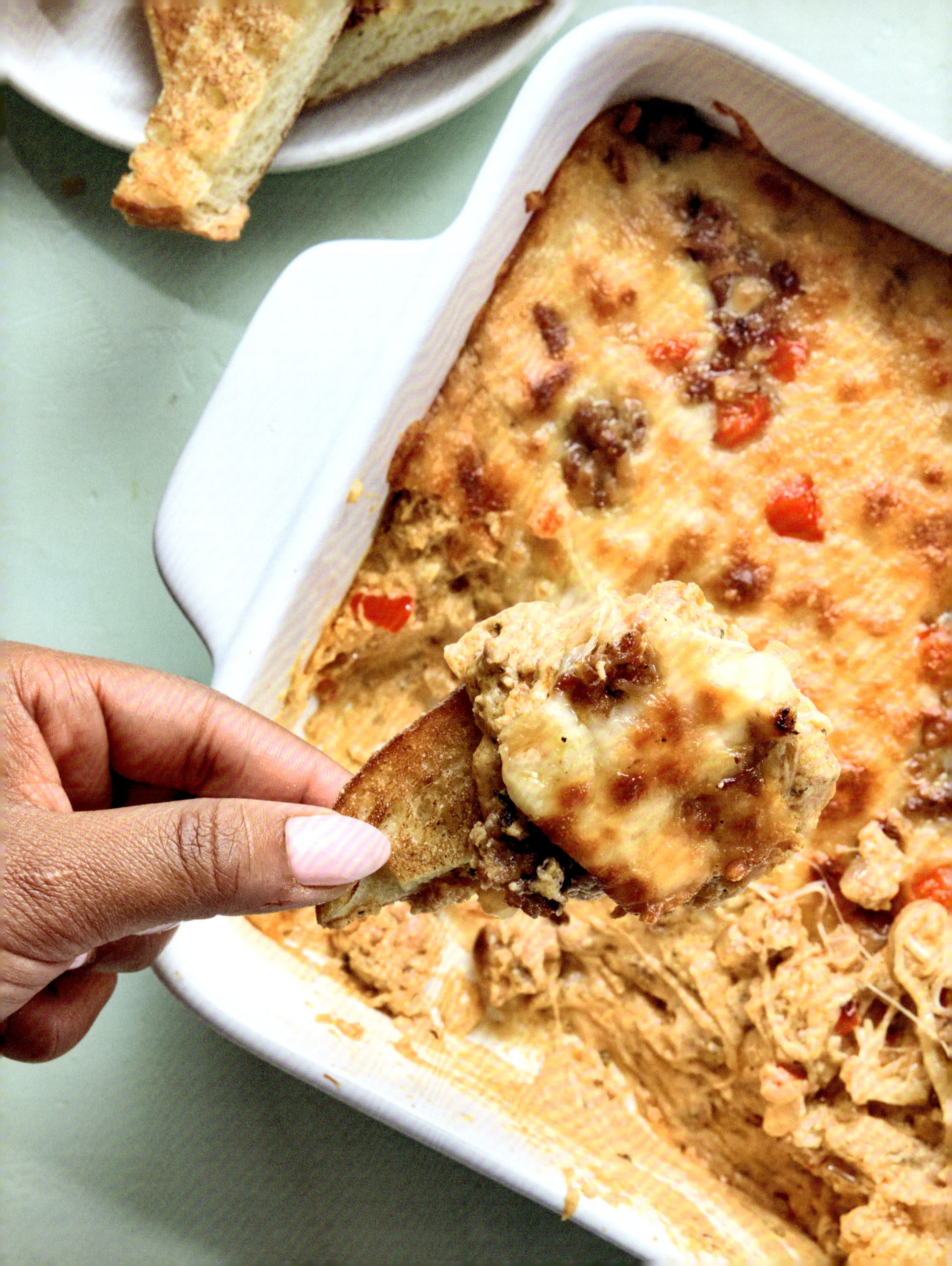

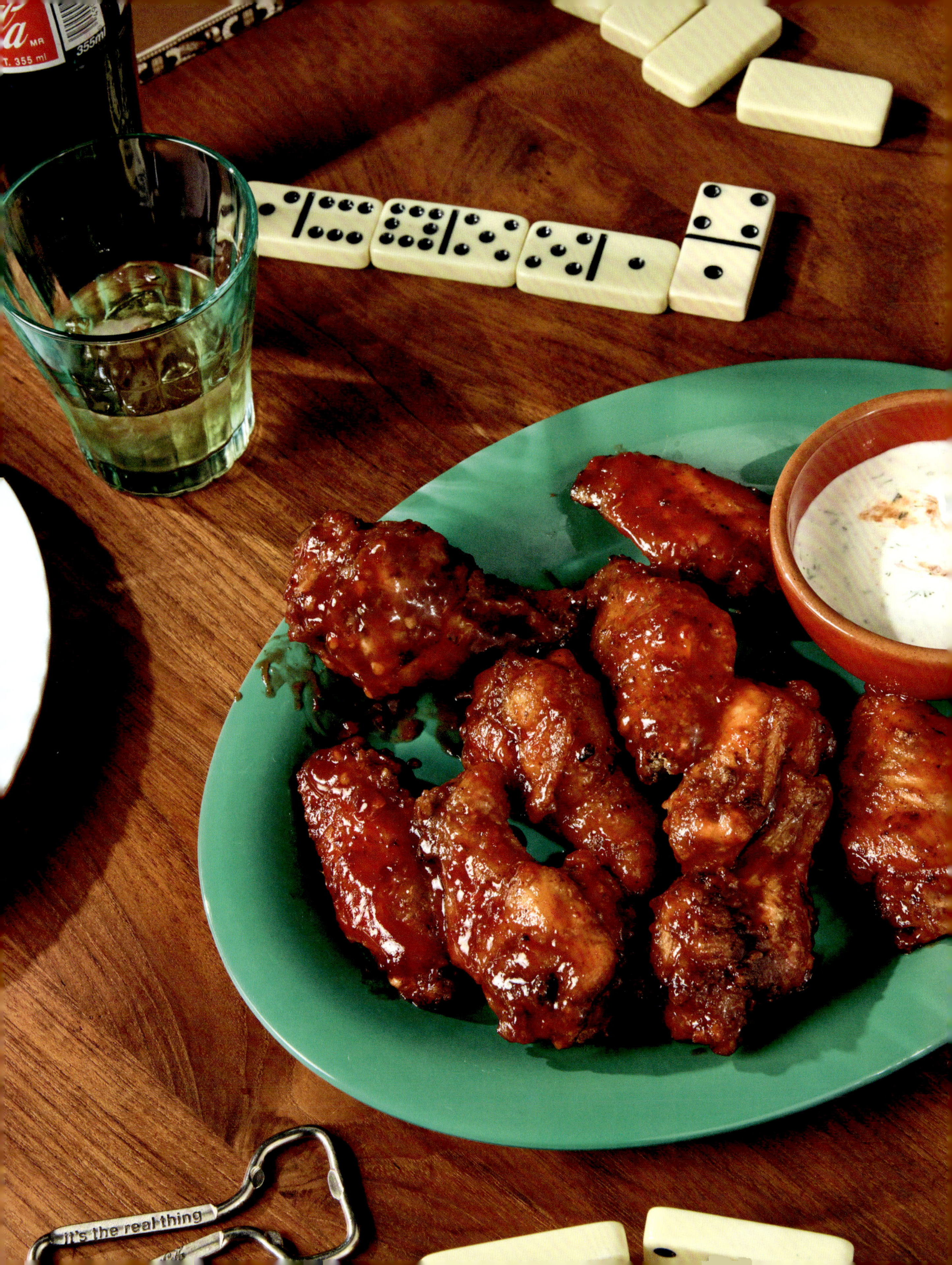
355ml
it's the real thing

Rum and Cola Wings

Serves 6

If you're from the East Coast, are Puerto Rican, or come from a party family like mine (or all of the above), then you might already know that rum and Coke is an essential drink for get-togethers that always hits the spot. It's sweet, strong, and perfect for any occasion. When I was in college, my friends and I would play Spades and drink rum and Coke for hours, always ending the night with me cooking up something because after all that laughing and drinking and gossiping, we needed nourishment! One night, all I had in my fridge was a pack of wings, so with a couple of pantry staples, a tipsy spirit, and some creativity, I came up with this recipe—which, I have to say, is fight-over-the-last-wing-worthy. I double-fry the wings to create the extra-crunchy, mouth-dropping goodness that takes them up two more notches. Trust me, it's worth it if you're looking to really impress!

Vegetable oil, for deep-frying

Wings
2 pounds chicken wings (about 14 pieces of wing, both drums and flats)
5 teaspoons smoked paprika
2 teaspoons garlic powder
3 teaspoons kosher salt
1 tablespoon vegetable oil
1½ cups all-purpose flour
¾ cup cornstarch

Glaze
1 (12-ounce) can Coke
¾ cup honey or agave syrup
½ cup ketchup
¼ cup Bacardi Gold rum
1 tablespoon lower-sodium soy sauce
2 teaspoons sambal oelek
½ teaspoon red food coloring (optional)
½ teaspoon kosher salt
1 tablespoon cornstarch

Your favorite dipping sauce (optional; see tip), for serving

Heat the oil: Pour enough oil into a large, deep pot or Dutch oven to come halfway up the sides. Clip a candy/deep-fry thermometer to the side and heat the oil over medium-high until it reaches 350°F. Line a wire rack with paper towels and have near the stove.

Meanwhile, season and dredge the wings: Line a baking sheet with parchment paper. In a large bowl, season the chicken wings with 3 teaspoons of the smoked paprika, the garlic powder, 1 teaspoon of the salt, and the vegetable oil. Toss to evenly coat the chicken.

In a medium bowl, whisk together the flour, cornstarch, remaining 2 teaspoons smoked paprika, and remaining 2 teaspoons salt. Coat the wings all over in the dry batter mixture and place the chicken on the lined baking sheet.

Make the glaze: In a small saucepan, whisk together the Coke, honey, ketchup, rum, soy sauce, sambal, food coloring (if using), and salt. Cook over medium-high heat for about 15 minutes, stirring occasionally, until it's reduced slightly.

In a small bowl, whisk together the cornstarch with 1 tablespoon water. Whisk the cornstarch mixture into the sauce and cook for 5 minutes, stirring occasionally, until the sauce thickens to your desired consistency. Transfer to a large bowl.

Fry the wings: Dip the battered wings into the dry batter again. Working in batches to avoid overcrowding, deep-fry the wings for 5 to 7 minutes, until golden brown. Transfer the wings to the paper towels to rest for 10 minutes.

Again working in batches, fry the wings a second time for 3 minutes. Line the rack with new paper towels, then transfer the wings there for 1 minute to soak up any excess oil. Add the wings to the large bowl with the glaze and toss to coat the wings all over. Serve right away with dipping sauce, if you like.

Chef's Kiss: Try dipping the wings in The Real MVP Ranch Dressing on page 241.

Little Detail, BIG Impact: If you're buying your wings from a butcher, you can ask them to remove the tips and separate the drums from the flats to save you time.

Start with Something Special

Cajun Crab-Stuffed Oysters

Makes **12** oysters

These are a whole vibe. Oysters can seem intimidating, but throwing them on the grill is a party trick that's perfect for summer. It's easy, impressive, and the smoky flavor from the grill just takes them to another level. The filling? Buttery, flavorful, and packed with crabmeat and cheese—chef's kiss. Now, shucking oysters might feel like a challenge, but trust me, once you get the hang of it (thanks, YouTube University!), you'll be good. Or, if you want to keep it simple, ask your seafood person to shuck them for you and then keep them on ice for the ride home. Once you get those oysters stuffed and on the grill, it's game over. Perfect for any summer cookout! And if you don't have a grill, or it's not summer, don't worry, I got you covered.

4 tablespoons (½ stick/2 ounces) unsalted butter
½ small yellow onion, diced (about ¼ cup)
3 garlic cloves, minced (about 1 tablespoon)
4 ounces frozen chopped spinach, thawed and drained (about ½ cup)
4 ounces lump crabmeat, picked over for shells
½ cup heavy cream
1½ teaspoons no-salt Cajun seasoning
1 teaspoon Old Bay seasoning
2 ounces mild Cheddar cheese, freshly shredded (about ¼ cup)
⅔ cup panko bread crumbs
Rock salt (optional), for baking
12 oysters, shucked and on the half shell
1 ounce Parmesan cheese, freshly shredded (5 tablespoons)
Chopped fresh parsley, for serving
Lemon wedges, for serving

Make the filling: In a medium skillet, melt 2 tablespoons of the butter over medium heat. Add the onion and sauté, stirring frequently, for 3 to 4 minutes, until softened and translucent. Add the garlic and cook for 30 seconds, or until fragrant.

Stir in the spinach and cook for 2 minutes to remove excess moisture. Stir in the crab, cream, Cajun seasoning, and Old Bay and cook for 2 to 3 minutes, stirring occasionally, until the mixture thickens slightly. Remove from the heat and stir in the Cheddar until melted and evenly combined.

If grilling: Preheat a grill to high heat.

If baking: Preheat the oven to 450°F. Line a baking sheet with rock salt or a bed of crumpled foil to keep the oysters stable.

Meanwhile, toast the panko: In a small skillet, melt the remaining 2 tablespoons butter over medium heat. Add the panko and stir constantly for 2 minutes, until golden brown. Set aside on a plate to cool slightly.

Stuff the oysters: Place the shucked oysters on the prepared baking sheet and spoon the crab and spinach filling into each oyster shell, filling generously and dividing evenly among the oysters. Dividing evenly, top with the toasted panko and the Parmesan.

To bake: Bake for 10 to 12 minutes, until the bread crumbs and cheese are browned and the oysters are heated through. Remove from the oven and let cool for 1 minute.

To grill: Lay the oysters on the grill and cook for 10 to 12 minutes, until the topping is golden brown and the oysters are heated through.

Serve garnished with fresh parsley and lemon wedges for squeezing.

Little Details, BIG Impact: When it comes to shucking oysters, safety first! Use an oyster knife and protect your hand with a towel or glove—trust me, you don't want to slip.

If you're buying preshucked oysters, make sure to use them within a few hours, as they can lose freshness quickly. Keep them on ice from the store to home to keep them in top shape.

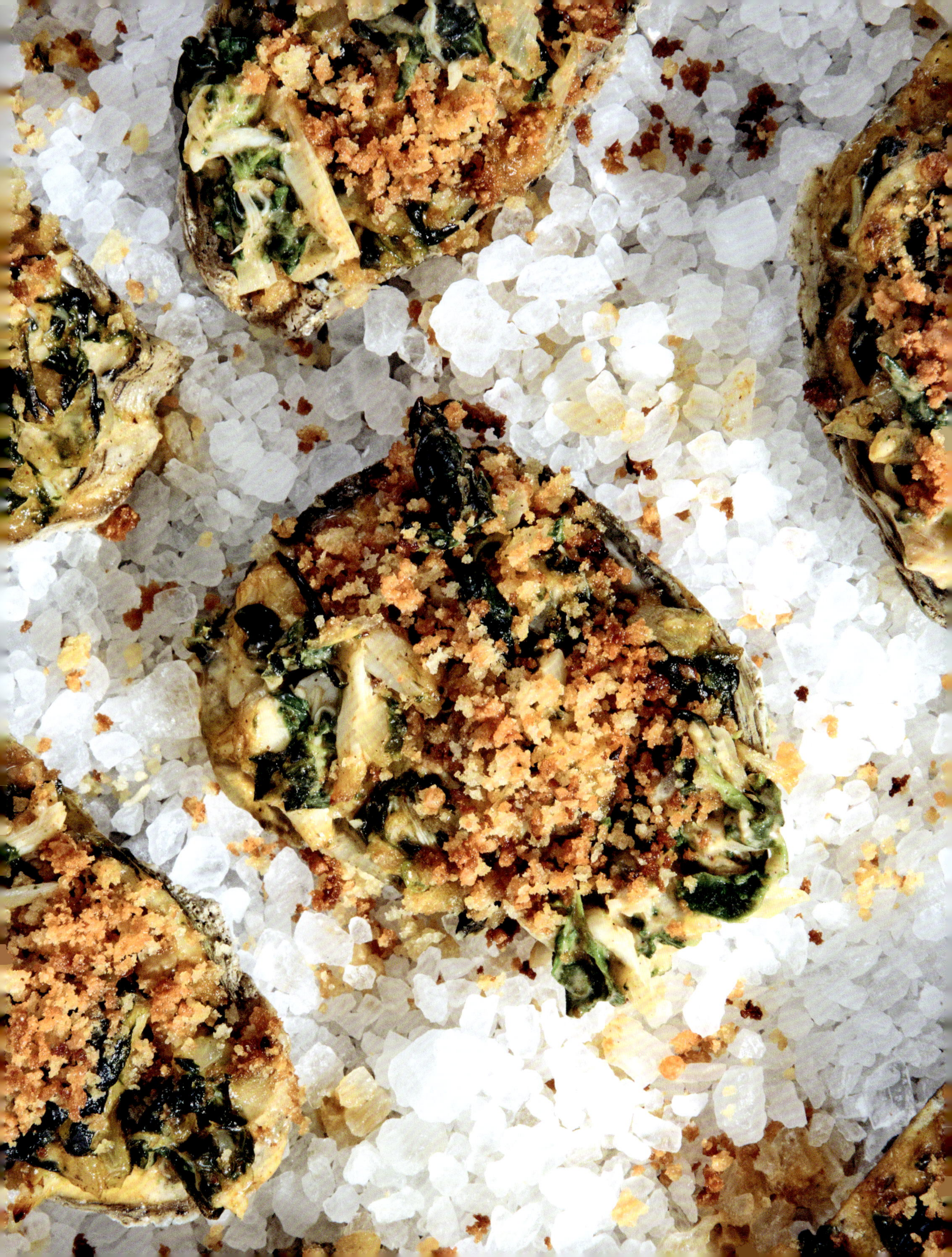

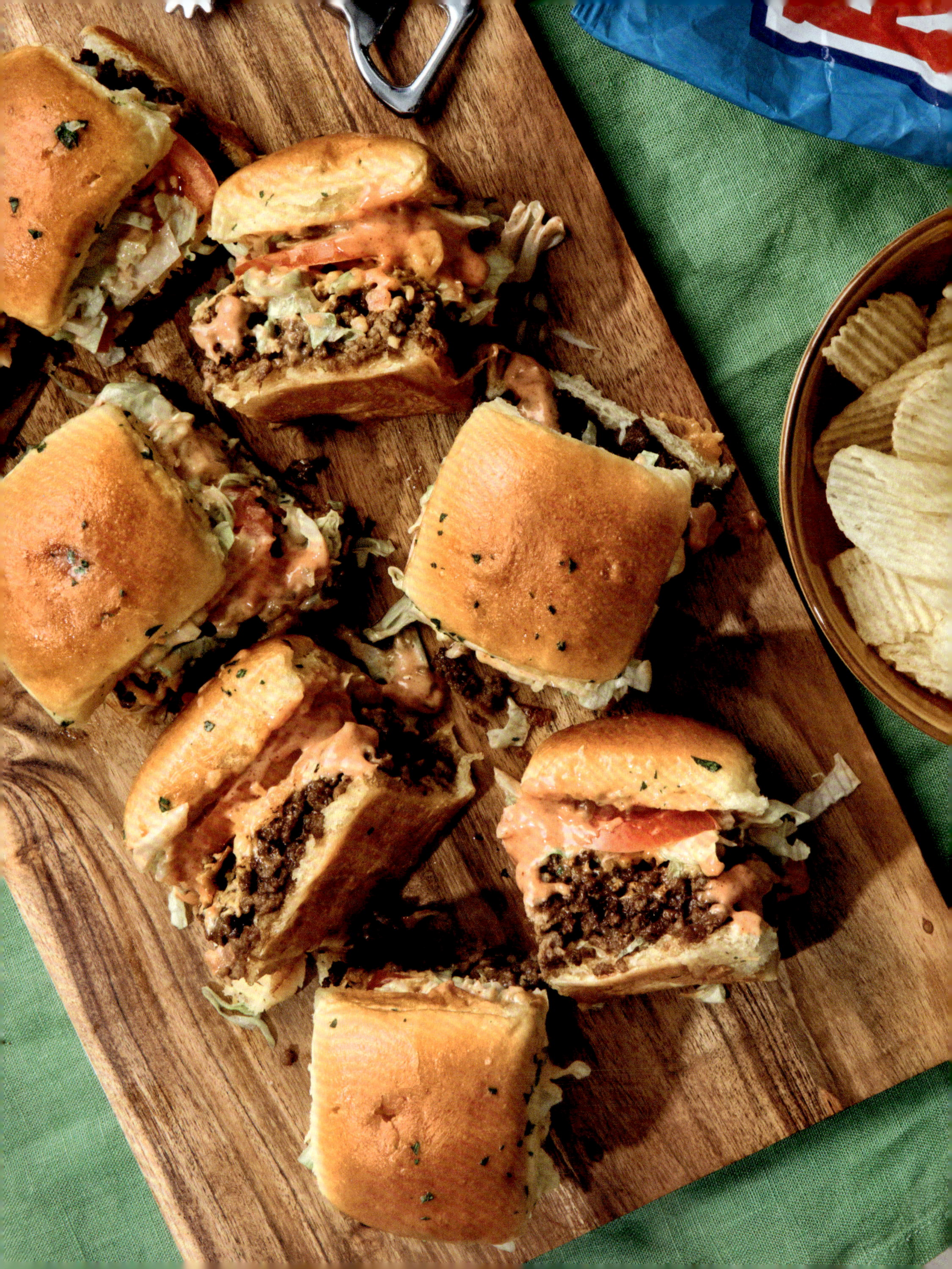

Chopped Cheese Sliders

Makes **12** sliders

If you know, you know—there's nothing like a classic chopped cheese. It's all about that seasoned ground beef, melted cheese, and perfect balance of fresh lettuce, juicy tomatoes, and a killer sauce. It's simple, but it packs in so much flavor.

To switch things up, I turned the chopped cheese into sliders for when I'm hosting. They've got everything you love about the original—savory beef, melty cheese, and all the fixings—but in bite-size form. These sliders always get people talking, and even if they've never had the real deal, they'll be hooked after the first bite. Perfect for sharing, and a great way to bring that NYC flavor to the table.

Beef-Cheese Topping

1 tablespoon extra-virgin olive oil
1 small white onion, finely diced (about 1 cup)
1½ pounds ground beef (80/20)
1 tablespoon Worcestershire sauce
1 teaspoon garlic powder
1 teaspoon onion powder
1 teaspoon seasoning salt
1 teaspoon adobo seasoning
¼ teaspoon kosher salt
8 ounces sharp Cheddar cheese, freshly shredded (2 cups)

Sliders

12 Hawaiian slider rolls (from Honey Butter Hawaiian Rolls, page 24)
4 ounces sharp Cheddar cheese, freshly shredded (1 cup)
2 tablespoons (1 ounce) unsalted butter
1 teaspoon Italian seasoning
½ cup mayonnaise
½ cup ketchup
¼ cup sweet relish
1 teaspoon no-salt Cajun seasoning
2 cups shredded iceberg lettuce
1 medium tomato, cut into 12 thin slices (about ⅛ inch thick)

Preheat the oven to 350°F. Line a 9 × 13-inch baking dish with parchment paper.

Make the beef-cheese topping: In a large skillet, heat the oil over medium heat until hot and shimmering. Add the onions and cook, stirring occasionally, for about 7 minutes, or until soft and translucent. Add the beef and cook for about 5 minutes, breaking it up with a spatula as it cooks into small pieces, until it starts to brown. Stir in the Worcestershire sauce, garlic powder, onion powder, seasoning salt, adobo seasoning, and kosher salt. Reduce the heat to low and cook for another 5 minutes, stirring occasionally, until the beef is browned and cooked through. Add the Cheddar and stir for 1 minute, until the cheese is melted and fully incorporated. Remove from the heat.

Assemble the sliders: Slice the slider rolls in half horizontally to separate the tops of the rolls from the bottoms. Place the bottom halves of the rolls in the lined baking dish. Evenly spread the meat mixture over the bottom halves of the rolls. Sprinkle with the Cheddar.

In a small skillet, melt the butter over medium heat. Stir in the Italian seasoning, then brush the tops of the slider buns with the seasoned butter and place them on a baking sheet.

Place the baking dish with the meat-topped buns and the baking sheet with the buttered tops in the oven. Bake for about 5 minutes, or until the cheese is melted and the tops are slightly toasted.

Meanwhile, make the sauce: In a medium bowl, whisk together the mayonnaise, ketchup, sweet relish, and Cajun seasoning. Set aside.

To serve, sprinkle the lettuce evenly over the top of the cheesy beef mixture. Set 1 slice of tomato on top of each roll. Drizzle the sauce evenly over the lettuce and tomatoes. Place the top halves of the rolls on top. Use a bread knife, if needed, to separate the sliders, and serve warm.

Chef's Kiss: My famous honey butter trick is a game changer here. Just melt 2 tablespoons honey with 2 tablespoons butter and brush it on for that golden glow at the end. It's the perfect finishing touch!

Start with Something Special

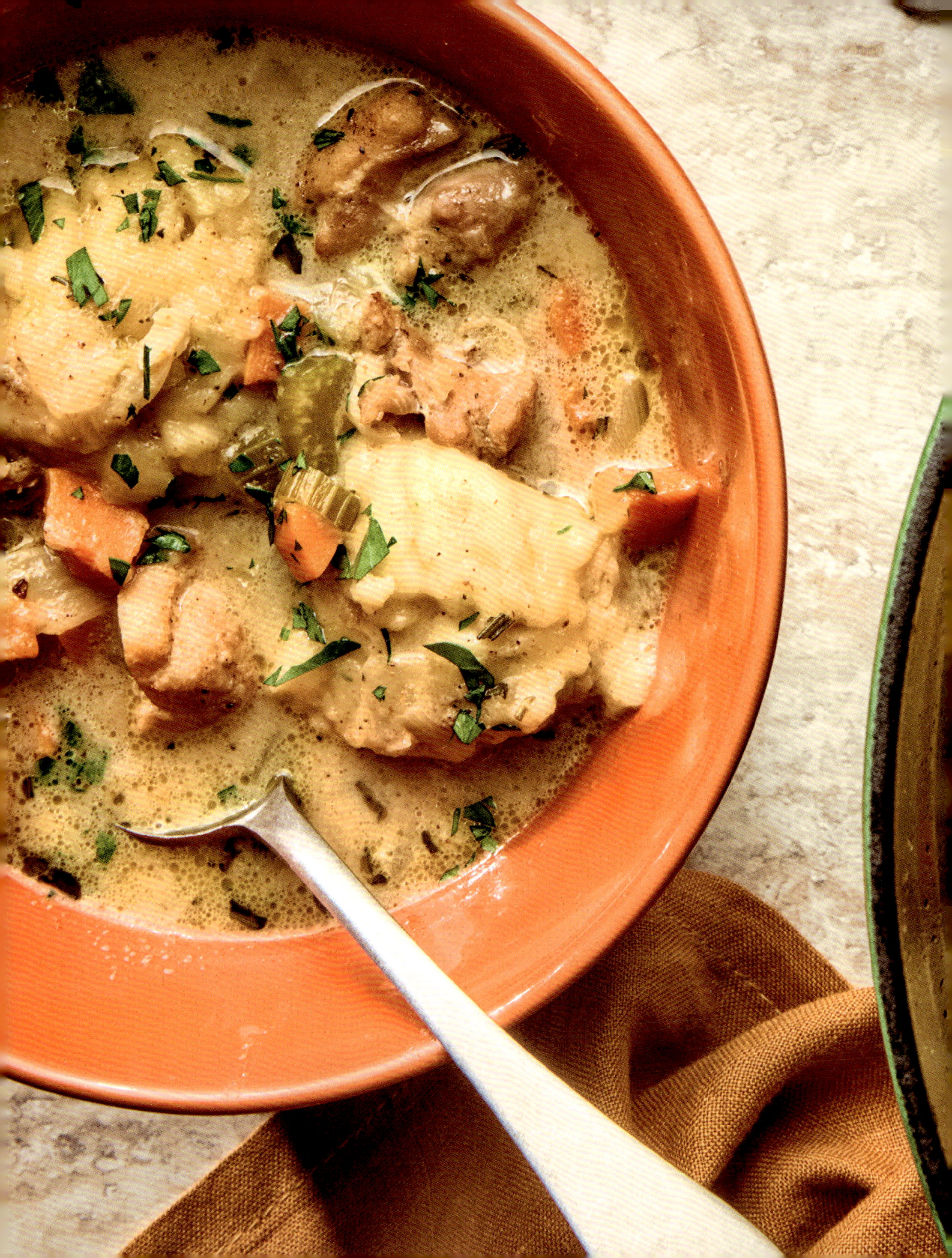

2

Soulful Soups

Soups were a staple in my life when I was growing up. My abuelita Edie always had a pot of asopao—a Puerto Rican soup made with chicken, sofrito, and pumpkin—or some other kind of soup simmering on the stove. Somehow, no matter what she threw into the caldero (a traditional cooking pot; see page 18), it would become a flavorful pot of magic—colorful, rich, and comforting, just like her. My love for soups can be traced back to my childhood and her kitchen table. Soups have continued to be a cornerstone of my cooking for a few reasons. First, I absolutely love slow-cooking. Building flavor from scratch is like writing a book; chapter by chapter, you're building a masterpiece. Second, I'm a homebody, meaning home is where it's at for me, especially in the winter, when soup making becomes one of my favorite things to do (who doesn't love a comforting bowl of chicken soup when it's cold out?). And third, soups are usually budget-friendly. Whether you have leftovers from last night's dinner, canned or frozen vegetables you aren't sure what to do with, or a limited budget, anyone can make a tasty and filling soup without breaking the bank. Soups are mostly quick to put together, packed with flavor, and keep well in the fridge—many even taste better after a day or two as the flavors deepen.

This chapter is a ballad of broths—from Caribbean and Hispanic-inspired soups like The Very Best Pozole Verde (page 55) to rich, creamy American-style soups like The Ultimate Loaded Baked Potato Soup (page 63). When you're under the weather, you'll make my abuelita's famous Kick the Cold Soup (page 52), because Grandma knows best. When you want to stay in and binge-watch your favorite show with your boo, a warm bowl of Marry Me Chicken Soup (page 59) is perfect for date night (invite me to your wedding if you get a ring). On those winter nights, when you just want something quick and comforting, my Island Pasta Soup (page 60) does the trick. And since these recipes are so hearty, you can be sure you'll have enough for yourself *and* to spread the love. Why not make someone's day and give a mason jar to friends, family, or a neighbor; or if you're greedy like me, keep it all and have plenty for seconds, thirds, and fourths.

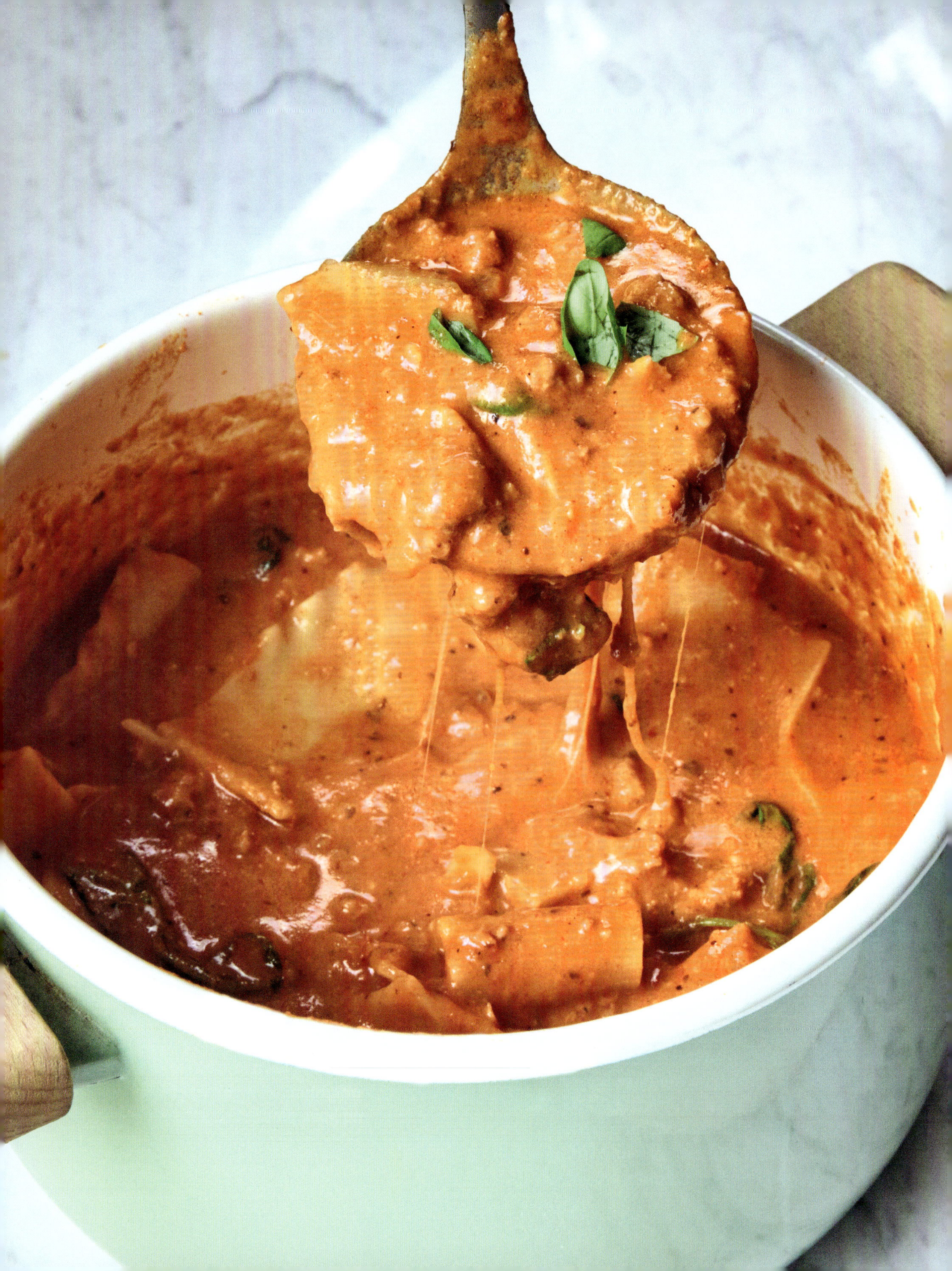

Spicy Lasagna Soup

Serves **8**

When I first saw the lasagna soup trend blow up on TikTok, like everyone else, I was instantly hooked. A creamy, rich, pasta-forward soup? That sounded like a win to me. There were so many versions out there, but I knew if I was gonna make it my own, it couldn't just be easy, it needed depth, and more important, some heat. With all that cream, tomatoes, and cheese, I knew it could handle a little spice. So I went for it with hot Italian sausage *and* chorizo, and trust me, it was the right call. The soup turned out incredible, but if spice isn't your thing, you can always dial it back with mild sausage. Either way, you're in for something exceptional.

2 tablespoons extra-virgin olive oil
1 small yellow onion, finely chopped (about 1 cup)
9 garlic cloves, minced (about 3 tablespoons)
8 ounces fresh chorizo sausage, casings removed
1 pound hot Italian sausage, casings removed (or mild Italian sausage for less heat)
2 cups canned tomato sauce
½ cup tomato paste
2 teaspoons sugar
1 teaspoon Italian seasoning
1 teaspoon garlic powder
1 teaspoon onion powder
1 teaspoon kosher salt, or more to taste
½ teaspoon red pepper flakes
5 cups low-sodium chicken broth
8 ounces lasagna noodles, broken into 1-inch pieces
6 ounces mozzarella cheese, freshly shredded (1½ cups), plus more for serving
1 ounce Parmesan cheese, freshly grated (about ¼ cup)
½ cup heavy cream
½ cup fresh basil leaves, roughly chopped, plus more for serving

Cook the sausage: In a large pot, heat the oil over medium heat until hot and shimmering. Add the onion and garlic and sauté, stirring frequently, for 5 to 7 minutes, until soft and translucent.

Add the chorizo and Italian sausage and cook for 5 to 7 minutes, breaking up the meat with a spoon as it cooks and stirring occasionally, until browned. Stir in the tomato sauce and tomato paste until well combined with the meat. Stir in the sugar, Italian seasoning, garlic powder, onion powder, salt, and pepper flakes. Cook for 2 to 3 minutes, stirring occasionally, to allow the flavors to meld.

Make the soup: Pour in the chicken broth and stir in the broken lasagna. Bring the soup to a gentle boil, then reduce the heat to low and simmer uncovered for 30 minutes, stirring occasionally, until the pasta is al dente.

Stir in the mozzarella and Parmesan until melted, then stir in the heavy cream and basil until well combined. Simmer for 5 minutes to heat through. Taste and adjust the seasoning if needed.

Serve the lasagna soup hot, garnished with additional shredded mozzarella and fresh basil.

Abuelita's Chicken Soup
(aka Kick the Cold Soup)

Serves 4

My abuelita Edie meant everything to me. So much of what I know in the kitchen came from her. Her cooking style was soulful and layered. She built flavor from scratch and had that special touch that made everything she cooked taste incredible. Especially her chicken noodle soup. Whenever any of us felt under the weather, she would make it with her own special touches. She added sofrito, which gives the soup that Latin flavor; she also liked to use tomato sauce and lime juice, as the acidity complements the chicken (she said the acidity also helped if you were feeling under the weather). And there's hot sauce, of course, because the women in my family are known for being spicy! The soup was like a shot of espresso—vibrant and just what you needed to make you feel alive. Whether I'm feeling under the weather or just craving a taste of home, Abuelita's chicken soup is always the perfect remedy.

1 pound bone-in, skinless chicken drumsticks and thighs
1 tablespoon chicken bouillon powder
2 teaspoons adobo seasoning
1 teaspoon dried oregano
1 teaspoon Goya Sazón (culantro y achiote)
1 teaspoon freshly ground black pepper
1 tablespoon extra-virgin olive oil
1 medium yellow onion, finely chopped (about 1 cup)
½ cup canned tomato sauce
¼ cup Abuela's Green Sofrito (page 233)
6 garlic cloves, minced (about 2 tablespoons)
3 cups low-sodium chicken broth, plus more as needed
3 celery stalks, finely chopped (about 1¼ cups)
2 medium carrots, chopped (about 1 cup)
1 teaspoon dried thyme
1 bay leaf
8 ounces vermicelli noodles, broken into small pieces
3 sprigs cilantro, plus more chopped for garnish
Juice of ½ lime
Hot sauce and lime wedges, for serving

Cook the chicken: Season the chicken all over with the chicken bouillon powder, 1 teaspoon of the adobo seasoning, the oregano, Sazón, and pepper. In a large Dutch oven, heat the olive oil over medium heat until hot and shimmering. Add the chicken and sear for 2 to 3 minutes on each side, until golden brown (it will finish cooking later). Leave the fat in the pot, transfer the chicken to a plate, and set aside.

Make the soup: In the same pot, add the onion, tomato sauce, sofrito, and garlic and sauté over medium heat, stirring frequently, for 2 minutes, until fragrant. Return the chicken to the pot and add the chicken broth and 3 cups water. Cook uncovered for 20 to 25 minutes, stirring a few times, until the chicken is cooked through and an instant-read thermometer inserted into the thickest part of the chicken reads 165°F. Use tongs or a slotted spoon to transfer the chicken from the pot to a large bowl, and remove and discard all the bones. Shred the meat with two forks.

Finish the soup: Add the celery, carrots, remaining 1 teaspoon adobo seasoning, the thyme, bay leaf, and broken noodles to the pot. If needed, add water or additional chicken broth so that the broth covers all the ingredients. Bring to a boil, then reduce the heat to medium-low and simmer for 15 minutes to allow the flavors to meld, stirring every few minutes and using a spoon to skim off any excess fat that rises to the top.

Remove the bay leaf from the soup and return the shredded chicken to the pot. Stir in the cilantro sprigs and lime juice and simmer for 5 minutes, or until the noodles and vegetables are tender.

Divide among bowls, top with extra cilantro, and serve with hot sauce and lime wedges on the side.

Abuelita Says: "Taste as you go, add your own little *sazón*."

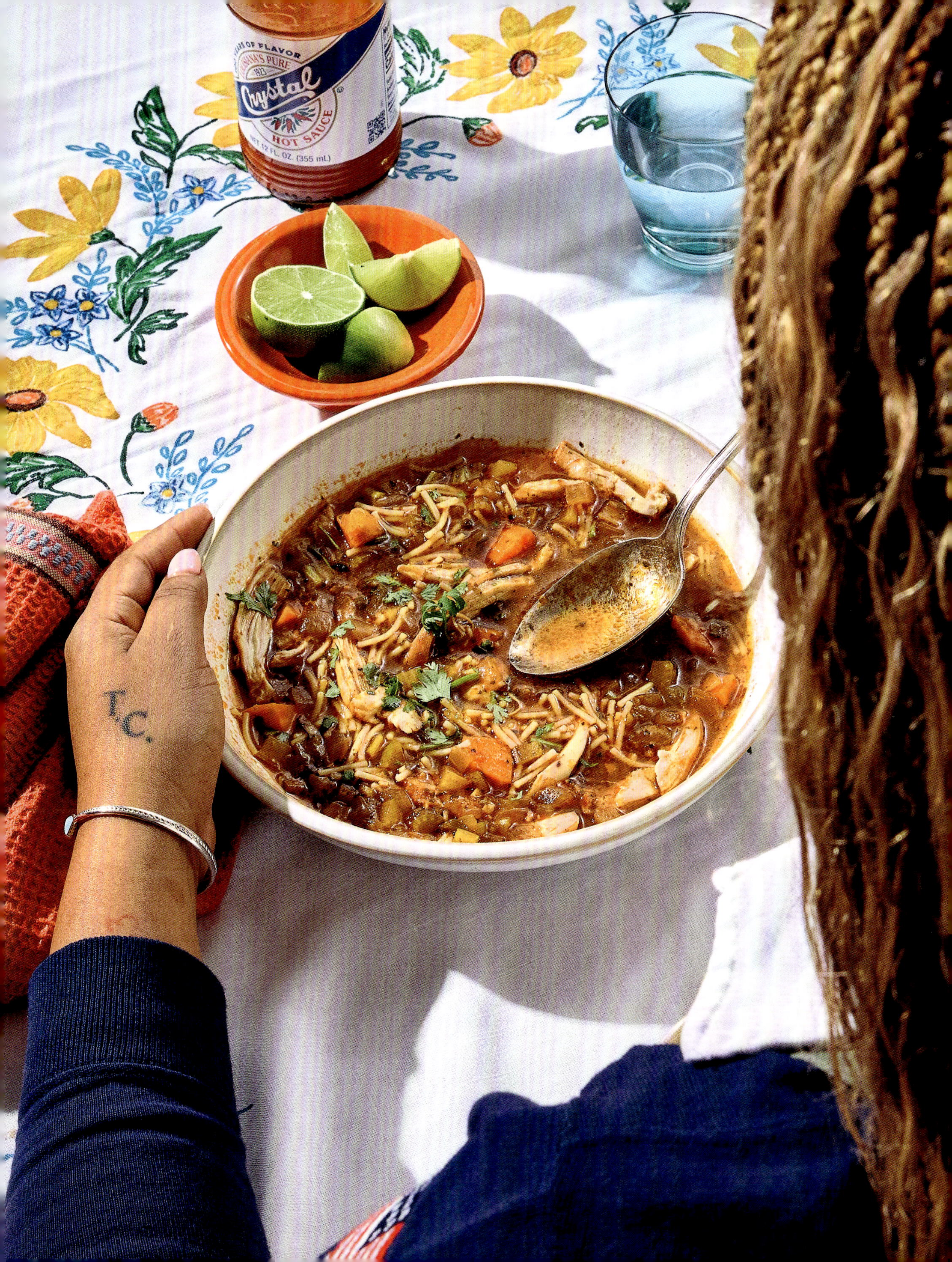

1923
Crystal
HOT SAUCE

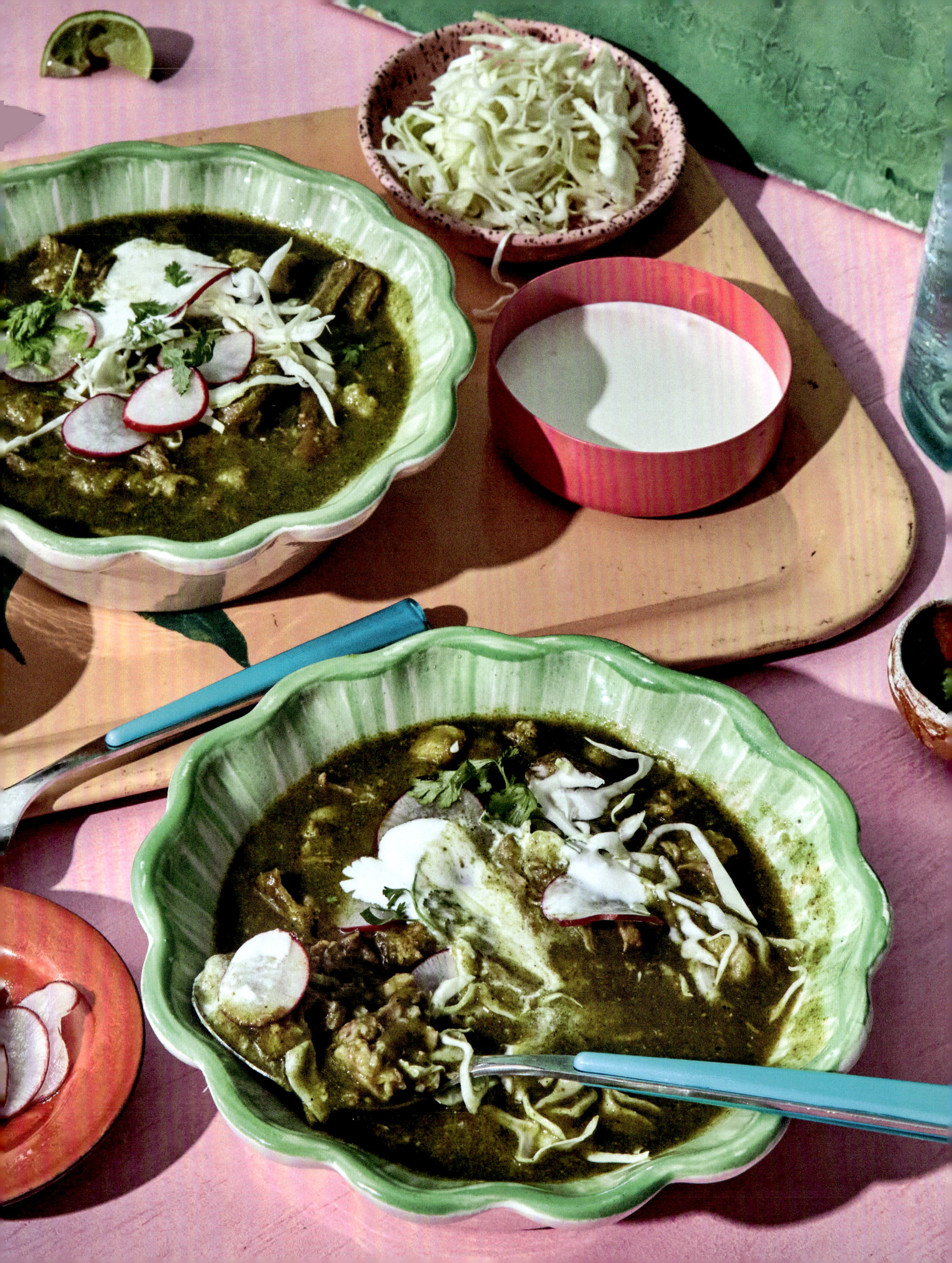

The Very Best Pozole Verde

Serves 8

This is by far my favorite soup recipe in the chapter and is an ode to my love for Mexican culture and cuisine. Pozole verde is one of Mexico's most beloved soups. It's so hearty it's almost like a stew, with a cilantro-based broth flavored with a green salsa (salsa verde). The salsa verde is made by roasting jalapeños, tomatillos, green bell peppers, garlic, and poblano peppers and blending them, then stirring the salsa into the soup so it can flavor every bite. Sometimes when I make this soup, I'm sneaking spoonfuls of the sauce as I cook—it's that good. If I could take a bath in one soup broth, this would be the one. Even though the broth is light, the pork shoulder and the hominy give it depth, making it so comforting. Now, for toppings, this is where I'm heavy-handed. Be generous with sour cream, radishes, and lime wedges for a creamy, citrusy, fresh bowl of goodness.

Soup

3 pounds boneless pork shoulder, cut into 4-inch chunks
2 teaspoons kosher salt
½ teaspoon ground cumin
½ teaspoon freshly ground black pepper
2 tablespoons extra-virgin olive oil
½ medium yellow onion, roughly chopped (about ½ cup)
6 garlic cloves, minced (about 2 tablespoons)
6 bay leaves
6 cups chicken broth

Salsa Verde

6 tomatillos, husked
3 large poblano peppers
2 small jalapeños
1 large green bell pepper, quartered
½ medium yellow onion, quartered
8 garlic cloves, peeled but whole
2 tablespoons extra-virgin olive oil
1⅛ teaspoons kosher salt
3 cups fresh cilantro leaves (from about 2 bunches, stemmed)
2 teaspoons chicken bouillon powder
1 teaspoon dried Mexican oregano
1 teaspoon onion powder
1 teaspoon garlic powder

To Finish

2 cups drained canned hominy
Sour cream
Sliced radishes
Shredded cabbage
Lime wedges

Make the soup: Season the pork all over with the salt, cumin, and black pepper. In a 5-quart Dutch oven, heat the olive oil over medium-high heat until hot and shimmering. Working in batches to avoid overcrowding (which would cause the pork to steam rather than brown), sear the pork for 3 to 4 minutes per side, until browned all over. Transfer the pork to a plate.

Reduce the heat to medium-low, return all the pork back to the pot and add the onion, garlic, and bay leaves. Pour in the chicken broth, cover, and cook for about 1½ hours, stirring every 30 minutes, until the pork is tender and easily breaks apart. While cooking, add additional water, 1 cup at a time, as needed while the broth reduces, making sure the meat is always submerged in the liquid.

Meanwhile, make the salsa verde: Preheat the oven to 400°F. Line a baking sheet with aluminum foil.

Place the tomatillos, poblanos, jalapeños, bell pepper, onion, and garlic on the lined baking sheet. Drizzle with the olive oil and sprinkle with ⅛ teaspoon of the salt. Toss to coat. Roast for 20 to 25 minutes, until the vegetables are charred. Allow the roasted vegetables to slightly cool, about 10 minutes.

In a blender, combine the cooled vegetables, cilantro, chicken bouillon powder, oregano, onion powder, garlic powder, and remaining 1 teaspoon salt. Scoop out ½ cup of broth from the soup and add to the blender. Blend until smooth, cracking the lid away from you or opening up the steam vent to let the steam escape.

To finish: Once the meat is tender, remove it from the pot with tongs or a slotted spoon, shred it with two forks, and return it to the pot. Pour in the salsa verde and add the hominy. Simmer for 20 minutes, stirring occasionally, to blend the flavors.

Spoon the pozole verde into bowls and top with sour cream, sliced radishes, and shredded cabbage. Serve with lime wedges on the side for squeezing.

Chef's Kiss: If you *really* want to take this soup up a notch, serve with warm tortilla chips or tostadas for adding a crunchy element that complements the freshness, brightness, and creaminess of the soup. The balance of textures and flavors is amazing!

Soulful Soups

Creamy Chicken and Dumplings

Serves **8**

When the craving for comfort food hits, nothing warms the soul quite like a bowl of chicken and dumplings. This soup combines juicy, boneless chicken thighs with a creamy, flavorful broth packed with fresh vegetables and aromatic herbs. The real magic happens when you add the dumplings to soak up all that deliciousness, creating a meal that feels like a warm hug on a chilly day. Perfect for family gatherings or a relaxing night in, this recipe is a true showstopper that's sure to become a favorite in your home.

Chicken

- 2 pounds boneless, skinless chicken thighs, cubed
- 2 tablespoons extra-virgin olive oil
- 1 tablespoon onion powder
- 1 tablespoon garlic powder
- 1 tablespoon sweet paprika
- 1 tablespoon kosher salt
- 1 tablespoon freshly ground black pepper

Soup

- 8 tablespoons (1 stick/4 ounces) unsalted butter
- 3 small carrots, diced (about 1½ cups)
- 3 celery stalks, diced (about 1 cup)
- 2 small yellow onions, diced (about 1 cup)
- ½ cup all-purpose flour
- 6 garlic cloves, minced (2 tablespoons)
- 1 tablespoon Worcestershire sauce
- 1 tablespoon kosher salt
- 4 cups low-sodium chicken broth
- 1 cup heavy cream
- 3 sprigs thyme, leaves picked and finely chopped
- 1 sprig rosemary, leaves picked and finely chopped
- 1 sprig sage, finely chopped

Dumplings

- 2 cups all-purpose flour, plus more as needed
- 2 tablespoons chopped fresh parsley
- 1 tablespoon garlic powder
- 2 teaspoons baking powder
- 2 teaspoons kosher salt
- 6 tablespoons (3 ounces) unsalted butter, cubed
- 1 cup whole milk

Cook the chicken: In a large bowl, combine the chicken thighs, 1 tablespoon of the olive oil, the onion powder, garlic powder, paprika, salt, and pepper. Toss to coat the chicken all over.

In a large pot or Dutch oven, heat the remaining 1 tablespoon olive oil over medium heat until hot and shimmering. Add the chicken and cook for 3 to 4 minutes, stirring occasionally, until browned on all sides. Transfer the chicken to a plate and set aside.

Make the soup: In the same pot, melt the butter over medium heat. Stir in the carrots, celery, onions, flour, garlic, Worcestershire sauce, and salt. Cook for 5 minutes, stirring occasionally, until the vegetables are softened. Stir in the chicken broth, heavy cream, thyme, rosemary, and sage. Let the mixture simmer over medium-low heat for 10 minutes, stirring occasionally, to allow the flavors to combine.

Meanwhile, make the dumpling dough: In a large bowl, mix together the flour, parsley, garlic powder, baking powder, and salt. Add the butter and use a fork or dough cutter to incorporate the butter into the flour mixture, until pieces no larger than a pea remain. Make a well in the middle of the mixture and pour in the milk. Mix with your hands just until combined. If your dough sticks to your hands, add a sprinkle of flour. Do not overmix. Use a tablespoon to scoop dollops of dough onto a plate. You should have about 20 balls.

Cook the dumplings: Add the chicken to the pot along with 2 cups water. Stir and add the dumplings. Cover tightly with a lid and cook for 20 minutes, until the dumplings are cooked through. Do not open the lid while cooking. Serve hot.

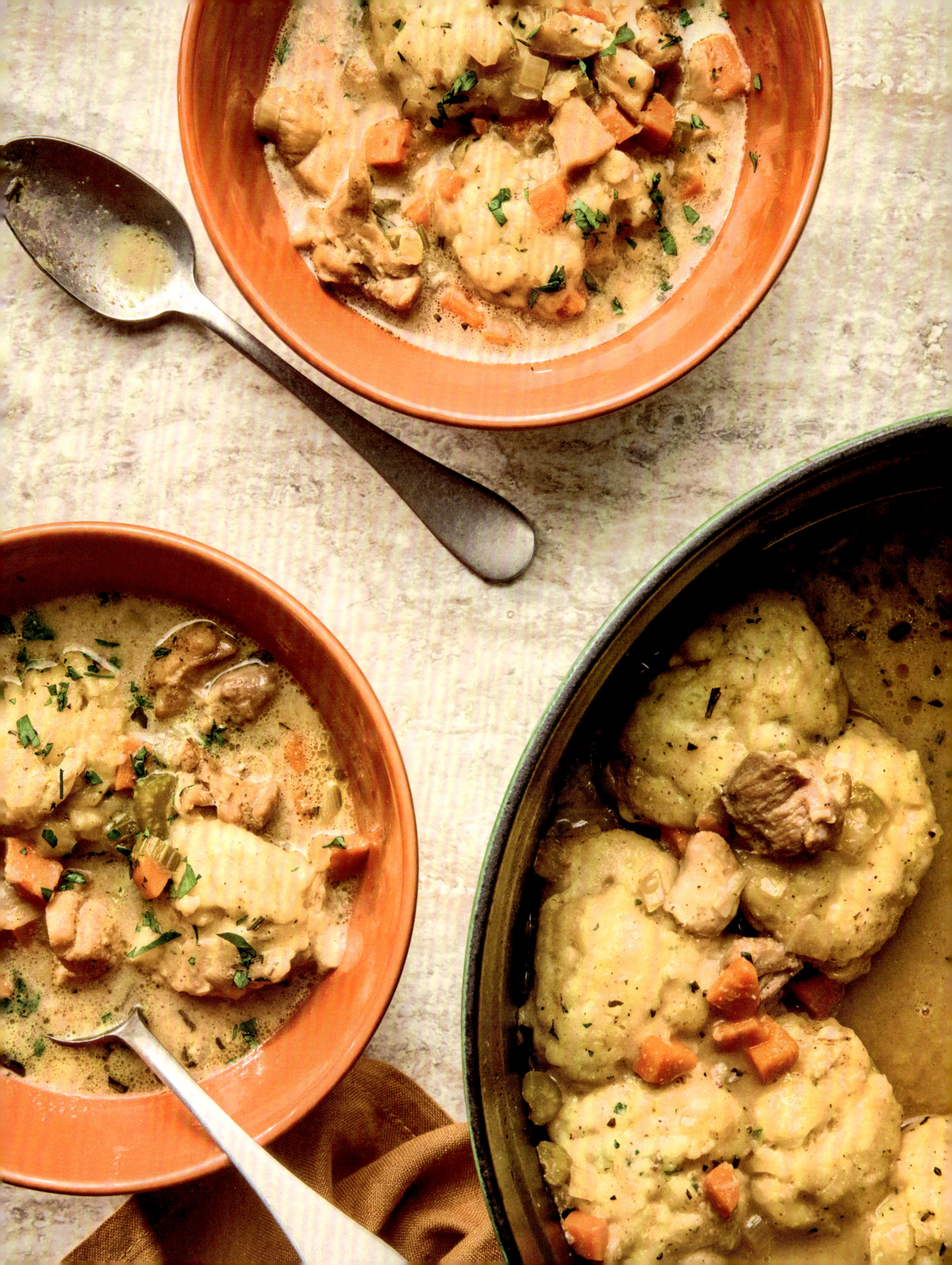

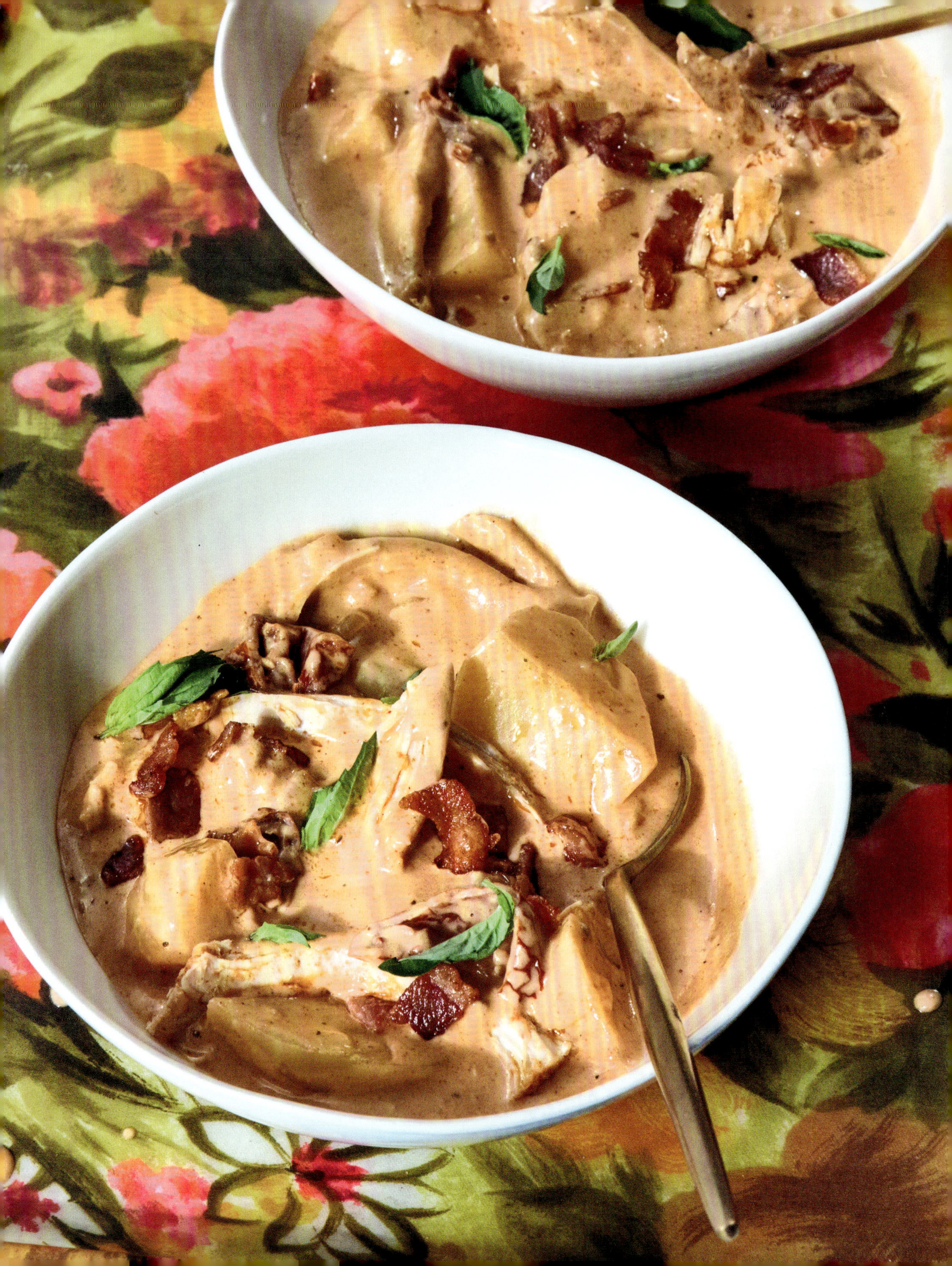

Marry Me Chicken Soup

Serves 6

For me, the perfect comfort meal has a few things: 1. Bacon—let's be real, bacon makes everything better; 2. Butter, because without butter, how would I live?; and 3. Cheese, because cheese holds the key to my heart. All of these ingredients combined make for an "mmm" kinda meal. The term "Marry Me" came from a chicken recipe that allegedly is so good, it would get you a ring. This soup takes the "Marry Me Chicken" even further by using all of my favorite ingredients. If that chicken gets you a ring, this soup will get you the white picket fence, two-point-five kids, and a cute goldendoodle. Use it wisely.

4 slices bacon (optional), chopped

Chicken

1 pound boneless, skinless chicken cutlets (about 3)
2 teaspoons sweet paprika
1 teaspoon garlic powder
1 teaspoon onion powder
1 teaspoon all-purpose seasoning
½ teaspoon no-salt Cajun seasoning
½ teaspoon kosher salt
2 tablespoons extra-virgin olive oil (optional; use only if not using bacon)

Soup

4 tablespoons (½ stick/2 ounces) unsalted butter
½ medium yellow onion, diced (about ½ cup)
8 garlic cloves, minced (about 3 tablespoons plus 2 teaspoons)
½ cup all-purpose flour
4 cups heavy cream
3 cups low-sodium chicken broth
1 (7-ounce) jar sun-dried tomatoes, drained
2 teaspoons sweet paprika
2 teaspoons kosher salt
1 teaspoon onion powder
1 teaspoon garlic powder
1 teaspoon Italian seasoning
½ teaspoon no-salt Cajun seasoning
2 pounds Yukon Gold potatoes, peeled and cut into 1-inch pieces
4 ounces Parmesan cheese, freshly shredded (1 cup)
½ cup roughly chopped fresh basil leaves

Cook the bacon (if using): Line a plate with paper towels and have near the stove. In a large pot or Dutch oven, sauté the bacon over medium-high heat, stirring and flipping occasionally, for 5 to 7 minutes, until crisp. Remove the cooked bacon from the pan and place it on the paper towels. Leave the bacon fat in the pot (or, if you didn't use bacon, you'll use olive oil for cooking the chicken).

Cook the chicken: Season the chicken cutlets with the paprika, garlic powder, onion powder, all-purpose seasoning, Cajun seasoning, and salt.

In the pot, heat the bacon fat (or olive oil) over medium-high heat until shimmering. Sear the seasoned chicken for 4 to 5 minutes per side, until browned all over, cooked through, and an instant-read thermometer inserted into the thickest part of the chicken reads 165°F. Transfer the cooked chicken to a plate and set aside.

Make the soup: Add the butter to the same pot you used to sear the chicken. Once melted, add the onion and garlic and sauté for about 5 minutes, stirring often, until soft. While stirring constantly, sprinkle in the flour to make a roux. Keep stirring for 2 to 3 minutes, until the mixture turns golden brown and velvety.

Stir in the heavy cream, chicken broth, sun-dried tomatoes, paprika, salt, onion powder, garlic powder, Italian seasoning, and Cajun seasoning. Bring the mixture to a simmer over low heat, stirring occasionally. Add the potatoes and let the soup simmer, uncovered and stirring occasionally, for 15 to 20 minutes, until the potatoes are fork-tender and the soup has thickened. Stir in the Parmesan until melted.

Shred the cooked chicken and add it to the soup. Let the soup simmer for 5 minutes, until the chicken is heated through. Stir in the basil just before serving. Ladle into bowls and garnish with the bacon (if using).

Soulful Soups

Island Pasta Soup

Serves **8**

This soup is everything you love about rasta pasta, just cozier and in a bowl. It's got all the signature flavors—creamy coconut milk, bold jerk seasoning, and the warmth of fresh thyme—mixed with tender pasta and a medley of peppers and onions that bring that vibrant island vibe. And let's not forget the protein! You can add shrimp, chicken, or even just keep it veggie; it's flexible and packed with flavor no matter what.

This soup is rich, creamy, and perfect for those nights when you want something comforting but still with a little spice and personality. It's like wrapping yourself in a Caribbean hug, and the best part? It's simple to make. This is the kind of soup that feels like a vacation in a bowl, no passport required.

8 slices bacon, roughly chopped
1 pound Italian sausage links, casings removed (I like half hot, half sweet)
1 tablespoon unsalted butter
1 small green bell pepper, diced (about ½ cup)
1 small red bell pepper, diced (about ½ cup)
1 small yellow onion, diced (about ½ cup)
3 garlic cloves, minced (about 1 tablespoon)
¼ cup all-purpose flour
4 cups low-sodium chicken broth
2 tablespoons jerk seasoning
2 tablespoons roughly chopped fresh oregano
4 sprigs thyme
1 tablespoon onion powder
1 tablespoon garlic powder
2 teaspoons kosher salt, plus more to taste
19 ounces frozen cheese tortellini
1 (13.5-ounce) can full-fat coconut milk
1 cup heavy cream
Juice of 1 lime
Freshly ground black pepper
¼ cup chopped fresh cilantro, for serving
Freshly grated Parmesan cheese, for serving
Lime wedges (optional), for serving

Cook the bacon and sausage: Line a plate with paper towels and have near the stove. In a large pot or Dutch oven, cook the bacon over medium heat for 5 to 7 minutes, stirring occasionally, until crispy. Use a slotted spoon to transfer the bacon to the paper towels to drain, leaving the bacon fat in the pot.

Add the sausage to the pot. Cook for 7 to 8 minutes, until browned and cooked through, breaking up the sausage with a spoon and stirring frequently as it cooks. Use a slotted spoon to transfer the sausage to the plate with the bacon, leaving the fat in the pot.

Make the soup: Melt the butter in the fat. Add the bell peppers and onion and sauté, stirring frequently, for 3 to 5 minutes, until the peppers are softened and the onion is translucent. Add the garlic and cook, stirring constantly, for 1 to 2 minutes, until fragrant.

Sprinkle the flour in the pot and stir well to coat the vegetables and make a roux. Cook for 1 to 2 minutes, stirring constantly, until the roux starts to bubble and thicken. Slowly pour in the chicken broth and 2 cups water, stirring constantly to prevent lumps. Bring the mixture to a simmer and cook for 10 minutes, until the soup thickens slightly.

Return the sausage and bacon to the pot. Stir in the jerk seasoning, oregano, thyme, onion powder, garlic powder, and salt. Simmer for 5 minutes to meld the flavors.

Add the tortellini to the soup and cook according to the package directions (usually 7 to 9 minutes).

Stir in the coconut milk and heavy cream. Simmer for 5 minutes to heat through. Stir in the lime juice and season with salt and black pepper to taste.

To serve, discard the thyme stems, ladle the soup into bowls, and sprinkle with the cilantro and grated Parmesan. Serve hot with a wedge of lime, if desired.

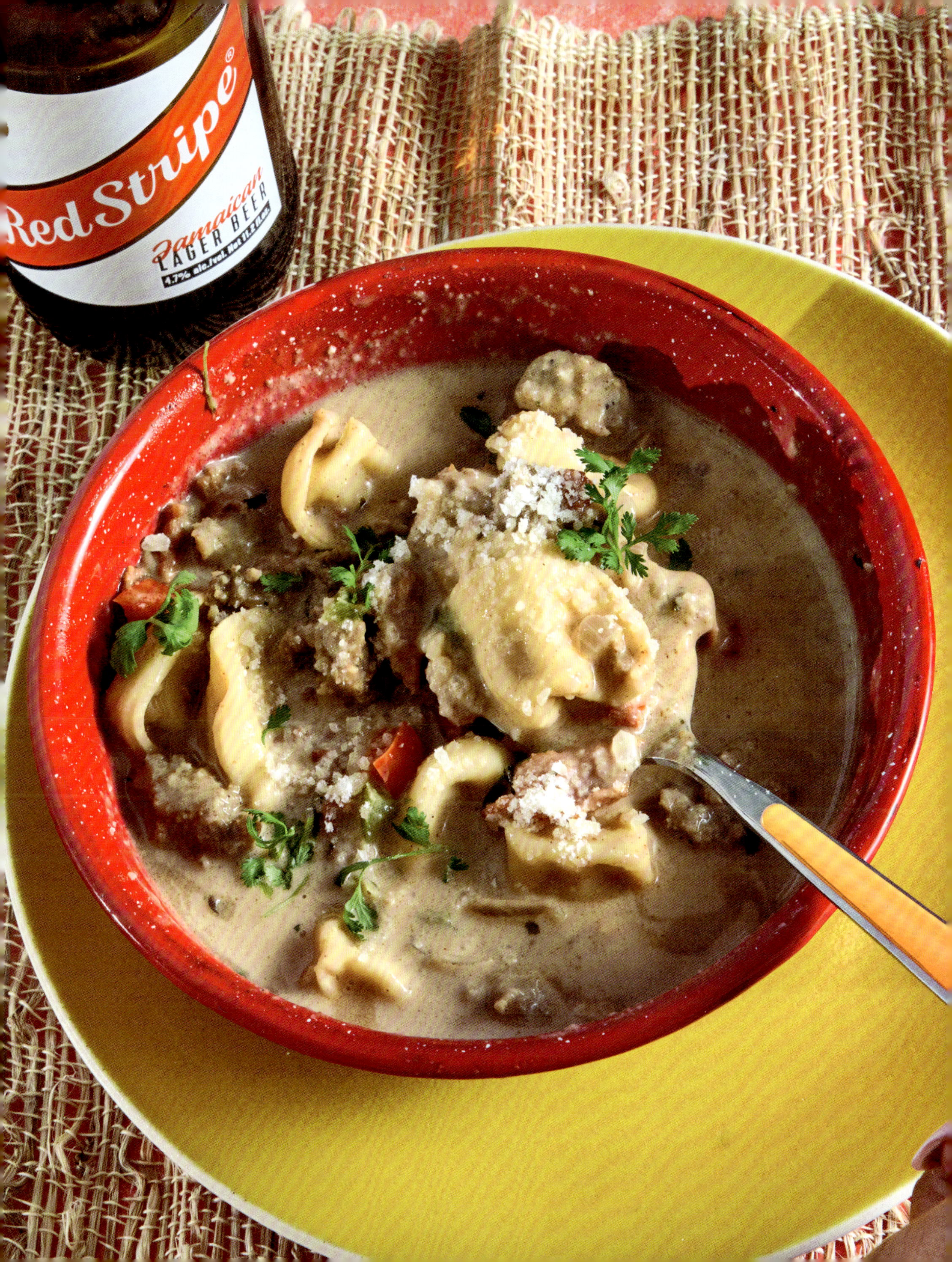
Red Stripe
Jamaican
LAGER BEER

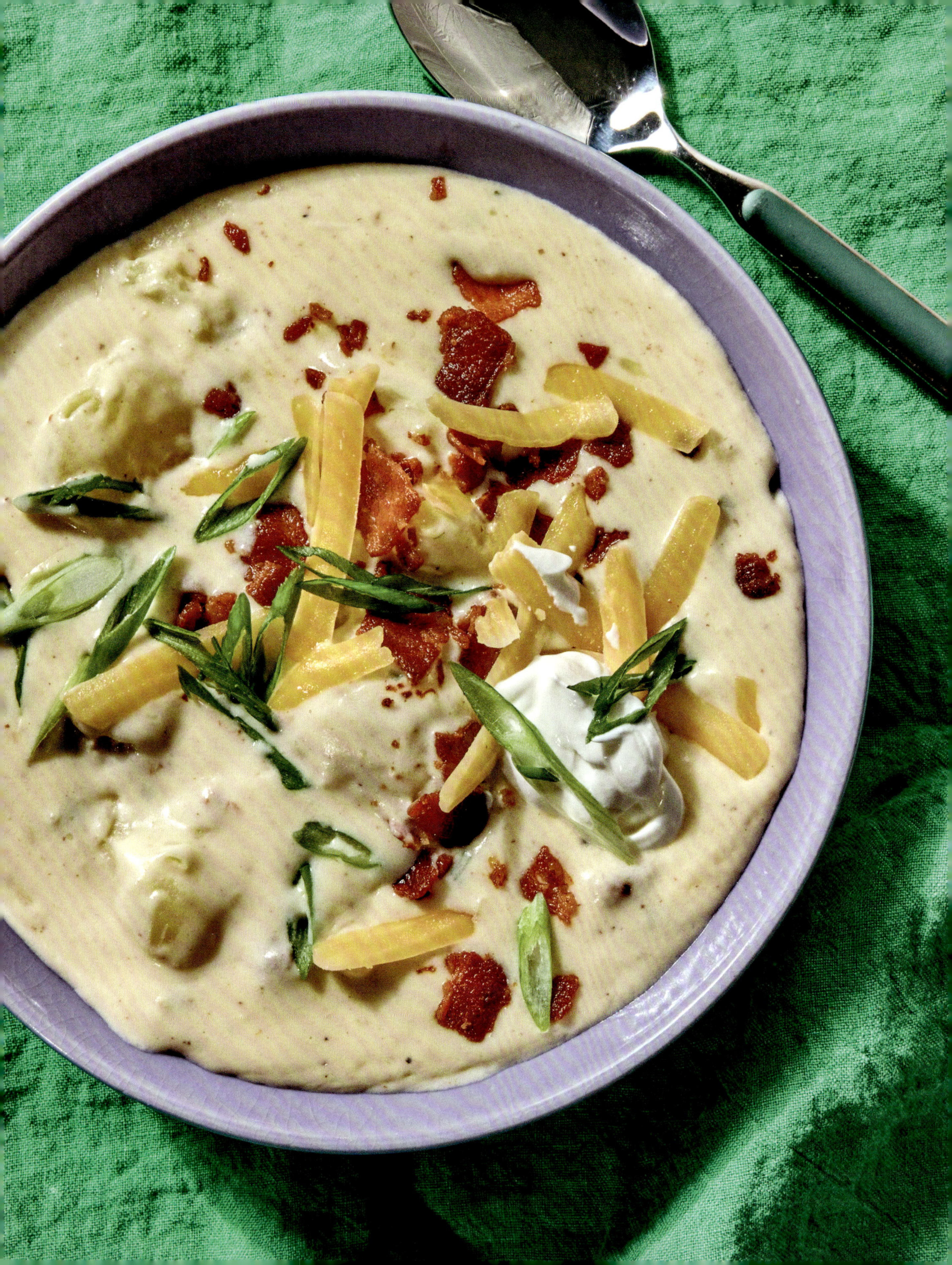

The Ultimate Loaded Baked Potato Soup

Serves **8**

I had no idea this soup would blow up the way it did, but the moment I posted it, it was everywhere. There's just something about loaded baked potatoes—they're as American as it gets, and turning them into a soup? That had everyone excited. While mine wasn't the first version of this classic, it stands out with its layers of flavor. It all starts with a roux made from bacon fat, setting the stage with that rich, smoky goodness. Then I go all in with heavy cream and cheese (you'll thank me later), and Yukon Gold potatoes add the perfect soft, buttery texture. It's the kind of soup that feels familiar, but with enough depth to make it unforgettable.

1 pound bacon, sliced into ½-inch pieces
12 garlic cloves, minced (about ¼ cup)
¼ cup finely chopped scallions
¼ cup all-purpose flour
4 cups heavy cream
2 cups low-sodium chicken broth, plus more as needed
1 cup whole milk
1 teaspoon adobo seasoning
Kosher salt and freshly ground black pepper
3 pounds Yukon Gold potatoes, peeled and cut into 1-inch cubes
8 ounces sharp Cheddar cheese, freshly grated (2 cups), plus more for serving
Sour cream, for serving
Sliced scallions, for serving

Cook the bacon: Line a plate with paper towels and have near the stove. In a large pot or Dutch oven, cook the bacon over medium heat for 5 to 7 minutes, stirring occasionally, until crispy. Use a slotted spoon to transfer the bacon to the paper towels to drain, leaving the bacon fat in the pot.

Make the soup: In the same pot, combine the garlic, chopped scallions, and flour and whisk over medium-low heat for 2 minutes to make a roux, until the mixture is golden and smooth. Stir in the heavy cream, chicken broth, milk, adobo seasoning, and salt and pepper to taste. Add the potatoes and more chicken broth, if needed, to cover the potatoes. Cook, uncovered, for 20 minutes, stirring occasionally, until the potatoes are fork-tender. Stir in the Cheddar, reduce the heat to low, and simmer for 15 minutes, stirring frequently, until the cheese is melted.

Ladle the hot soup into bowls and serve with sour cream, Cheddar, sliced scallions, and the bacon sprinkled over the top.

Parmesan Garlic Breadsticks

Makes 12 breadsticks

These buttery breadsticks are the stuff dreams are made of—soft, pillowy, and just the right amount of golden on the outside. I love using them to soak up the delicious flavorful broth in my soups. They might remind you of Olive Garden (you know the ones), but trust me, these are better. They're so rich and buttery, you'll want to eat them straight out of the oven, but they're also perfect for dunking into soups, stews, or even mopping up that last bit of sauce on your plate. Yes, they take a little time, but they're worth every minute. The dough is foolproof—easy to work with and forgiving, even for beginners. Plus, you can freeze them, so a fresh batch of breadsticks is always just a reheat away. Trust me, once you make these, you'll find yourself planning meals just to have an excuse to bake them again.

Breadsticks

1¼ cups warm water (about 110°F)
2 tablespoons dark brown sugar
1 packet instant yeast (2¼ teaspoons)
3 cups all-purpose flour, plus more for dusting
4 ounces Parmesan cheese, freshly grated (about ½ cup)
2 teaspoons kosher salt
4 tablespoons (½ stick/2 ounces) unsalted butter, melted and cooled, plus more for greasing and brushing

Garlic Butter

4 tablespoons (½ stick/2 ounces) unsalted butter, melted
1 tablespoon garlic powder

Freshly grated Parmesan cheese, for serving
Chopped fresh parsley (optional), for serving

Make the breadstick dough: In a large bowl, combine the warm water and brown sugar, stirring until the sugar is dissolved. Sprinkle the yeast over the water and let it sit for 10 minutes, until it foams.

In a separate large bowl, stir together the flour, Parmesan, and salt. Make a well in the middle of the mixture and add the melted butter and the yeast mixture. Stir well until fully combined and the dough starts to come together.

Transfer the dough to a floured surface and knead for about 10 minutes, until the dough is smooth and elastic. (Alternatively, use a stand mixer with the dough hook and mix on medium speed for 5 minutes.)

Lightly grease a large bowl with butter. Place the dough in the bowl, cover with a clean kitchen towel or plastic wrap, and let rise in a warm place until it doubles in size, about 1 hour.

Bake the breadsticks: Preheat the oven to 400°F. Line a baking sheet with parchment paper.

Punch down the dough with your hand to release any air bubbles, then divide it into 12 equal portions. Roll each portion into a breadstick 6 to 8 inches long. Place the breadsticks on the lined baking sheet, spacing them 1 inch apart. Cover the breadsticks with a kitchen towel and let them rise for 15 to 20 minutes, until they're slightly puffed up.

Brush the tops with melted butter and bake for 12 to 15 minutes, until they are golden brown.

Meanwhile, make the garlic butter: In a small bowl, whisk together the melted butter and garlic powder.

After the breadsticks come out of the oven, immediately brush them with the garlic butter. Serve sprinkled with additional Parmesan and some parsley, if desired.

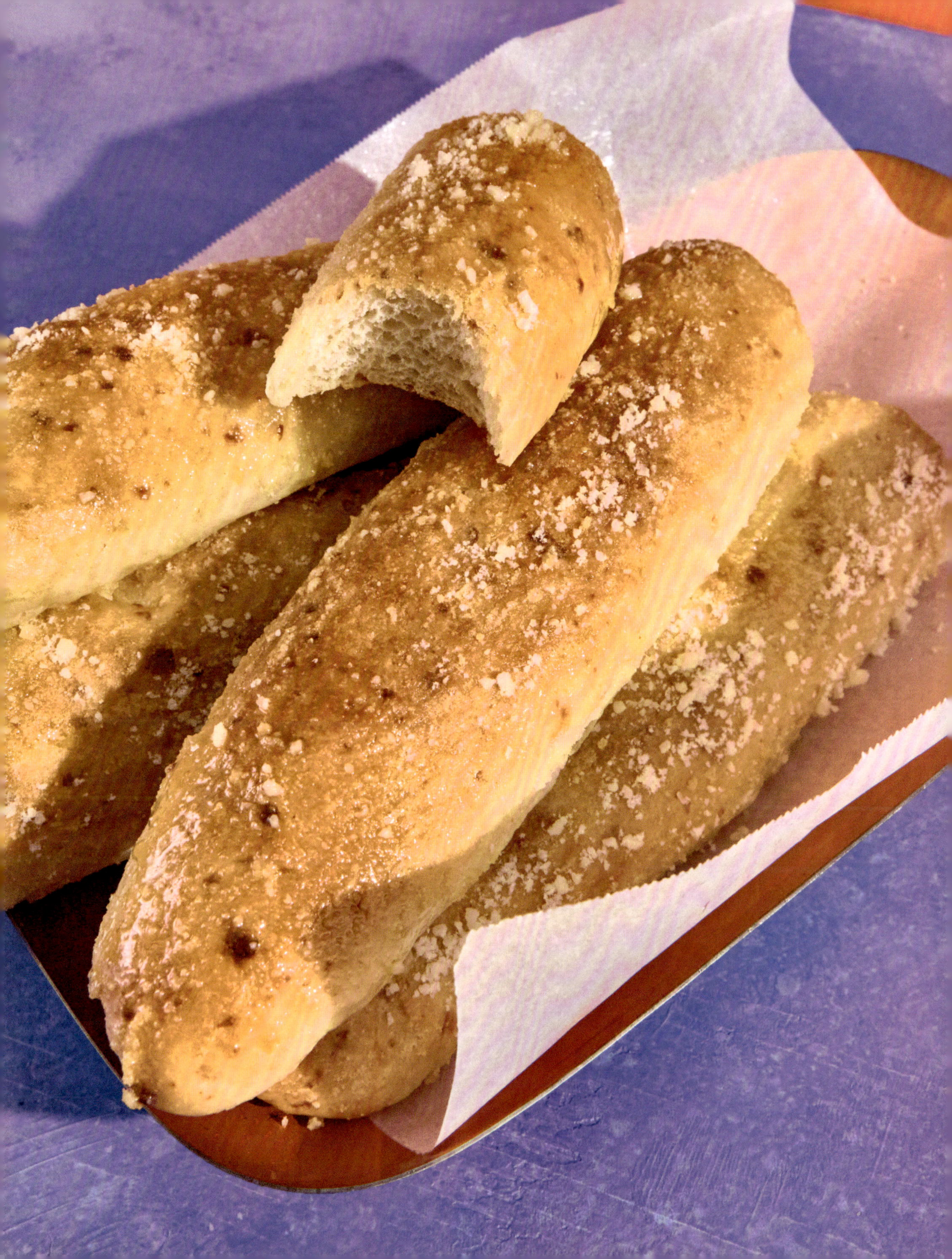

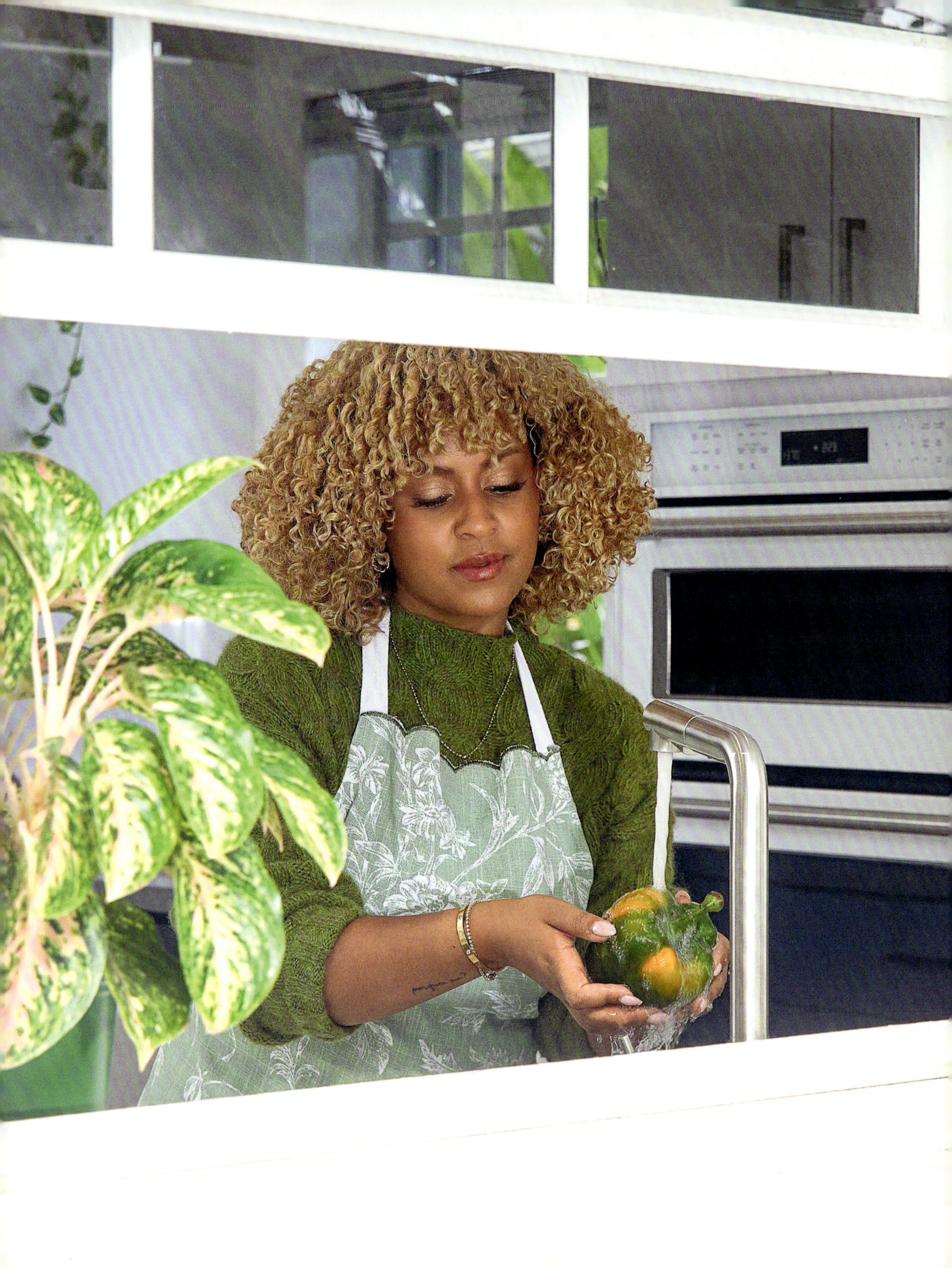

3
On a Lighter Note
(Bright and Easy)

Growing up in the inner city, fresh fish, herbs, fruits, and veggies weren't always on the menu. A typical meal at our house was a stewed meat, plenty of rice, and maybe a root veggie or platano or a piece of bread. And honestly? I loved it. I ate meals like this every day, completely happy and unaware of what I was missing.

Fast-forward to 2023, when I moved from Jersey City to Miami, and everything changed. My social media feed, my cooking style, my pantry—it all got an upgrade. Suddenly, I was surrounded by vibrant ingredients and began making my own marinades, vinaigrettes, sauces, and spice blends. That was the start of my obsession with brighter, fresher recipes. Saturdays became my favorite day of the week because I'd stroll through the Coconut Grove farmers' market, where the fresh snapper, ripe quenepas (a small Caribbean fruit), fragrant citrus, and straight-from-the-source coconut water sparked something new in me. And then there was The Mango House, the first home I moved to in Miami, named for the mango, lime, lemon, and coconut trees on the property. Every day, I was inspired by the bounty around me, experimenting and creating recipes that felt like home but with a brighter, fresher twist.

That's why I had to dedicate a whole chapter to these dishes. They're easy to prepare, packed with fresh, bold flavors, and still comforting enough to feel like me. Think cilantro's cooling taste, the sweetness of diced mango, the heat of a Scotch bonnet pepper, and the bold zest of lime. Need to impress for Taco Tuesday? My Shrimp and Mango Ceviche (page 75) brings that perfect balance of sweet, light, and heat—serve it with chips and beers, and you'll be the host of the century. For a quick weeknight favorite, my Lemon-Butter Cod (page 79) is pure magic—it's my personal favorite, and I'd bet it'll become yours, too. Or take a flavor-packed trip to the islands with my famous Caribbean-Style Jerk Chicken (page 80), bursting with spices and that unmistakable Caribbean freshness.

These recipes are the type you'll want to make two or three times a week. Lighter, brighter, but still cozy and full of flavor, they made me fall in love with cooking again and I hope they do the same for you.

Goes-with-Everything Salad

Serves 6

My cucumber salad is one of those easy sides that goes with everything. It's crisp, fresh, and the perfect way to sneak some veggies into your meal. Pair it with rice or any of my stews, and it balances out the richness with a light, refreshing crunch. The best part? The addition of the creamy feta and Dijon vinaigrette makes it taste indulgent—you almost forget it's actually good for you! Simple to throw together but it hits every time.

Vinaigrette

½ cup extra-virgin olive oil
¼ cup red wine vinegar
4 garlic cloves, minced (about 4 teaspoons)
1 tablespoon Dijon mustard
1 tablespoon freshly squeezed lemon juice
1 tablespoon chopped fresh dill
1 heaping teaspoon honey
1 teaspoon kosher salt
1 teaspoon Italian seasoning
½ teaspoon freshly ground black pepper

Salad

2 large cucumbers, cut into ½-inch cubes
12 ounces grape or cherry tomatoes, quartered
¾ large red onion, thinly sliced
8 ounces feta cheese, crumbled

Make the vinaigrette: In a medium bowl, whisk together the olive oil, vinegar, garlic, mustard, lemon juice, dill, honey, salt, Italian seasoning, and pepper.

Assemble the salad: In a large bowl, combine the cucumbers, tomatoes, and onion. Pour the vinaigrette over the vegetables and toss until well coated. Gently stir in the feta and chill in the fridge for at least 30 minutes or up to 1 day before serving.

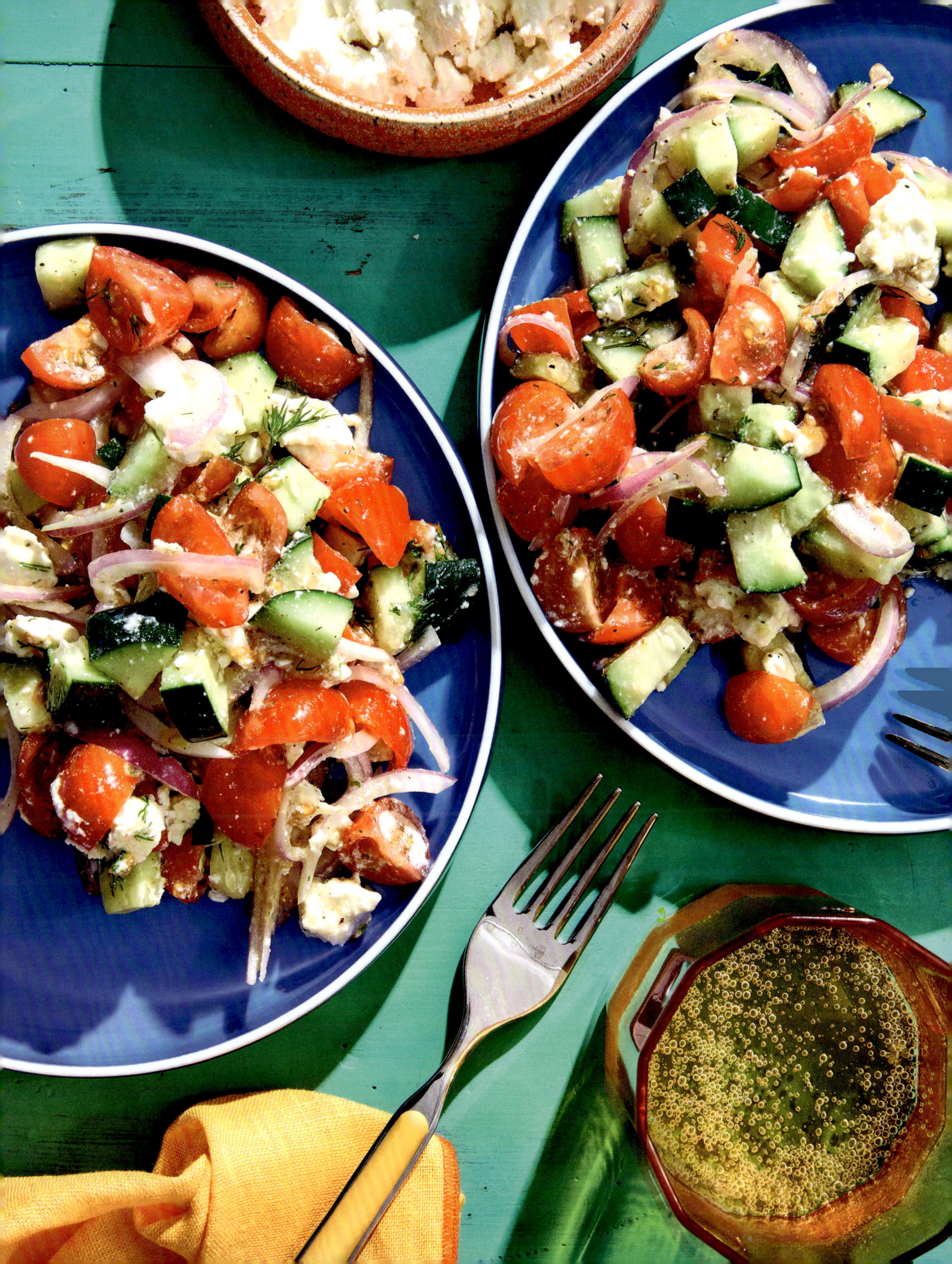

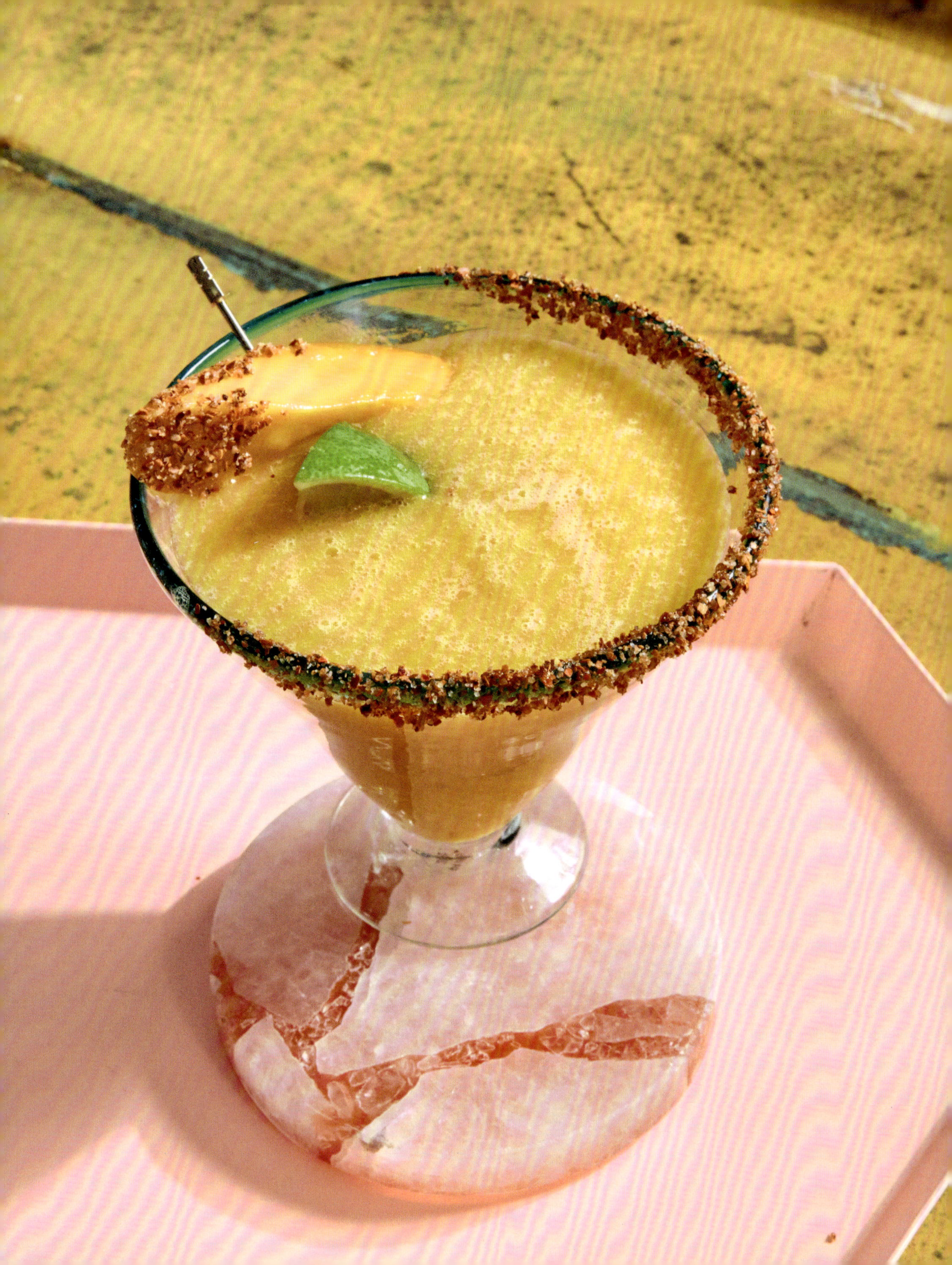

Mango House Margarita

Makes **1** cocktail

This got its name from where it all started—right at the first place I lived in Miami, which we call The Mango House because of the big mango tree on the property. Whenever I had friends or family over, I'd grab some fresh mangoes and whip up this sweet and tangy margarita. It became a bit of a tradition, and the drink took on a life of its own. The ripe mangoes, mixed with the bright lime and a little heat, turned into something everyone who comes over looks forward to. It's more than just a cocktail—it's a nod to the good times shared at my house, with fresh-picked mangoes and a margarita in hand.

1 lime wedge
1 tablespoon Tajín seasoning, plus more (optional) for garnish
1 mango, diced, with 1 slice set aside for garnish
Ice
¼ cup freshly squeezed lime juice (about 2 limes)
2 ounces tequila
2 tablespoons agave syrup

Rub the lime wedge around the rim of a cocktail glass. Cover a small plate with the Tajín. Dip the glass into the Tajín to coat the rim. Fill the glass with ice.

Add the mango to a cocktail shaker and use the flat end of a wooden spoon or cocktail muddler to mash the mango and release the juices. Add a handful of ice, then the lime juice, tequila, and agave. Shake well and strain into the prepared glass. Serve garnished with the reserved mango slice dipped in extra Tajín, if desired.

Cajun Lemon Pepper Corn

Serves 6

At any barbecue in America, you'll probably find grilled corn, a staple that everyone makes but not everyone makes well (no shade)! Most corn is usually overcooked or lacking in flavor—two things I wanted to address! So, I came up with this recipe on the fly one night. I had some friends over, we were laughing, drinking, and politicking, and I wanted to make a sauce for the corn I was grilling. I grabbed a few ingredients, and voilà, this lemony-spicy sauce was born. It's a little sweet, spicy, and tangy, with a great punch from the cilantro. Serve this certified banger at your next barbecue.

6 ears sweet corn
8 ounces (2 sticks) unsalted butter
¼ cup honey
Juice of ½ lemon
1 tablespoon finely chopped fresh cilantro
1 tablespoon Old Bay seasoning
1 tablespoon sweet paprika
1 teaspoon adobo seasoning
1 teaspoon lemon pepper

Preheat a grill to medium-high heat.

Prep the corn: Peel back the corn husks, leaving them attached at the base of each ear of corn. Remove the silks and rinse the corn, then pat dry.

Grill the corn: Place the corn on the grill and cook for 10 to 15 minutes, turning every couple of minutes. You'll know it's perfect when the kernels are tender and have those deep charred marks—like little bursts of caramelized gold. Pierce a kernel with a knife to check for tenderness, and keep turning until you've got that perfect balance of char and sweetness.

Meanwhile, make the butter: Set a 12-inch cast-iron skillet on the grill and melt the butter. When the butter is melted, stir in the honey, lemon juice, cilantro, Old Bay, paprika, adobo seasoning, and lemon pepper until smooth and fully combined.

Baste the corn: Once the corn is grilled on all sides, use a basting brush to brush it generously with the seasoned butter. Serve hot.

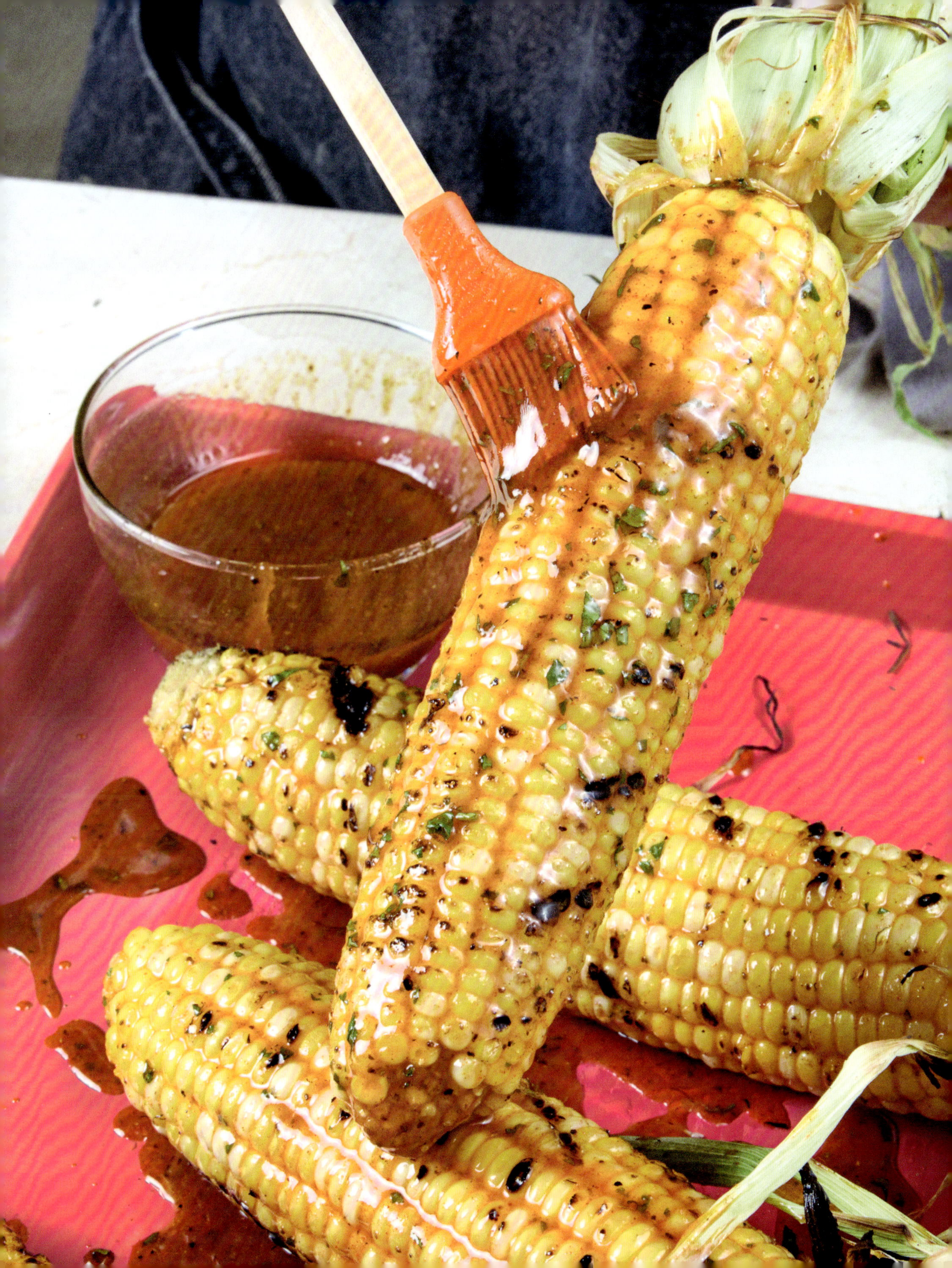

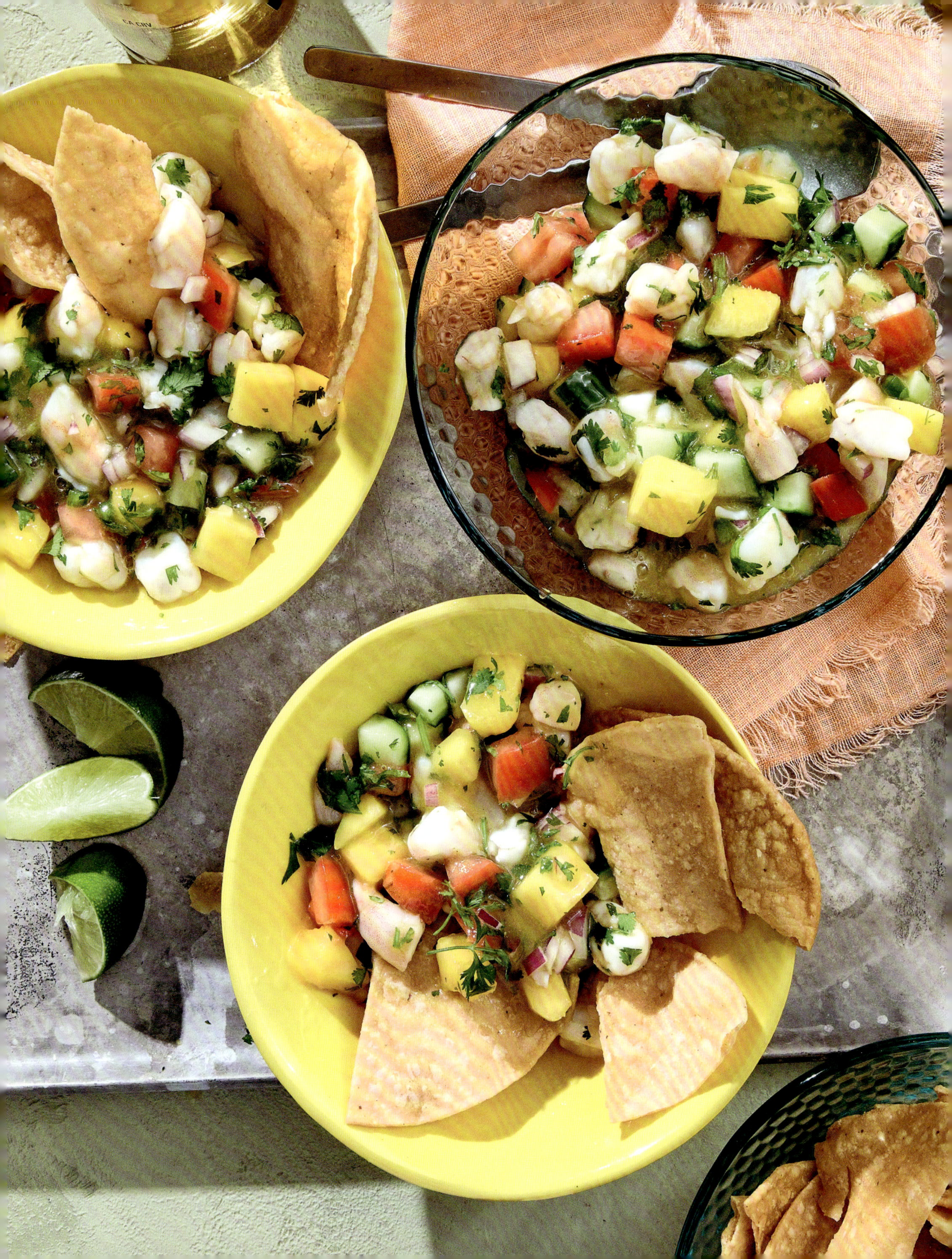

Shrimp and Mango Ceviche

Serves **8**

Living in Miami, I've had some of the best ceviche in the country, no question. And over the years, I've picked up all the tips and tricks to make it right at home. Most people think ceviche is intimidating, but like with most of my recipes, I'm here to show you it's not. Ceviche is really just seafood "cooked" in a whole lot of lime juice. That's it! No heat, no stress. The lime does the work, and the rest is all about building flavor. I like to keep things fresh with jalapeños, cucumbers, red onions, tomatoes, and my little secret weapon—mango. The sweetness of the mango balances out the acidity of the lime perfectly, and the jalapeños bring that extra kick. It's a twist on the classic that hits all the right notes—crunchy, sweet, spicy. Remember when we talked about the elements of great cooking on page 17? This dish is the perfect balance of flavors, and trust me, it's so good you'll wonder why you ever thought ceviche was hard to make.

Ceviche

2 pounds shrimp (21/25 count), peeled and deveined, tails off, diced
1 cup freshly squeezed lime juice (about 8 limes), plus more as needed
2 teaspoons kosher salt
1 teaspoon freshly ground black pepper
2 medium mangoes, finely diced
1 large cucumber, peeled, seeded, and finely diced
2 Roma tomatoes, seeded and finely diced
½ small red onion, finely diced
1 jalapeño, finely diced, or more for extra heat
½ cup fresh cilantro leaves, finely chopped

Mango Sauce

1 mango, roughly chopped
¼ cup freshly squeezed lime juice (about 2 limes), plus more to taste
2 tablespoons Clamato tomato cocktail (optional)
6 to 8 dashes Maggi seasoning, plus more to taste
1 teaspoon kosher salt, plus more to taste

Tortilla chips or tostadas, for serving
Lime wedges, for serving

"Cook" the shrimp: In a large bowl, stir together the shrimp and lime juice. Add more lime juice, if needed, to cover the shrimp completely. Season with salt and pepper. Marinate in the refrigerator for at least 2 hours and up to 4 hours, until the shrimp is opaque. Once the shrimp have turned opaque, drain off any excess lime juice.

Assemble the ceviche: Add the diced mangoes, cucumber, tomatoes, onion, jalapeño, and cilantro to the bowl with the marinated shrimp.

Make the mango sauce: In a blender, combine the mango, lime juice, Clamato (if using), Maggi seasoning, and salt. Blend until smooth. Adjust the seasonings to taste, adding more lime juice, Maggi, or salt as desired.

Pour the mango sauce over the shrimp mixture and toss until well combined and evenly coated with the sauce.

Chill the ceviche: Cover the bowl with plastic wrap and refrigerate for 30 minutes to allow the flavors to meld together.

Serve the ceviche cold as an appetizer or light meal with tortilla chips on top and a squeeze of lime.

Good Vibes Rum Punch

Serves 8

Bright, citrusy, and just the right amount of sweet, rum punch tastes like summer in a glass. Pineapple, orange, and lime juices blend perfectly with the bold kick of strong rum, while a little grenadine adds a pop of color and sweetness. It's refreshing yet rich, the kind of drink that feels like a celebration with every sip. A staple of the Caribbean, rum punch has roots that go back centuries, born from the islands' fresh fruits and legendary rum-making tradition. It's a must-have at any BBQ, beach party, or family gathering. One sip and you're on island time, surrounded by good vibes and sunshine.

2 cups orange juice
2 cups pineapple juice
¾ cup spiced rum
½ cup Wray & Nephew rum
¼ cup grenadine
1 orange, cut into thin slices
2 limes, cut into thin slices
6 allspice berries
Ice, for serving

In a large pitcher, mix together the orange juice and pineapple juice until well combined. Pour in both rums and stir gently to combine. Slowly add the grenadine to the pitcher. It will sink to the bottom, creating a beautiful gradient effect. Toss in the oranges, limes, and allspice berries. Lightly stir to distribute the fruit and spices. Refrigerate for 1 hour until well chilled.

To serve, add ice to the pitcher just before serving to keep the punch cold without diluting it too quickly. Pour the punch into glasses, dividing evenly among the glasses, and serve.

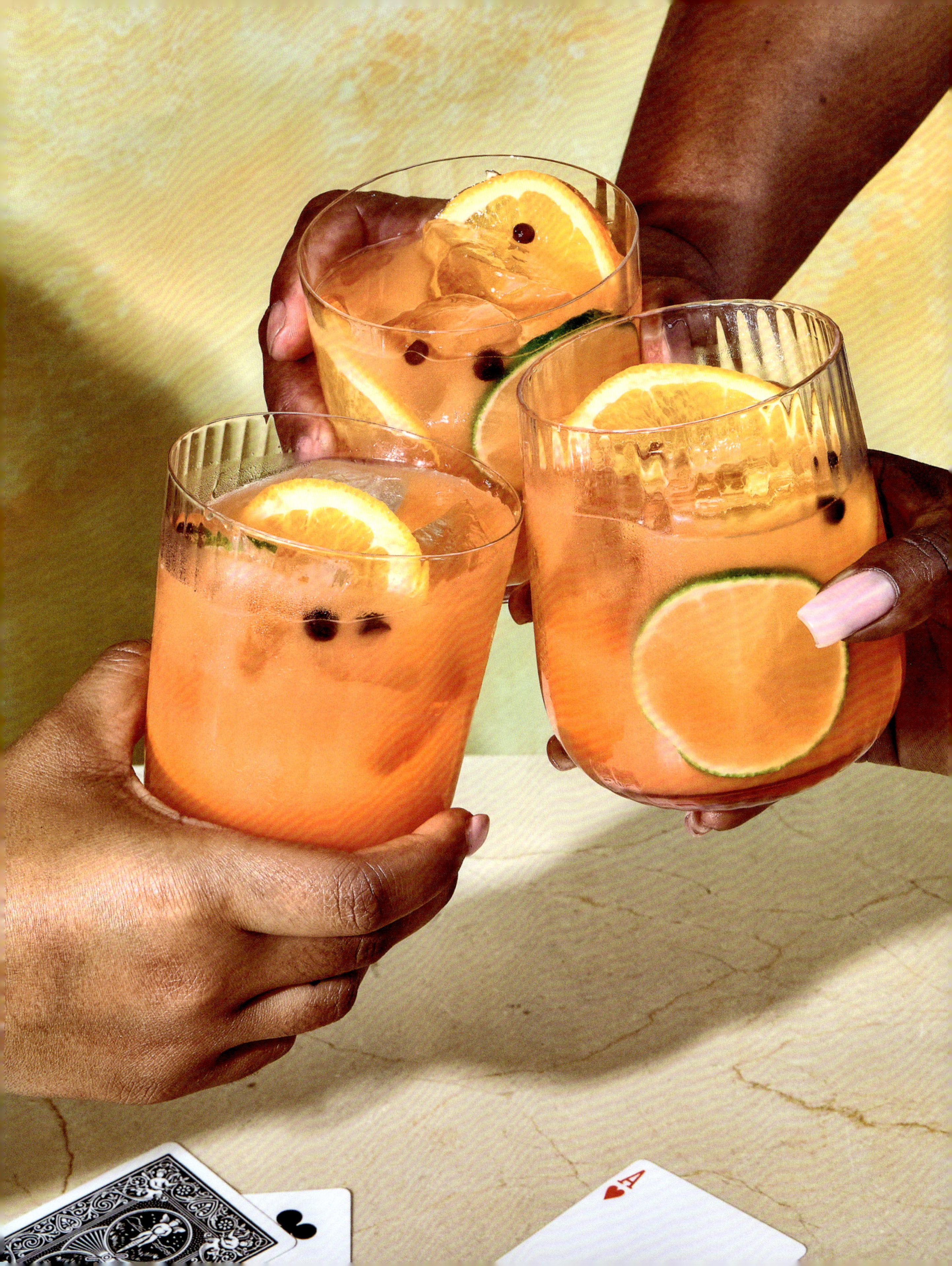

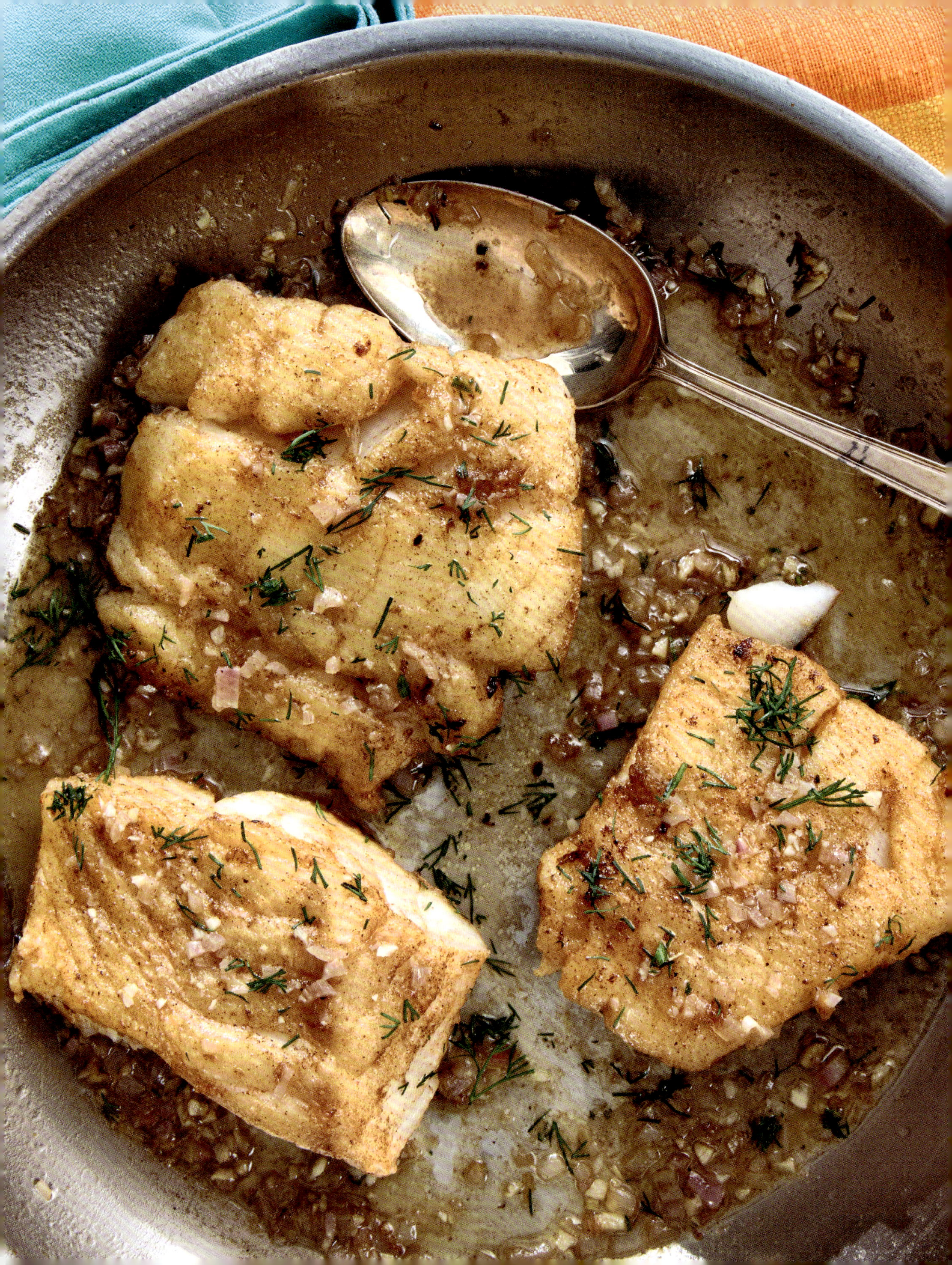

Lemon-Butter Cod

Serves **6**

At The Mango House, the first place I lived in Miami, the mango, lime, and lemon trees became my best friends. Besides making a ton of Mango House Margaritas (page 71), I used fresh citrus in almost all my cooking, as in this recipe for lemon-butter cod, which perfectly balances some of my favorite flavors—citrus, dill, and butter. There have been a few times where I've eaten half of this recipe in one sitting, it's that good! I usually serve this with air-fried potatoes, rice, or a green salad.

Cod

6 (6-ounce) cod fillets
2 teaspoons kosher salt
Freshly ground black pepper
¼ cup all-purpose flour
1 teaspoon sweet paprika
1 tablespoon unsalted butter
1 tablespoon extra-virgin olive oil

Sauce

3 tablespoons (1½ ounces) unsalted butter
2 small shallots, finely chopped (about ¼ cup)
6 garlic cloves, minced (about 2 tablespoons)
¼ cup dry white wine, such as Chardonnay
¼ cup low-sodium chicken broth
1 teaspoon grated lemon zest
Juice of ½ lemon
2 tablespoons finely chopped fresh dill, for serving

Cook the cod: Pat the cod dry with a paper towel and season with 1 teaspoon of the salt and a pinch of pepper.

In a shallow dish, whisk together the flour, paprika, and remaining 1 teaspoon salt until well combined. Dredge the cod fillets in the flour mixture, shaking off any excess.

In a large skillet, heat the butter and oil over medium-high heat. When the butter is melted, add the cod fillets and cook for 3 to 4 minutes on each side, until golden brown and cooked through and the fish flakes apart with a fork. Transfer the cod to a plate and set aside.

Make the sauce: In the same skillet, melt the butter over medium-high heat. Add the shallots and garlic and sauté, stirring frequently, for 2 to 3 minutes, until softened and fragrant. Pour in the white wine and simmer, stirring occasionally, for 2 to 3 minutes to reduce slightly. Add the chicken broth, lemon zest, and lemon juice to the skillet. Stir to combine and simmer for 2 to 3 minutes, until the sauce is fully incorporated.

Return the cod to the skillet, spooning the sauce over each fillet, and cook for 2 to 3 minutes to allow the flavors to meld. Transfer the cod to plates and serve with the sauce and a sprinkling of dill.

Little Detail, BIG Impact: The secret to this recipe is making sure the cod is perfectly cooked. Insert the tines of a fork into the fish at a 45-degree angle. Gently twist the fork to pull up some of the fish. If it flakes easily without pushing or tugging, then it is done and ready to eat.

Chef's Kiss: Add a little more lemon zest on top before serving.

Caribbean-Style Jerk Chicken

Serves 4

Jerk chicken was a staple in my neighborhood growing up, thanks to the Caribbean spots that always smelled like smoky, spicy heaven. I've eaten a lot of jerk chicken over the years, and here's what I've learned along the way. First things first—making the jerk seasoning from scratch is nonnegotiable. Trust me, the fresh spices and herbs make all the difference (you'll thank me later). Second, grab a Red Stripe or Guinness and pour it on the chicken while it cooks—it's a small touch, but it gives the meat that authentic, smoky-sweet flavor. And finally, don't rush it! Let the chicken marinate overnight so the spices really sink in. Whether you're grilling it over an open flame or baking it in the oven, this jerk chicken is guaranteed to bring the heat, the flavor, and the vibe.

- 2 pounds bone-in chicken (mixed pieces)
- 1 cup Jerk Marinade (page 239)
- ½ cup dark beer (if grilling), such as Red Stripe or Guinness

In a large bowl, marinate the chicken in the jerk marinade for at least 1 hour or ideally overnight.

To grill: Preheat a grill to medium-high heat (about 400°F). Lightly oil the grates and place the marinated jerk chicken on the grill, skin-side down. Grill for 5 to 7 minutes on each side, turning occasionally to prevent burning. While the chicken grills, pour some beer over the top. Grill for a total of 20 to 25 minutes, until an instant-read thermometer inserted into the dark meat reads 165°F. Remove the chicken from the grill and let rest for 2 to 3 minutes, then serve warm.

To bake: Preheat the oven to 375°F. Line a baking sheet with parchment paper. Place the marinated jerk chicken on the prepared pan. Bake for 40 to 50 minutes, until an instant-read thermometer inserted into the dark meat reads 165°F. Remove the chicken from the oven and rest for 2 to 3 minutes, then serve warm.

Chef's Kiss: Baste the chicken with leftover marinade during the last few minutes. Letting the chicken rest before serving locks in all those juicy flavors.

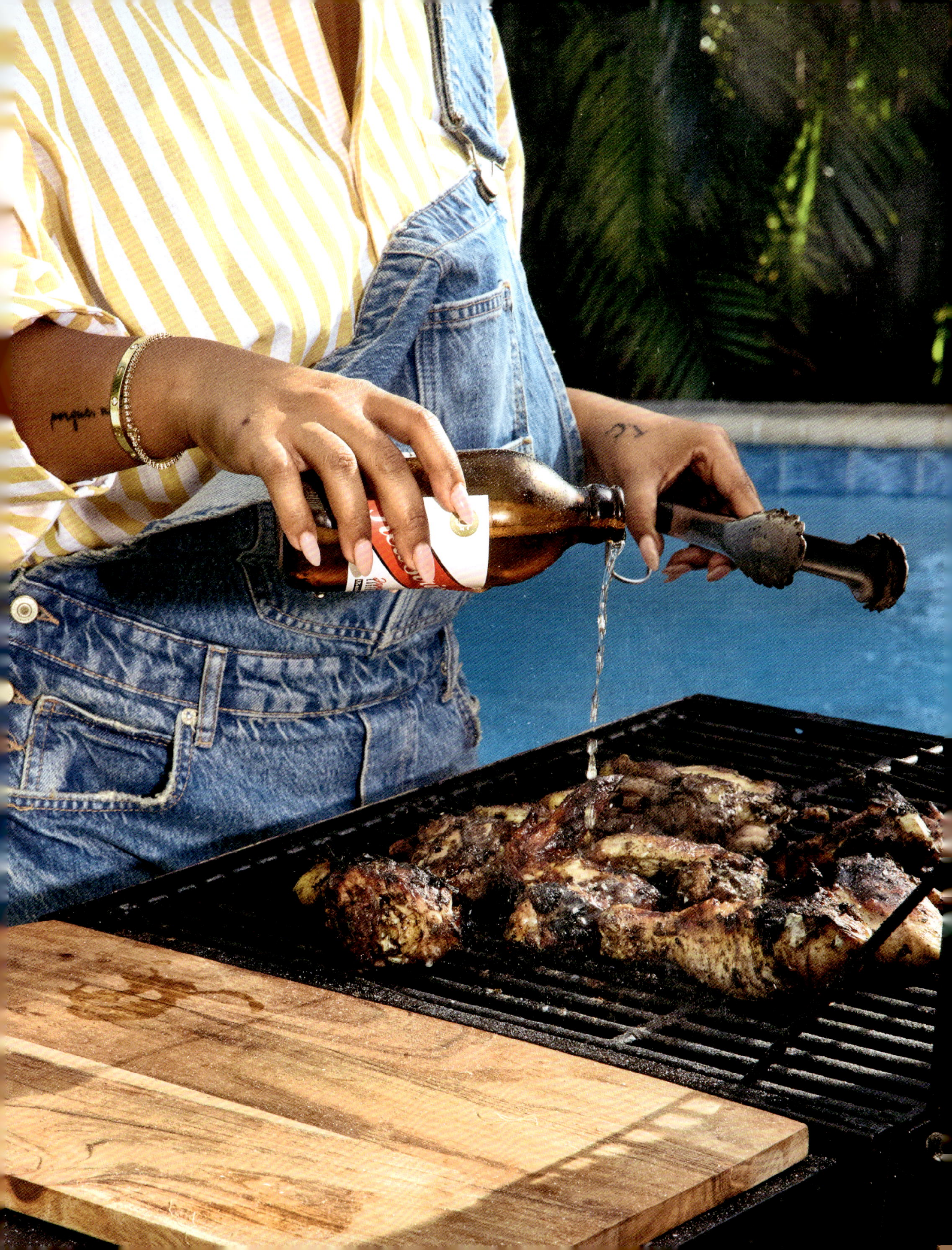

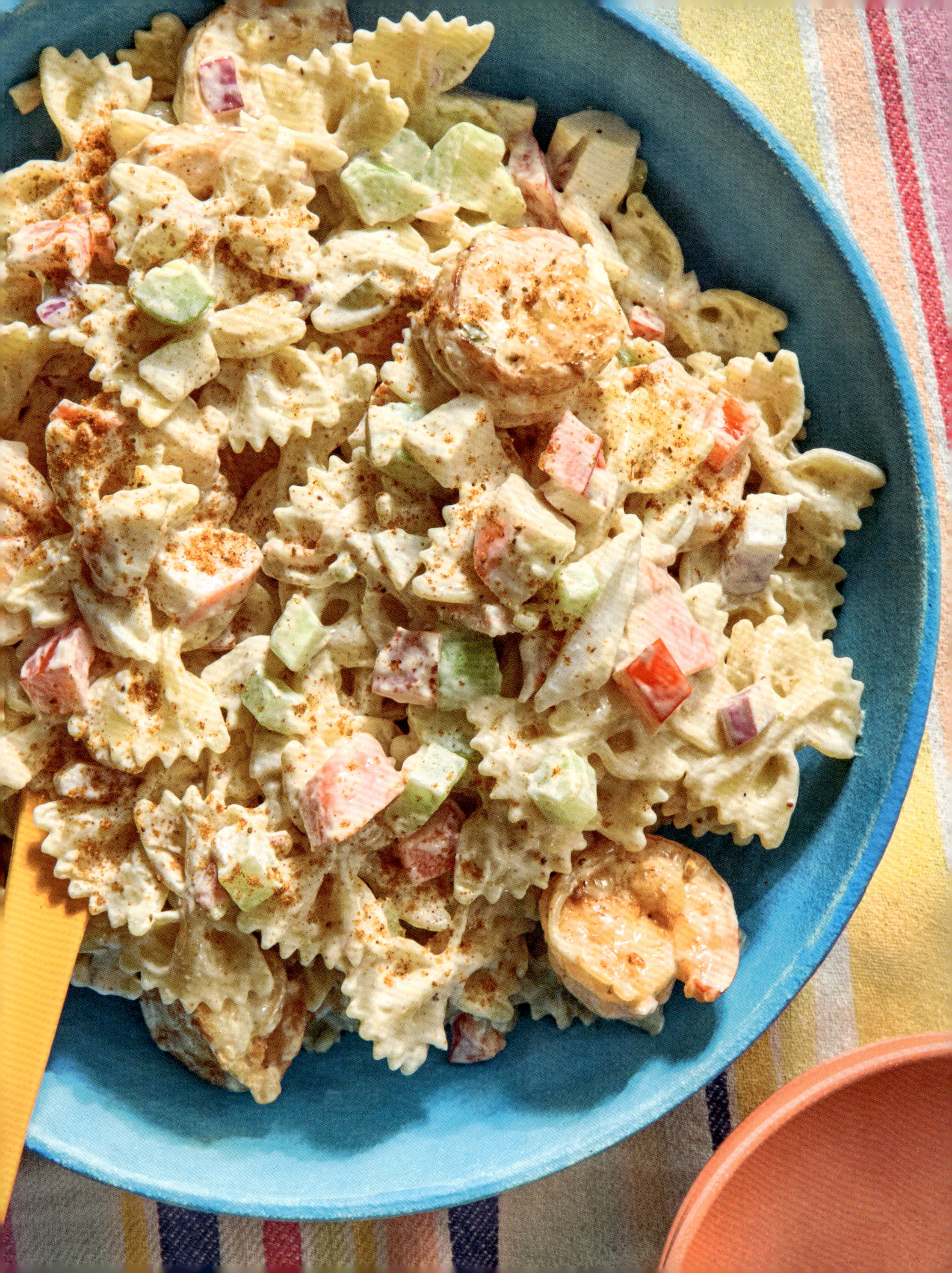

Papi's Seafood Pasta Salad

Serves 6

My papi proudly serves his famous seafood salad at every family gathering. While most dads have their secret BBQ sauce or chili recipe, Papi's specialty is this salad, the two most important ingredients being love (of course) and Hellmann's mayo. I know a lot of people have their opinions on the best mayo, but for this recipe to be like Papi's, you *have* to use Hellmann's.

1 pound bow tie pasta
1 pound shrimp (21/25 count), peeled and deveined, tails off
1¼ teaspoons Old Bay seasoning
¼ teaspoon garlic powder
2 tablespoons (1 ounce) unsalted butter
2 cups Hellmann's mayonnaise (Papi says!)
2 tablespoons Dijon mustard
2 tablespoons sweet relish
1 tablespoon freshly squeezed lemon juice
2 teaspoons Worcestershire sauce
3 celery stalks, diced (about 1 cup)
1 medium red bell pepper, chopped (about 1 cup)
½ medium red onion, finely chopped (about ½ cup)
8 ounces imitation crabmeat, coarsely chopped (about 2 cups)

Cook the pasta: Bring a large pot of water to a boil. Cook the pasta according to the package directions. Drain and let it cool completely.

Cook the shrimp: Put the shrimp in a large bowl, season with ¼ teaspoon of the Old Bay and the garlic powder, and toss to coat all over.

In a large skillet, melt the butter over medium heat. When the butter is melted, place the shrimp in the pan in a single layer and cook for 2 to 3 minutes, until they are pink and opaque. Flip and continue cooking for another 1 to 2 minutes, until they're pink all over and just cooked through. Transfer the shrimp to a plate and set aside to cool completely.

Make the salad: In a large bowl, whisk together the mayonnaise, mustard, relish, lemon juice, and Worcestershire sauce. Add the celery, bell pepper, onion, pasta, and shrimp and toss until everything is well coated. Gently fold in the crab and season with the remaining 1 teaspoon Old Bay.

Chill: Cover the bowl and refrigerate the pasta salad until chilled, for at least 1 hour and up to overnight, before serving.

Papi Says: If you want to be extra fancy, you can use fresh crabmeat, or even lobster (be sure to pick through for any shell fragments) instead of imitation crabmeat. You do you!

Plantain and Cream Cheese–Stuffed Pork Chops with Guava Sauce

Serves 2

This dish makes you feel like Abuela just cooked you a meal straight from the heart. That's the vibe here. Let's say it's Friday night. You've had a long week, and you want something that feels special. Make these stuffed pork chops, and trust me, they're nothing like your regular chuletas. These are next-level. The pork is first seasoned to perfection with Sazón and adobo before being pan-seared until crispy and golden. Then sweet plantains and cream cheese are tucked into those chops, and a simple sauce made of guava paste goes on top. The flavors come together in this perfect mix of savory and sweet that'll have you wondering why you ever made plain pork chops to begin with. Serve the pork chops with Arroz con Gandules (page 170).

Pork Chops

2 bone-in center-cut pork chops, at least 1 inch thick
2 teaspoons Goya Sazón (culantro y achiote)
1 teaspoon adobo seasoning
1 teaspoon kosher salt
3 tablespoons vegetable oil

Filling and Sauce

Vegetable oil, for frying
1 ripe yellow plantain, sliced into 1-inch pieces
Kosher salt
4 tablespoons (2 ounces) cream cheese (¼ block)
2 tablespoons guava paste

Cilantro leaves, for garnish

Preheat the oven to 350°F.

Sear the pork chops: Insert a sharp knife horizontally into the pork chops and cut a large slit to make a deep pocket for the stuffing. Do not cut all the way through.

In a small bowl, mix together the Sazón, adobo, and salt. Rub the seasoning mix onto the pork chops, ensuring it gets into the slits as well. Drizzle the pork chops with 1 tablespoon of the oil and rub it into the meat, coating well.

In a large, deep skillet, heat the remaining 2 tablespoons oil over medium-high heat until hot and shimmering. Sear the pork chops for 4 minutes per side, until they are golden brown. Transfer the pork chops to a plate.

Make the filling: Pour 2 inches of oil into the same skillet and heat over medium-high heat to 350°F. Fry the plantains for 5 to 6 minutes total, until fully cooked and golden brown. Transfer to a large bowl, add a pinch of salt, and then immediately mash with a pilón or potato masher until the texture reaches a paste-like consistency.

Bake the pork chops: Add ¼ cup of mashed plantains and half of the cream cheese into each pork chop, filling the slits. Transfer the pork chops to a baking sheet.

In a microwave-safe bowl, heat the guava paste with 2 tablespoons water for 1 minute. Stir until combined to make a sauce. Pour half of the guava sauce over the stuffed pork chops.

Bake for 30 minutes, or until the pork is cooked through and an instant-read thermometer inserted sideways into the pork reads 145°F. Switch the oven to low broil.

Add the remaining guava sauce on top of the pork chops and broil for about 2 minutes, making sure not to burn, until the sauce is bubbling. Garnish with cilantro and serve warm.

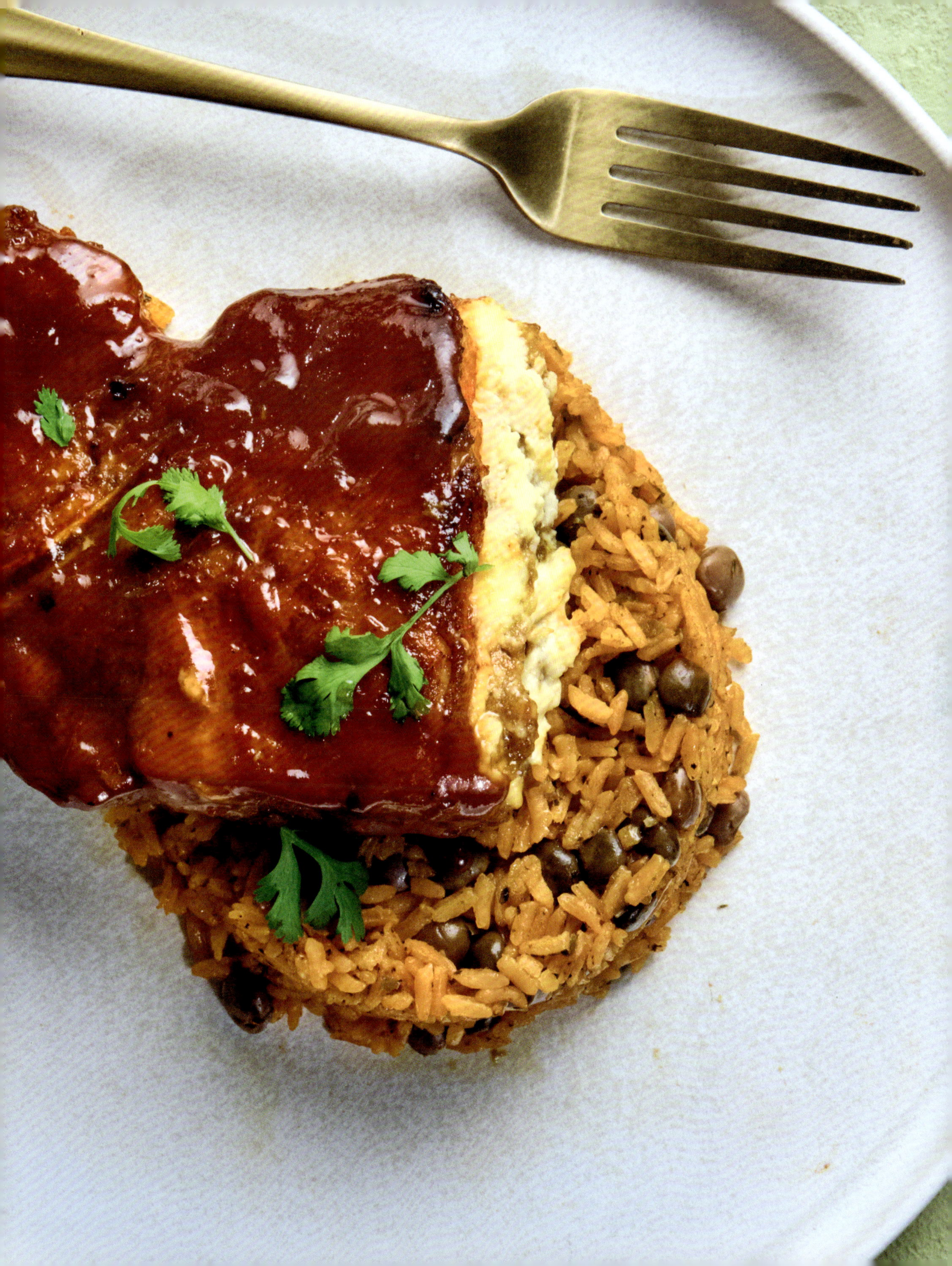

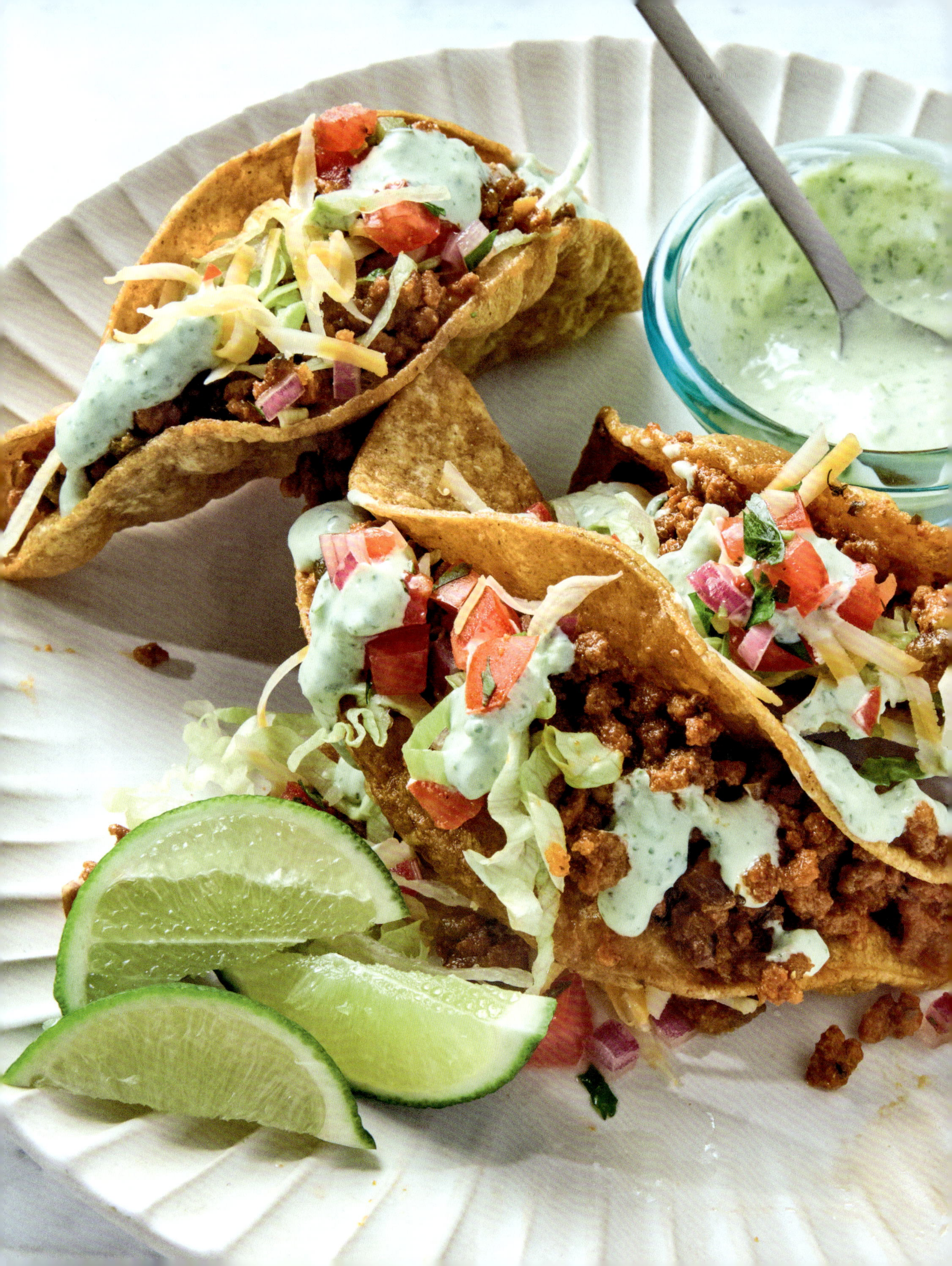

Crunchy Beef Tacos

Makes **8** tacos

Taco Bell–style tacos are always my guilty pleasure! That crunchy hard shell with perfectly seasoned beef? Whew, I could easily take down six. But as I grew as a chef and foodie, I wanted to make them my own. Turns out, you can make crunchy tacos at home, and you can take them to the next level with fresh pico, sour cream, cheese, and any of my sauces. In this recipe I use the Peruvian Ají Verde Sauce for the perfect balance of flavor.

This recipe will satisfy any Taco Bell craving, and trust me, once you put them on the table, they disappear fast. You might want to plan on making extras because these get eaten real quick!

Beef Filling

1 pound ground beef (80/20)
½ small green bell pepper, finely diced (about ¼ cup)
½ small red onion, finely diced (about ¼ cup)
3 garlic cloves, minced (about 1 tablespoon)
1 tablespoon tomato paste
½ cup canned tomato sauce
4 teaspoons Goya Sazón (culantro y achiote)
2 teaspoons garlic powder
2 teaspoons ground cumin
2 teaspoons dried oregano
2 teaspoons onion powder
2 teaspoons kosher salt, or more to taste
1 teaspoon sugar

Tacos

4 cups vegetable oil, for shallow-frying
8 (6-inch) yellow corn tortillas
Toppings: shredded lettuce, diced tomatoes or Pico de Gallo (page 88), shredded Cheddar cheese

Peruvian Ají Verde Sauce (page 242), for serving

Cook the beef filling: In a large skillet, cook the ground beef over medium-high heat for 5 to 7 minutes, breaking up the meat into small pieces and stirring frequently, until the beef is browned and no longer pink. Drain the excess fat from the pan, leaving the meat in the pan.

Reduce the heat to medium and add the bell pepper, onion, garlic, and tomato paste and cook for 3 to 4 minutes, stirring occasionally, until the vegetables soften. Stir in the tomato sauce, Sazón, garlic powder, cumin, dried oregano, onion powder, salt, sugar, and ¼ cup water. Reduce the heat to medium-low and simmer for 5 to 7 minutes, stirring occasionally, until the mixture thickens slightly. Taste and adjust the seasoning if needed.

Meanwhile, make the taco shells: While the beef mixture is simmering, pour ½ inch of oil into a large skillet and heat until it reaches 350°F. Line a plate with paper towels.

Once the oil is hot, place a tortilla flat in the oil for 30 seconds. Use tongs to flip it over and then fold the tortilla in half, using the other hand to hold a spoon in the middle of the shell so it doesn't close completely, and hold in place until crispy, about 30 seconds. Transfer the taco shell to the paper towels and repeat with the remaining tortillas.

Assemble the tacos: Dividing evenly, spoon the beef mixture inside the taco shells. Top with lettuce, tomatoes or pico de gallo, and cheese.

Serve the tacos immediately with the Peruvian ají verde sauce on the side for dipping or drizzling.

Pico de Gallo

Makes 4½ cups

Pico de gallo is my go-to all-purpose topping that takes just about anything to the next level. Tacos? Obviously. A crisp, fresh spoonful on fish or grilled meat? Perfection. Over a plate of fries? Game changer. I always keep a batch prepped and ready because it's the kind of thing you'll want to throw on everything. I especially love it piled high on my Crunchy Beef Tacos (page 87) or tucked into my Cheesy Chipotle Chicken Quesadillas (page 129)—it adds that fresh, tangy kick that ties everything together. It's simple, it's fresh, and it's just plain good. Once you have it ready, you'll be finding excuses to use it everywhere.

4 medium tomatoes, finely diced (3 cups)
1 medium red onion, finely diced (about 1 cup)
1 jalapeño, seeded and finely chopped
½ cup cilantro sprigs, finely chopped
2 tablespoons freshly squeezed lime juice (about 1 lime)
½ teaspoon kosher salt
¼ teaspoon freshly ground black pepper

In a medium bowl, combine the tomatoes, onion, jalapeño, and cilantro. Drizzle the lime juice over the mixture and sprinkle with the salt and pepper. Gently toss everything together until well combined. Taste and adjust the seasoning, if needed.

Pico de gallo is best fresh, but you can store leftovers in an airtight container in the refrigerator for up to 3 days. Stir well before serving, as the juices may separate during storage.

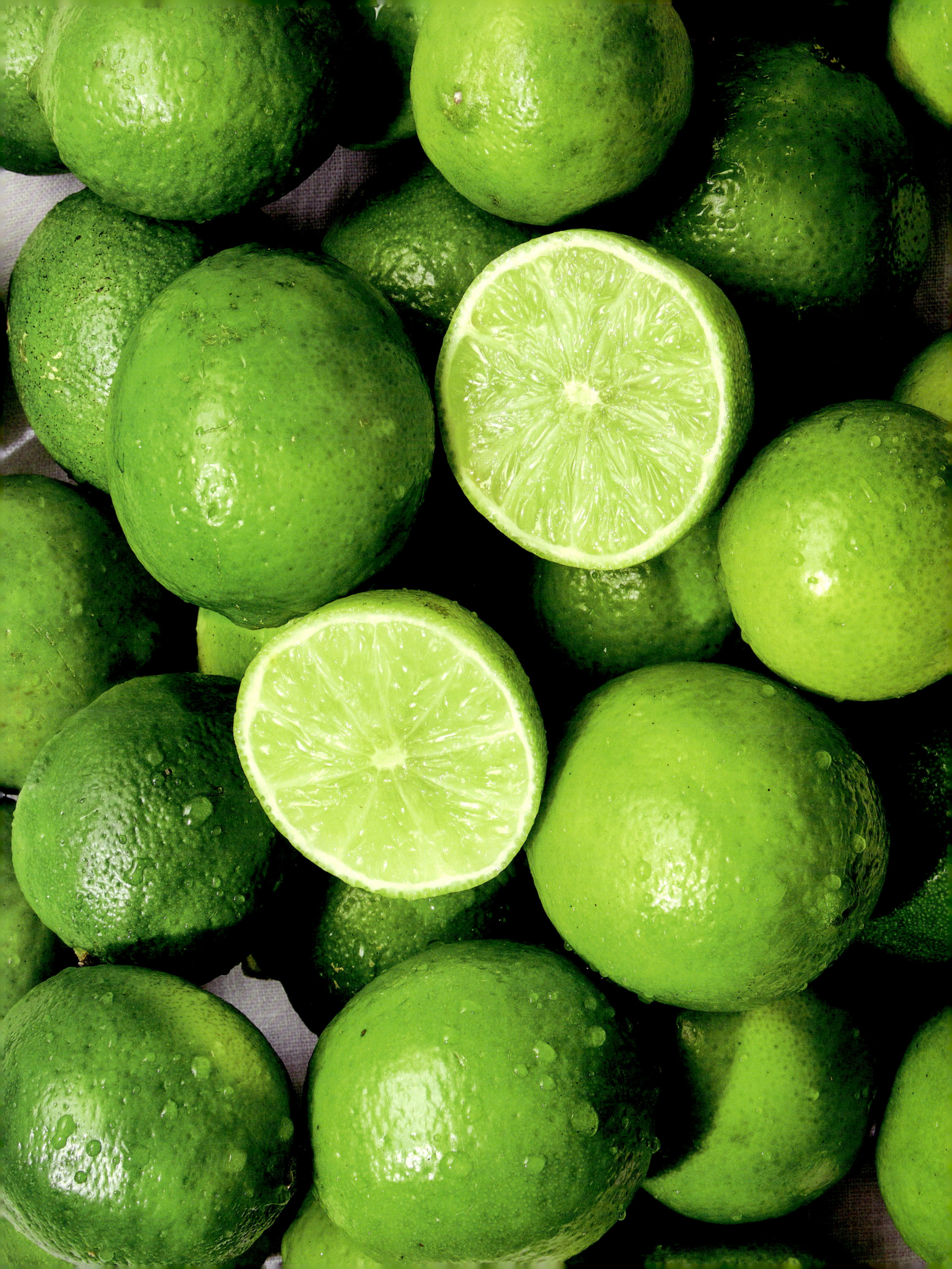

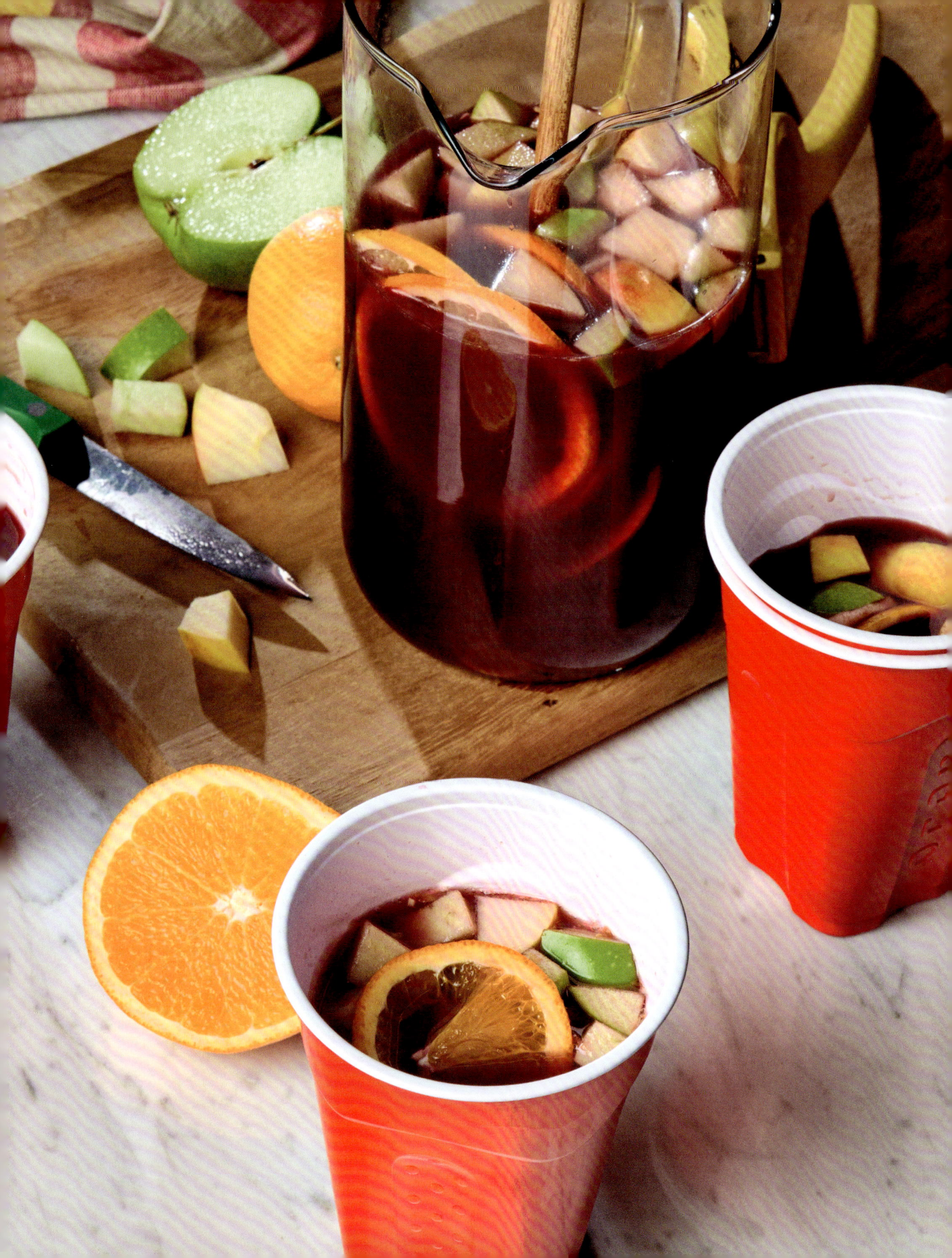

Sip Slow Sangria

Serves 6

This is my all-year-round, perfect-for-any-dinner-or-celebration cocktail. It's sweet, deep, and packed with flavor; and trust me, it'll have you feeling *real* nice. Packed with oranges and apples, it's fruity and bright. You can use any dark liquor you're into, but I love using Hennessy for that extra kick. I also love adding a splash of Sprite. Nontraditional—but it works. The key to this drink is to let it sit. Overnight is where the magic happens, letting all that fruit soak into the wine and turn this into a rich, flavorful beverage. Whether it's a BBQ, holiday, or just a night in with friends, sangria is always the right move.

1 (750ml) bottle red wine, such as Merlot or Cabernet
1 cup orange juice
⅔ cup packed dark brown sugar
½ cup Sprite
¼ cup Cognac (I like Hennessy)
2 tablespoons Grand Marnier
1 apple, cut into 1-inch cubes
1 orange, thinly sliced

In a large pitcher, combine the wine, orange juice, brown sugar, Sprite, Cognac, and Grand Marnier. Add the apple cubes and orange slices. Stir well until the sugar is dissolved. Refrigerate for at least 6 hours or up to overnight. Serve chilled.

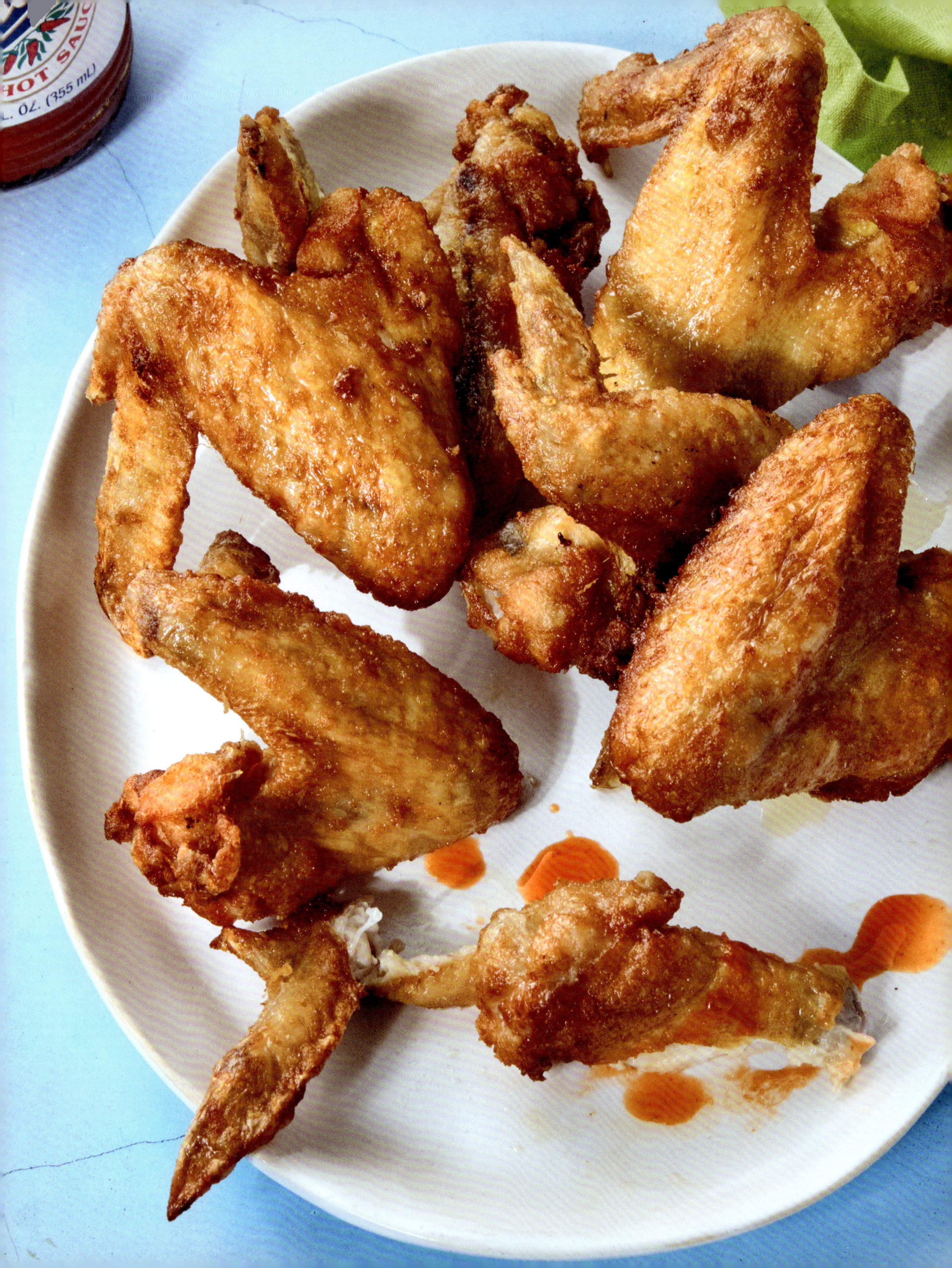

4

Takeout Classics

One of my earliest, most vivid food memories is from a random weeknight after school. Money was tight, and it was time for dinner. We lived in a neighborhood that was tough, but it was rich in culture and food—everything from Chinese takeout and pizza to plates from the local Spanish spot. Dad looked at me and said, "We've got $7 for dinner—what's it gonna be? Chinese wings, a few slices of pizza, or a plate from the Spanish restaurant?" I don't remember what we chose, but I remember eating *good* that night.

I've always loved ordering in. It's a comfort thing—whether it was Friday nights at home, long study sessions, or even date nights, takeout has always been nostalgic. Some of my favorite foods are takeout dishes, and re-creating them at home has been a huge part of my cooking style. It's personal for me. Whether it's the freezer breakfast sandwiches—a quick and easy breakfast staple—the extra-crispy chicken wings with duck sauce that were a childhood treat, or the enchiladas I would walk ten blocks to get during college, takeout classics are my ultimate comfort food. They always made me happy.

This chapter is dedicated to the classic takeout dishes—the ones you order on a snow day, off Uber Eats, or grab on those nights when you want to collapse on the couch. It's a mix of American Chinese takeout, fast-food favorites, NYC grab-and-go classics, and a little bit of everything in between. These recipes are so close to the real thing, they'll leave you speechless. I spent time perfecting these because I wanted to nail those little details that make takeout so irresistible—the ones you can't always put your finger on.

These recipes *feel* like a Friday night—they feel like home. When you're craving Chinese takeout, my General Tso's Chicken (page 99) with Pork Fried Rice (page 95) brings back that NYC takeout-spot vibe. For something shareable, my Halal Cart Chicken and Rice Bowls (page 109) are perfect for feeding a crowd, packed with flavor and way better than what you get on the street. And when you're craving smash burgers but haven't had the confidence to try making them, my easy, no-fuss recipe gives you that crispy, juicy burger that's impossible to resist.

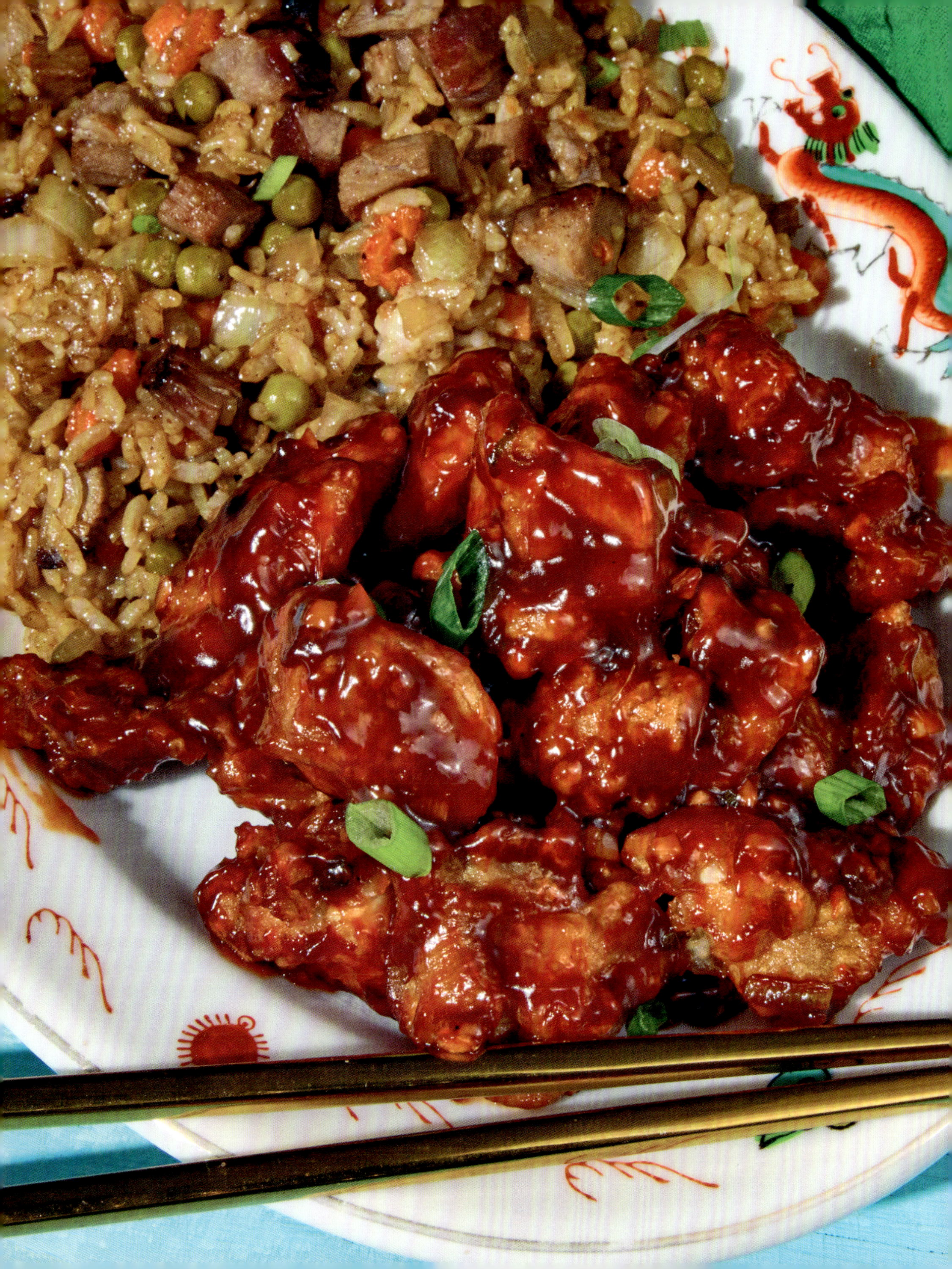

Pork Fried Rice

Serves 6

That char siu from page 106? Yep, we're taking little chunks of it and turning them into the most flavorful fried rice you've ever had. It pairs perfectly with my General Tso's Chicken (page 99), hot and crunchy Shrimp Egg Rolls (page 96), or even Popeyes fried chicken. It sounds like a weird combo, but it works! This fried rice hits all the right notes: salty, umami-forward, with a touch of sweetness from the pork. It's authentic, delicious, and brings everything together on the plate.

¼ cup lower-sodium soy sauce
1 tablespoon dark brown sugar
2 teaspoons rice vinegar
1 teaspoon Shaoxing wine
1 teaspoon toasted sesame oil
1 teaspoon kosher salt
¼ teaspoon Chinese five-spice powder
2 tablespoons vegetable oil
½ small yellow onion, finely chopped (about ¼ cup)
½ cup canned peas and carrots, drained
1 cup finely chopped cooked Char Siu Pork (page 106)
3 cups Classic White Rice (page 140), cold or room temperature

Make the sauce: In a small bowl, whisk together the soy sauce, brown sugar, vinegar, Shaoxing wine, sesame oil, salt, five-spice powder, and 2 tablespoons water until the sugar dissolves and the mixture is well combined.

Make the fried rice: In a large skillet or wok, heat the vegetable oil over medium-high heat until hot. Add the onion and sauté for 2 to 3 minutes, stirring frequently, until softened and fragrant. Add the peas and carrots and cook for 2 to 3 minutes, stirring frequently. Add the pork and cook for 2 minutes, stirring frequently, to heat through.

Stir in the cooked rice, breaking up any clumps. Cook for 3 to 4 minutes, stirring occasionally, until the rice is heated through and lightly toasted.

Pour the sauce over the rice and stir until everything is evenly coated. Cook for 2 to 3 minutes, stirring frequently, to allow the flavors to meld. Serve hot.

Shrimp Egg Rolls

Makes **6** egg rolls

In high school, the Chinese takeout spot across the street from me was *always* packed. It didn't matter if it was pouring rain, scorching hot, or freezing cold—people crammed in shoulder to shoulder, all for one thing: the egg rolls. That spot was the place to be after school, and for $1.25 I'd grab a shrimp roll (or two) with extra duck sauce, sometimes paired with a Chinese iced tea if I was feeling fancy. Those hot, crunchy, salty rolls were the perfect snack to hold me over until dinner. Now, making shrimp rolls at home reminds me of those afternoons. The trick is in the filling—it has to be tender and flavorful. I blanch the veggies and shrimp, then shock them in an ice bath to keep everything fresh before patting them dry. After that, it's all about rolling them up in store-bought egg roll wrappers (because cheat codes), then frying until they're golden and crispy. They're just like the ones that got me through high school, but even better.

Filling
- 1 cup finely shredded cabbage
- 1 cup shredded carrots
- ½ pound medium-large shrimp (36/40 count), peeled, deveined, and cut into bite-size pieces
- 2 tablespoons hoisin sauce
- 2 teaspoons lower-sodium soy sauce
- 1 teaspoon rice vinegar
- 1 teaspoon Shaoxing wine
- ½ teaspoon ground ginger

Egg Rolls
- 4 to 6 cups vegetable oil, for frying
- 6 egg roll wrappers
- Duck Sauce (page 249), for serving

Make the filling: Bring a large pot of water to a rolling boil. While the water is heating up, set up a large bowl of ice and water and have near the stove.

Once the water is boiling, carefully add the cabbage, carrots, and shrimp to the pot. Cook for 2 minutes 30 seconds, or until the vegetables are just tender and the shrimp is opaque. Using a slotted spoon, quickly transfer the blanched vegetables and shrimp to the bowl of ice water to stop the cooking process. Let them sit in the ice water for 1 minute, then use the slotted spoon to transfer to another large bowl and pat them dry with a paper towel.

In a small bowl, whisk together the hoisin sauce, soy sauce, vinegar, Shaoxing wine, and ginger. Pour the sauce over the blanched shrimp and vegetables and toss to coat evenly.

Assemble the egg rolls: Fill a Dutch oven or wok halfway with oil and heat over medium-high heat to 350°F. Line a plate with paper towels and have near the stove.

Fill a small bowl with water and put it by you on the counter. Lay out an egg roll wrapper in a diamond shape with a corner facing you. Place about ¼ cup of the filling onto the bottom center of the wrapper. Fold the corner closest to you up over the filling, then fold the sides of the wrapper over the filling. Roll it up tightly, sealing the edges with water. Repeat with the rest of the wrappers.

Fry the egg rolls: Add the egg rolls to the hot oil and cook for 5 minutes, turning occasionally, until golden brown. Use tongs to carefully remove the egg rolls from the oil and transfer to the paper towels for 1 to 2 minutes.

Serve hot with duck sauce for dipping.

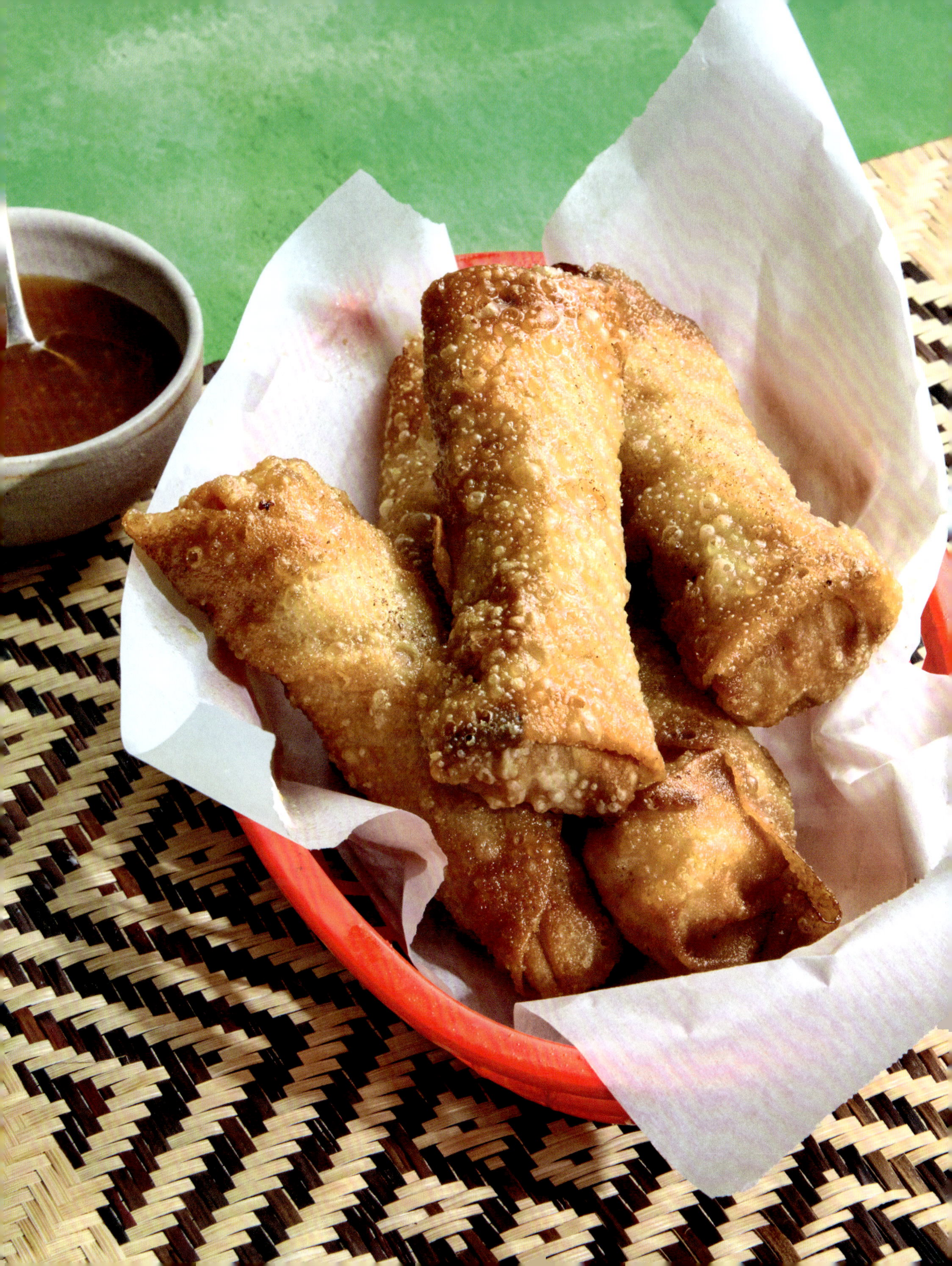

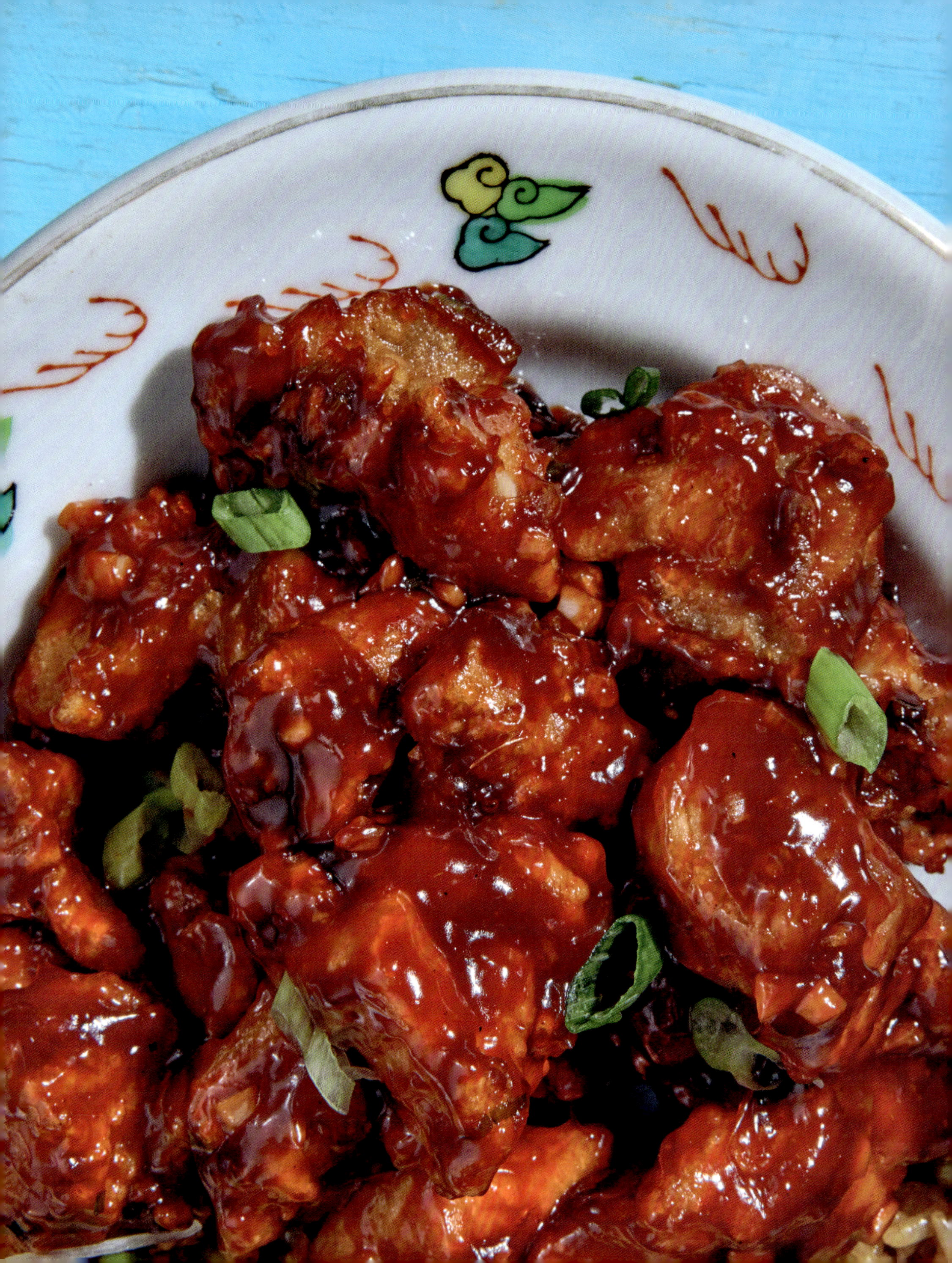

General Tso's Chicken

Serves 4

General Tso's chicken was the dish I missed most when I left the East Coast. It had gotten me through everything—college, breakups, girls' nights, and all those little moments in between. That sauce, with its bold, bright red color, hits just the right balance of sweet and heat. But the real magic is in the chicken. It's always juicy on the inside and perfectly crunchy on the outside, thanks to a cornstarch batter that gets it extra crispy as it fries. And here's the best part: When you pour that sauce over the top, the chicken doesn't get soggy. It soaks up all that flavor while keeping that irresistible crunch. Making it at home now, I love that I can control every element—the sweetness, the heat, even the salt. It's the kind of meal that wraps me up in comfort, bringing back all those memories from late-night takeout runs and weekend hangouts. But this version has a little extra love, a little more flavor, because there's nothing like cooking it up in your own kitchen.

Marinated Chicken

2 pounds boneless, skinless chicken thighs, cut into 1-inch cubes
¼ cup cornstarch
2 tablespoons lower-sodium soy sauce
1 tablespoon rice vinegar
1 large egg

Sauce

½ cup lower-sodium soy sauce
5 tablespoons dark brown sugar
¼ cup ketchup
2 tablespoons cornstarch
1 tablespoon rice vinegar
½ teaspoon red food coloring (optional)

To Finish

5 cups vegetable oil, for frying
¼ cup cornstarch
1 tablespoon toasted sesame oil
2 tablespoons finely chopped scallions
6 garlic cloves, minced (about 2 tablespoons)
1 teaspoon peeled and minced fresh ginger

Marinate the chicken: In a large bowl, combine the chicken, cornstarch, soy sauce, vinegar, and egg and mix until smooth. Toss until the chicken is fully coated. Marinate for 30 minutes.

Make the sauce: In a small bowl, whisk together the soy sauce, brown sugar, ketchup, cornstarch, vinegar, and red food coloring (if using). Set aside.

To finish: In a wok or large skillet, heat the vegetable oil over medium-high heat to 350°F. Line a plate with paper towels and have near the stove.

Right before frying, add the cornstarch to the chicken and toss to coat the chicken all over.

Working in batches to avoid overcrowding, fry the chicken for 6 to 8 minutes, until golden brown and cooked through. Use tongs to transfer the chicken to the paper towels.

Heat a large skillet over medium heat and add the sesame oil. When the oil is hot and shimmering, add the scallions, garlic, and ginger and sauté for 2 minutes, stirring occasionally with a wooden spoon, until fragrant. Stir in the sauce and cook for 5 minutes, stirring occasionally, until the sauce thickens like a syrup.

Add the chicken to the sauce, toss until fully coated, and cook for 2 to 3 minutes, until the chicken is heated through. Serve hot!

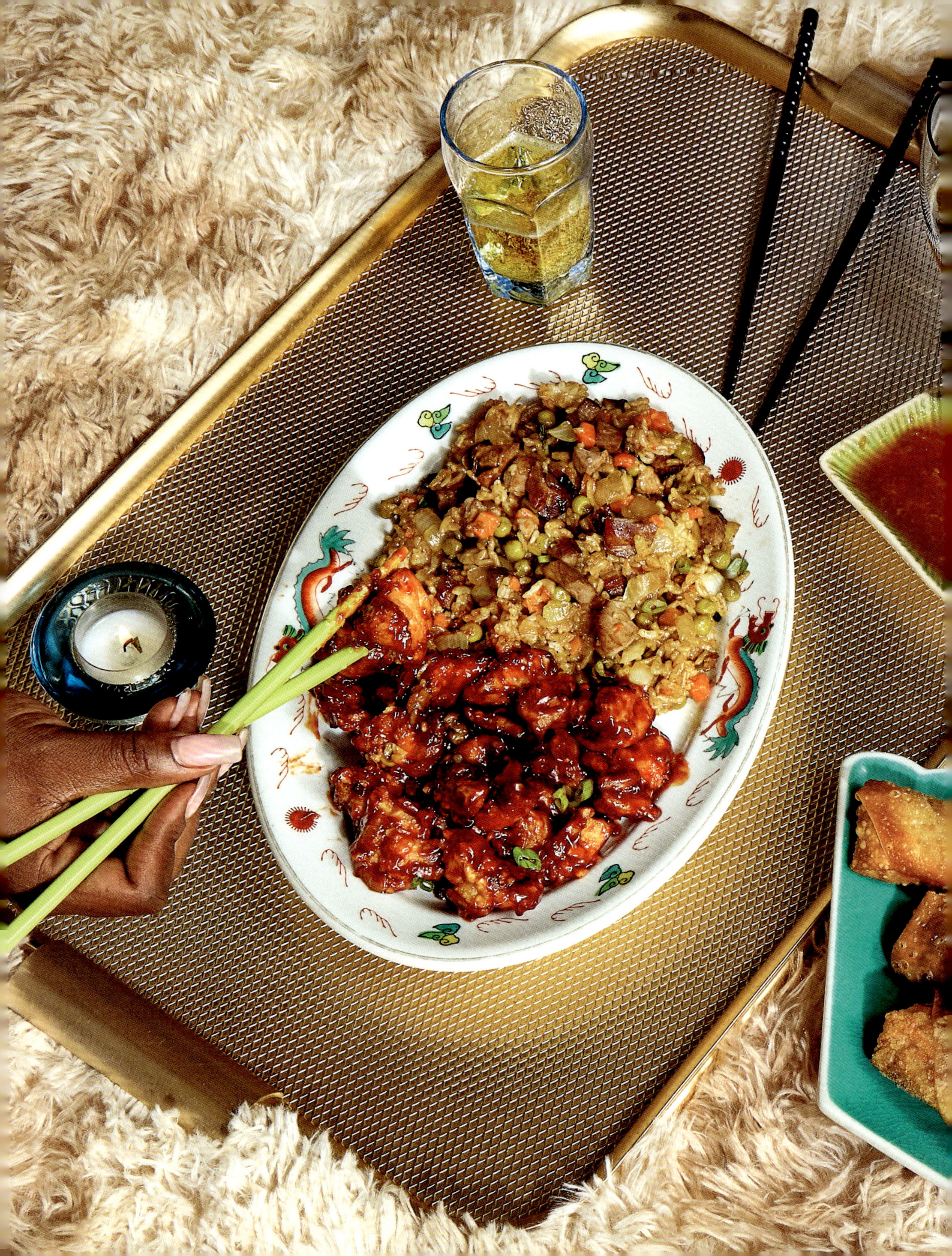

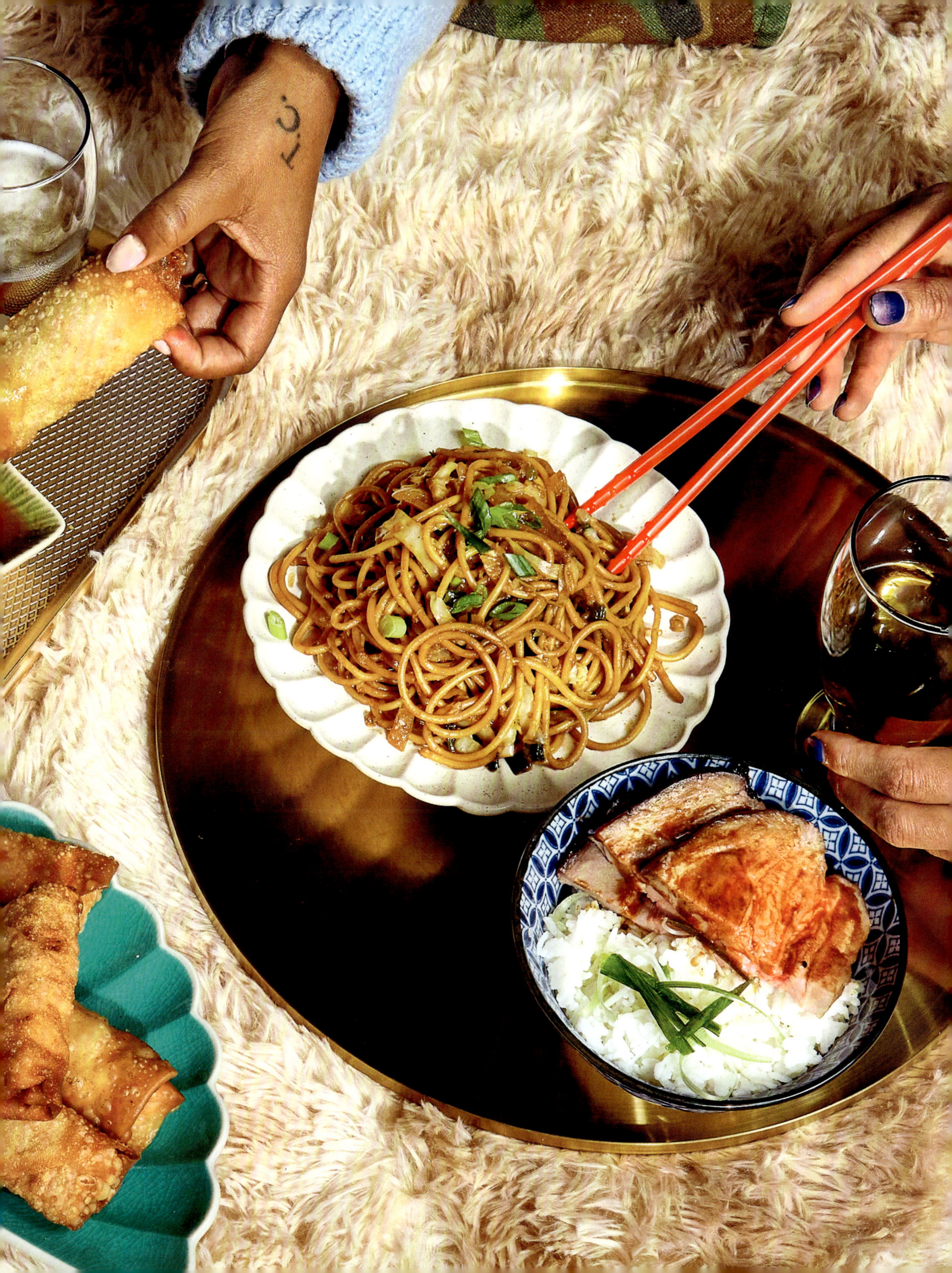

New York City–Style Chicken Wings
(aka Chinese Takeout Wings)

Makes 10 wings

Chicken wings from Chinese takeout spots are a neighborhood classic, part of the culture, and a staple I grew up eating. If you know, you know. And if you don't—you're about to find out! These wings are fried to perfection—extra crunchy and crispy, with just the right balance of salty goodness and a hint of sweetness. You could drench them in any sauce you want. Back in the day, you could grab five wings for $2.75, and I ate them *all* the time; but of course I had to try to perfect them at home. Now, if you know anything about the local Chinese takeout spots, you know their recipes are locked down tight. Figuring out the right flavors was no easy task. After a lot of trial and error, I found the key—soy sauce, Shaoxing wine, and sugar form the base of these wings. As for that signature crunch? Cornstarch is key! It keeps them light, crispy, and provides that satisfying crunch that lasts. I like to serve these with garlic toast and a lot of duck sauce.

1 large egg
1 tablespoon Shaoxing wine
1 tablespoon toasted sesame oil
1 tablespoon soy sauce
1 teaspoon sugar
1 teaspoon garlic powder
1 teaspoon freshly ground black pepper
10 whole chicken wings (about 2½ pounds)
3 tablespoons cornstarch
2 tablespoons all-purpose flour
Vegetable oil, for deep-frying
2 teaspoons kosher salt, plus more to taste
Duck Sauce (page 249), for serving
Crunchy Garlic Toast (page 31), for serving

Coat the wings: In a large bowl, whisk together the egg, Shaoxing wine, sesame oil, soy sauce, sugar, garlic powder, and pepper. Add the wings and toss to coat the chicken all over. Add 2 tablespoons of the cornstarch and the flour. Toss the wings again to coat the chicken all over. Cover and set aside for 10 to 15 minutes to bring the wings to room temperature.

Add the remaining 1 tablespoon cornstarch to the wings and toss to coat the chicken all over.

Fry the wings: Pour enough oil into a large, deep pot or Dutch oven to come up halfway. Clip a candy/deep-fry thermometer to the side and heat the oil over medium-high until it reaches 350°F. Line a plate with paper towels and have near the stove.

Working in batches to avoid overcrowding, fry the wings for 10 to 12 minutes, until golden brown and cooked through. Use tongs to transfer the wings to the paper towels. When the wings are hot, sprinkle them with the salt.

Serve with duck sauce for dipping and garlic toast.

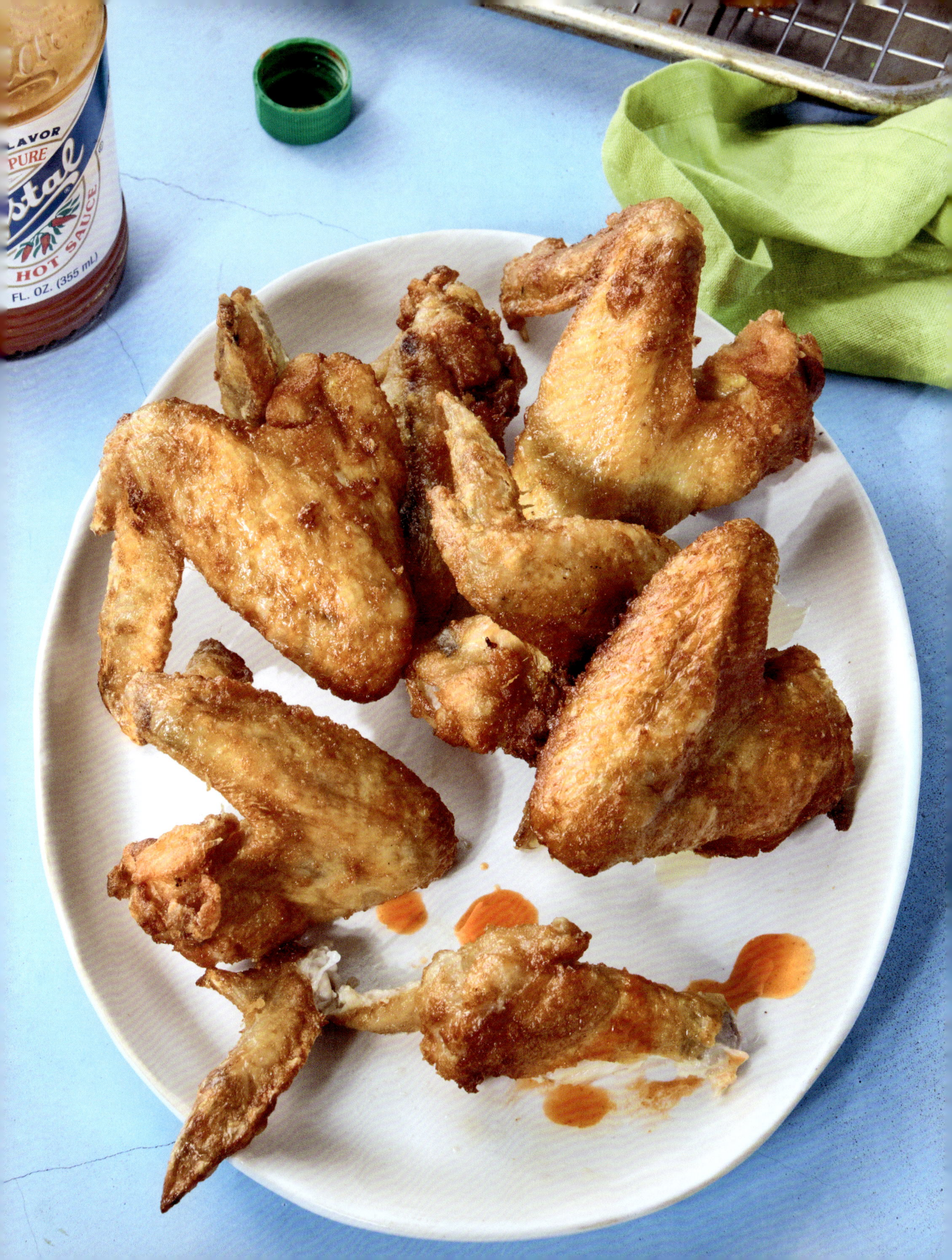
PURE
HOT SAUCE
FL. OZ. (355 mL)

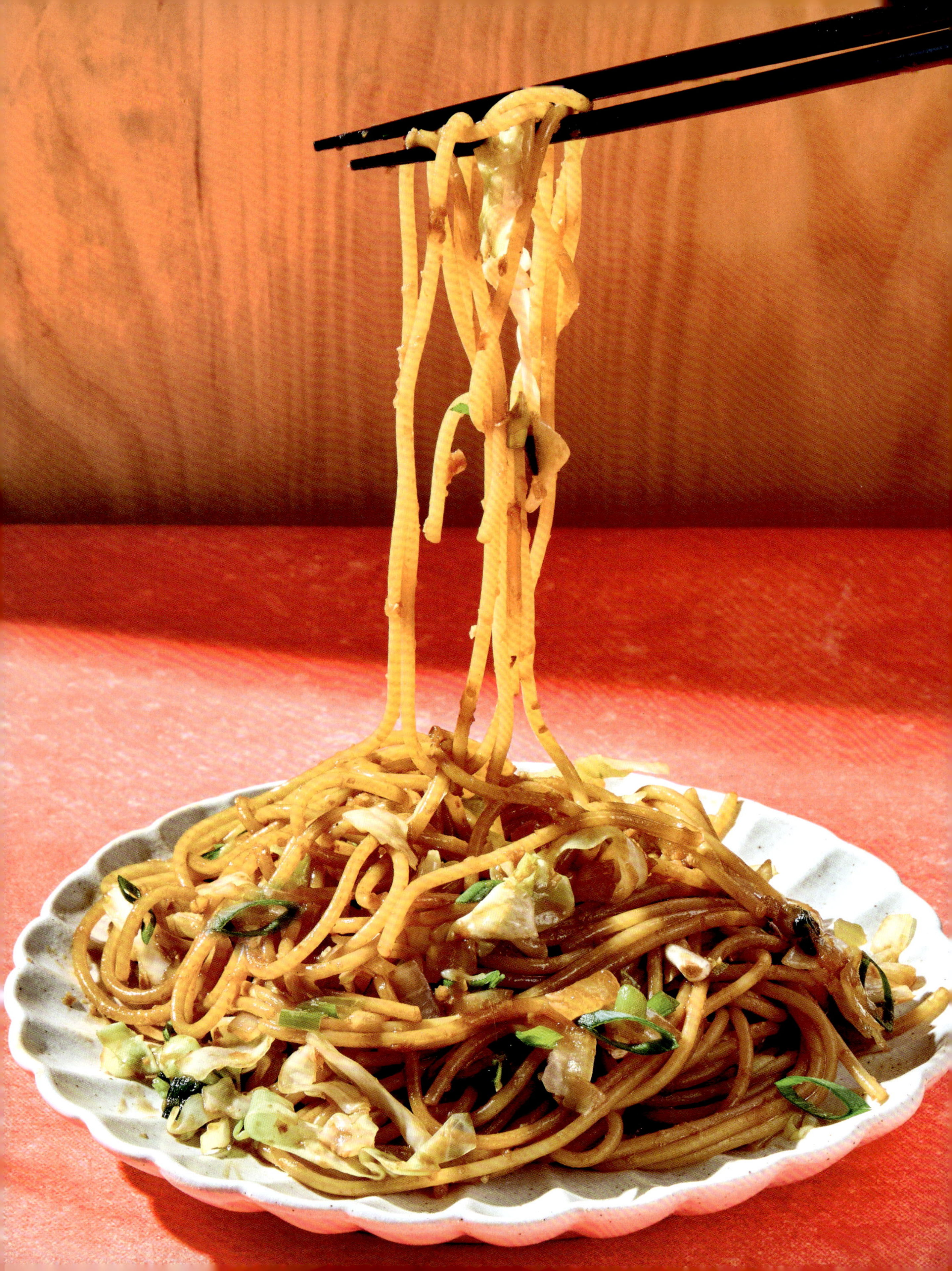

Copycat Panda Chow Mein

Serves 4

I've always loved Panda Express's chow mein, and this is my copycat version. It has that perfect balance of sweet and savory. The tender noodles soak up the rich, garlicky sauce, while the crunchy cabbage adds just the right amount of bite, making it the perfect side or even a main dish. Whether I'm pairing it with General Tso's Chicken (page 99) or enjoying it on its own, this chow mein is one of my go-to recipes when I'm craving the best noodles ever.

Kosher salt
8 ounces spaghetti
½ cup lower-sodium soy sauce
¼ cup honey
6 garlic cloves, minced (about 2 tablespoons)
1-inch piece fresh ginger, peeled and minced (1 tablespoon)
1 tablespoon oyster sauce
2 teaspoons toasted sesame oil
½ teaspoon browning sauce
2 tablespoons vegetable oil
1 medium onion, diced (about 1 cup)
¼ head green cabbage, sliced (about 2 cups)
½ cup diced scallions, reserving 1 tablespoon for garnish

Cook the pasta: Bring a large pot of salted water to a boil. Add the spaghetti and cook al dente according to the package directions. Drain and rinse the pasta under cold water to stop the cooking process. Set aside.

Make the sauce: In a small bowl, whisk together the soy sauce, honey, garlic, ginger, oyster sauce, sesame oil, and browning sauce until well combined. Set aside.

Cook the vegetables: In a large wok or skillet, heat the vegetable oil over medium-high heat until hot and shimmering. Add the onion and cook for 2 to 3 minutes, stirring occasionally, until softened. Add the cabbage and sauté, stirring occasionally, for 4 to 5 minutes, until the cabbage is tender but still slightly crisp. Add the scallions and cook for 1 to 2 minutes. Transfer the vegetables to a plate and set aside.

To finish: In the same wok or skillet, combine the cooked spaghetti and the sauce and use tongs to toss the pasta to evenly coat with the sauce, cooking over medium heat for 2 to 3 minutes, until the pasta absorbs some of the sauce.

Return the vegetables to the wok and toss everything together until well combined. Cook for 1 to 2 minutes to heat through.

Garnish with reserved scallions for a fresh finish.

Char Siu Pork

Serves 6

Some know it as "rib tips," others as "char siu pork," and some call it "boneless spare ribs," but whatever you call the famous Chinese American–style roast pork, we all love it. This is my spin on it. Originally, I wanted to learn how to make this recipe because I've always been obsessed with pork fried rice and thought it'd be perfect diced up in rice dishes. But then, I realized just how versatile this pork really is, and I knew it deserved to be in the spotlight. You can throw it in stir-fries, salads, or just eat it straight off the plate—it's that good. The key to making it is all in the marinade. Letting the pork soak up all that sweet, savory, umami-packed goodness is what makes the flavor pop. Then it's straight into the oven, where it caramelizes and turns tender and juicy. If you can't find the Chinese red bean curd, it's all good—use what you have (but P.S.—your local Asian supermarket or even Amazon usually has everything you need).

- 4 tablespoons Ah-So Chinese-style sauce
- 3 tablespoons Chinese red bean curd
- 2 tablespoons dark brown sugar
- 2 tablespoons lower-sodium soy sauce
- 2 tablespoons red food coloring (optional)
- 1 tablespoon Shaoxing wine
- 1 tablespoon toasted sesame oil
- 1 tablespoon granulated sugar
- 2 teaspoons Chinese five-spice powder
- 4 pounds boneless pork shoulder

Marinate the pork: In a large bowl, whisk together 2 tablespoons of the Ah-So sauce, the red bean curd, brown sugar, soy sauce, red food coloring (if using), Shaoxing wine, sesame oil, granulated sugar, and five-spice powder. Add the pork to the bowl and toss to coat all over. Cover and marinate the pork in the refrigerator for at least 4 hours or preferably overnight for the best flavor.

Cook the pork: Preheat the oven to 325°F. Set a roasting rack over a baking sheet. Remove the pork from the fridge and let it come to room temperature for 30 minutes.

Place the pork on the rack. Discard the remaining marinade. Roast the pork for 45 minutes, basting with the remaining 2 tablespoons Ah-So sauce every 15 minutes, until the pork is tender and an instant-read thermometer inserted in a cube reads 190°F.

Remove the pork from the oven and let it rest for 15 minutes. Slice it into 1-inch-thick pieces and serve warm.

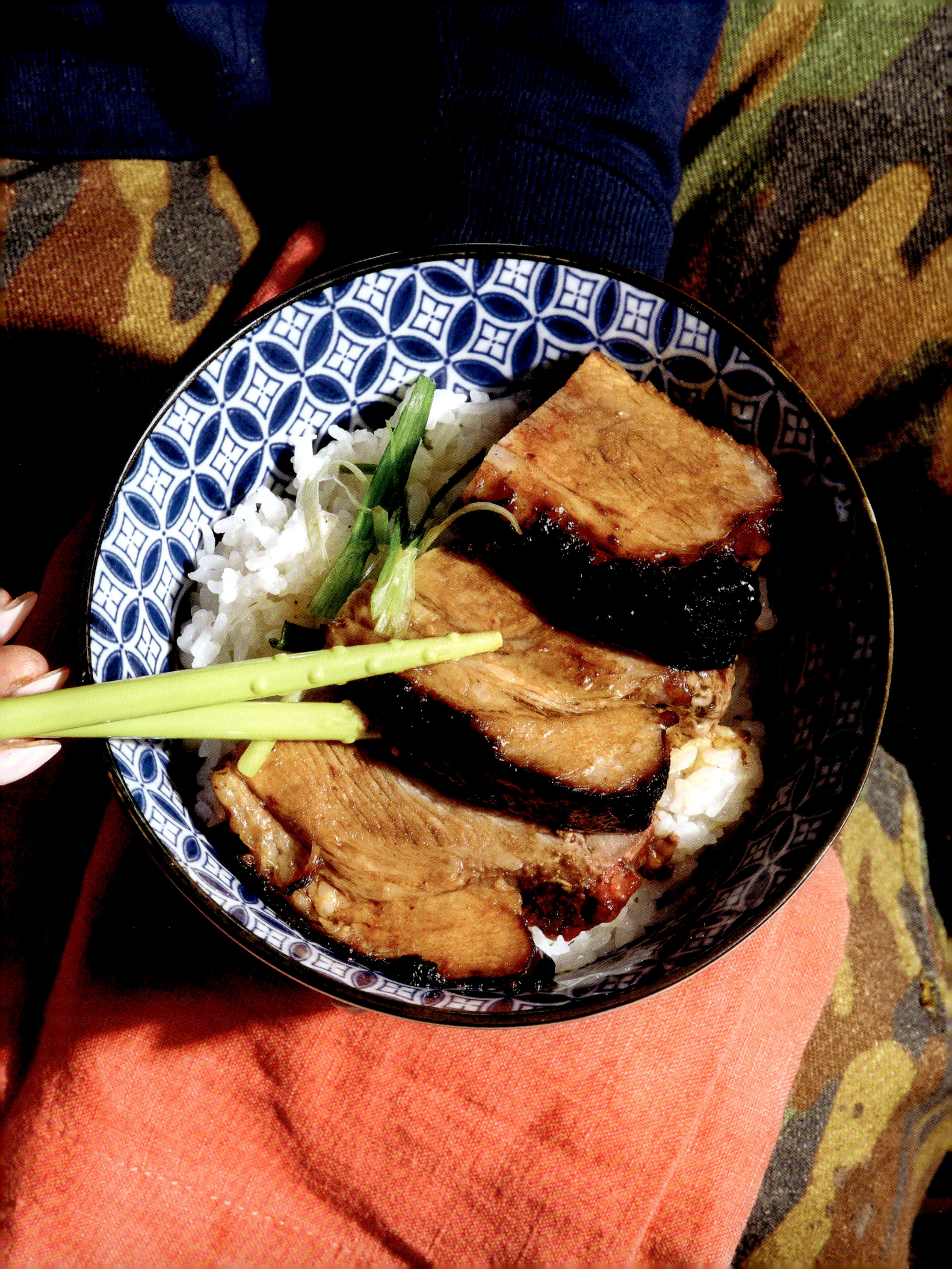

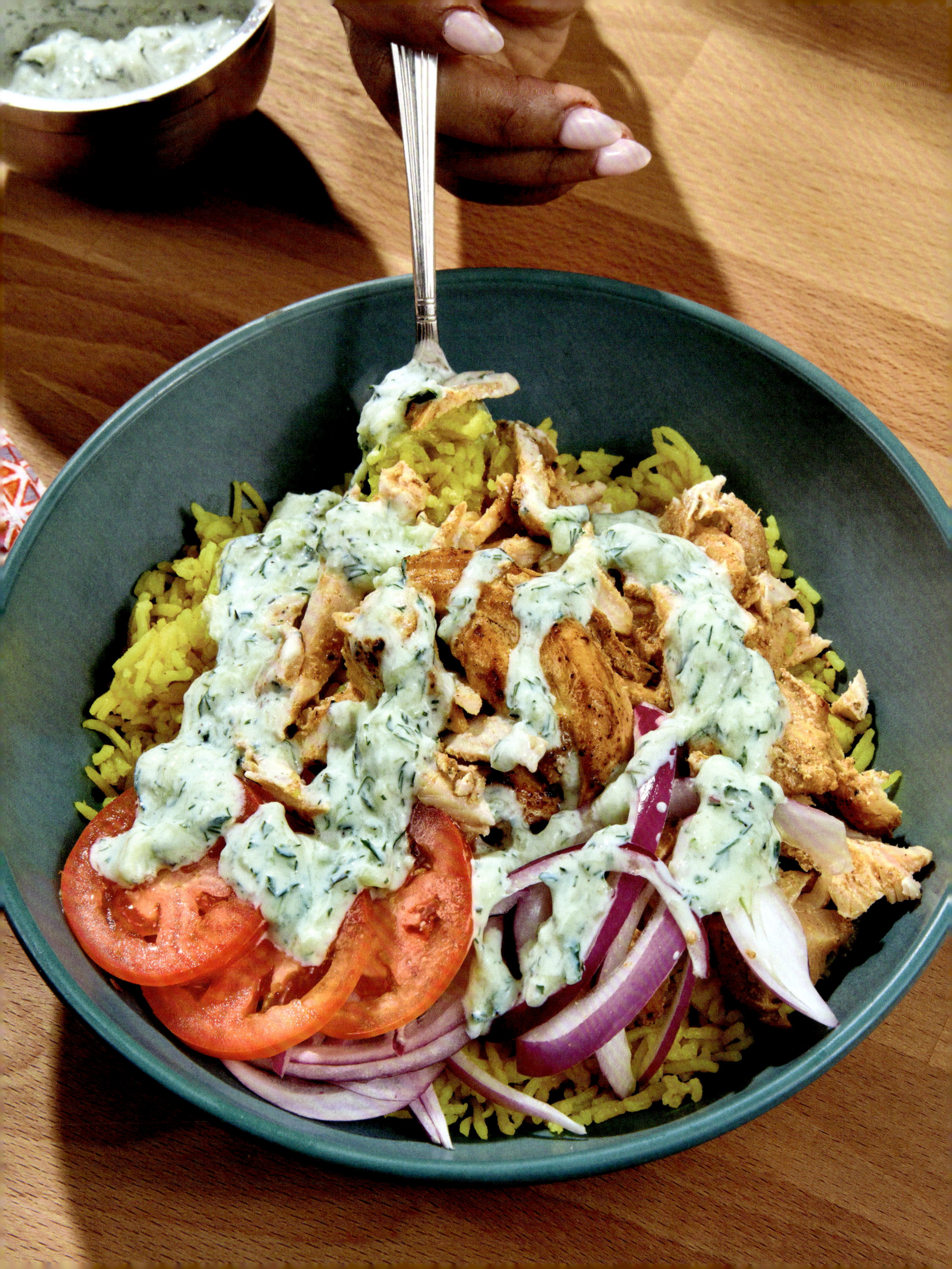

Halal Cart Chicken and Rice Bowls with Tzatziki Sauce

Serves 4

In NYC, there's a famous street cart called The Halal Guys that always has people lined up around the block. To be honest, I never waited in that line to find out what made their food stand out. Instead, I figured out how to make those delicious platters right at home. I had to start with making my own shawarma in the oven. The key? Take two skewers and stick them into an onion for a sturdy base. Then layer thinly sliced meat onto the skewers and let it cook. Once it's done, you shave the meat off with a knife, giving you that perfect shawarma texture and flavor, just like you'd get from the street carts. Serve it over my delicious turmeric-spiced rice with fresh tomatoes and, of course, don't sleep on that creamy tzatziki.

Chicken Shawarma

- 3 pounds boneless, skinless chicken breasts, thinly sliced
- ¾ cup full-fat plain Greek yogurt
- 2 tablespoons extra-virgin olive oil
- 2 tablespoons sweet paprika
- 1 tablespoon honey
- 1 teaspoon ground cumin
- 1 teaspoon Italian seasoning
- 1 teaspoon Goya Sazón (culantro y achiote; optional)
- 1 teaspoon kosher salt
- 1 teaspoon freshly ground black pepper
- Juice of ½ lemon
- ½ onion (any kind), for shawarma stand
- 2 (12-inch) wooden skewers

Rice

- 2½ cups basmati rice
- 2 tablespoons extra-virgin olive oil
- 1 small yellow onion, finely diced
- 2 teaspoons ground turmeric
- 1 teaspoon ground ginger
- 1 teaspoon ground cumin
- 4½ teaspoons kosher salt

Tzatziki Sauce

- 1½ cups plain full-fat Greek yogurt
- 1 cucumber, grated
- 2 tablespoons finely chopped fresh dill
- 2 tablespoons extra-virgin olive oil
- 1 tablespoon freshly squeezed lemon juice
- 1 tablespoon finely chopped fresh mint
- 2 garlic cloves, grated (2 teaspoons)
- 2 teaspoons kosher salt
- 1 teaspoon freshly ground black pepper

Make the chicken shawarma: In a large bowl, combine the chicken, yogurt, olive oil, paprika, honey, cumin, Italian seasoning, Sazón (if using), salt, pepper, and lemon juice. Toss to evenly coat the chicken all over. Marinate for at least 10 minutes or up to 1 hour.

Preheat the oven to 350°F. Remove the top rack from the oven to make room for the shawarma stand.

Place half an onion, flat-side down, on a baking sheet and press two skewers about 3 inches apart into the top of the onion, so they are standing up. Push the pieces of chicken onto the skewers, tightly packed.

Carefully transfer to the bottom rack of the oven and bake for 20 to 30 minutes, until the juices run clear and an instant-read thermometer poking down through the layers of the chicken reads 165°F.

Meanwhile, make the rice: In a large bowl, soak the basmati rice in cold water for 20 minutes. Drain and rinse the rice under cold running water until the water runs clear. This helps remove excess starch and prevents the rice from becoming sticky.

In a medium pot, heat the oil over medium heat until shimmering. Add the onion and sauté for 3 to 4 minutes, stirring frequently, until soft and translucent. Stir in the turmeric, ginger, and cumin and cook for 1 to 2 minutes, stirring frequently, until fragrant. Stir in the rinsed rice and cook for 1 minute to toast the rice.

Increase the heat to high. Pour in 4 cups water and add the salt. Stir well to combine, then bring the mixture to a boil. Reduce the heat to low, cover, and simmer for 15 to 18 minutes, until the rice is tender and the water is fully absorbed. Remove from the heat and let it sit, covered, for 5 minutes to allow the rice to steam. Use a fork to fluff the rice before serving. Keep warm.

Meanwhile, make the tzatziki: In a medium bowl, whisk together the yogurt, cucumber, dill, olive oil, lemon juice, mint, garlic, salt, and pepper. Cover and refrigerate until serving time.

To serve: Divide the rice evenly among four bowls. Use a knife to slice the chicken off the skewers. Place the chicken over the rice. Serve with tzatziki sauce.

Jamaican-Style Oxtail with Rice and Peas

Serves 8

Of all the incredible dishes from the Caribbean, Jamaican-style oxtail is hands-down my favorite. I've driven an hour (from Jersey City to Brooklyn, which is like driving to another country) to get oxtail that tastes just right—and I'd do it again, too. The key to stewed oxtail is the marinade, which is made from a blend of fresh ginger, garlic, Scotch bonnet pepper, thyme, and ketchup. After marinating overnight, the oxtail is browned to develop even more flavor before it cooks for a few hours—the combination of the marinade, the extra sear, plus the low and slow cooking makes the dish even more special. Trust me, your patience will be rewarded. Just turn up the music (and it better be Buju Banton!) and simmer away. While the oxtails simmer, it's the perfect time to make my famous rice and "peas" (kidney beans). Packed with coconut cream, coconut milk, allspice, ginger, and thyme, it's a flavorful rice dish that will help soak up all of those oxtail juices. And, if I'm feeling ambitious, I'll pair it with my Good Vibes Rum Punch (page 76)—because why not? BIG UP Jamaica for creating one of the best dishes of all time.

Oxtail

- 3 to 4 pounds beef oxtail (10 to 12 pieces), cut into ½-inch sections (see tip), fat trimmed
- ½ large red bell pepper, diced (about ½ cup)
- ½ large green bell pepper, diced (about ½ cup)
- ½ small yellow onion, diced (about ¼ cup)
- 8 scallions, minced (about ¼ cup)
- 3 tablespoons ketchup
- 6 garlic cloves, minced (about 2 tablespoons)
- 2-inch piece fresh ginger, peeled and minced (about 2 tablespoons)
- 2 tablespoons browning sauce (see tip)
- 1 Scotch bonnet pepper, thinly sliced (see tip)
- 1½ tablespoons allspice berries
- 1 tablespoon garlic powder
- 1 tablespoon onion powder
- 1 tablespoon powdered oxtail seasoning
- 1 beef or chicken bouillon cube, crushed (see tip)
- 3 teaspoons kosher salt
- 1 teaspoon freshly ground black pepper
- 3 sprigs thyme
- 2 tablespoons extra-virgin olive oil

Marinate the oxtails: In a large bowl, combine the oxtails with both bell peppers, the onion, scallions, ketchup, minced garlic, ginger, browning sauce, sliced Scotch bonnet pepper, allspice, garlic powder, onion powder, oxtail seasoning, crushed bouillon cube, salt, black pepper, and thyme. Toss to coat the oxtails evenly. Cover the bowl and marinate the oxtails overnight in the refrigerator.

Cook the oxtails: In a large pot or Dutch oven, heat the oil over medium-high heat until hot and shimmering. Working in batches to avoid overcrowding, add the oxtails, letting the extra marinade drip back into the bowl, and sear for about 3 minutes on each side, until browned. Transfer the browned oxtails to a plate. Reserve the marinade in the bowl.

Make the stew: Return all the meat to the pot and add 3 cups water to the bowl and mix with the extra marinade. Pour the marinade mixture into the pot. If needed, add more water to completely cover the oxtails. Add the thyme, crushed bouillon cube, bay leaves, and whole Scotch bonnet pepper. Cover and cook over medium-low heat for 1 hour, stirring every 15 minutes, then check to make sure the water in the pot still covers the oxtails; add more if needed. Cook covered for an additional 1½ to 2 hours, until the oxtails are juicy and tender. During the last 30 minutes, remove the lid to let the steam evaporate and the sauce thicken. Taste and adjust the salt if needed.

Meanwhile, make the rice and peas: In a large pot, combine the soaked beans and 4 cups water. Cover and cook over medium heat, stirring occasionally, for 50 minutes, or until all of the water is evaporated.

Stir in the coconut milk and creamed coconut and simmer for 10 minutes. Add the scallions, ginger, minced garlic, chicken bouillon powder, salt, garlic powder, thyme, and allspice, and stir until combined. Simmer uncovered for 10 minutes, stirring occasionally, to allow the flavors to combine. Add the

Stew

3 sprigs thyme
1 beef or chicken bouillon cube, crushed (see tip)
2 or 3 bay leaves
1 Scotch bonnet pepper, left whole
Kosher salt

Rice and Peas

14 ounces dried kidney beans, soaked overnight, drained, and rinsed
1 (15-ounce) can full-fat coconut milk
2 tablespoons creamed coconut or coconut butter (see tip)
¼ cup chopped scallions
1-inch piece fresh ginger, peeled and minced
6 garlic cloves, minced (about 2 tablespoons)
2 teaspoons chicken bouillon powder (see tip)
1 tablespoon kosher salt
2 teaspoons garlic powder
5 sprigs thyme
7 allspice berries
3 cups long-grain parboiled rice
1 small Scotch bonnet pepper

rinsed rice to the pot and stir until everything is combined. Pour in enough water to reach the first knuckle of your finger, about 3½ cups. Add the small Scotch bonnet pepper and stir well to combine. Cook for 10 minutes, until the water is reduced by half. Reduce the heat to low, cover, and cook for 30 minutes, until the rice is tender.

Fluff the rice with a fork and serve warm with the oxtails.

Chef's Kiss: Browning sauce is a darkening agent found in Caribbean and Hispanic supermarkets in the sauce aisles. If you can't find browning sauce, skip it in the marinade. Instead, before you sear the oxtails, heat 3 tablespoons dark brown sugar with 2 tablespoons neutral oil (like canola or vegetable oil) over medium heat in the Dutch oven and stir until it's dark like chocolate, about 2 minutes. Sear the marinated oxtail in this and continue with the recipe as directed.

Bouillon is interchangeable; you can use crushed or powder.

Creamed coconut is a type of coconut fat commonly used in Caribbean and Latin American cooking. It has a rich coconut aroma and adds depth to dishes like rice, beans, and stews. If you can't find it, coconut oil (especially unrefined) is the best substitute since it has a similar texture and flavor.

Little Details, BIG Impact: Ask your butcher to cut your oxtail into the ½-inch sections for you. A really thick oxtail can be on the tough side, but cutting it into ½-inch sections is the sweet spot, because there is a higher proportion of meat to bone.

The color of the Scotch bonnet will indicate its spiciness. For a milder flavor, opt for green or orange Scotch bonnets. If you like it extra spicy—like me—choose red. If a Scotch bonnet pepper bursts, it could make your dish overly spicy, so use with caution and choose the color based on your desired level of chile heat. Using a medium to mild pepper is my recommendation if you want to play it safe.

Takeout Classics

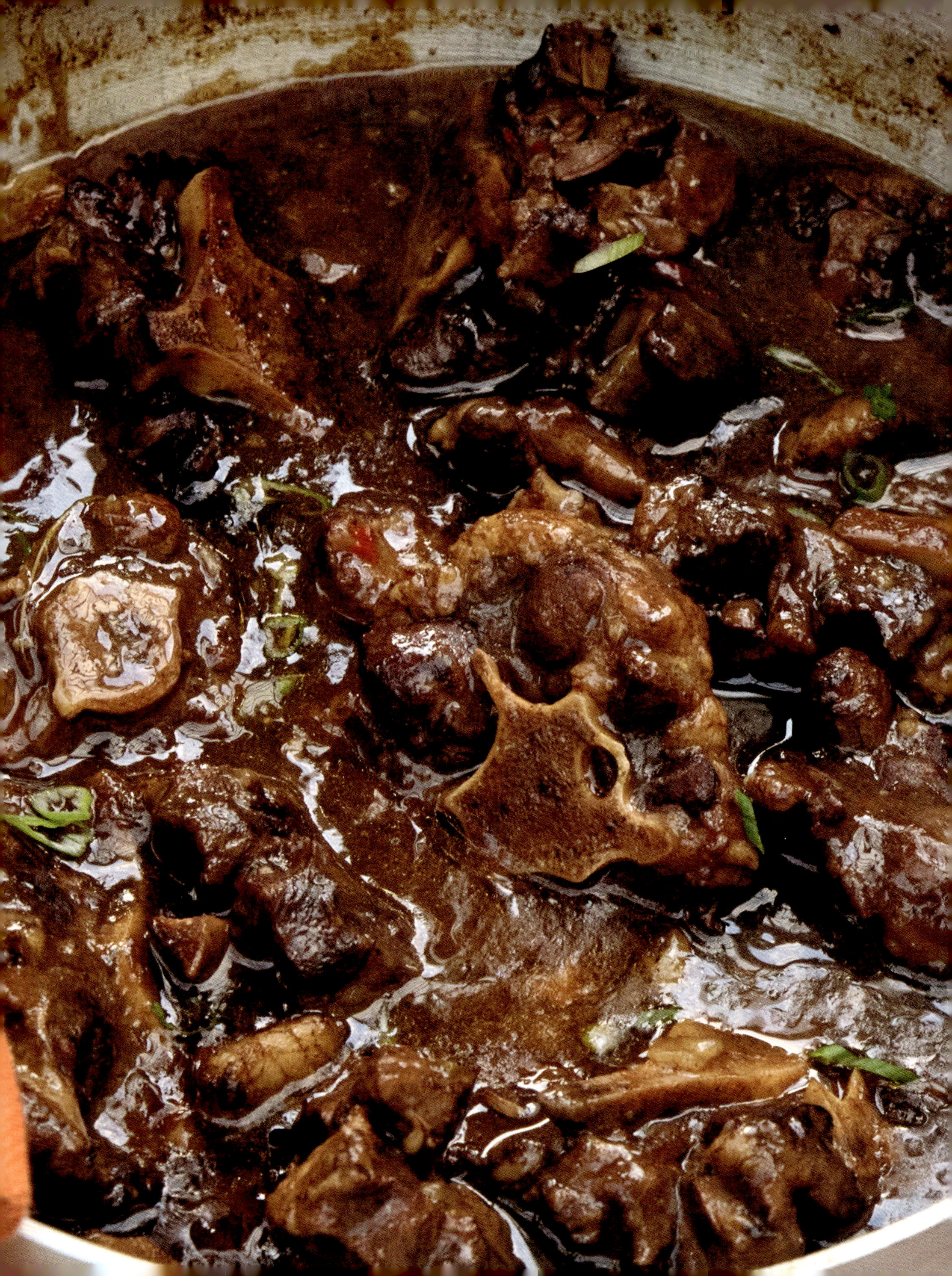

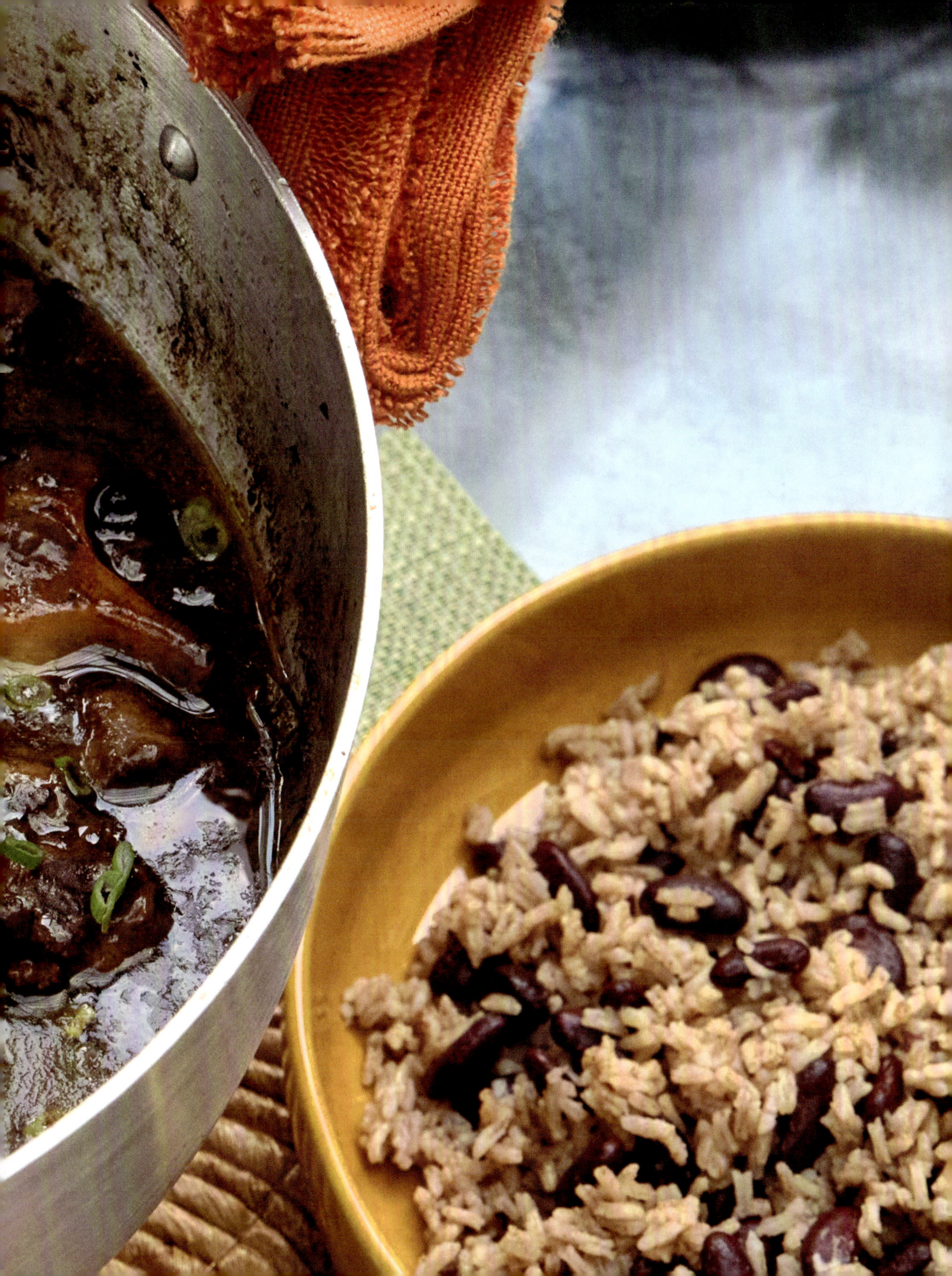

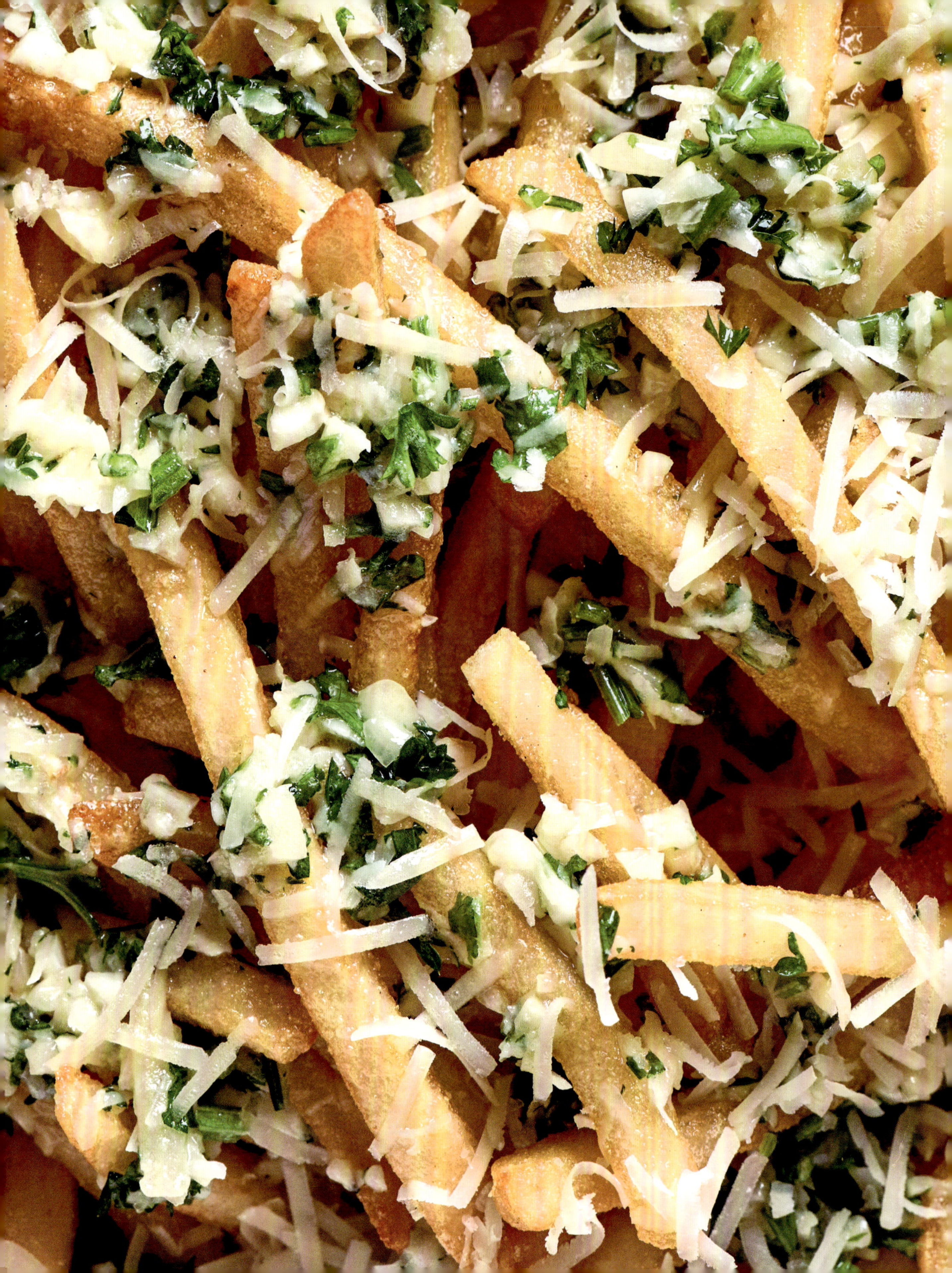

Garlic Parmesan French Fries

Serves 4

French fries are hands down the GOAT of side dishes. They go with everything, and I'm not here for any arguments about it. But let's be real—not all fries taste the same. Soggy takeout fries? Bland, unseasoned ones? No thanks. That's why these fries hit different—they fix both of those problems, and then some.

Perfect fries at home take a little patience, but here's the game changer: You can prep them ahead of time. Do the first fry, freeze them until you're ready to cook them, and then fry them up when you're ready to eat. I like to use peanut oil for its subtle flavor, but any neutral oil will do the trick. Then we level up—because you know I don't do basic—with a buttery garlic Parmesan coating that'll have you questioning why you ever settled for plain fries. These fries aren't just a side—they're a whole moment.

- 6 medium russet potatoes (about 3 pounds)
- Neutral oil (I like to use peanut oil), for deep-frying
- 4 tablespoons (½ stick/2 ounces) unsalted butter
- 3 garlic cloves, minced (about 1 tablespoon)
- ½ cup freshly grated Parmesan cheese
- 1 tablespoon kosher salt, or more to taste
- 1 tablespoon chopped fresh parsley

Prepare the potatoes: Peel the potatoes and cut them into 1-inch-wide sticks. Soak the cut potatoes in a large bowl of ice water for about 30 minutes. This will help remove excess starch and make the fries crispier. After soaking, thoroughly dry the potato slices with a clean kitchen towel or paper towels.

First fry: Pour enough oil into a large, deep pot or Dutch oven to come up halfway. Clip a candy/deep-fry thermometer to the side and heat the oil over medium-high until it reaches 325°F. Line a plate with clean paper towels and have near the stove.

Working in batches to avoid overcrowding, carefully fry the potatoes for 4 to 5 minutes, until they are light golden brown. Remove the partially fried fries from the oil and place them on the paper towels to drain the excess oil. Let them cool to room temperature. Transfer the partially fried fries to a baking sheet and place them in the freezer. Allow them to freeze for at least 30 minutes.

Make the garlic Parmesan coating: In a large skillet, melt the butter over medium heat. Slowly stir in the minced garlic, stirring constantly, until fragrant, 2 to 3 minutes. Stir in ¼ cup of the Parmesan.

Second fry: Once the fries are frozen, heat the oil to 375°F. Line a plate with clean paper towels.

Working in batches to avoid overcrowding, carefully add the frozen fries to the hot oil and fry for 2 to 3 minutes, until golden brown and crispy. Remove the fries from the oil and place them on the paper towels to drain.

Place the hot fries in a large bowl, sprinkle them with the salt, and evenly pour the sauce over the fries. Shake the bowl so that the fries are coated all over. Garnish with the remaining ¼ cup Parmesan and the parsley. Add more salt to taste. Serve the hot fries with any of my delicious sauces (see tip).

Chef's Kiss: These garlic Parmesan fries are so flavorful on their own, but when I'm making them for guests, I love to prepare a few of my favorite sauces—like ranch, ají verde, or duck sauce—to serve them with. The combo of the sauces with hot and crunchy garlic Parmesan fries is elite.

Straight-Fire Smash Burgers

Serves 4

A really good burger is a gift you don't get often, but when you do, it sticks with you. My boy Mateo, who ran the food truck Stacked in Jersey City, is all about burgers. Before his business took off, he loved experimenting with recipes, and one night we decided to get together to try out different spices, sauces, and techniques for his food truck. We invited a few friends over, and let me tell you—it was a vibe.

That night I saw why smash burgers are so universally loved. They're easy to make, full of flavor, and juicy every single time. My recipe is all about that. The sauce is sweet with a little kick. The potato buns are toasted light and perfect for that authentic feel. And when you put it all together, you'll know why I call it straight fire. This burger isn't just good, it's unforgettable.

Burger Sauce

¼ cup finely diced dill pickles
1 teaspoon dill pickle juice
3 tablespoons mayonnaise
2 tablespoons ketchup
1 teaspoon hot sauce
1 teaspoon Dijon mustard
1 teaspoon red wine vinegar

Burgers

1 pound ground beef (85/15)
2 teaspoons kosher salt
1 teaspoon garlic powder
1 teaspoon onion powder
1 teaspoon Worcestershire sauce
¼ teaspoon freshly ground black pepper

Assembly

2 tablespoons (1 ounce) unsalted butter
4 potato hamburger buns or sandwich rolls, split
4 slices mild or sharp Cheddar cheese
¼ pound white onions, thinly sliced
4 slices tomato
2 cups shredded iceberg lettuce

Make the sauce: In a small bowl, whisk together the pickles, dill pickle juice, mayonnaise, ketchup, hot sauce, mustard, and vinegar until smooth and well combined. Set aside.

Make the burgers: In a large bowl, combine the ground beef, salt, garlic powder, onion powder, Worcestershire sauce, and pepper. Use a spoon to gently mix until combined, being careful not to overwork the meat. Divide the mixture into 4 equal portions, shaping each into a loose ball.

Assemble: In a large skillet or griddle, melt the butter over medium heat. When the butter is melted, add the potato buns, cut-side down, and toast for 1 to 2 minutes, until golden brown and crispy, working in batches if you need to. Remove and set aside.

Cook the burgers: Increase the heat under the skillet to medium-high. Place the beef balls in the hot skillet, working in batches, if needed. Using a large spatula or burger press, smash each ball down to a ¼-inch thickness. Press down firmly to create a nice crust. Cook for 2 to 3 minutes without moving, until the edges are crispy and browned. Flip the burgers and place a slice of cheese on top of each patty. Cook for 1 to 2 minutes, until the cheese is melted and the burgers are cooked through. Remove from the pan, set aside, and reduce the heat to medium.

In the same pan, cook the onions for 2 to 3 minutes, stirring frequently and scraping up any browned bits from the pan, until softened and caramelized.

Spread a generous amount of the burger sauce on the tops and bottoms of the toasted buns. Place a burger patty on each bottom bun and top with onions, a tomato slice, and some lettuce. Place the top buns over the stacks and serve immediately.

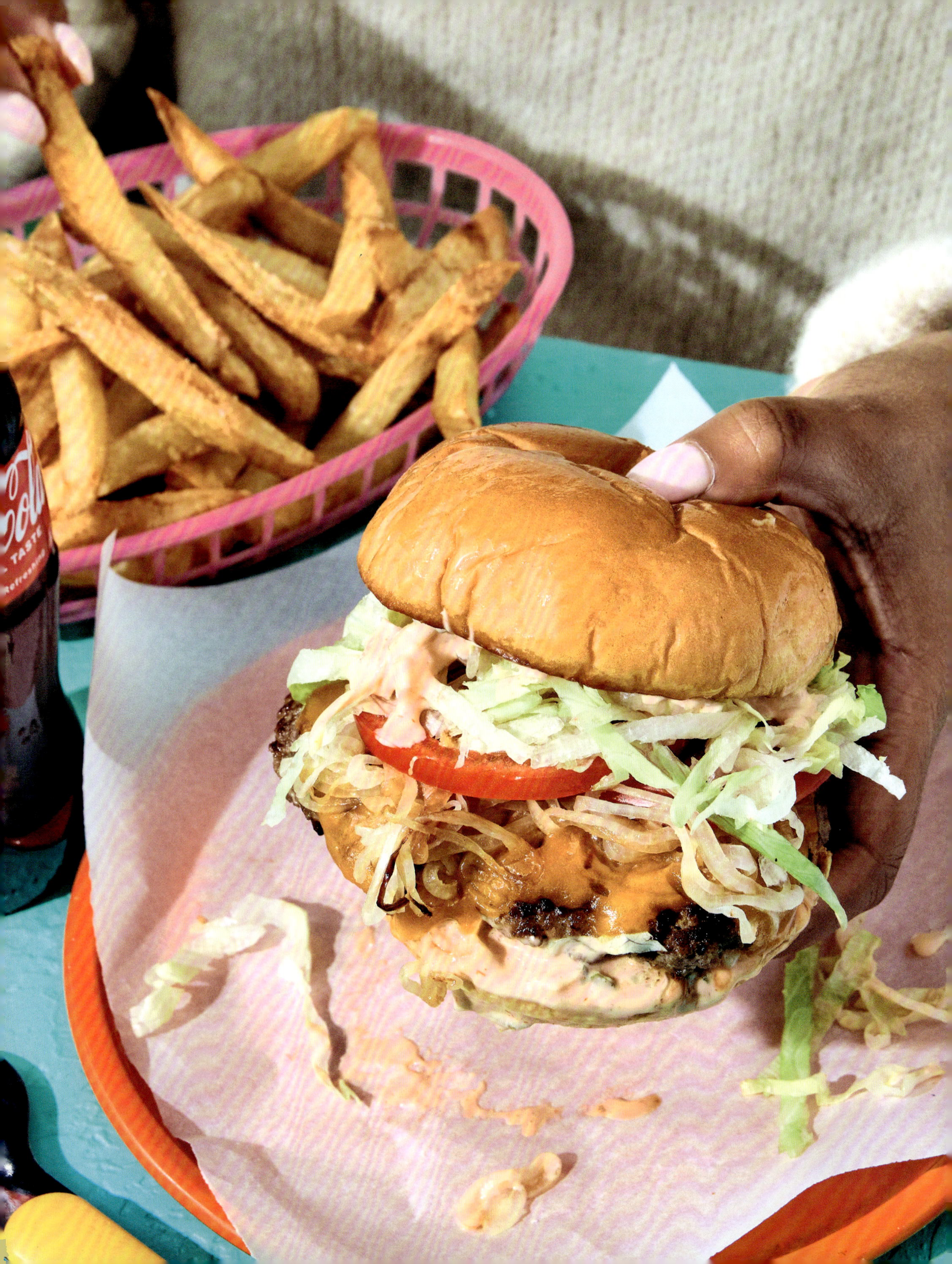
TASTE

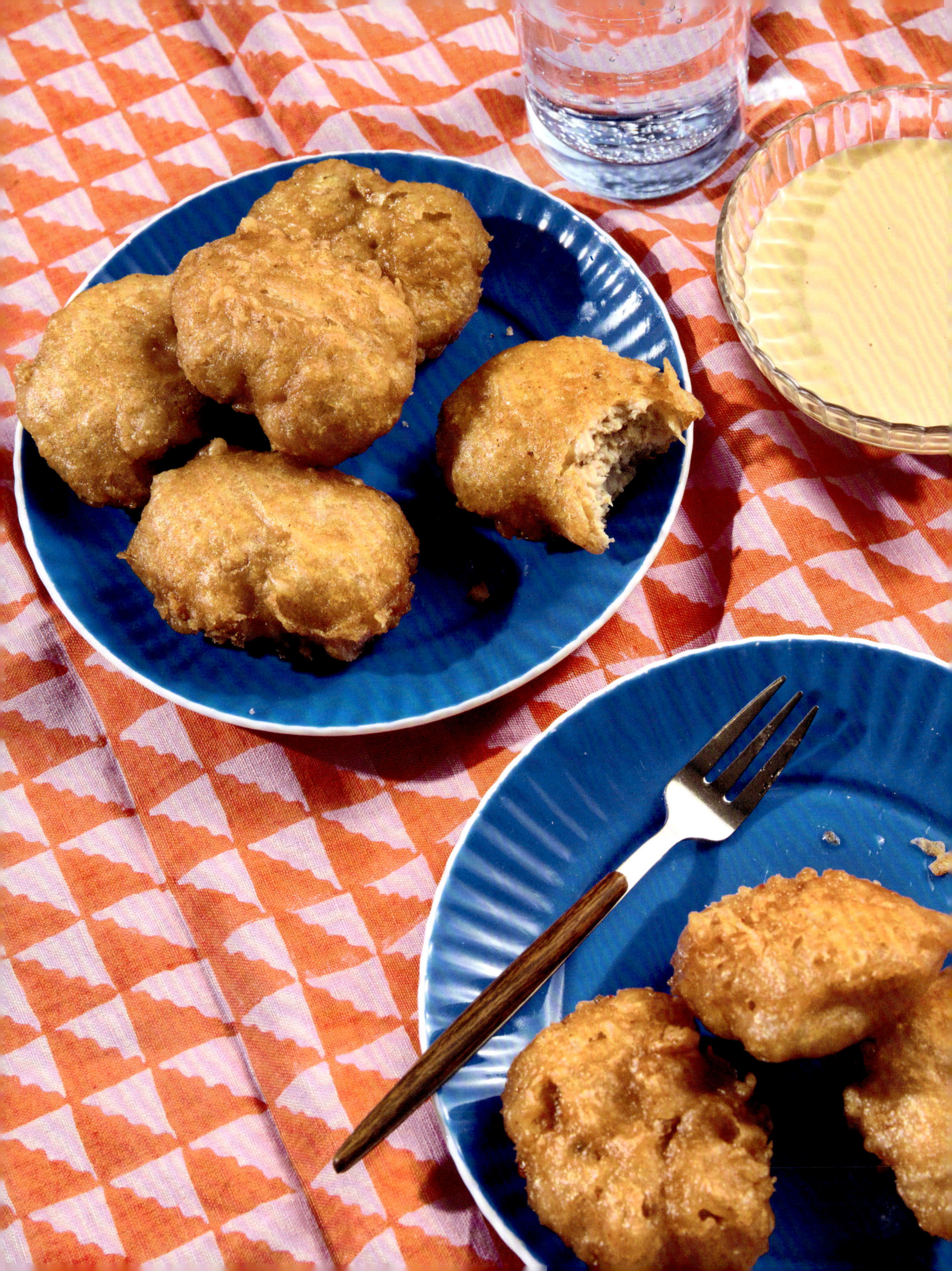

Drive-Thru Chicken Nuggets

Makes **16** nuggets

"You got McDonald's money?" That question always hit hard. Sitting in the back seat, watching Mickey D's pass by, feeling all kinds of sad when my dad wouldn't stop for a Happy Meal. If you know that struggle, this dish is your childhood on a plate. After all those missed McDonald's runs, I decided to learn how to make these nuggets myself as an adult—call it redemption. Now, I can whip them up whenever I want—no permission needed! Pair them with my homemade ranch (see page 241) for that perfect dipping sauce—and trust me, it's better than anything from the drive-thru. Mad good!

Chicken
- 1½ teaspoons kosher salt
- 1 teaspoon sweet paprika
- 1 teaspoon garlic powder
- 2 pounds boneless, skinless chicken thighs, roughly chopped

For Frying
- Vegetable oil, for deep-frying
- 1 cup cornstarch, plus more for coating the nuggets
- 1 cup all-purpose flour
- 1 tablespoon sweet paprika
- 2 teaspoons kosher salt
- 1 teaspoon garlic powder
- 1¾ cups club soda

Prepare the chicken: Line a baking sheet with parchment paper. In a small bowl, mix together the salt, paprika, and garlic powder until combined.

In a food processor, pulse the chicken just until finely ground, being careful not to overprocess to a paste. Add the seasoning mixture to the ground chicken and pulse until well combined.

Shape the seasoned chicken into small nugget shapes (about 2 tablespoons) and place them on the prepared baking sheet. Transfer the sheet to the freezer and freeze the shaped nuggets for 30 minutes.

Meanwhile, set up the frying station: Pour enough oil into a large, deep pot or Dutch oven to come up halfway. Clip a candy/deep-fry thermometer to the side and heat the oil over medium-high until it reaches 350°F. Line a plate with paper towels and have near the stove.

In a large bowl, whisk together the cornstarch, flour, paprika, salt, and garlic powder. Gradually stir in the club soda until the batter is smooth.

Coat the nuggets in some cornstarch, shaking off any excess. One at a time, dredge the cornstarch-coated nuggets in the batter, allowing any excess batter to drip off. Working in batches to avoid overcrowding, add the battered nuggets to the oil and fry for 6 to 8 minutes, until golden brown and the chicken reaches an internal temperature of 165°F. Use a slotted spoon to transfer the nuggets to the paper towels to drain.

Freezer Door Breakfast Sandos

Makes **6** sandwiches

When I was little, all I needed was fifty cents to grab a little something from the bodega to start my day, and I always chose a "butter roll." It was a warm, toasted piece of bread with so much butter it'd melt right through the wrapper. I'd pick one up every day before rushing off to school. It was all we could afford, but Dad always made sure I had something in my stomach to kick off the day. Now as an adult, these freezer sandwiches give me that same vibe but with a lot more protein, way more nutrition, and definitely better flavor. Whip 'em up on a Sunday and you're set for the week. Just do a little prep, wrap them (maybe even with a cute little note), and toss in the freezer. What I love about this recipe is the versatility—swap in any cheese or breakfast meat you're into. Having these on hand for those hectic mornings is a total game changer.

Eggs
12 large eggs
¼ cup whole milk
1 teaspoon kosher salt
1 teaspoon ground white pepper

Sausage Patties
1 pound ground beef (80/20)
1 pound bulk breakfast sausage
1 tablespoon dark brown sugar
1 teaspoon Italian seasoning
1 teaspoon garlic powder
1 teaspoon onion powder
½ teaspoon red pepper flakes
1 tablespoon extra-virgin olive oil

Sandwiches
6 English muffins, split
2 tablespoons (1 ounce) unsalted butter, melted
Maple syrup
6 slices sharp Cheddar cheese

Preheat the oven to 350°F. Line a 9 × 13-inch baking dish with parchment paper.

Bake the eggs: In a large bowl, whisk together the eggs, milk, salt, and white pepper until smooth. Pour the mixture into the prepared dish and bake for about 20 minutes, or until the eggs are set. Use the top of a drinking glass or a 3- to 4-inch round cookie cutter to cut the egg into 6 rounds.

Meanwhile, make the sausage patties: In a medium bowl, combine the beef, breakfast sausage, brown sugar, Italian seasoning, garlic powder, onion powder, and pepper flakes. Divide the mixture into 6 equal portions and shape into patties that are slightly larger than the English muffins, as they will shrink during cooking.

In a large skillet, heat the oil over medium heat until hot and shimmering. Sear the patties for 5 to 6 minutes per side, until cooked through and no longer pink. Transfer to a plate.

Assemble the sandwiches: Toast the English muffins, then spread the inside of each with the melted butter and a drizzle of syrup to taste. Layer the bottom half of each sandwich with one round of baked egg, a slice of Cheddar, and a cooked sausage patty. Close the sandwiches with the English muffin tops. Wrap the sandwiches individually in parchment paper, then store in a freezer-safe bag, pressing all of the air out.

When ready to have a sandwich, thaw in the refrigerator overnight. Unwrap and bake in the oven or air fryer at 375°F for 10 to 12 minutes until heated through.

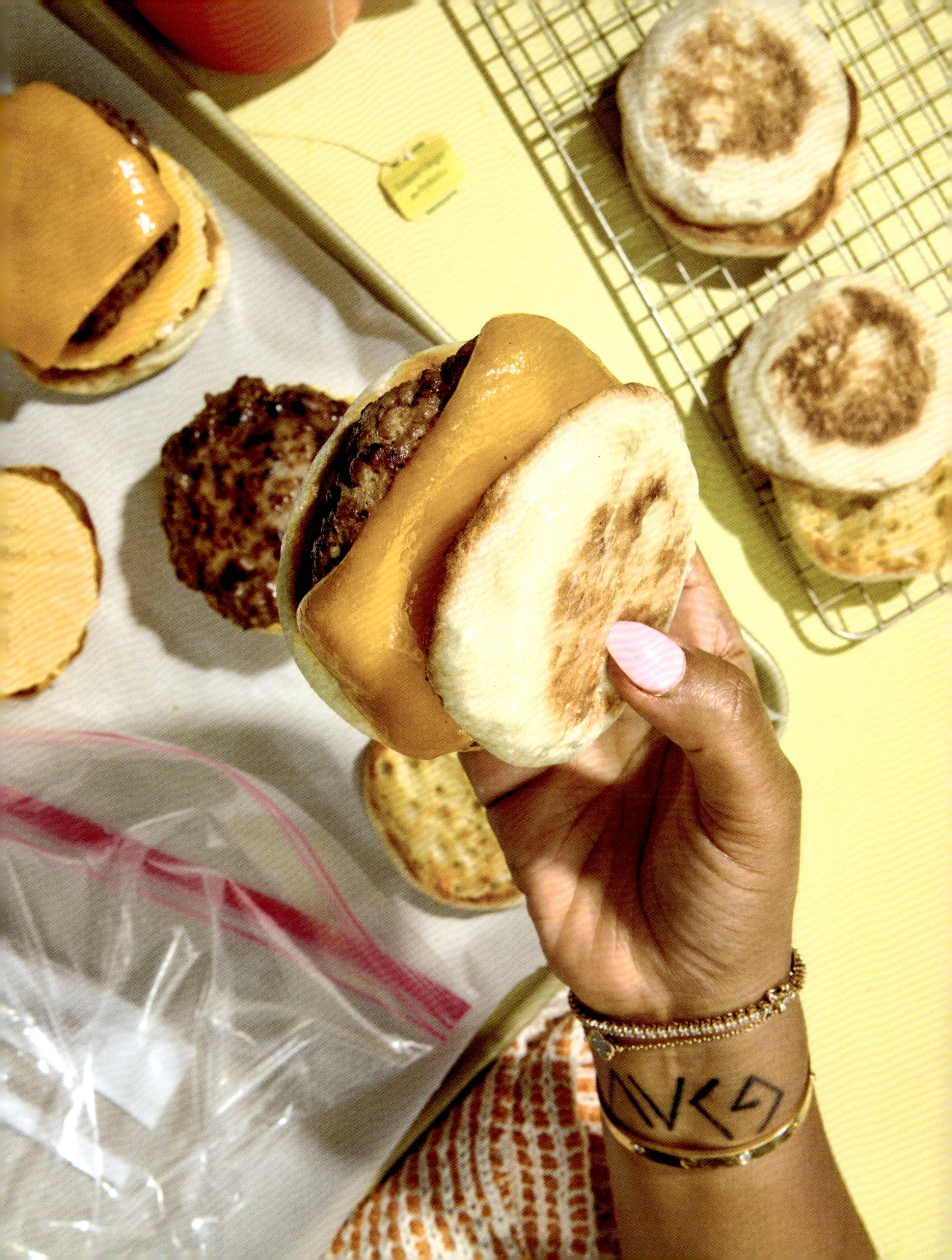

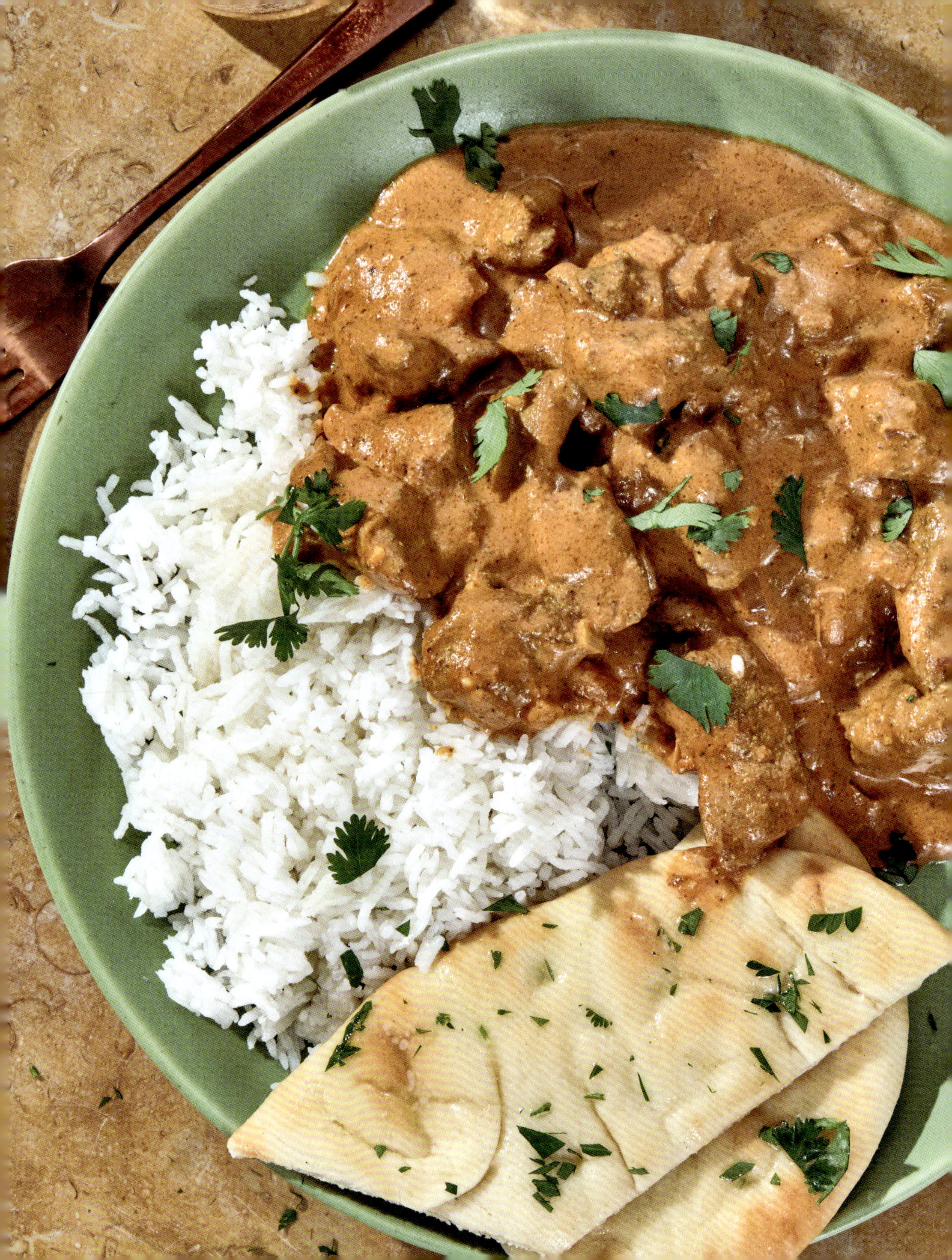

Indian-Style Chicken

Serves 4

If you've always wanted to make your own butter chicken but didn't know where to start, I got you. My first time trying this classic Indian dish (also known as murgh makhani) was in college at a potluck, and after just one bite, I knew I had to figure it out. That rich, creamy sauce with tender chicken? Unforgettable. At first, I thought it'd be complicated, but once you've got your spice cabinet stocked, it's way easier than you'd think. I grab store-bought naan, heat it up, and let it soak up all that sauce. Butter chicken has become one of my go-to comfort dishes, bold in flavor but straightforward to make. Once you try my take, you'll be hooked, too.

Chicken

- ½ cup plain full-fat Greek yogurt
- 2 teaspoons ground turmeric
- 1 teaspoon ground cloves
- 1 teaspoon ground cinnamon
- 1 teaspoon ground ginger
- 1 teaspoon ground cumin
- 2 pounds boneless, skinless chicken thighs, cut into 1½-inch pieces
- 2 tablespoons (1 ounce) unsalted butter

Sauce

- 2 tablespoons (1 ounce) unsalted butter
- 1 small yellow onion, finely diced (about ½ cup)
- 6 garlic cloves, minced (about 2 tablespoons)
- 1 cup canned tomato puree
- 1 tablespoon tomato paste
- 1 cup heavy cream
- 2 teaspoons kosher salt
- 1 teaspoon chili powder
- 1 teaspoon ground cumin

Classic White Rice (page 140), made with basmati, for serving
Chopped fresh cilantro, for serving
Naan (optional), for serving

Marinate the chicken: In a large bowl, whisk together the yogurt, turmeric, cloves, cinnamon, ginger, and cumin. Add the chicken pieces and toss well to coat the chicken all over. Cover and refrigerate for at least 1 hour or up to overnight for the best results.

Cook the chicken: In a large skillet, melt the butter over medium heat. Use tongs to add the chicken to the skillet, shaking off any excess marinade first. Cook for 5 to 6 minutes, stirring frequently, until browned on all sides. Transfer the chicken to a plate and set aside.

Make the sauce: In the same skillet, melt the butter over medium heat. Add the onion and cook for 5 minutes, stirring frequently, until translucent. Add the garlic and cook for 1 to 2 minutes, stirring frequently, until fragrant. Stir in the tomato puree and tomato paste. Cook for 5 minutes, stirring occasionally, until the sauce thickens slightly. Reduce the heat to low.

Stir in the heavy cream, salt, chili powder, and cumin. Simmer for 5 minutes, stirring occasionally, until slightly thickened. Return the browned chicken to the skillet with the sauce and stir gently to coat the chicken all over. Simmer for 5 minutes, allowing the flavors to meld together and the chicken to finish cooking.

Serve the butter chicken hot over cooked basmati rice, garnished with cilantro, with naan on the side, if desired.

Creamy White Chicken Enchiladas with Salsa Verde

Serves 4

I've always had a love for Mexican flavors, and these enchiladas? They're everything—zesty, fresh, and paired with a creamy sauce that takes them over the top. Back when I lived in Jersey City, down the block from this little Mexican spot, they made the softest, creamiest enchiladas I've ever had. You could get a half-pan for $15, and I'd eat them throughout the week when life got busy. When I left Jersey City, I couldn't find enchiladas like that anywhere. So I had no choice but to learn how to make them myself. It all starts with the sauce—the salsa verde, one of my favorite flavors. We're talking onion, garlic, tomatillos, green peppers, jalapeños, cilantro—super fresh, with a bit of heat. We add that salsa verde to everything in this recipe—into the cream sauce, mixed with the chicken, and layered at the bottom of the dish. There's no escaping the flavor, and honestly, why would you want to? These enchiladas bring it all home.

- 2 pounds boneless, skinless chicken breasts
- 1½ teaspoons kosher salt
- 1¾ cups Salsa Verde (page 238)
- 3 tablespoons (1½ ounces) unsalted butter
- 2 cups low-sodium chicken broth
- 2 tablespoons all-purpose flour
- ½ cup sour cream
- 4 ounces cream cheese (½ block)
- ½ teaspoon dried oregano
- ¼ teaspoon ground cumin
- 8 (12-inch) flour tortillas, preferably white flour
- 2 cups mozzarella cheese
- Chopped fresh cilantro, for serving
- Sliced jalapeño, for serving

Cook the chicken: Bring a large pot of water to a boil over high heat. Lower the heat to a simmer and add the chicken and 1 teaspoon of the salt. Cook for 15 minutes, or until the chicken is cooked through and an instant-read thermometer reads 165°F. Transfer the chicken to a large bowl and shred with two forks. Add 1½ cups of the salsa verde and stir until well combined. Set aside.

Make the enchiladas: Preheat the oven to 350°F.

In a large skillet, melt the butter over medium-low heat. In the same skillet, whisk together the chicken broth and flour until no lumps remain. Add the sour cream and cream cheese and stir until the cheeses are completely melted. Stir in 2 tablespoons of the salsa verde, the oregano, remaining ½ teaspoon salt, and cumin.

Lay a tortilla on the counter. Add ¼ cup of the chicken mixture and sprinkle 3 tablespoons of the mozzarella over the chicken. Roll the tortilla into an enchilada and transfer to a 9 × 13-inch baking dish, seam-side down. Repeat this process until you have made all 8 enchiladas. Fill the side gaps in the baking dish with any leftover chicken meat.

Pour the creamy sauce over the enchiladas and smooth it out with a spatula. Drizzle the remaining 2 tablespoons salsa verde on top and cover with the remaining ½ cup mozzarella cheese.

Bake for 30 minutes, or until the cheese is melted and bubbling. Switch the oven to low broil and broil for 2 to 3 minutes for a golden finish. Serve, topped with chopped cilantro and sliced jalapeño.

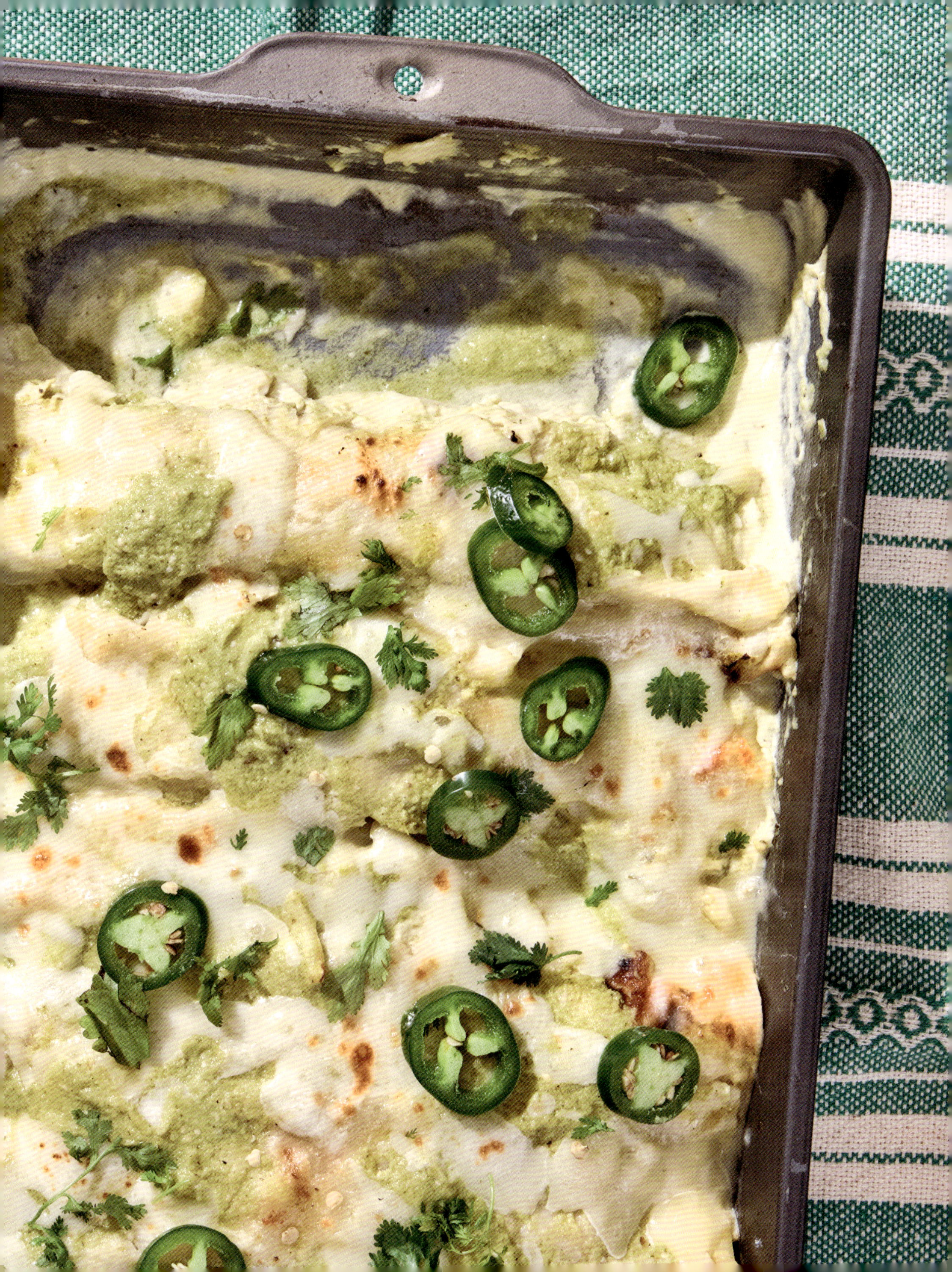

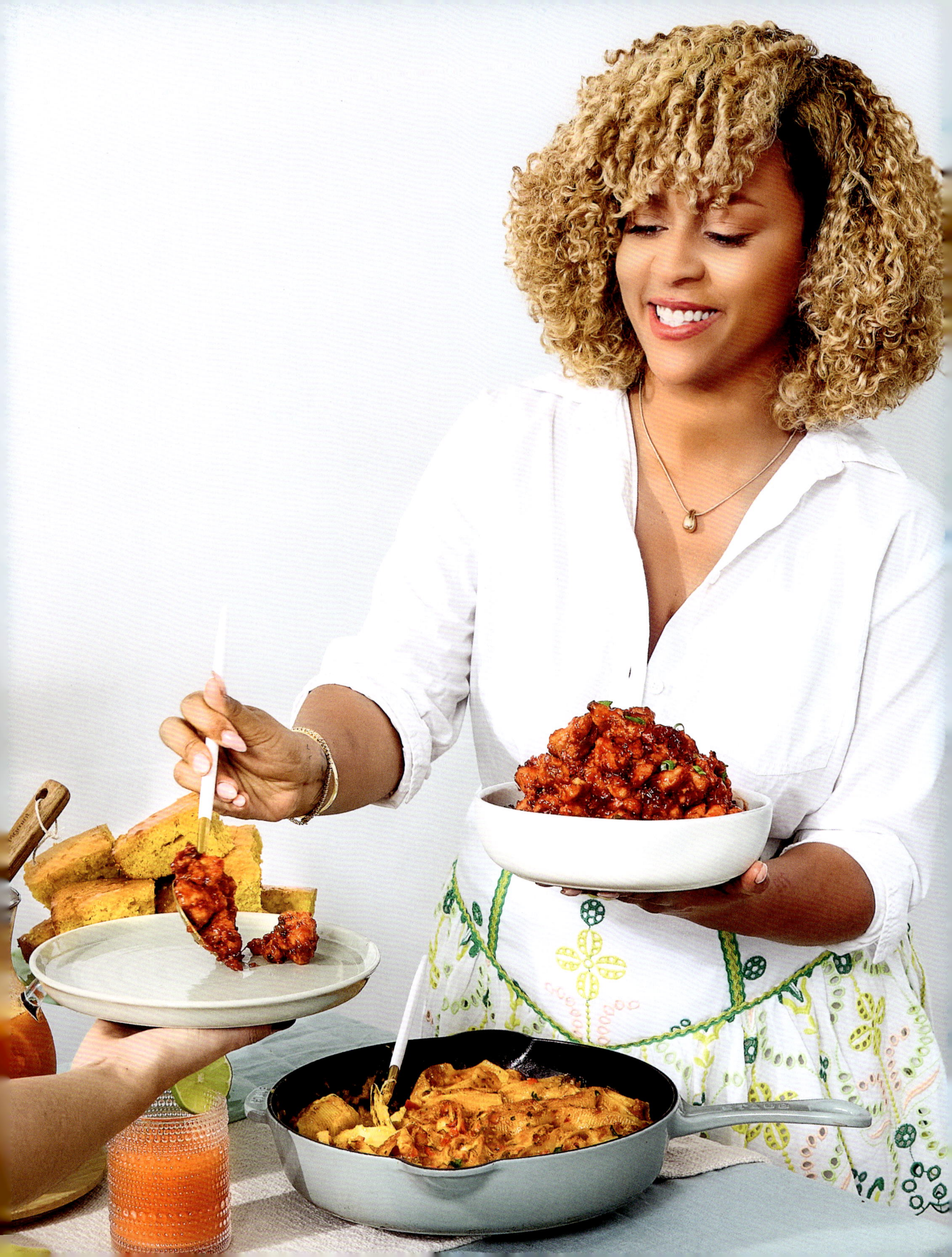

5
What's for Dinner?

Some dinners stick with you—they're the ones you look forward to all day, the ones that make your whole house smell incredible, and the ones that make everyone at the table pause after the first bite and say, "Damn, this is good." That's what this chapter is about. These recipes aren't just meals; they're the kind of dinners that comfort you, impress your date, or get you through a hectic week with leftovers that somehow taste even better the next day.

I've been helping people master the art of flavorful weeknight dinners since 2016, so trust me—I know what works. At nineteen years old, I started my meal-delivery business, Tonicooks, with one mission: to deliver fresh, delicious meals that made weeknight dinners something to look forward to. Whether it was juicy chicken thighs, cheesy tacos, or quick pastas, people loved the idea of delicious comfort dinners. That mission is still at the core of everything I do. Along the way, I've learned that great dinners don't have to be fussy, but they do have to be memorable, and they should always feel like something you want to sit down and savor.

This chapter is full of recipes for every kind of dinner moment. Need something impressive for date night? My Creamy Shrimp and Crab–Stuffed Shells (page 138) are rich, indulgent, and guaranteed to set the mood. Want a one-pan wonder that's cozy enough for Sunday dinner but practical enough to meal-prep for the week? My Garlic Parmesan Chicken Thighs and Potatoes (page 143) has you covered. For those nights when you're craving comfort, my triple-threat Classic Chili (page 134)—loaded with three types of meat and packed with layers of flavor—will take care of you. And when you need a quick favorite that works for the whole family, my Cheesy Chipotle Chicken Quesadillas (page 129) are smoky, melty perfection.

These recipes are here for you—weekends, weeknights, or whenever you want to sit down to something delicious and feel like you've done something good for yourself. Because great food doesn't just feed your body—it feeds your soul.

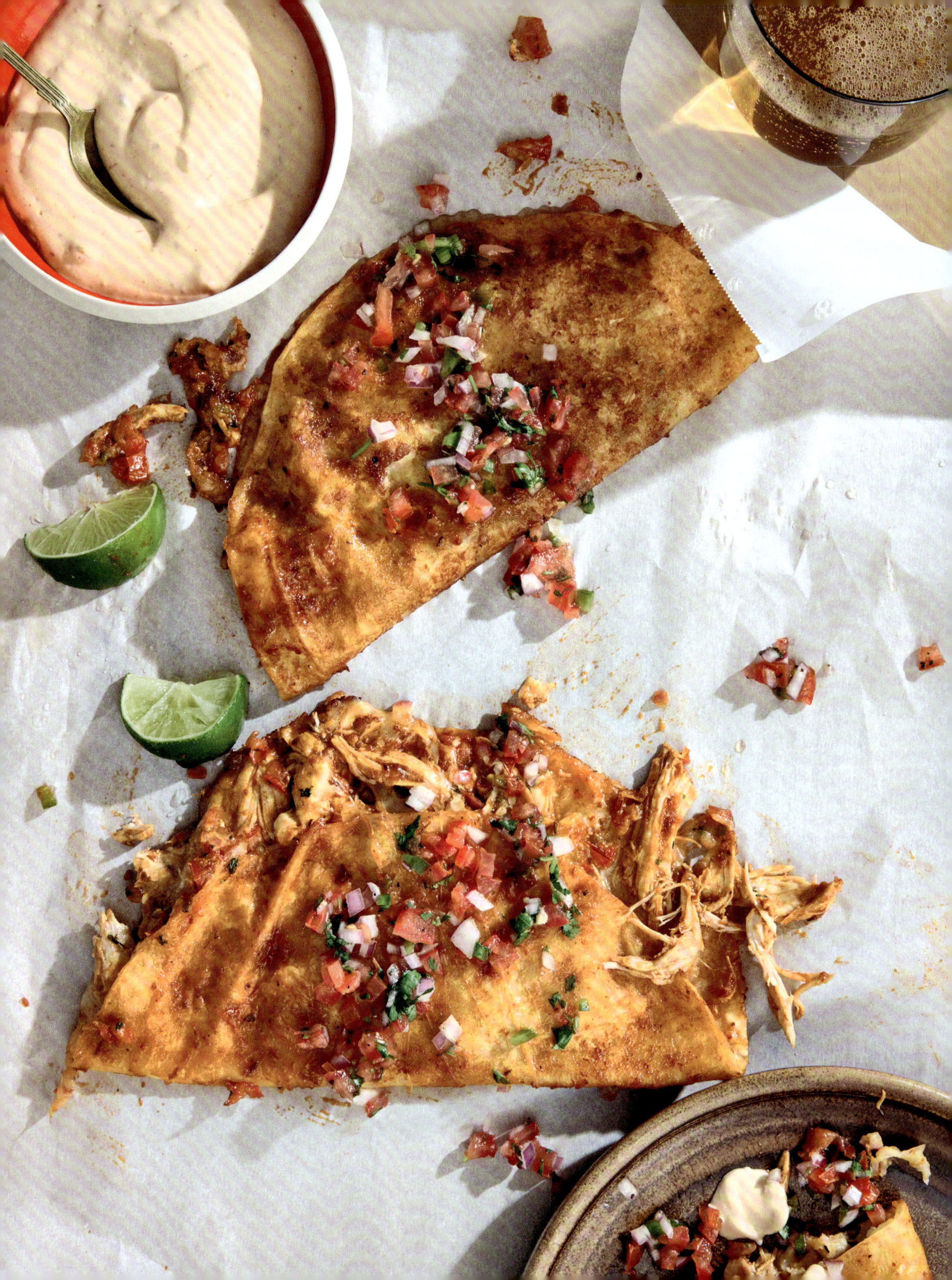

Cheesy Chipotle Chicken Quesadillas

Serves 6

Quesadillas are the ultimate lazy comfort food, perfect for those nights when all you want to do is binge your favorite show and eat something good. This chipotle chicken version is all about the flavorful chipotle sauce pulling all the weight. First, I toss rotisserie chicken in it (because, hello, we're saving time), then it turns into a creamy aioli for dipping your quesadillas in, and finally, I use it in the pan to sear the quesadillas until they're crispy and full of flavor.

Top it with fresh pico de gallo for that perfect balance—fresh and bright against the saucy, cheesy quesadillas. A quick, no-fuss dinner that's guaranteed to hit the spot.

Chipotle Sauce

- 1 (7-ounce) can chipotle peppers in adobo sauce
- 2 tablespoons honey
- 1 tablespoon red wine vinegar
- Juice of 1 lime
- 1 teaspoon garlic powder
- 1 teaspoon ground cumin
- 1 teaspoon kosher salt

Chicken Filling and Quesadillas

- 2 cups shredded rotisserie chicken
- ½ cup mayonnaise
- 2 tablespoons (1 ounce) unsalted butter
- 6 (8-inch) flour tortillas
- 1 cup plus 2 tablespoons freshly shredded mozzarella cheese
- ¾ cup Pico de Gallo (page 88), plus more for serving

Make the chipotle sauce: In a blender, combine the chipotle peppers in adobo sauce, honey, vinegar, lime juice, garlic powder, cumin, and salt. Blend until completely smooth and no chunks remain. Set aside.

Make the chicken filling: In a medium skillet, combine ½ cup of the chipotle sauce, the shredded rotisserie chicken, and ¼ cup water. Bring to a simmer over medium heat and cook for 5 minutes, stirring occasionally, until the chicken is heated through and well coated in the sauce. Set aside.

Make the chipotle aioli: In a small bowl, whisk the mayonnaise with 1 tablespoon of the chipotle sauce until well combined. Set aside.

Cook the quesadillas: In a large skillet, melt 1 teaspoon of the butter over medium heat. Spread 1 teaspoon chipotle sauce in the pan. Place a tortilla on top of the sauce. On one half of the tortilla, layer ⅓ cup chicken filling, 3 tablespoons mozzarella, and 2 tablespoons pico de gallo. Drizzle additional chipotle sauce over the filling to taste.

Use a spatula to carefully fold the tortilla in half and press down to close. Cook for 2 to 3 minutes on each side, until golden brown and crispy. Repeat with the remaining tortillas to make 6 quesadillas.

Cut each quesadilla into 3 wedges. Serve warm with a dollop of chipotle aioli or more fresh pico on the side.

Seared Salmon with Creamy Lemon Orzo and Spinach

Serves 4

Let me tell you, orzo surprised me. I didn't try it until I was in my twenties, and the second I did, I realized I'd been missing out. Tender orzo loves soaking up every bit of flavor you throw at it—which makes it perfect for my style of cooking, where it's all about building flavor from the ground up. And this recipe is a favorite because it's all about those layers. First, you cook the salmon, and while it's resting, all those seasoned juices hang tight, just waiting to do their thing. Then we build the base for the orzo—shallot, a whole lot of garlic, butter, heavy cream, white wine, and Parmesan. But here's where the magic happens—we take all those salmon drippings and mix them into the base, turning it into a pot of straight-up greatness. This dish was a reminder to me to never be afraid to try something new in the kitchen. Sometimes stepping out of your comfort zone is exactly how you end up creating a masterpiece like this one-pot dinner. If you haven't tried orzo yet, trust me, this is the recipe to kick it off with.

- 4 (6-ounce) salmon fillets, skinned and any pin bones removed
- 3 tablespoons extra-virgin olive oil
- 1 teaspoon sweet paprika
- 1 teaspoon kosher salt, plus more to taste
- Freshly ground black pepper
- 2 tablespoons (1 ounce) unsalted butter
- ½ large shallot, minced (about ¼ cup)
- 12 garlic cloves, minced (about ¼ cup)
- ¼ cup dry white wine, such as Chardonnay
- 20 ounces orzo pasta (about 3⅓ cups)
- 2½ cups low-sodium chicken broth, plus more as needed
- 2 cups loosely packed baby spinach
- ½ cup heavy cream
- ½ cup freshly grated Parmesan cheese (2 ounces)
- Grated zest and juice of ½ lemon, plus lemon slices for garnish
- 1 teaspoon Italian seasoning
- 1 teaspoon garlic powder
- 1 teaspoon red pepper flakes

Cook the salmon: Coat the salmon with 1 tablespoon of the olive oil and season with the paprika, ½ teaspoon of the salt, and pepper to taste.

In a large skillet, heat the remaining 2 tablespoons olive oil over medium-high heat until hot and shimmering. Add the salmon fillets and cook for 2 minutes on each side, until browned. Transfer the salmon to a plate and set aside.

Cook the orzo: In the same skillet, melt the butter over medium-high heat. When the butter is melted, add the shallot and minced garlic and reduce the heat to medium-low. Cook, stirring frequently, for 2 to 3 minutes, until softened. Pour in the white wine and let it reduce, stirring occasionally, for 2 to 3 minutes, until the shallots are tender. Add the orzo and stir to combine. Add the chicken broth and bring to a simmer. Stir in the spinach, heavy cream, Parmesan, lemon zest, lemon juice, Italian seasoning, garlic powder, pepper flakes, and remaining ½ teaspoon salt. Simmer for 10 minutes, stirring constantly, until the orzo is almost tender, adding more broth if needed to keep the pasta covered.

To finish: Reduce the heat to low, add the salmon pieces and any juices to the pan, and cook for 10 minutes, uncovered, or until the pasta is fully tender and the salmon is opaque on the outside but still slightly translucent on the inside.

Divide the orzo into bowls, top with the salmon and lemon slices, and serve.

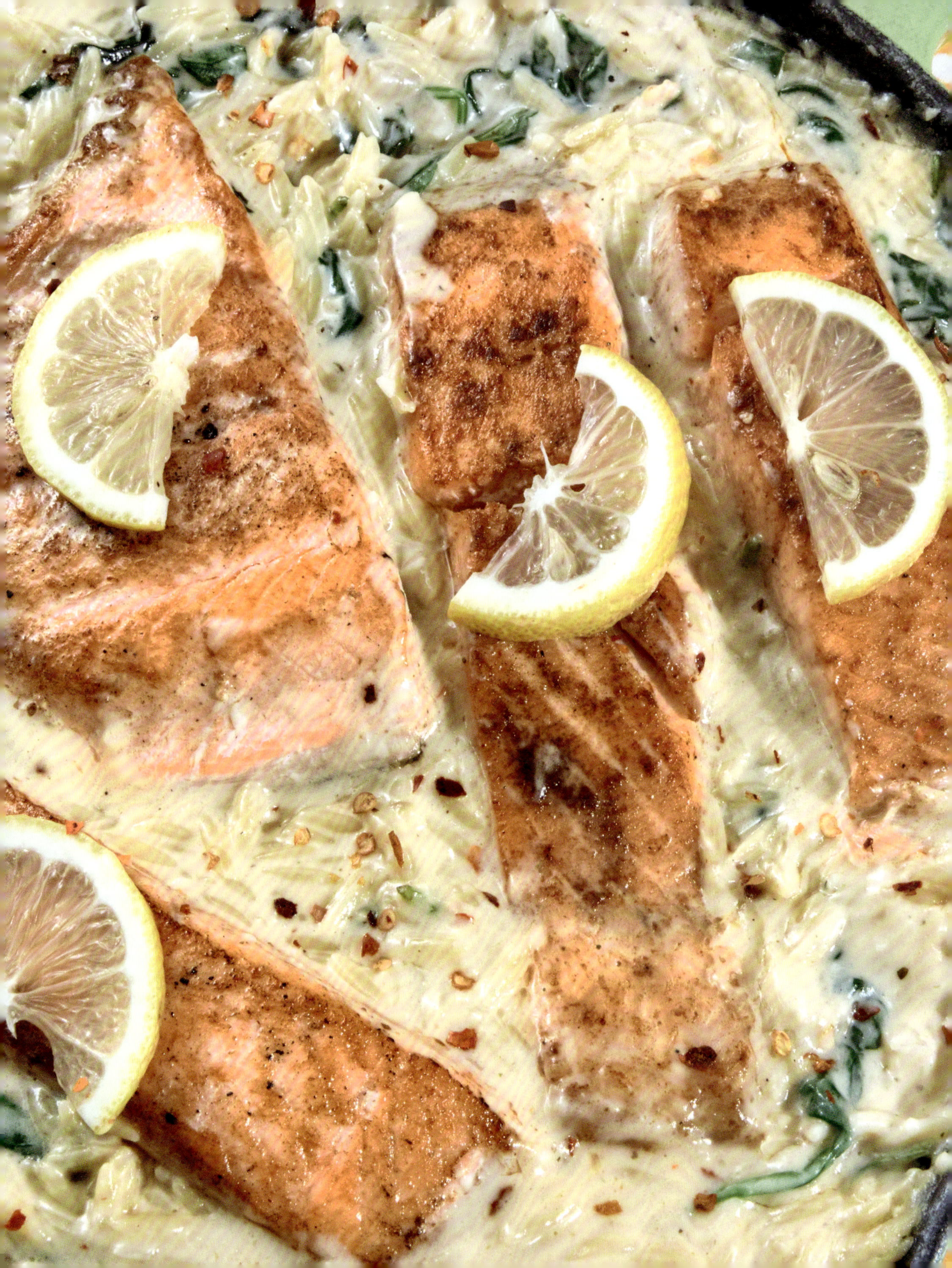

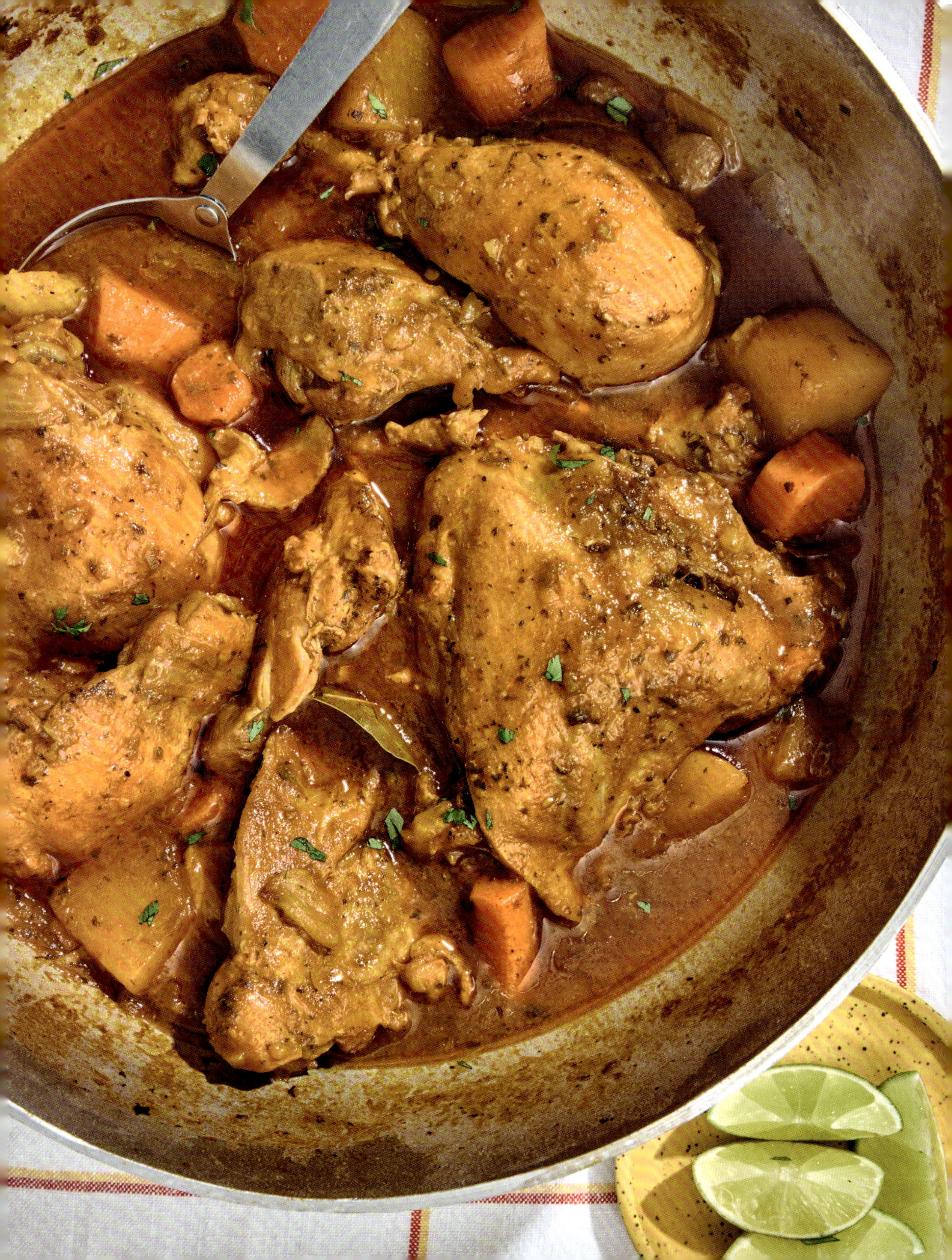

The Perfect Pollo Guisado

Serves **4**

Growing up, we ate pollo guisado all the time, and it was never just "dinner." It was comfort, culture, and connection all in one pot. My grandmother, Edie, always made it in her caldero, that sacred pot every Puerto Rican kitchen is built around. The smell of garlic, onion, and fresh sofrito simmering on the stove is something you don't just remember—you feel it. And in true Puerto Rican fashion, everyone in the family swore their version was the best. I'll just say this—my recipe holds its own.

The key to nailing it? Two things: fresh sofrito and a splash of beer. Sofrito is the soul of this dish, and making it from scratch takes it to another level. My grandmother would've laughed me out of the kitchen if I had dared to use the jarred stuff. And the beer? A little Corona adds a depth you didn't know was missing—it's that secret sazón that makes you say *wow*.

With tender, fall-off-the-bone chicken and a thick, savory gravy infused with garlic, onion, and sofrito, this dish is pure Puerto Rican comfort food. Serve it with arroz blanco, tostones, and avocado, and you've got a meal that speaks to generations of love, tradition, and flavor. It's simple, soulful, and the kind of recipe that turns dinner into something unforgettable.

Marinated Chicken

- 3 pounds bone-in, skinless chicken drumsticks and thighs
- 2½ teaspoons Goya Sazón (culantro y achiote)
- 1 teaspoon adobo seasoning
- 1 teaspoon garlic powder
- 1 teaspoon kosher salt
- ½ teaspoon freshly ground black pepper
- 1 tablespoon extra-virgin olive oil

Stew

- 2 tablespoons extra-virgin olive oil
- 1 cup Goya canned tomato sauce
- ¼ cup Abuela's Green Sofrito (page 233)
- ¼ small yellow onion, finely diced (about 2 tablespoons)
- 2 teaspoons Goya Sazón (culantro y achiote)
- 1 teaspoon adobo seasoning
- 1 teaspoon dried oregano
- ½ teaspoon kosher salt
- 3 cups low-sodium chicken broth
- 1 chicken bouillon cube
- ½ cup beer, such as Corona, well chilled
- 3 sprigs cilantro
- 3 bay leaves
- 2 small russet potatoes, peeled and chopped (about 2 cups)
- 2 medium carrots, chopped (about 1 cup)
- Classic White Rice (page 140), for serving

Marinate the chicken: Put the chicken in a large bowl and season all over with the Sazón, adobo seasoning, garlic powder, salt, and pepper. Cover the bowl and marinate the chicken in the refrigerator for at least 1 hour or up to overnight.

Cook the chicken: In a 4-quart caldero (see page 18) or large Dutch oven, heat the olive oil over medium-high heat until hot and shimmering. Working in batches to avoid overcrowding, sear the chicken for 2 to 3 minutes on each side, until browned all over. Use tongs to transfer the chicken to a plate and set aside.

Make the stew: In the same pot, heat the olive oil over medium heat until hot and shimmering. Add the tomato sauce, sofrito, and onion. Stir and scrape up any browned bits from the bottom of the pot, then reduce the heat to medium-low and simmer for 5 minutes, stirring frequently, until fragrant. Add the Sazón, adobo seasoning, oregano, and salt. Stir in the chicken broth and chicken bouillon. Simmer for 5 minutes.

Return the chicken to the pot and stir in the beer, cilantro, and bay leaves. Reduce the heat to low, cover, and cook for 30 minutes. Then, add in the potatoes and carrots and continue cooking for another 20 minutes, stirring occasionally, until the potatoes and carrots are fork-tender and the chicken is cooked through.

Discard the bay leaves. Serve with white rice.

Classic Chili

Serves 6 to 8

This classic chili is a triple-threat—literally. With Italian sausage, ground beef, and ground pork, it's a texture lover's dream. I know, three meats might sound extra, but trust me, it makes all the difference. Each bite is packed with bold, smoky flavor, thanks to a perfect mix of spices, a splash of dark stout, and layers of aromatics that bring it all together.

This chili is hearty, comforting, and anything but basic. It's the kind of dish that works for anything—game day, a cozy dinner, or feeding a hungry crowd. And if you really want to set it off, pair it with my Honey Butter Corn Bread (page 182). Don't skimp on the toppings either—cheese, sour cream, jalapeños, whatever you've got.

- 2 tablespoons extra-virgin olive oil
- 3 celery stalks, diced (about 1½ cups)
- 1 small yellow onion, diced (about ½ cup)
- 1 (6-ounce) can tomato paste
- 6 garlic cloves, minced (about 2 tablespoons)
- 1 pound bulk mild Italian sausage
- ½ pound ground beef (80/20)
- ½ pound ground pork
- 1 (28-ounce) can crushed tomatoes
- 2 (10-ounce) cans diced tomatoes with green chilies, drained
- 1 (15-ounce) can dark red kidney beans, drained and rinsed
- 1 cup low-sodium beef broth
- ½ cup dark beer (optional; see tip), such as Guinness
- 2 sprigs oregano
- 3 bay leaves
- 3 tablespoons chili powder
- 2 tablespoons dark brown sugar
- 1 tablespoon smoked paprika
- 1 tablespoon garlic powder
- 1 tablespoon onion powder
- 1 tablespoon Worcestershire sauce
- 2 teaspoons ground cumin
- 2 teaspoons kosher salt, plus more to taste
- ½ teaspoon liquid smoke (optional)
- Freshly ground black pepper
- Toppings: shredded Cheddar cheese, sour cream, sliced jalapeños

Cook the meat and veggies: In a large pot or Dutch oven, heat the olive oil over medium heat until hot. Add the celery, onion, tomato paste, and minced garlic. Cook, stirring frequently, for 5 minutes, or until the onion is translucent and the tomato paste has caramelized. Add the Italian sausage, ground beef, and ground pork and cook for 8 to 10 minutes, breaking up the meat into small pieces and stirring occasionally, until the meat is browned and no longer pink.

Make the chili: Stir in the crushed tomatoes, diced tomatoes, kidney beans, beef broth, beer (if using), oregano, bay leaves, chili powder, brown sugar, smoked paprika, garlic powder, onion powder, Worcestershire sauce, cumin, salt, liquid smoke (if using), and black pepper to taste. Stir everything together and bring the chili to a simmer. Reduce the heat to low, cover, and simmer for 45 minutes to 1 hour, stirring occasionally, until the chili is thick and all of the flavors have melded.

Ladle into bowls and top with shredded Cheddar, sour cream, and sliced jalapeños.

Chef's Kiss: I love adding 3 to 4 ounces of dark Guinness stout when I add in all my spices. This gives the chili a little va-va-voom! Although optional, it's worth it.

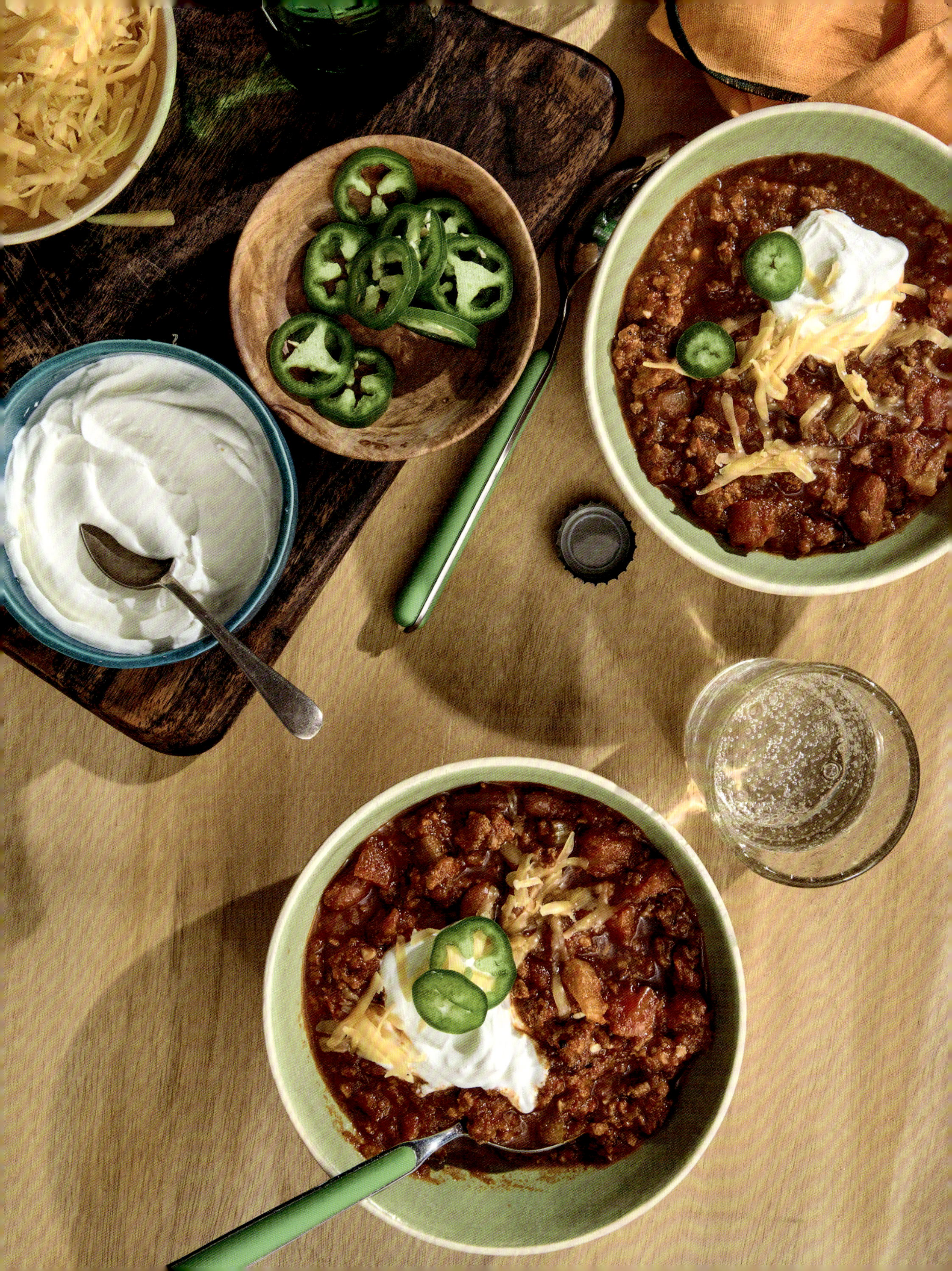

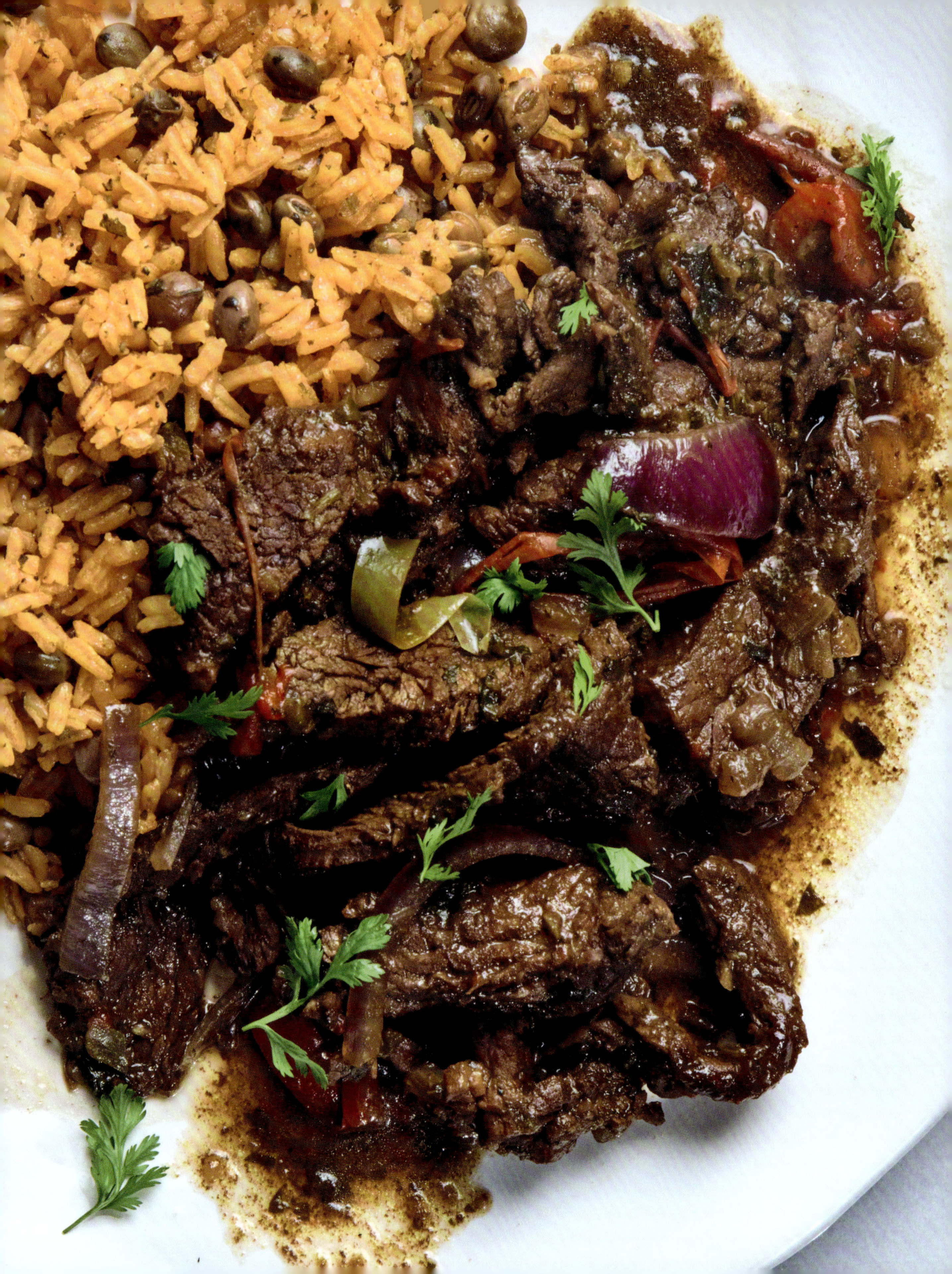

Puerto Rican Pepper Steak

Serves 4

Puerto Rican pepper steak is the kind of dish that feels like a warm hug from the island. Tender strips of steak, sweet bell peppers, and onion simmered in a rich sauce seasoned with Maggi, adobo, and fresh sofrito—it's the definition of Latin comfort food. A splash of vinegar cuts through the richness, making every bite perfectly balanced and full of flavor.

This was one of those dishes growing up that could stretch to feed a crowd, always served over arroz con gandules to soak up every last drop of that saucy goodness. It's quick enough for a weeknight meal but has all the soul and depth of a dish that's been slow-cooked with love.

Steak

- 3 pounds flank steak, sliced against the grain into thin strips
- ⅓ cup Abuela's Green Sofrito (page 233)
- ¼ cup chopped fresh cilantro
- 8 garlic cloves, peeled and crushed
- 1 tablespoon vegetable oil
- 2 teaspoons Maggi seasoning or 2 teaspoons kosher salt
- 1 teaspoon dried oregano
- 1 teaspoon adobo seasoning
- 1 teaspoon chicken bouillon powder
- 1 teaspoon freshly ground black pepper
- ½ teaspoon ground cumin

To Finish

- 1 tablespoon vegetable oil
- ½ medium red bell pepper, sliced into thin strips
- ½ medium green bell pepper, sliced into thin strips
- ½ medium red onion, sliced
- 2 tablespoons browning sauce (optional)
- 3 bay leaves
- Chopped fresh cilantro, for serving
- Arroz con Gandules (page 170) or Classic White Rice (page 140), for serving

Marinate the steak: In a large bowl, combine the steak, sofrito, cilantro, garlic, oil, Maggi seasoning, oregano, adobo seasoning, chicken bouillon powder, black pepper, and cumin. Toss until the steak is coated all over and the seasonings are evenly distributed. Cover and marinate in the fridge for at least 1 hour or up to overnight.

To finish: In a large pot, heat the oil over medium-high heat until hot and shimmering. Add the steak with the marinade and sauté for 5 to 7 minutes, stirring occasionally, until the natural juices release. Add both bell peppers, the onion, browning sauce (if using), and bay leaves. Reduce the heat to medium. Add 2 cups water to the same bowl you seasoned your meat in and swirl to incorporate any lingering marinade, then pour the water into the pot. Cook for 10 minutes, stirring occasionally, until the water reduces by half. Reduce the heat to low, cover, and cook for 1 hour, or until the meat is tender.

Garnish with cilantro and serve hot with the rice of your choice.

Creamy Shrimp and Crab-Stuffed Shells

Serves **6 to 8**

When I was young, my grandmother dated a man named Frank. All I remember about Frank is that he loved pasta, owned a funeral home, and made my grandmother really happy. My grandmother loved cooking for Frank. The dish that stands out most in my memory is her stuffed shells.

Normally, my grandmother was a strong, no-nonsense woman, but in the kitchen, making those stuffed shells, she softened. It was a labor of love—she made delicious, cheesy stuffed shells with love.

When my grandmother passed away, I found myself thinking about the times when she seemed happiest. In my grief, when I couldn't do much but celebrate her life, I decided to make her beloved dish—with a twist. I added seafood—shrimp and crab—to elevate it. I wanted the recipe to stay rich, so I went with a creamy sauce seasoned with pepper, Cajun spices, and adobo. For color, I tossed in some bell peppers, and of course I finished it off with plenty of Parmesan and mozzarella cheese.

This recipe is my love letter to my grandmother, to Frank, to their union, and to the meal I ate to cope. To this day it's my favorite comfort dish.

Shells
1 teaspoon kosher salt
18 jumbo pasta shells (about 9 ounces)

Shrimp
1 pound peeled and deveined shrimp (21/25 count), tails off
1 teaspoon no-salt Cajun seasoning
1 teaspoon adobo seasoning
2 tablespoons extra-virgin olive oil

Sauce
4 tablespoons (½ stick/2 ounces) unsalted butter
½ red bell pepper, diced
½ green bell pepper, diced
¼ cup diced yellow onion
3 garlic cloves, minced
4 cups heavy cream
1 tablespoon sweet paprika
1 teaspoon no-salt Cajun seasoning
1 teaspoon adobo seasoning
1 teaspoon kosher salt
¼ teaspoon ground white pepper
8 ounces shredded mozzarella (2 cups)
4½ ounces Parmesan cheese, freshly shredded (1½ cups)
1 pound lump crabmeat, picked over for shells
½ bunch of parsley, chopped, for serving

Cook the pasta shells: Bring a large pot of water to a boil and stir in the salt. Carefully add the shells and cook for 8 to 10 minutes, until al dente. Drain and set aside.

Preheat the oven to 350°F.

Cook the shrimp: In a large bowl, combine the shrimp with the Cajun seasoning and adobo seasoning and toss to coat.

In a large skillet, heat the olive oil over medium heat until hot and shimmering. Add the shrimp and sauté for 3 to 5 minutes, stirring occasionally, until opaque and fully cooked. Use a slotted spoon or tongs to transfer the shrimp to a cutting board. Chop the shrimp, transfer to a plate, and set aside.

Make the sauce: In the same skillet, melt the butter. Add both bell peppers, the onion, and garlic and sauté for 2 to 3 minutes, until softened. Whisk in the heavy cream, whisking constantly to prevent lumps. Bring to a simmer and whisk in the paprika, Cajun seasoning, adobo seasoning, salt, and white pepper. Reduce the heat to medium-low and simmer for 5 to 7 minutes, stirring occasionally, until the sauce thickens slightly.

Stir in 1½ cups of the mozzarella and 1 cup of the Parmesan until melted and smooth. Reduce the heat to low and stir in the cooked shrimp. Simmer for 5 to 10 minutes, until thickened. Gently fold in the crabmeat.

Assemble and bake: Spread ½ cup of the cream sauce on the bottom of a 12-inch or 13-inch cast-iron skillet. Stuff the shells with the cream sauce and place them into the skillet, open-side up. Evenly spoon any remaining cream sauce over the stuffed shells.

Sprinkle the remaining ½ cup mozzarella and ½ cup Parmesan over the top. Cover with foil and bake for 20 minutes. Uncover and bake for about 10 minutes more, until the cheese is golden and bubbling. Garnish with fresh parsley before serving.

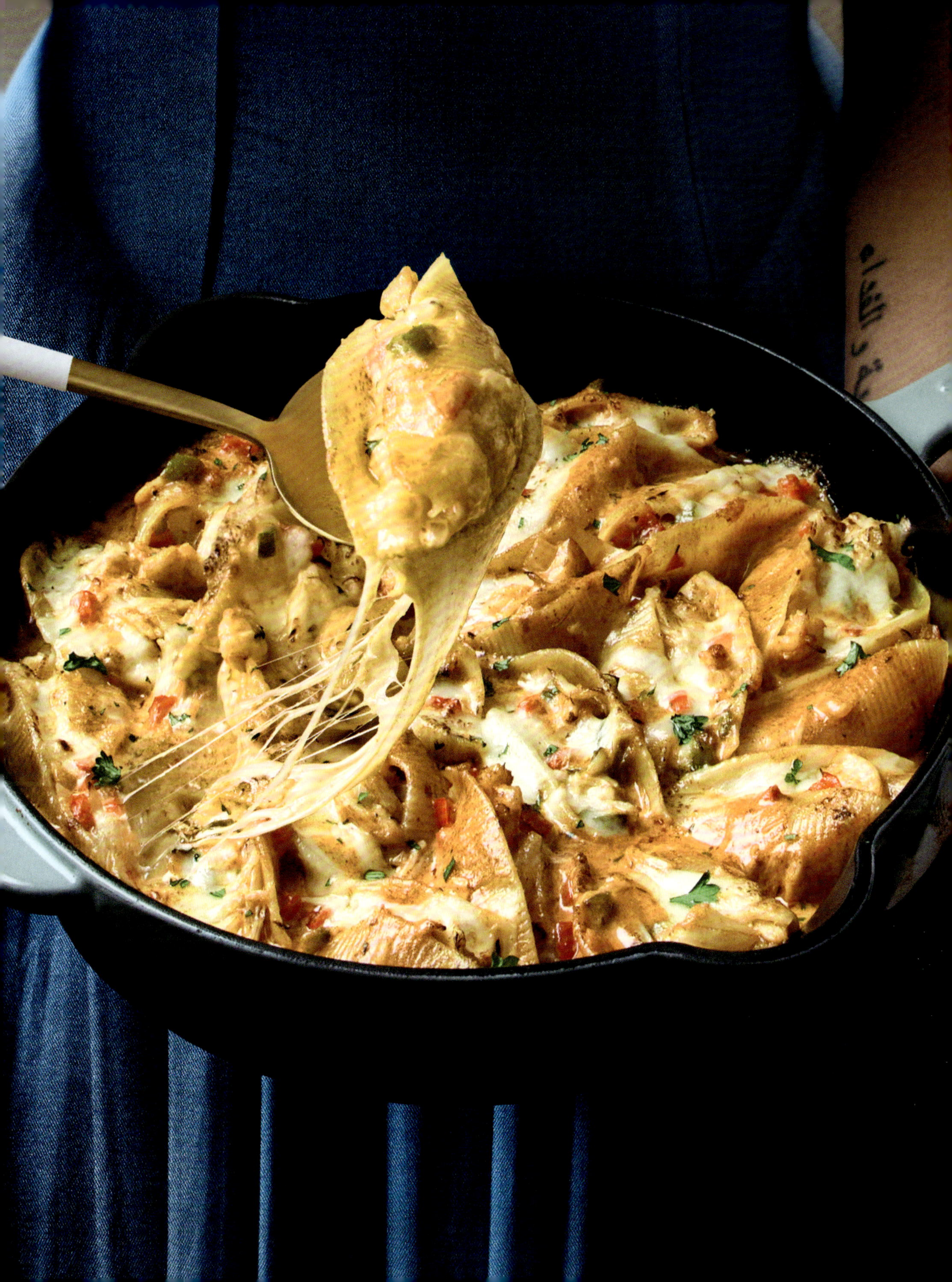

How to Make Rice 101

So many of the recipes in this book aren't complete until you add simple steamed rice. There are a million ways to make it—here are a few of my favorites.

No matter how you're cooking it, wash your rice first. Start by placing the rice in a fine sieve. Rinse the rice under cold running water for 2 to 3 minutes, or until the water runs clear. This process helps to remove excess starch, which is essential for preventing the rice from becoming too sticky.

And a trick I swear by for measuring water is using the first line of your index finger. (Trust me, it works.) Once you've added the water to the rice, just place your index finger on top of the rice, and the water should come up to that first line.

Classic White Rice

White rice is the perfect side dish for so many of the recipes in this book. Here's how to nail it.

Put the washed rice in a large saucepan, then add water. For medium- and long-grain rice, I use a 1:2 ratio. So, for every 1 cup rice, add 2 cups water. I also add 2 teaspoons neutral oil (like canola or vegetable oil) and 1 teaspoon kosher salt for every 1 cup rice.

Bring the water to a boil over high heat, then reduce the heat to low, cover, and let it simmer for 25 minutes without lifting the lid. It's important not to disturb the rice while it's cooking to ensure the rice cooks evenly. Remove the pan from the heat and let it sit covered for an additional 5 minutes to allow the steam to finish cooking the rice. Fluff the rice with a fork before serving, and you'll have perfectly cooked rice, every time. Every 1 cup of uncooked rice makes 3 cups cooked.

Cilantro-Lime Rice

Just a few extra ingredients adds a zesty flavor to white rice and goes with countless dishes, making it a must-have side in your culinary collection!

Make a pot of Classic White Rice with 2 cups rice, using the instructions at left. Set aside to cool slightly. In a separate bowl, mix together ¼ cup finely chopped fresh cilantro, 3 tablespoons freshly squeezed lime juice (about 1½ limes), 2 teaspoons kosher salt, and 1 teaspoon grated lime zest. Fluff the cooked rice with a fork and then gently fold in the cilantro-lime mixture until well combined. Makes 6 cups. (This can easily be scaled up to feed more people.)

Spanish-Style Yellow Rice

The perfect side for Latin and Caribbean dishes. Making it is so easy!

In a large pot, heat 1 tablespoon neutral oil (like canola or vegetable oil) over medium heat until hot and shimmering. Add ¼ cup finely chopped yellow onion and sauté, stirring frequently, for 8 minutes or until translucent. Add 2 cups washed rice and 2 teaspoons Goya Sazón to the pan and stir to coat the rice with the seasoned oil. Add 4 cups water. Stir the rice well to ensure the seasoning is evenly distributed. Bring the water to a boil, then reduce the heat to low, cover, and simmer for 25 minutes without lifting the lid. Once the rice is cooked, let it sit covered for an additional 5 minutes to allow the flavors to meld. Fluff the rice with a fork before serving. Makes 6 cups. (This can easily be scaled up to feed more people.)

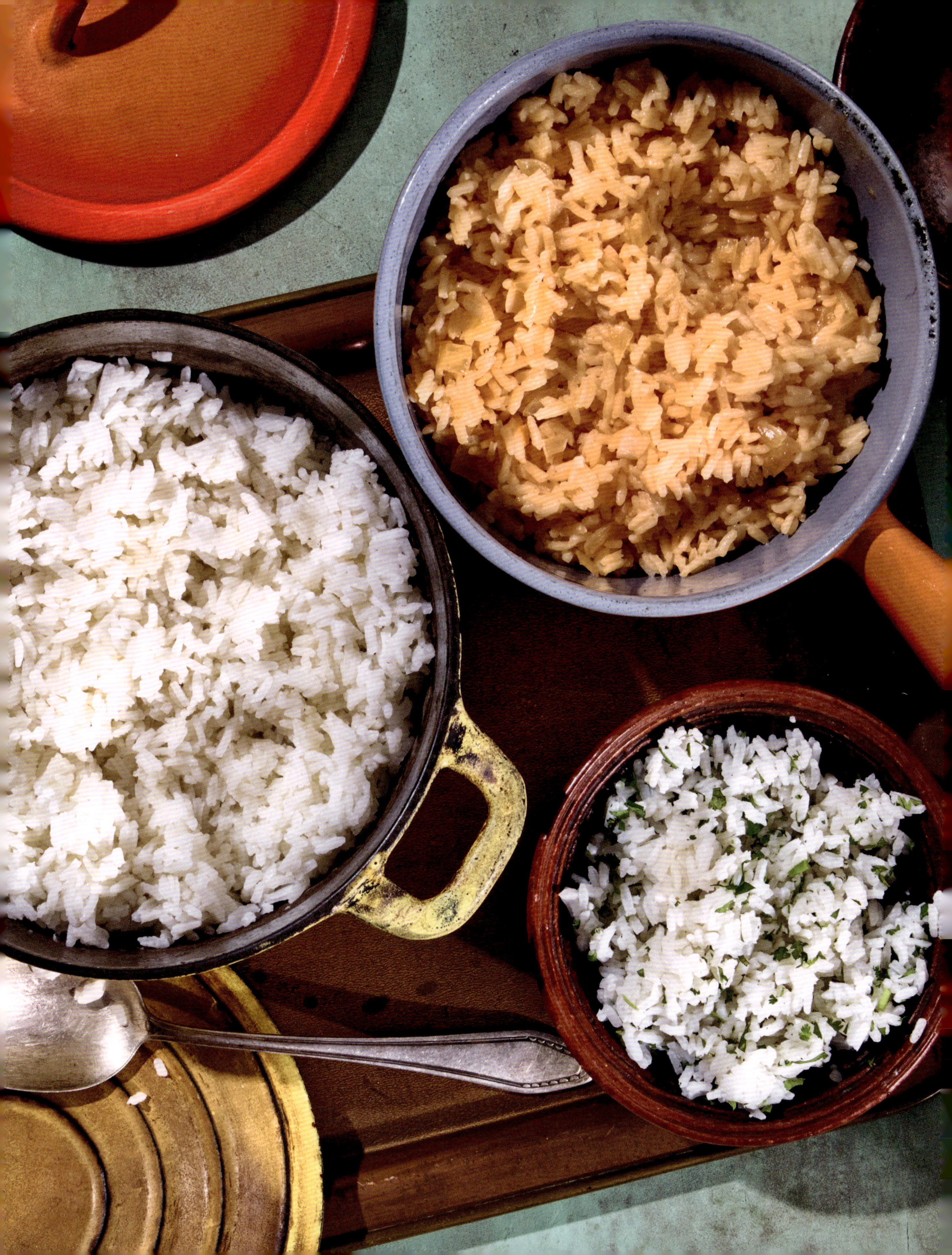

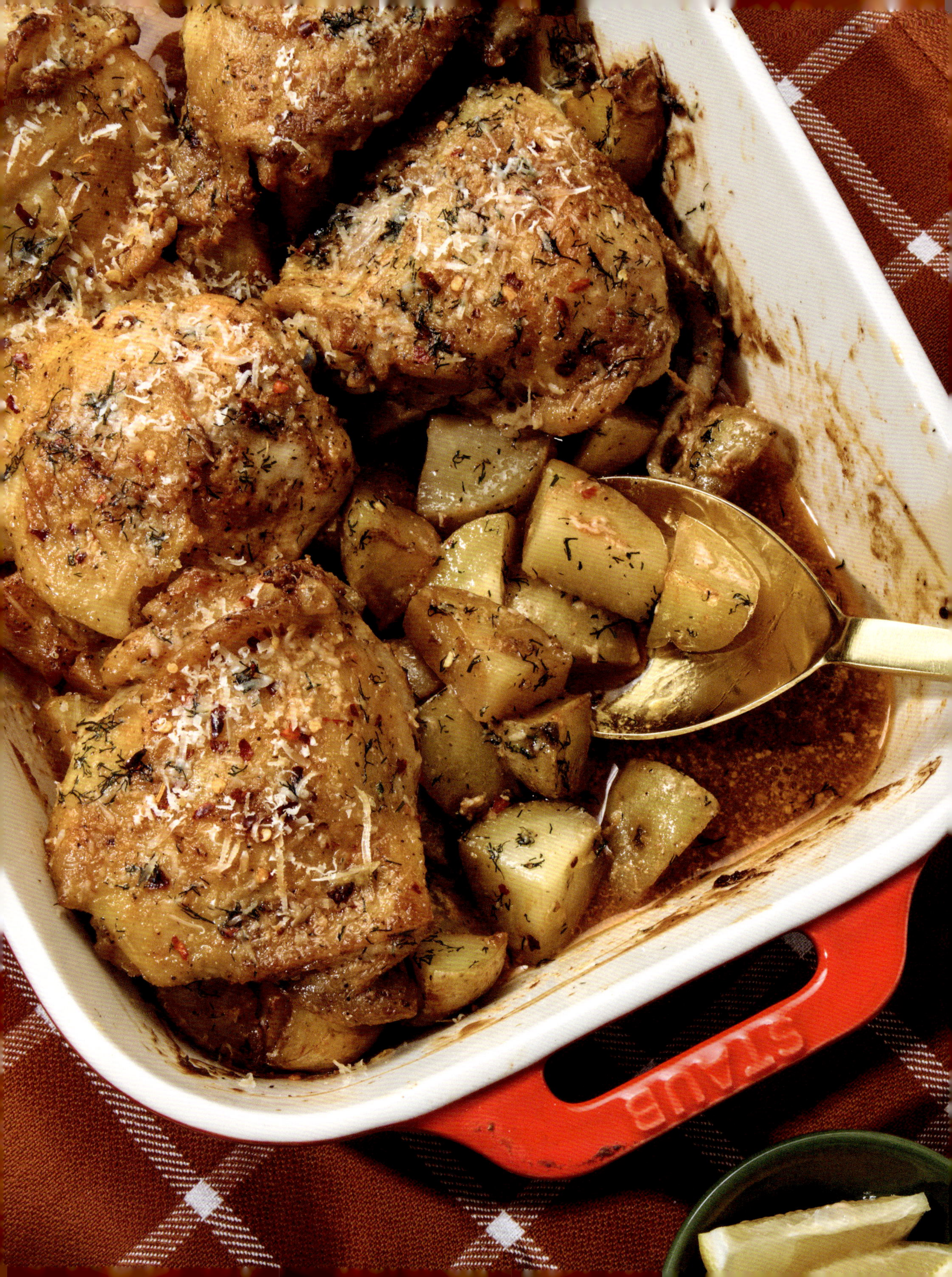
STAUB

Garlic Parmesan Chicken Thighs and Potatoes

Serves 6

I've cooked and tested my way through this entire cookbook many times, but this is the recipe I keep coming back to. Somehow, some way, it does so much with very little. I'm not sure if it's the soft, flavorful, and creamy Yukon Gold potatoes, the crispy Parmesan-topped chicken that's juicy with hints of lemon and dill, or the fact that it's ridiculously easy (there are only *three* steps). Maybe it's because no matter how many times I make it, I love it just as much every time. It's perfect for date nights when you want to impress, or lazy nights on the couch when you barely want to lift a finger. Whatever it is, I know it's one of my favorites—and soon, it'll be one of yours, too.

Potatoes

2 pounds Yukon Gold potatoes, cut into 1-inch cubes
1 teaspoon sweet paprika
1 teaspoon garlic powder
1 teaspoon onion powder
1 teaspoon kosher salt

Chicken

6 bone-in, skin-on chicken thighs (about 1½ pounds)
½ cup mayonnaise
2 tablespoons Dijon mustard
½ teaspoon grated lemon zest
2 teaspoons freshly squeezed lemon juice, plus ½ lemon for serving
1 teaspoon garlic powder
1 teaspoon onion powder
1 teaspoon Italian seasoning
1½ teaspoons kosher salt
1¼ teaspoons sweet paprika
¼ teaspoon freshly ground black pepper
4 ounces Parmesan cheese, freshly grated (1 cup)
1 tablespoon chopped fresh dill

Preheat the oven to 350°F.

Prep the potatoes: In a large bowl, combine the potatoes, paprika, garlic powder, onion powder, and salt. Toss well to coat the potatoes all over. Add the potatoes in an even layer to a 9 × 13-inch baking dish.

Prep the chicken: In another large bowl, combine the chicken thighs, mayonnaise, mustard, lemon zest, lemon juice, garlic powder, onion powder, Italian seasoning, salt, paprika, and pepper. Toss well to coat the chicken all over and evenly distribute the seasonings. Place the chicken thighs on top of the potatoes.

Bake and serve: Bake uncovered for 1 hour, or until cooked through and the juices run clear. Sprinkle with the Parmesan and dill and squeeze the half lemon over the top. Serve warm.

Cola-Braised Short Ribs

Serves **4 to 6**

Coca-Cola is my emotional support drink while I'm recipe testing. When I'm deep in the process of developing recipes or writing, it's my little pick-me-up—a treat for all my hard work. While I was working on a short rib recipe that called for red wine, I realized that I had run out. I looked at the can of cola in my hand, shrugged, and thought "YOLO" as I poured the entire can into the mixture and continued to cook, not entirely sure of what the outcome would be. To my surprise, the result was a sweet and sticky braised short rib recipe that not only exceeded my expectations but also paired perfectly with a serving of white rice.

Short Ribs

3 tablespoons vegetable oil
1 tablespoon dried oregano
1 tablespoon adobo seasoning
1 tablespoon sweet paprika
1 tablespoon garlic powder
1 tablespoon onion powder
2 teaspoons kosher salt
1½ teaspoons dried thyme
1 teaspoon ground cumin
3 pounds beef short ribs
½ cup diced yellow onion
3 garlic cloves, minced (about 1 tablespoon)
4 cups beef broth
1 (12-ounce) can Coca-Cola
2 sprigs sage
1 sprig rosemary
1 sprig thyme

Gravy

4 tablespoons (½ stick/2 ounces) unsalted butter
¼ cup all-purpose flour
½ cup Coca-Cola
2 tablespoons dark brown sugar
1 teaspoon burnt sugar syrup
¼ teaspoon kosher salt
Freshly ground black pepper

Classic White Rice (page 140), for serving
Finely chopped fresh chives or fresh parsley, for serving

Season the short ribs: In a small bowl, mix together 1 tablespoon of the oil, the oregano, adobo seasoning, paprika, garlic powder, onion powder, salt, thyme, and cumin until a paste-like mixture forms.

Rub the spice mixture all over the beef short ribs. Cover and marinate in the refrigerator for at least 2 hours or overnight for the best flavor.

Cook the ribs: Preheat the oven to 325°F.

In a medium Dutch oven or heavy ovenproof pot, heat the remaining 2 tablespoons oil over medium-high heat until hot. Working in batches to avoid overcrowding, sear the ribs on all sides and brown for 3 to 4 minutes on each side, until they are golden brown. Transfer the ribs to a plate and set aside.

To the same pot, add the onion and cook, stirring frequently, for 3 to 4 minutes, until softened. Stir in the minced garlic and cook for 1 minute, stirring frequently, until fragrant. Stir in the beef broth, 2 cups water, and the Coca-Cola. Add the sage, rosemary, and thyme. Return the ribs to the pot, adding more water if necessary to make sure they are submerged in the liquid.

Cover the pot and transfer to the oven. Cook for 2 to 3 hours, or until the ribs are tender and falling off the bone. Transfer the ribs to a plate and set aside.

Use a fine-mesh sieve to strain the warm liquid from the pot into a large heatproof bowl.

Make the gravy: In the same pot, melt the butter over medium heat. Whisk in the flour and cook for 1 minute until lightly golden. Whisk in 3 cups of the strained cooking liquid and the Coca-Cola. Add the brown sugar and burnt sugar and whisk for 5 to 7 minutes, until the gravy thickens. Season with the salt and pepper to taste.

Serve the short ribs with plenty of gravy over rice. Finish with chives or parsley.

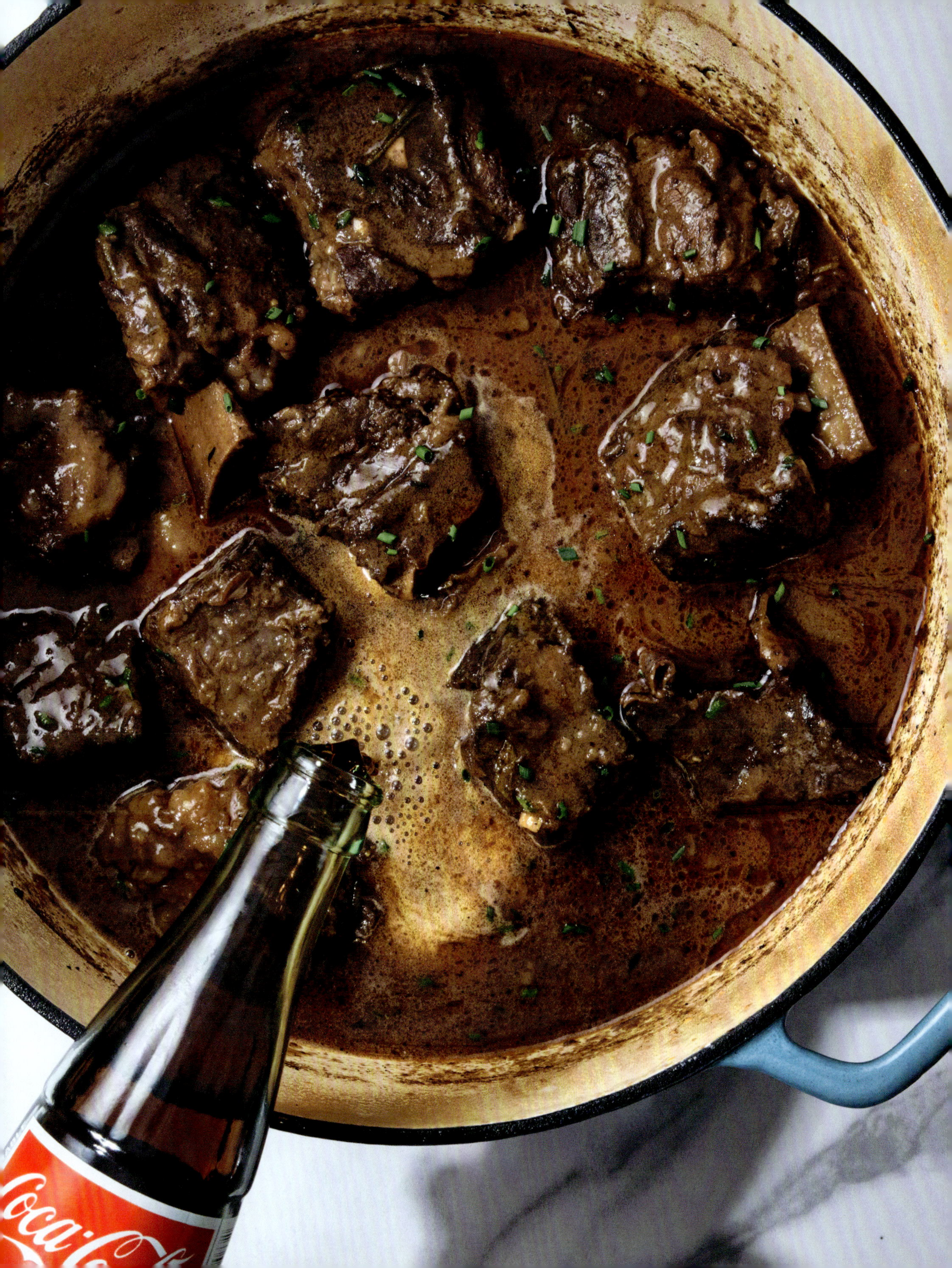

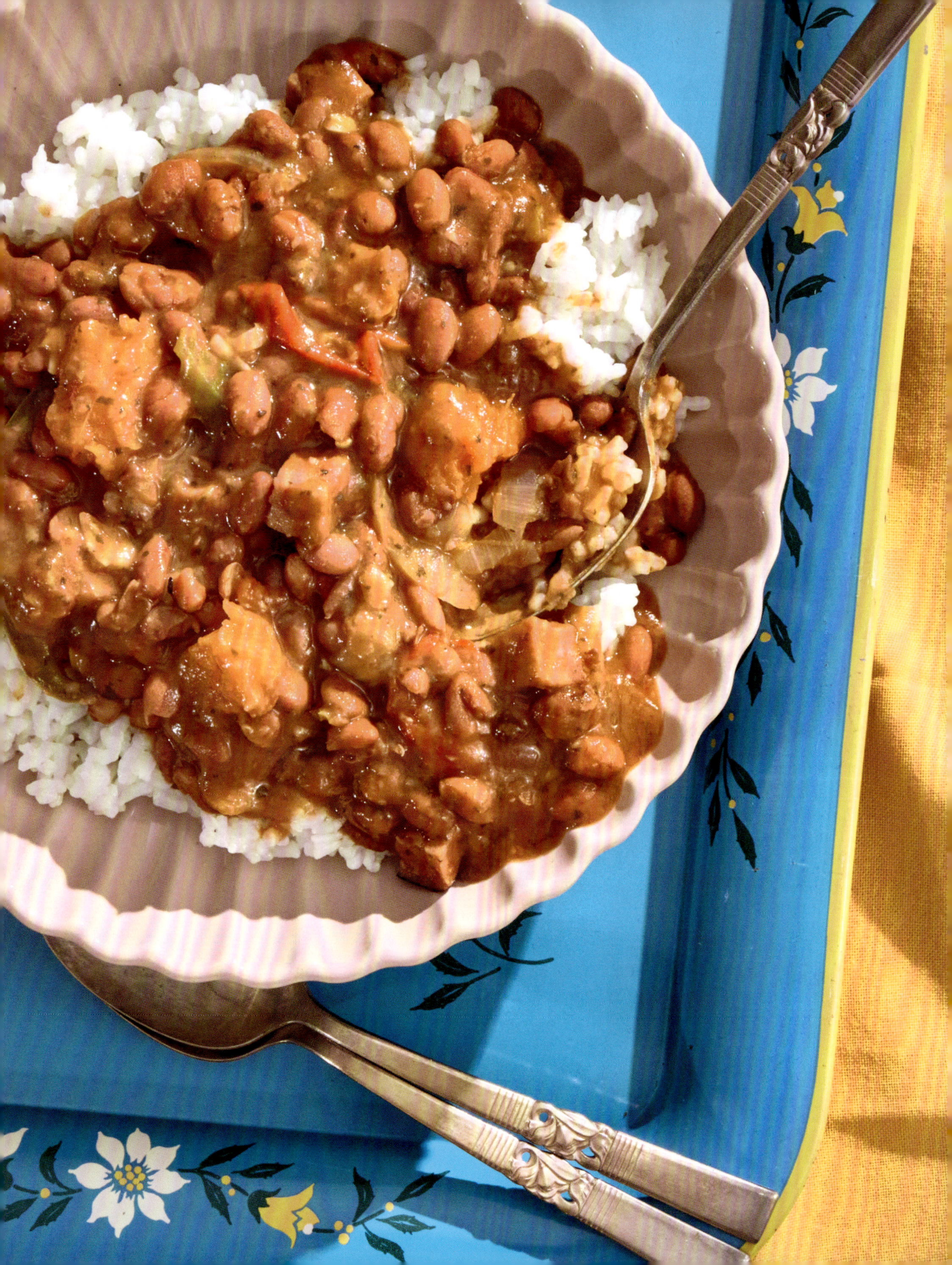

Habichuelas Guisadas
(Puerto Rican Beans)

Serves 6

I can still smell the beans, hot and steamy, from when I'd go to the little restaurant in my neighborhood where, for $2, they'd fill up a Styrofoam cup to the brim. I'd run home, pour those beans over a plate of white rice, and just sit there, eating what felt like the coziest, most comforting meal ever. It was simple, cheap, and straight-up soul-soothing.

My recipe brings that same energy, but with a little extra oomph. Yeah, we're using canned beans (because who has time to soak them on a random Tuesday?), but the flavor? Unmatched. Fresh sofrito, Sazón, tomato sauce, and sweet chunks of calabaza all come together to create a rich, flavorful pot of beans that tastes like it's been simmering for hours—even though it comes together in no time. I make these beans all the time because they go with *everything*. Pair them with my Plantain and Cream Cheese–Stuffed Pork Chops with Guava Sauce (page 84) for that perfect mix of sweet and savory, or ladle them next to The Perfect Pollo Guisado (page 133) for a classic Puerto Rican plate. And if it's a big occasion? These beans sitting next to a Pernil (page 166) are *chef's kiss*. This recipe is easy, foolproof, and filled with flavor—just the way I like it.

Garlic Paste

8 to 10 garlic cloves, minced (about 3 tablespoons)
Adobo seasoning
Extra-virgin olive oil

Beans

3 tablespoons extra-virgin olive oil
1 cup diced ham
½ red bell pepper, sliced
½ green bell pepper, sliced
½ medium onion, sliced
½ cup canned tomato sauce
3 tablespoons My Famous Red Sofrito (page 236)
2 teaspoons adobo seasoning
2 teaspoons Goya Sazón (culantro y achiote)
1 teaspoon dried oregano
1 teaspoon garlic powder
1 teaspoon freshly ground black pepper
1 (47-ounce) can or 3 (15-ounce) cans pink beans or red kidney beans, drained and rinsed
1½ cups peeled and cubed calabaza squash or winter squash
1 bunch of cilantro
1 bunch of culantro (see page 233)
2 bay leaves
Classic White Rice (page 140), for serving

Make the garlic paste: In a pilón, combine the minced garlic, a sprinkle of adobo, and a drizzle of olive oil. Mash the mixture into a paste.

Make the sauce for the beans: In a large pan, heat the olive oil over medium heat until hot and shimmering. Add the ham and sauté for 5 to 7 minutes, stirring frequently, until it starts to brown. Stir in the garlic paste, both bell peppers, and the onion and cook for 5 minutes, stirring frequently, until the vegetables soften.

Stir in the tomato sauce and sofrito and simmer for 5 minutes, stirring frequently, to meld the flavors. Add the adobo seasoning, Sazón, oregano, garlic powder, and black pepper, stirring well to incorporate everything. Pour in 3 cups water and bring the mixture to a gentle boil.

Cook the beans and squash: Once boiling, stir in the beans and squash. Add the cilantro, culantro, and bay leaves. Reduce the heat to low, cover, and simmer for 20 to 30 minutes, stirring occasionally, until the vegetables are tender. To thicken the sauce, scoop out ⅔ cup of the stew, transfer to a blender, and blend until smooth. Return the blended mixture to the pot and stir well to combine.

Discard the bay leaves and any large pieces of cilantro or culantro before serving. Serve with white rice.

Tuscan Chicken Meatballs with Sun-Dried Tomatoes and Spinach

Serves 4

Sometimes I want something that hits all the feels without a ton of effort, and this is that dish. It's rich and creamy enough to give you the comfort vibes you crave, but still practical enough for dinner. Don't panic—meatballs from scratch are not hard at all, and plus, you're getting a good protein punch. But the sauce? That's where the magic happens. It's garlicky, buttery, and packed with Parmesan, with just the right balance of creaminess to coat every bite perfectly. You can pair it with white rice (see page 140) or my amazing cabbage (see page 198)—or keep it cute and go low-carb by serving it over zucchini noodles or cauliflower rice. However you serve it, this dish is a straight-up banger!

Meatballs

1 pound ground chicken
½ cup fine dried bread crumbs
1 large egg, lightly beaten
1 tablespoon freshly grated Parmesan cheese
1 teaspoon ground cumin
1 teaspoon sweet paprika
1 teaspoon garlic powder
1 teaspoon onion powder
1 teaspoon dried oregano
1 teaspoon kosher salt
1 tablespoon extra-virgin olive oil

Sauce

1 garlic clove, minced
1 cup low-sodium chicken broth
1 cup heavy cream
1 teaspoon sweet paprika
1 teaspoon dried basil
1 teaspoon dried oregano
4 ounces Parmesan cheese, freshly grated (1 cup)
8 ounces baby spinach
3 ounces oil-packed sun-dried tomatoes, drained of oil and roughly chopped (⅓ cup)
Kosher salt and freshly ground black pepper

Make the meatballs: In a large bowl, combine the ground chicken, bread crumbs, egg, Parmesan, cumin, paprika, garlic powder, onion powder, oregano, and salt. Use a fork or large spoon to mix just until well combined. Shape the mixture into 9 large meatballs, 3 to 4 tablespoons per meatball.

In a large skillet, heat the oil over medium-high heat until hot and shimmering. Add the meatballs and cook for 5 to 6 minutes, turning occasionally, until browned all over and cooked through. Transfer the meatballs to a plate and set aside.

Make the sauce: In the same skillet (do not wipe clean), add the minced garlic and cook over medium heat, stirring frequently, for 30 seconds, until fragrant. Add the chicken broth, heavy cream, paprika, basil, oregano, and ½ cup water. Stir to combine and bring the mixture to a simmer. Reduce the heat to medium-low and let the sauce simmer for 5 minutes, stirring occasionally, until thickened.

Stir in the Parmesan and keep stirring until melted. Add the spinach and sun-dried tomatoes and cook for an additional 2 to 3 minutes, stirring occasionally, until the spinach wilts and the sauce thickens slightly.

Return the cooked meatballs to the skillet and gently toss until they are evenly coated. Season with salt and pepper to taste and cook for another 3 minutes to heat the meatballs through before serving.

Little Detail, BIG Impact: If you want to make the prep easier, air-fry the meatballs at 375°F for 12 minutes! YAS! When making the sauce, just add 2 tablespoons of olive oil to the skillet before cooking the garlic.

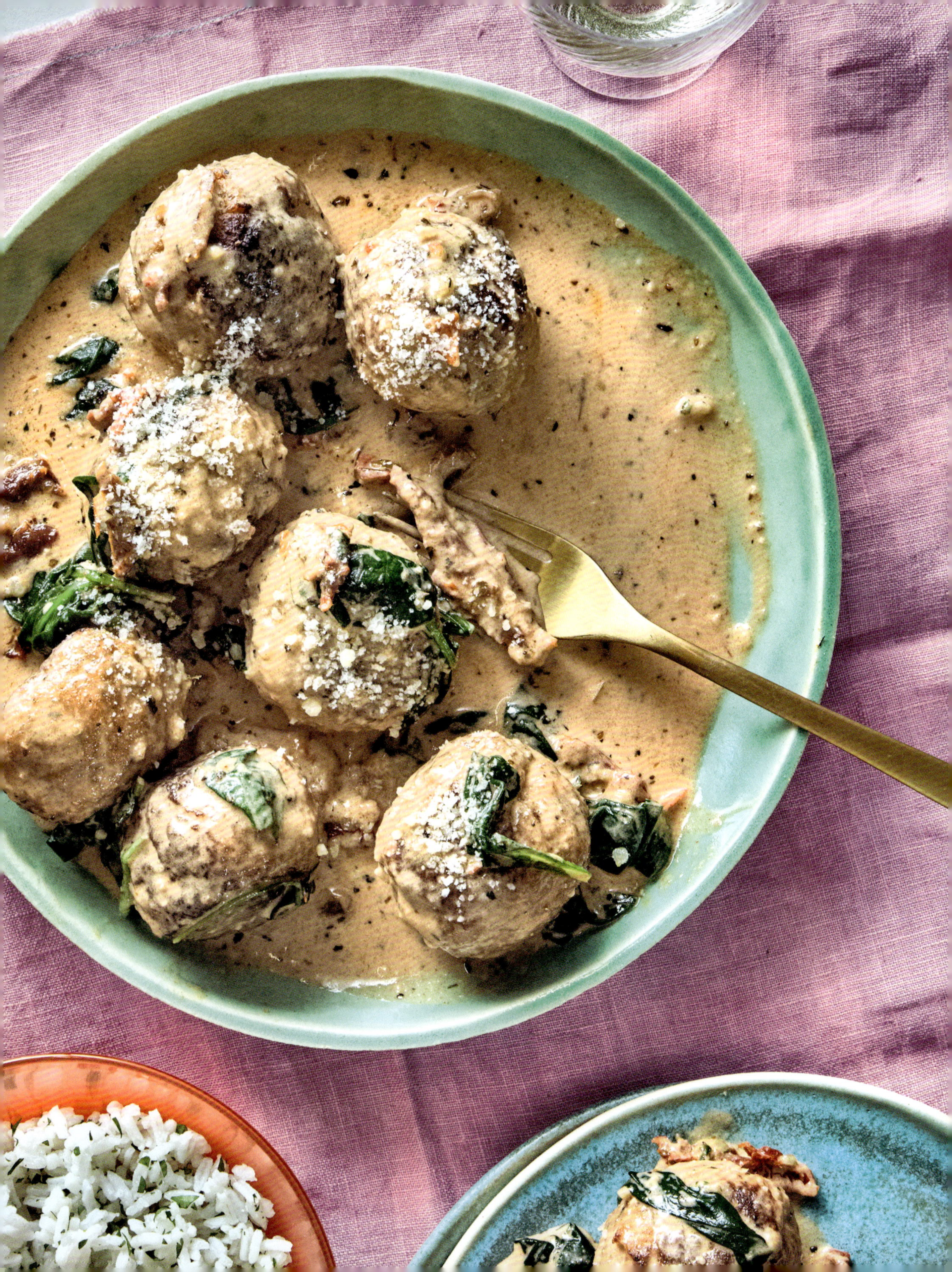

Little Detail, BIG Impact: If you can find them, gumbo crabs or blue crabs work best for this recipe. It's what is traditionally used for gumbo in Louisiana and we must respect tradition. If you can't find them, you can use snow crab, Dungeness crab, or Alaskan king crab.

GAH DAMN Gumbo

Serves **8**

I've always been inspired by the rich, soulful flavors of New Orleans. The depth, the spice, the Creole and Cajun influences—it all speaks to me and has shaped so much of my cooking. So, when I started writing recipes for this book, I knew seafood gumbo was at the top of the list. I started testing different versions and would share them with my neighbors, asking for their honest feedback. The first time I made it, I brought a batch to Cedric, a man in my neighborhood who knows good food. After a taste, he said, "It's good—but something's missing."

At first, I tried using boxed stock—because my recipes are all about keeping things easy—but this was one dish where I couldn't take shortcuts. I realized that making the stock from scratch was a game changer. Then, I took my time with the roux. A proper roux is everything in gumbo, and for this recipe, you'll want to let it cook low and slow until it's dark like chocolate. Finally, I took a page from Mr. New Orleans himself, Emeril Lagasse, and used a mix of seafood—shrimp, crabmeat, gumbo crabs, and a white fish like snapper or cod. When I brought the final version back to Cedric, he took one bite and said, "WELL GAH DAMN!" That's when I knew I had it. And now, here it is.

Shrimp Stock

1 pound shrimp (21/25 count), peeled and deveined, tails on
1 tablespoon vegetable oil
6 bay leaves
4 garlic cloves, minced
2 sprigs thyme
1½ tablespoons kosher salt

Gumbo

¾ cup plus 2 tablespoons vegetable oil
1 pound andouille sausage, sliced
1 cup plus 2 tablespoons all-purpose flour
3 celery stalks, roughly chopped
1 medium yellow onion, chopped
1 small green bell pepper, chopped
4 garlic cloves, minced
2 teaspoons no-salt Cajun seasoning
2 teaspoons kosher salt
1½ teaspoons garlic powder
1 teaspoon onion powder
1 teaspoon sweet paprika
⅛ teaspoon cayenne pepper
2 teaspoons Old Bay seasoning
8 ounces lump crabmeat, picked over
2 pounds gumbo crabs
1 pound white fish fillets (I like snapper or cod), cut into 2-inch squares

Classic White Rice (page 140), for serving

Make the shrimp stock: Remove the shrimp tails from the shrimp and set the shrimp aside in the refrigerator.

In a 5-quart Dutch oven or large pot, heat the oil over medium-high heat until hot and shimmering. Add the shrimp tails and sauté, stirring occasionally, for 1 minute, to extract the flavor from the tails. Add the bay leaves, minced garlic, thyme, and 7 cups water. Stir to combine and bring to a boil. Stir in the salt, then strain the liquid through a fine-mesh sieve into a large heatproof bowl. Set the broth aside and clean the Dutch oven.

Cook the andouille for the gumbo: Set the Dutch oven over medium-high and heat the 2 tablespoons oil. Add the andouille and cook for 4 to 5 minutes, stirring occasionally, until golden brown. Use a slotted spoon or tongs to remove the sausage from the pot and transfer to a plate.

Make the roux: In the same pot over medium-low heat, add the remaining ¾ cup oil and the flour and cook, stirring constantly with a wooden spoon, until the roux is smooth, velvety, and dark golden brown like chocolate, 12 to 15 minutes.

Assemble the gumbo: Stir in the celery, onion, and bell pepper and cook, stirring frequently, for 4 to 5 minutes, until softened. Stir in the minced garlic and cook for 2 to 3 minutes, stirring frequently, until fragrant.

Pour in the reserved shrimp stock and bring to a simmer. Stir in the Cajun seasoning, salt, garlic powder, onion powder, paprika, and cayenne. Cover and cook for 1 hour 30 minutes, stirring every 30 minutes, until the soup is dark and thickened.

Season the shrimp on both sides with the Old Bay. Add the shrimp, crabmeat, gumbo crabs, and fish to the pot. Cook for 20 minutes, or until the seafood is cooked through. Serve with white rice.

What's for Dinner?

Everything's Good

What's for Dinner?

153

Cajun-Spiced Potatoes

Serves 4

Potatoes were one of the first things I mastered in the kitchen. When I was little, it was all about boiling them, tossing them in a pan, and drowning them in ketchup—classic kid move. As I grew up, though, I gave the recipe a serious glow-up, too. Now, I use Yukon Golds, a generous amount of butter, and fry them up to crispy golden perfection, resulting in potatoes that are tender on the inside, crunchy on the outside, and bursting with flavor.

These potatoes go with everything in this book. Whether you're pairing them with my fried chicken or a breakfast burrito, they're the perfect sidekick. They've got enough flavor to stand on their own but blend effortlessly with anything on the plate. It's the kind of dish that makes those intentional, slow mornings even better.

- 2 pounds Yukon Gold potatoes, peeled and cut into ½-inch cubes
- 2 tablespoons vegetable oil
- ½ small yellow onion, diced (about ½ cup)
- ½ small red bell pepper, diced (about ½ cup)
- ½ small green bell pepper, diced (about ½ cup)
- 2 teaspoons kosher salt
- 1 teaspoon sweet paprika
- 1 teaspoon garlic powder
- 1 teaspoon onion powder
- 1 teaspoon Italian seasoning
- ½ teaspoon no-salt Cajun seasoning
- ½ teaspoon freshly ground black pepper
- ½ teaspoon chili powder
- 4 tablespoons (½ stick/2 ounces) unsalted butter
- ½ cup ketchup

Preheat the oven to 350°F. Line a baking sheet with parchment paper.

Bake the potatoes: Spread the potatoes out evenly on the lined baking sheet and bake for about 12 minutes, stirring once halfway through, until they are soft enough to be pierced with a fork.

In a large skillet, heat the oil over high heat until hot and shimmering. Add the potatoes and cook, stirring occasionally, for 8 to 10 minutes, until charred.

Add the onion and peppers and continue to cook and stir for another 4 to 5 minutes, until all of the vegetables are charred. Stir in the salt, paprika, garlic powder, onion powder, Italian seasoning, Cajun seasoning, black pepper, and chili powder. Add the butter and ketchup and cook for 2 to 3 minutes, stirring frequently, until the potatoes are deep golden brown on one or two sides.

Serve hot.

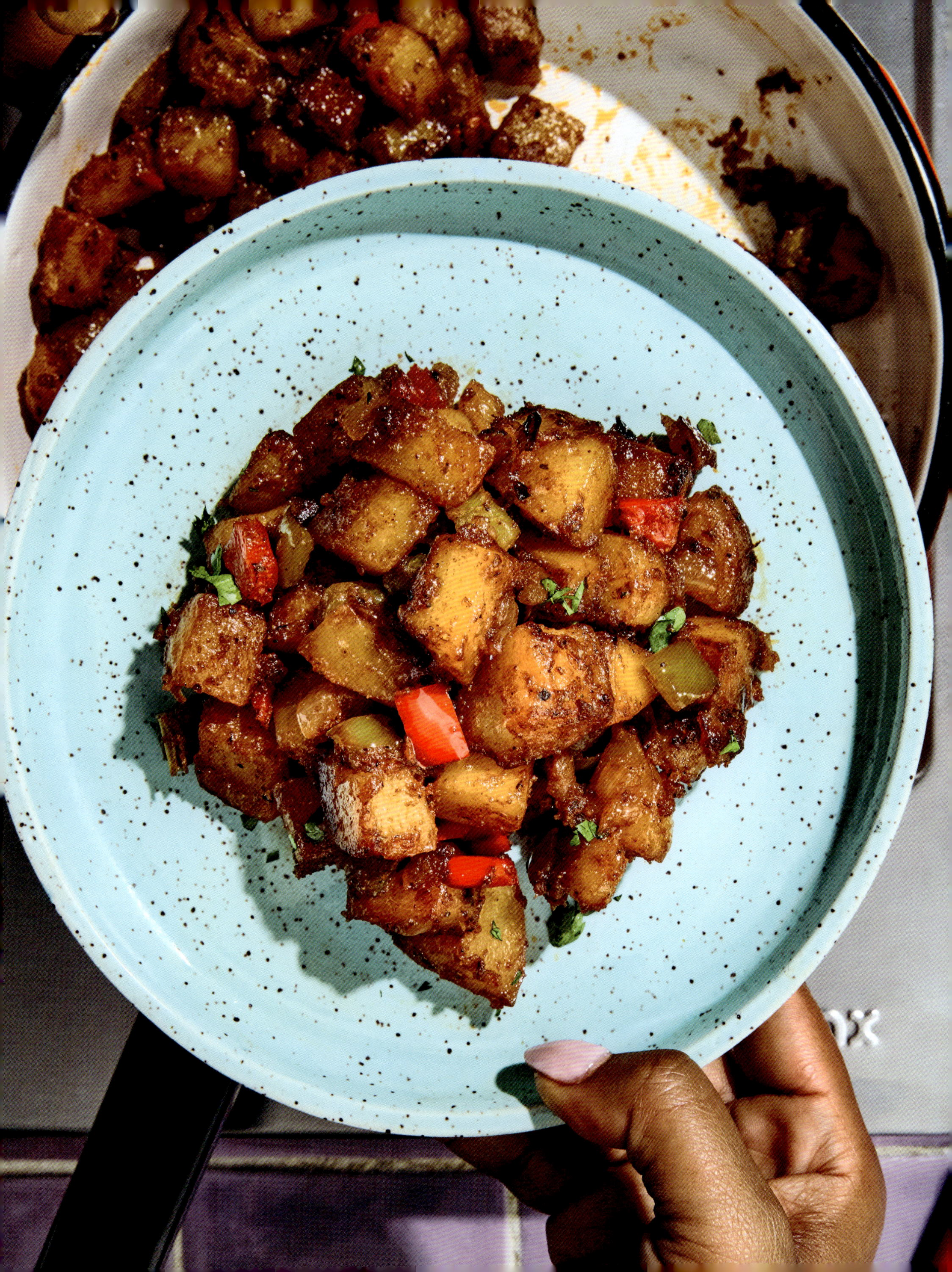

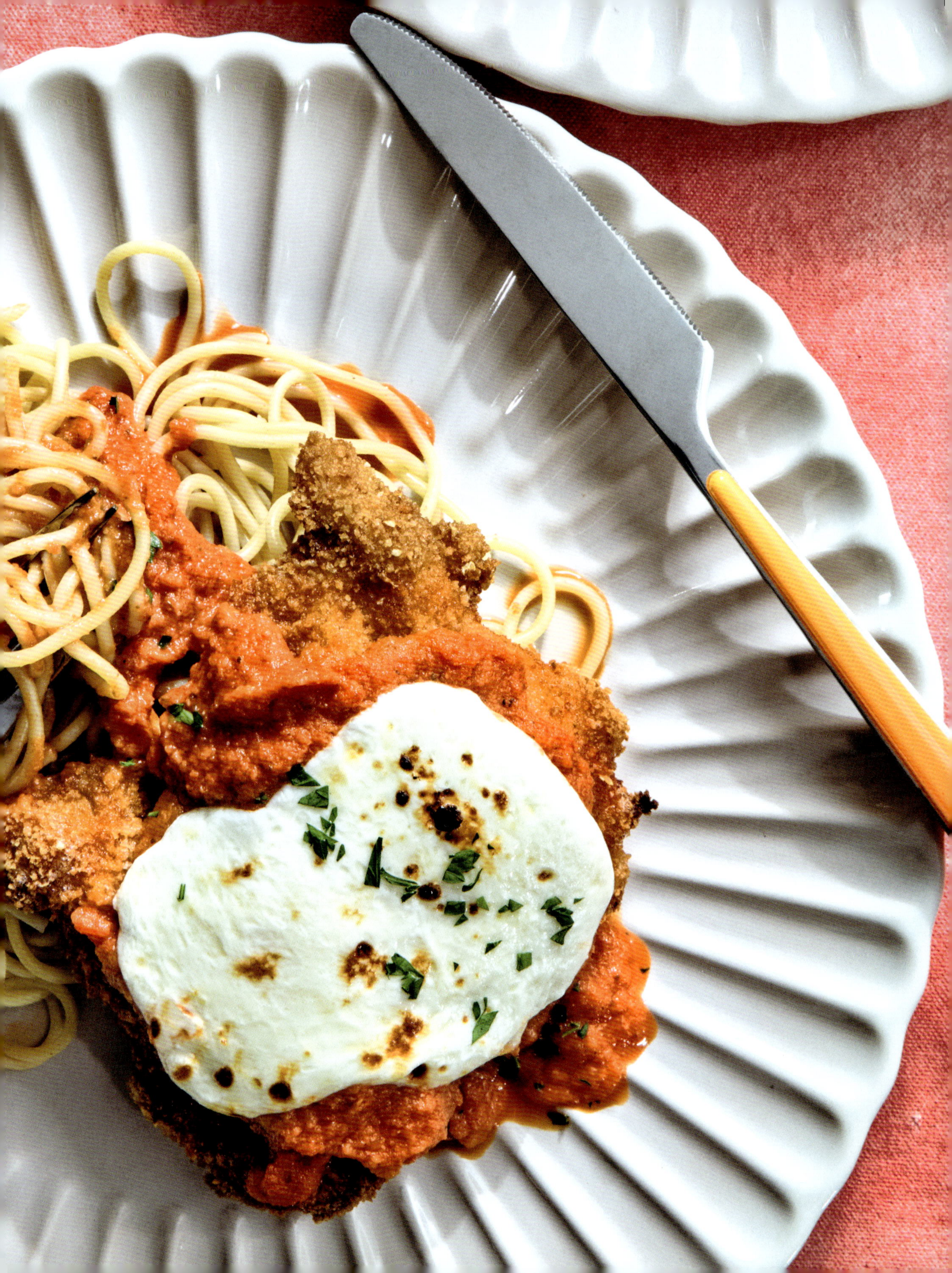

Secret Ingredient Chicken Parmesan

Serves 6

We all know chicken skin is the best part of the chicken thigh. I even used to hit up the butcher just to ask for leftover chicken skins so I could fry them up at home like potato chips—yeah, that's how deep my love goes. So when I wanted to level up a classic chicken parm, I knew I had to use chicken skin as the secret ingredient. Mixing it with bread crumbs and cheese to bread the chicken? Game changer. That little touch makes a *big* impact, and using chicken thighs instead of breasts means juicier, more flavorful parm every time.

Sauce

- 2 tablespoons extra-virgin olive oil
- ½ small yellow onion, finely diced (about ¼ cup)
- ¼ small green bell pepper, finely diced (about ¼ cup)
- ¼ small red bell pepper, finely diced (about ¼ cup)
- 3 garlic cloves, minced (about 1 tablespoon)
- 1 (24-ounce) jar marinara sauce (I use Rinaldi)
- 1 tablespoon garlic powder
- 1 tablespoon onion powder
- 1 teaspoon dried oregano
- 1 teaspoon Italian seasoning
- 1 teaspoon kosher salt
- 3 bay leaves
- 2 tablespoons freshly grated Parmesan cheese

Chicken

- 6 bone-in, skin-on chicken thighs
- 3 teaspoons kosher salt
- 2 teaspoons extra-virgin olive oil
- 1 teaspoon baking powder
- 1 teaspoon sweet paprika
- 1 teaspoon freshly ground black pepper
- 1 cup fine dried bread crumbs
- 1 ounce Parmesan cheese, finely grated (about ¼ cup)
- 2 cups all-purpose flour
- 3 large eggs, beaten
- 4 to 6 cups vegetable oil, for frying
- 1 pound fresh mozzarella cheese, cut into 12 slices
- Roughly chopped fresh basil, for serving

Preheat the oven to 425°F. Set a wire rack over a baking sheet.

Make the sauce: In a large saucepan, heat the olive oil over medium heat. Add the onion and both bell peppers and sauté for 5 to 7 minutes, until softened. Add the minced garlic and cook for 1 to 2 minutes, stirring frequently, until fragrant. Stir in the marinara sauce, garlic powder, onion powder, oregano, Italian seasoning, salt, and bay leaves. Bring the mixture to a simmer, then reduce the heat to low and simmer uncovered for 15 minutes, stirring occasionally. Discard the bay leaves and stir in the Parmesan.

Meanwhile, bake the chicken skin: Remove the skin from the chicken and set it aside in a large bowl. With a knife in one hand, hold the chicken bone-side up. Using the tip of the knife, gently remove the chicken from the bone and place the chicken thighs in another large bowl. Season the chicken skin with 1 teaspoon of the salt, 1 teaspoon of the olive oil, the baking powder, and paprika and toss to make sure it's evenly coated.

Place the seasoned skin flat on the wire rack and bake for 15 to 20 minutes, until lightly browned and crispy. Remove the skins from the oven and set aside to cool completely. Leave the oven on but reduce the temperature to 350°F. When the skins have cooled, pulse them in a blender for 3 seconds.

Season and dredge the chicken: Season the chicken thighs with the remaining 2 teaspoons salt, the remaining 1 teaspoon olive oil, and the black pepper.

Set up three shallow bowls. In one bowl, mix the chicken skin crumbs, bread crumbs, and Parmesan. Place the flour in a second bowl and the eggs in a third bowl. Coat each chicken thigh first in flour (shaking off excess), then in eggs (shaking off excess), and finally in the bread crumb mixture, making sure the chicken is completely coated. Put the chicken on a plate and repeat.

Fry then bake the chicken: Pour oil into a large skillet to come halfway up the sides and heat to 350°F. Set a wire rack over a baking sheet.

Working with 2 thighs at a time to avoid overcrowding, fry the chicken thighs for 5 to 7 minutes, until golden brown. Remove and place on the wire rack.

Once all the chicken is fried, spoon the sauce on top of each piece and add 1 or 2 slices of mozzarella cheese per thigh. Transfer the chicken to the oven and bake until the cheese is melted, about 10 minutes. Switch the oven to broil and broil for 1 minute. Serve garnished with fresh basil.

What's for Dinner?

Hooked-Up Hamburger Pasta

Serves 4

I grew up on Hamburger Helper. Being raised by a single dad, it was the cheap and easy meal Papi could throw together and feel proud of. We had it all the time, and even as an adult, I still get cravings for it. But let's be real—powdered cheese just doesn't cut it anymore, so I came up with my own version that's way better because of all the fresh ingredients it uses. Onion, peppers, and garlic make a flavorful base, plus a good dose of real Cheddar and cream keeps it rich and comforting. It's made from stuff you probably already have on hand, but the ingredients are the real deal. It's the grown-up version of a childhood classic, but still has that same easy, homey feel everyone loves.

Kosher salt
1 pound medium pasta shells
1 tablespoon extra-virgin olive oil
1 small red bell pepper, chopped (about ½ cup)
1 small green bell pepper, chopped (about ½ cup)
1 small onion, finely chopped (about ½ cup)
6 garlic cloves, minced (about 2 tablespoons)
1 pound ground beef (80/20)
2 tablespoons tomato paste
2 cups heavy cream
4 ounces Cheddar cheese, freshly shredded (1 cup)
1 teaspoon garlic powder
1 teaspoon onion powder
1 teaspoon Italian seasoning
Freshly ground black pepper
Chopped fresh parsley, for serving

Cook the pasta: Bring a large pot of water to a boil. Add a big pinch of salt and cook the pasta according to the package directions. Drain and set aside.

Meanwhile, make the sauce: In a large skillet, heat the olive oil over medium-high heat until hot and shimmering. Add both bell peppers, the onion, and minced garlic and cook, stirring occasionally, for 4 to 5 minutes, until the vegetables are tender. Add the ground beef and cook for 8 to 10 minutes, breaking up the meat into small pieces and stirring occasionally, until the beef is browned and no longer pink. Drain the excess fat from the pan, leaving the meat and vegetables in the pan.

Reduce the heat to medium and add the tomato paste to the pan, stirring frequently, until the tomato paste is evenly distributed and fully incorporated. Pour in the heavy cream, add the Cheddar, and stir until the cheese is melted and the mixture is smooth, 3 to 4 minutes. Add the garlic powder, onion powder, Italian seasoning, 2 teaspoons salt, and black pepper to taste. Stir to combine.

Add the cooked pasta to the skillet and stir to coat the pasta evenly. Simmer for 3 minutes to heat through. Serve hot, sprinkled with parsley.

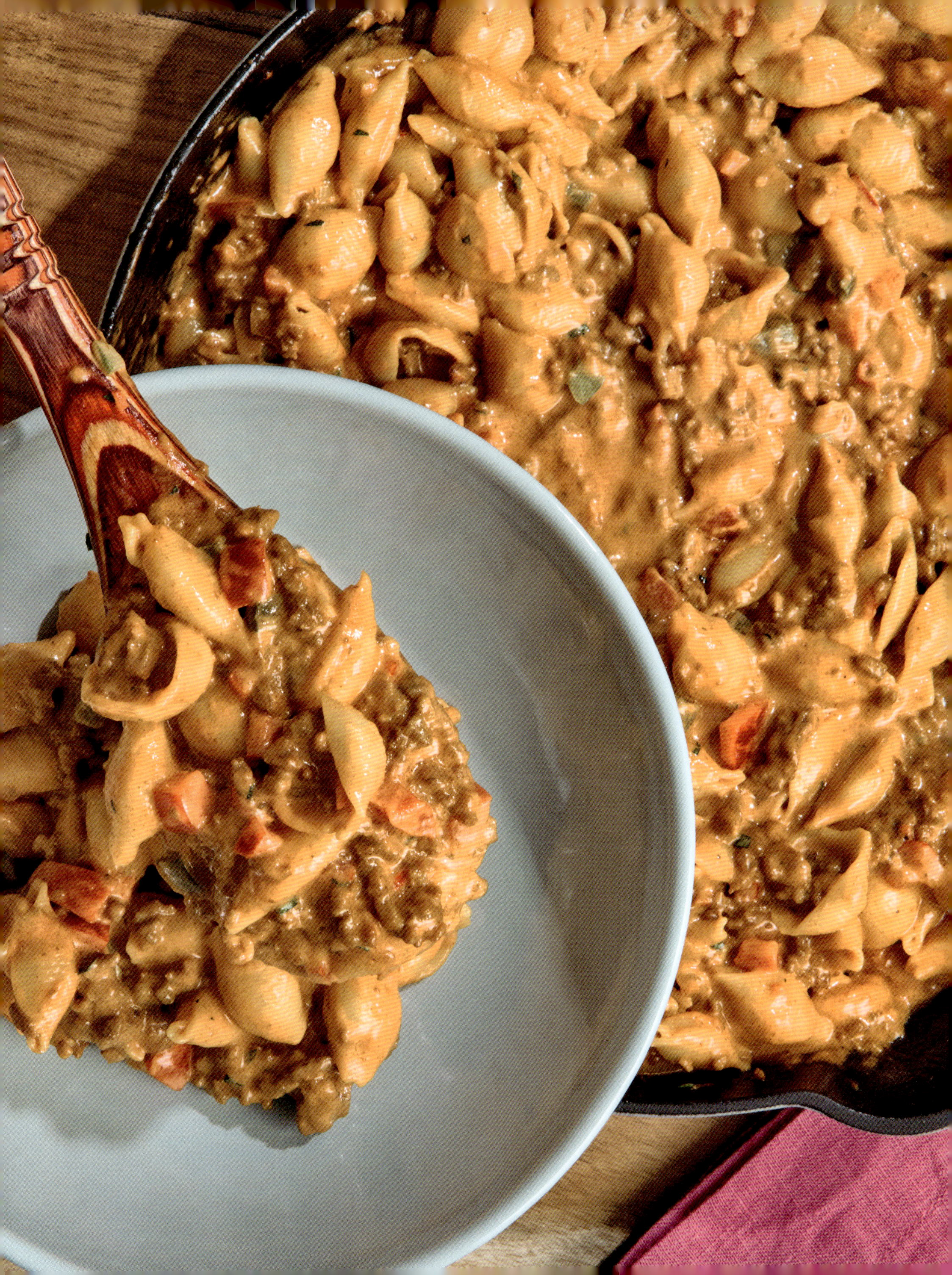

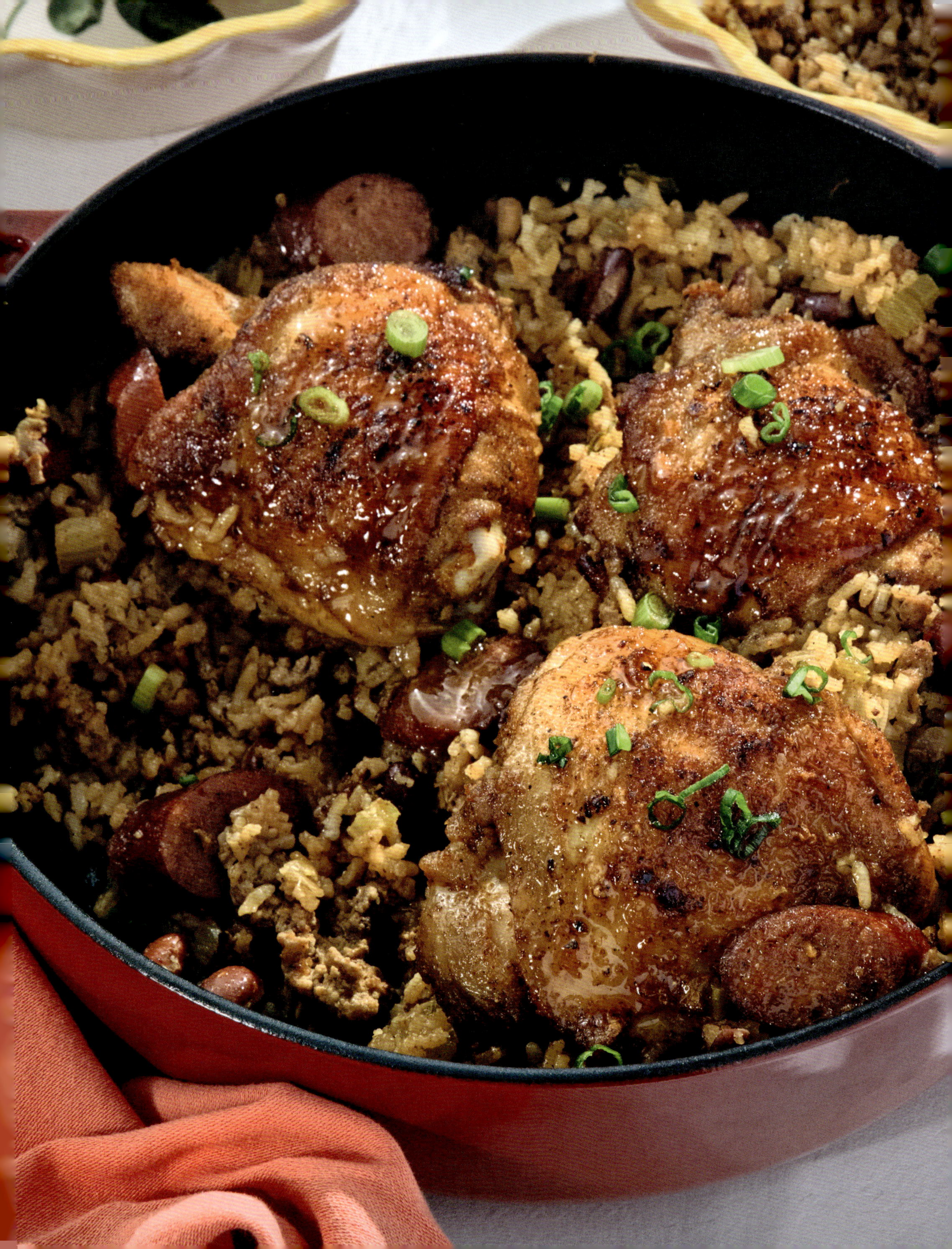

One-Pot Dirty Rice with Chicken and Sausage

Serves 4

This dish has a little bit of everything and is perfect for those nights when you need something full of flavor and soul. It's got beef, chicken, sausage, and beans, so it's packed with protein—ideal for meal-prepping and keeping you going all week. And let's be real, adulting is a lot more appealing when dinner is this easy to throw together. Bold spices, smoky andouille sausage, and the holy trinity of onions, bell peppers, and celery give it all the right vibes. Each bite is loaded with flavor, and trust me, when you're heating this up at work, your co-workers will be side-eyeing your lunch out of jealousy like, "What *is* that?" Plus, it's a one-pot situation—fewer dishes, more leftovers, and plenty to share with your work bestie if you're feeling generous.

Chicken and Sausage

4 bone-in, skin-on chicken thighs (about 1½ pounds)
1½ teaspoons smoked paprika
1 teaspoon no-salt Cajun seasoning
1 teaspoon onion powder
1 teaspoon garlic powder
1 teaspoon kosher salt
1 teaspoon freshly ground black pepper
1 tablespoon extra-virgin olive oil
12 ounces andouille sausage, sliced

Rice

½ pound ground beef or ground turkey (90/10)
1 small yellow onion, finely diced (about ½ cup)
2 celery stalks, finely diced (about ½ cup)
½ medium green bell pepper, finely diced (about ½ cup)
3 garlic cloves, minced (about 1 tablespoon)
2 cups low-sodium chicken broth
1 cup long-grain rice, rinsed (see How to Make Rice 101, page 140)
½ cup canned red kidney beans, drained and rinsed
1 tablespoon unsalted butter
1 teaspoon kosher salt
½ teaspoon no-salt Cajun seasoning

Chopped scallions, for serving

Prep the chicken: Pat the chicken dry with a paper towel. In a large bowl, season the chicken thighs with the smoked paprika, Cajun seasoning, onion powder, garlic powder, salt, and black pepper.

In a large skillet or Dutch oven, heat the olive oil over medium-high heat until it's hot and shimmering. Place the chicken thighs in the skillet, skin-side down, and sear for 4 to 5 minutes, undisturbed, until the skin is golden and crispy. Flip and sear the other side for another 2 to 3 minutes, until golden and crispy. Transfer the chicken to a plate, keeping in mind that it's not fully cooked yet.

Cook the sausage: In the same skillet, cook the sliced sausage over medium heat for 2 to 3 minutes, flipping occasionally, until browned on both sides. Transfer the sausage to the plate with the chicken and set aside.

Make the rice: In the same skillet, combine the ground beef, onion, celery, bell pepper, and minced garlic and cook for 8 to 10 minutes, stirring frequently, until the beef is browned and the vegetables soften. Stir in the chicken broth, rinsed rice, beans, butter, salt, and Cajun seasoning. Nestle the chicken thighs (skin-side up) and browned sausage back into the skillet, placing them in a single layer on top of the rice mixture. Keep the chicken skin exposed to maintain its crispiness. Cover and simmer for 30 minutes without stirring, until the chicken is cooked through and the rice is tender and fluffy.

Serve immediately, topped with chopped scallions.

Chef's Kiss: If you want extra-crispy skin on the chicken, place the skillet under the broiler for 2 to 3 minutes after the rice is cooked. Let the dish rest for a few minutes, fluff the rice, and serve.

Blackened Fish and Grits

Serves 2

Growing up, cheesy grits were my Saturday morning go-to—didn't need anything else. They were flavorful, comforting, cheap, and easy to throw together. By the time I was seven, I could stand over the stove and whip up the creamiest, most velvety pot of grits you'd ever tasted.

As I got older, I decided to level up my childhood favorite. First, I worked on a sauce to pair with my cheesy grits—a creamy, tomato-based sauce that brought everything together. Then, I figured, if I'm going all in on a comfort breakfast, I might as well sneak in some protein, so I added a piece of fish, which is lightly seasoned and cooked to perfection. This is the kind of meal you make on a lazy Saturday when all you want to do is crawl back into bed and binge-watch your favorite show. It's the perfect choice for a slow, soulful morning.

Grits
- ½ teaspoon kosher salt
- 1 cup old-fashioned grits
- 1 cup heavy cream
- 4 ounces sharp Cheddar cheese, freshly shredded (1 cup)
- 3 tablespoons unsalted butter

Fish
- 1 (8-ounce) skinless catfish fillet, cut into 2 equal pieces
- 1 teaspoon blackened seasoning
- 2 tablespoons extra-virgin olive oil
- 2 tablespoons unsalted butter

Sauce
- 6 tablespoons unsalted butter
- 2 tablespoons all-purpose flour
- 3 celery stalks, finely diced (about 1 cup)
- 1 small white onion, finely diced (about ½ cup)
- ½ small green bell pepper, finely diced (about ½ cup)
- 3 garlic cloves, minced (about 1 tablespoon)
- 1½ cups low-sodium chicken broth
- ¼ cup canned petite diced tomatoes with liquid
- ¼ cup heavy cream
- 2 teaspoons no-salt Cajun seasoning, plus more (optional) for serving
- 2 teaspoons onion powder
- 2 teaspoons garlic powder
- 1 teaspoon sweet paprika
- 1 teaspoon kosher salt
- Chopped fresh chives, for serving

Cook the grits: In a medium saucepan, combine 3 cups water and the salt and bring to a boil over medium-high heat. Slowly stir in the grits, then reduce the heat to low and cook for 15 to 20 minutes, stirring occasionally, until the grits are tender and thickened. Remove from the heat and stir in the heavy cream, Cheddar, and butter until the cheese and butter are completely melted. Cover and keep warm.

Cook the fish: Pat the fish dry with a paper towel. Rub ½ teaspoon of the blackened seasoning on each piece of fish, coating both sides.

In a large skillet, heat the olive oil over high heat until hot and shimmering. Add the fish fillets and sear for 3 to 4 minutes, until a crust forms. Flip the fillets and reduce the heat to medium-low. Add the butter to the pan and cook for 2 minutes, occasionally basting the fish with the melted butter, until the fish is cooked through and flakes easily with a fork. Transfer the fish to a plate and set aside.

Make the sauce: In the same skillet, melt 2 tablespoons of the butter over medium-low heat. Add the flour and whisk constantly for 1 to 2 minutes, until a light brown roux forms. Add the celery, onion, and bell pepper and cook for 6 minutes, stirring occasionally, until the vegetables are softened. Add the minced garlic and cook for 1 minute, until fragrant.

Pour in the chicken broth, stirring constantly to prevent lumps. Add the diced tomatoes with liquid, heavy cream, and the remaining 4 tablespoons butter. Stir until the butter is melted. Stir in the Cajun seasoning, onion powder, garlic powder, paprika, and salt. Simmer for 5 to 7 minutes, stirring occasionally, until the sauce thickens slightly.

Serve the fish on top of the grits and pour the sauce over the top. Garnish with fresh chives and a sprinkle of Cajun seasoning, if desired.

Chef's Kiss: If you happen to have it on hand, a sprinkle of Gouda melted into the sauce (about ¼ cup grated) is my little secret that I never share with anyone, but of course I got you.

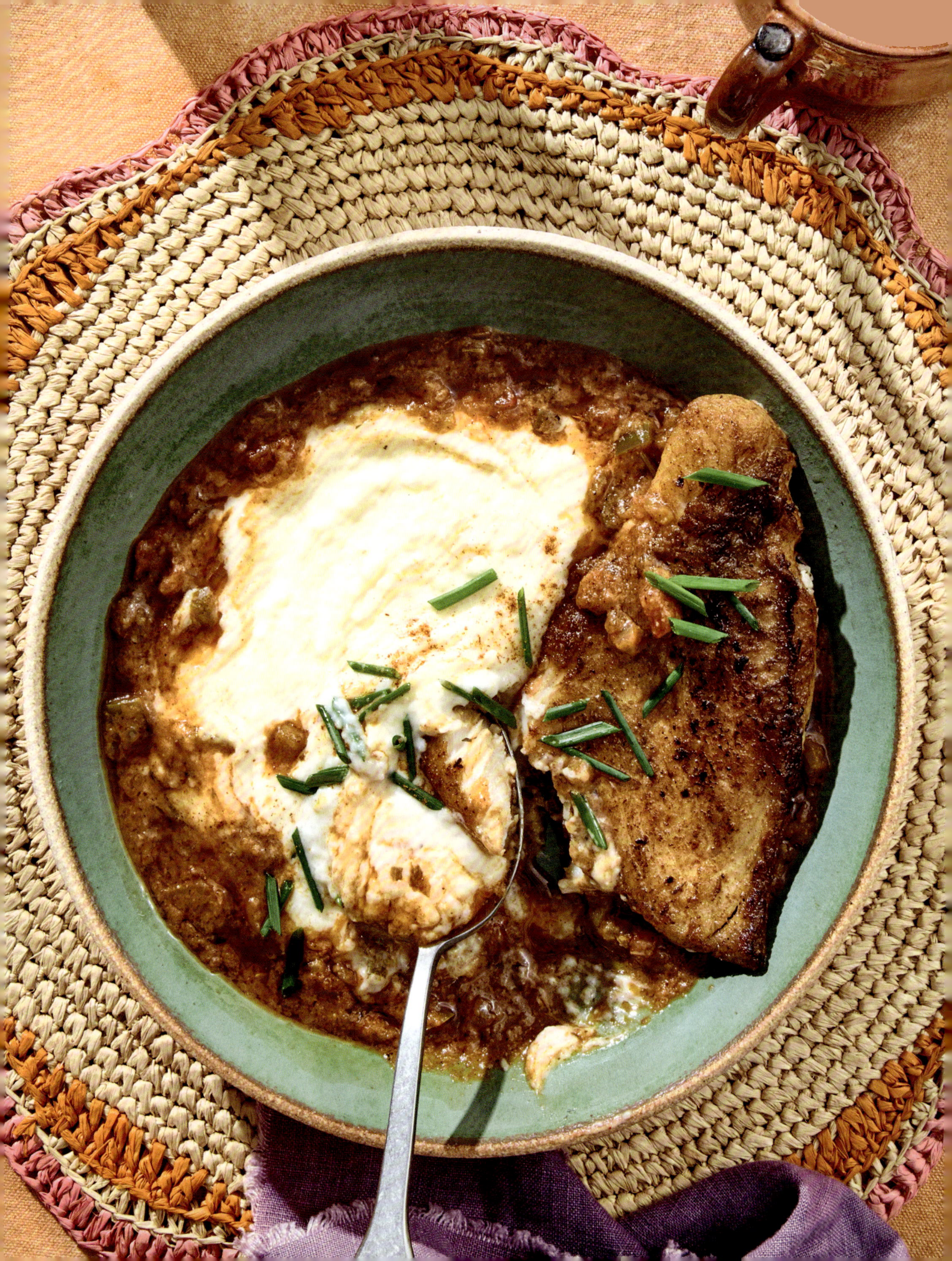

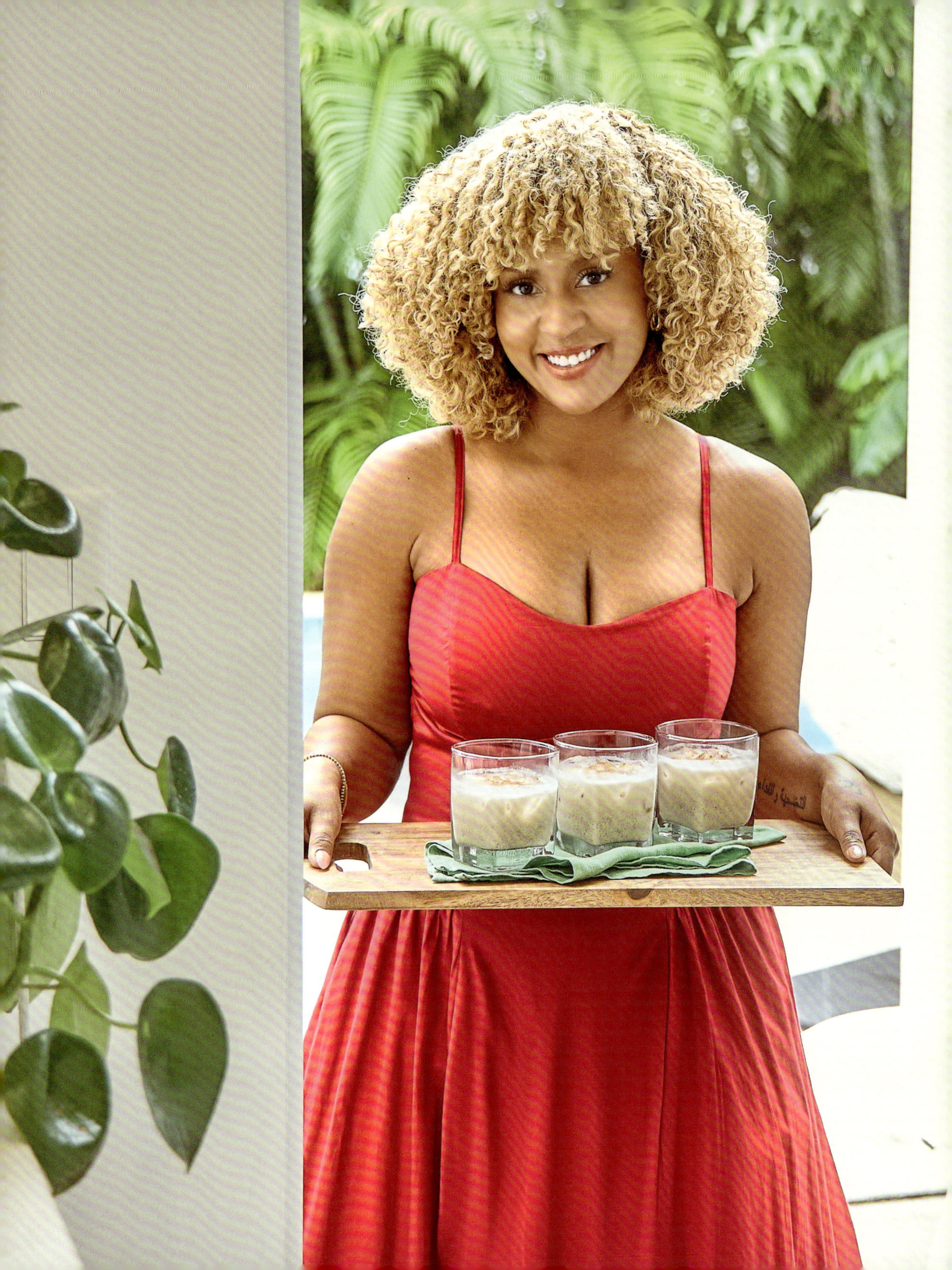

6
Family Style

There's a rhythm to my story—a beat that's distinctly Black, deeply Puerto Rican, and undeniably mine. Growing up, my grandmother would remind me that we are Black Latinas, and I've carried that identity like a badge of honor, a bridge between two histories that are one and the same. Our blood carries the lineage of resilience: African, Taíno, and Spanish threads interwoven through centuries of survival, migration, and tradition. And it all shows up in the food—our true inheritance.

In our house, food wasn't just nourishment, it was a language. My grandmother, the core of our family, spoke to me through her cooking. Every spoonful of sofrito, every pound of plantains she mashed into mofongo, carried whispers of our past. She'd remind me how the garlic came with the Africans, the plantains with the Taínos, and the flavors of olive oil and paprika with the Spaniards. Food was her way of keeping our story alive—a reminder that we are Black and Puerto Rican, always both, never either/or.

My dad, her son, was my rock, and idol. He cooked not just to feed but to nurture, to gather, to heal. I still remember the smell of his pernil, cooked low and slow until the meat fell off the bone, filling the house with an aroma that felt like family. Every Friday, he'd fry fish for the neighborhood, turning our kitchen into a place of connection. His cooking was humble yet profound, food that welcomed everyone and asked for nothing in return but laughter and togetherness.

My mother, though in and out of my life, was my connection to my African American heritage. Her family migrated from the South to Detroit, bringing their recipes along with them. Whenever I did get to see her, she was always in the kitchen—a sassy, confident cook with soulful recipes to match. She loved frying chicken, swore her mac and cheese was better than anyone's, and even though she grew up an orphan, it felt like Southern cooking was in her DNA. Her food was rich, comforting, and steeped in tradition, like an unspoken connection to the cooks who came before her.

For me, cooking is an act of preservation, a way to honor the people and cultures that shaped me. My food is where Puerto Rican adobo meets African American soul seasoning, where the crispy edges of a broiled mac and cheese sit beside the rich, garlicky depth of arroz con gandules. It's where fried fish meets mofongo, and where every bite tells a story of family, love, and resilience.

This chapter is a love letter to my roots and the meals that made me. These recipes are more than food—they're traditions, rituals, memories. They're the dishes that fill a room with laughter, the ones that make holidays feel like home, and the meals that turn strangers into family. Cooking them isn't just about taste; it's about getting it right, because in our culture, food is everything. It's how we mourn, how we celebrate, how we say, "I see you. I love you."

So, when you make my dad's juicy pernil or my mother's delicious collard greens that you pair with my Cajun butter turkey and honey butter corn bread, you're not just cooking—you're carrying a legacy. You're bringing people together, creating moments that linger long after the plates are empty. This chapter is about the flavors that define us, the love that binds us, and the stories that will always live on in the food.

Pernil
(Puerto Rican Roast Pork)

Serves 10 to 12

I remember the pernil wrapped in aluminum foil, waiting to be taken to my Titi Carmen's house on New Year's Eve. She made the best arroz con gandules, but my abuelita always brought the pork. I'd sneak into the kitchen, peel back the foil, and grab a piece of the cuerito, that crispy broiled skin. It was hot and would make the most satisfying crunching sound when I bit into it. When we finally got to Titi's and it was time to eat, I'd ask for the pernil with extra juices over my rice plus "a big piece of cuerito, please!" I'd run off with my plate, smiling to myself, knowing I'd already eaten most of the pork skin before we even got there.

Pernil is everything to me. It was the heart of the table at most gatherings, the beautifully roasted pork shoulder that everyone waited for. My version is exactly how it should be—juicy, full of flavor, with that perfect crispy skin. But to nail it, there are a few things you need to know: 1. Marinate it overnight. There's no getting around this—some dishes just take time. 2. Papi always said it's all about the marinade so be generous with it. "More garlic. Stick it in the holes," he'd say. "You can't overseason it, it's a big piece of meat." And he was right, so get in there and make sure every part of the pork is covered. 3. Don't rush cooking it—no shortcuts.

⅔ cup vegetable oil or extra-virgin olive oil
16 garlic cloves, smashed and peeled
¼ cup Abuela's Green Sofrito (page 233)
2 teaspoons adobo seasoning
2 teaspoons Maggi seasoning
2 teaspoons dried oregano
3 teaspoons kosher salt
2½ teaspoons Goya Sazón (culantro y achiote)
1 bone-in pork shoulder roast (8 to 10 pounds)

Marinate the pork: In a large bowl, whisk together the oil, garlic, sofrito, adobo seasoning, Maggi seasoning, oregano, 2 teaspoons of the salt, and 2 teaspoons of the Sazón.

Use a sharp knife to carefully peel back the skin of the pork, leaving it partially attached. Use the knife to evenly poke 8 holes all over the top of the meat (deep enough to insert garlic cloves). Flip the pork over and evenly poke 8 holes all over the bottom of the meat. Rub the marinade all over the pork, including underneath the skin, then place the large chunks of garlic inside the holes.

Pat the top of the skin dry with a paper towel. Season the top of the skin with the remaining 1 teaspoon salt and ½ teaspoon Sazón.

Place the pork in a large roasting pan and cover it with aluminum foil. Transfer to the refrigerator and marinate overnight.

Slow-roast the pernil: Preheat the oven to 325°F.

Remove the meat from the refrigerator and pat the skin dry with a paper towel. Re-cover the pork with aluminum foil and bake for 4 to 5 hours, until the meat is knife-tender.

Uncover the meat, increase the oven temperature to 375°F, and continue roasting for 1 hour, until the skin is crispy and an instant-read thermometer inserted into the thickest part of the pork reads 145°F.

Remove the pork from the oven. Let it rest for 15 minutes, then use ovenproof gloves or tongs to pull the meat off the bone and shred it. Serve each portion with a piece of skin on top.

Little Details, BIG Impact: Size matters! Depending on how large your pernil is, you'll need to adjust how much seasoning you use and the overall cook time. I definitely recommend an 8- to 10-pound pork shoulder, and if you want to serve more people, make two instead of buying a larger piece.

I've made many pernils in my lifetime. Along the way, I picked up a trick to give you more of that crunchy skin and to help it stay crispy: pinning down the skin. You can use potato baking nails, nails that come with injectors, or anything sharp enough to poke holes and secure the skin to the meat. Doing this ensures that the skin doesn't shrink and allows the skin to stay flat and even so that it gets nice and crispy.

Family Style

167

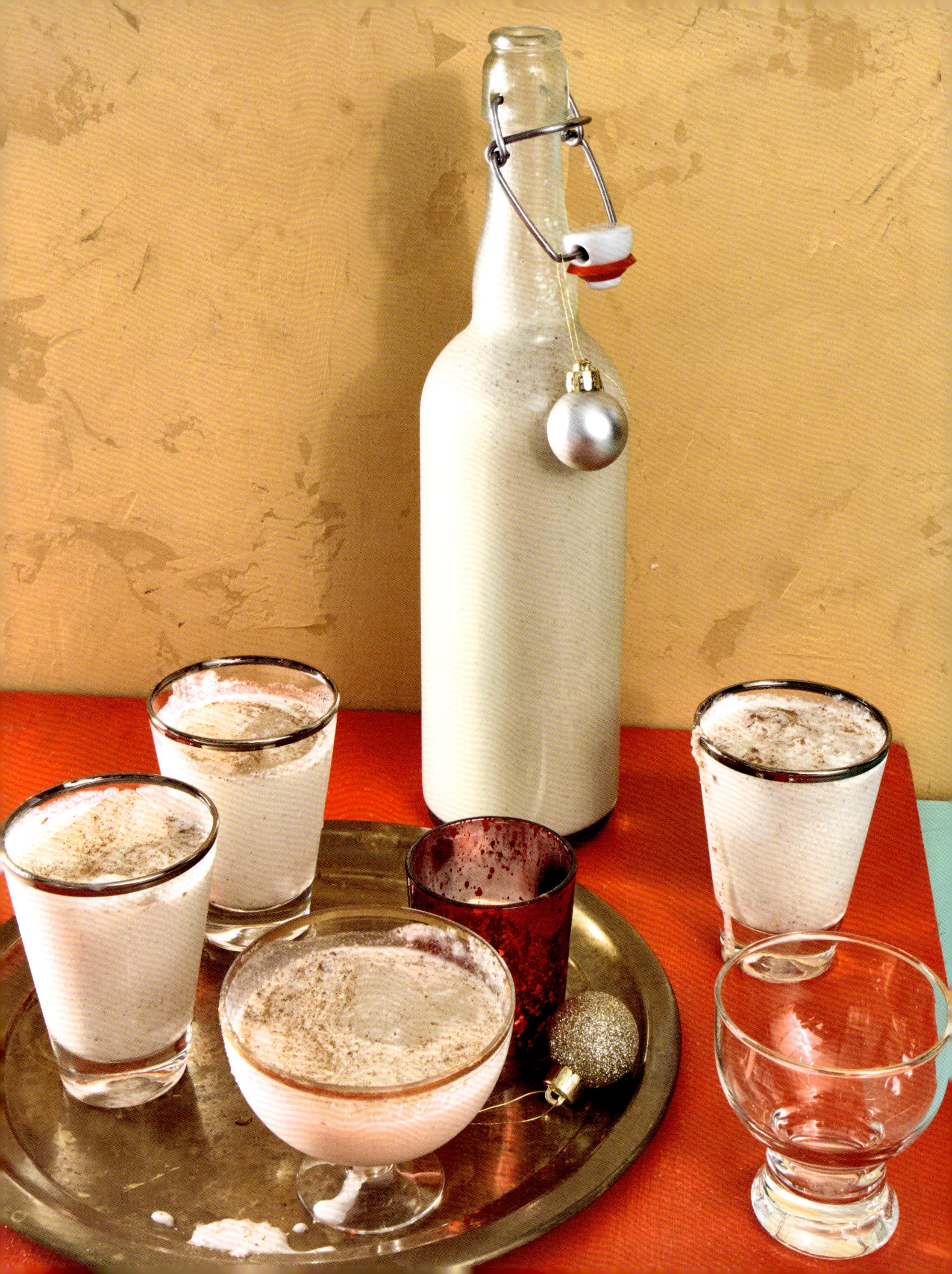

Coquito

Serves 8

Coquito isn't just a drink—it's Puerto Rico in a glass, a rich and festive tradition that embodies the warmth and joy of the holidays. Its roots trace back to colonial Puerto Rico, where it was inspired by Spanish eggnog but transformed into something distinctly ours. With the island's abundance of coconuts, we swapped the heavy cream for coconut milk, and added sweetened condensed milk, cinnamon, and of course, rum—because nothing says celebration quite like a bottle of Puerto Rican rum. Over generations, coquito became more than just a holiday staple; it's a symbol of togetherness, of family recipes passed down, and of homes filled with laughter and the clinking of glasses. It's not just a drink—it's a toast to our history and our culture.

I've been sipping coquito since I was eight years old. During Christmas, my tías would sneak me a little cup, whispering, "Shhh," as I ran down the hallway, giggling like I'd just gotten a taste of adulthood. It was a sweet, secret treat that made the holidays feel magical. By the time I was grown, I knew I had to perfect my own recipe.

In college, I turned coquito into a little hustle during Christmastime. I'd post on Instagram, "$25 bottles, pick up or delivery," and spend hours in the kitchen perfecting the ratios. Coquito might be simple, but getting it just right takes practice. This recipe is creamy, thick, and perfectly balanced—with just enough rum to warm your spirit and a cinnamon kick that keeps the good times rolling. And the best part? It makes enough for two bottles: one to gift and one to keep, because everyone deserves a little coquito magic during the holidays.

Spiced Tea
8 allspice berries
6 whole cloves
5 whole star anise
3 large cinnamon sticks
1 teaspoon ground cinnamon

Coquito
1 (15-ounce) can cream of coconut (Coco Lopez is the best!)
1 (14-ounce) can sweetened condensed milk
1 (13.5-ounce) can full-fat coconut milk
1 cup evaporated milk
1 tablespoon vanilla extract
¾ cup white rum (I use Don Q)
¼ cup spiced rum or dark rum, such as Captain Morgan Spiced Rum or Don Q 151
1 teaspoon ground cinnamon
1 teaspoon ground nutmeg

Make the spiced tea: In a medium saucepan, bring 1 cup water to a boil over medium heat. Remove from the heat and add the allspice, cloves, star anise, cinnamon sticks, and ground cinnamon. Let the tea rest for 20 minutes, then strain into a medium bowl and set aside to cool completely.

Make the coquito: In a blender, combine the cream of coconut, sweetened condensed milk, coconut milk, evaporated milk, and vanilla. Pulse until smooth and fully combined. Pour the mixture into a large bowl.

Whisk ⅓ cup of the tea mixture into the milk mixture. (Discard the remaining tea or use for additional batches of coquito.) Whisk in both rums, the cinnamon, and nutmeg until combined.

Pour the coquito into two 750ml bottles, close, and chill for at least 4 hours or up to 1 month. Shake before serving cold.

Arroz con Gandules

Serves
8

Arroz con gandules is the rice dish for Puerto Ricans—the one that's on every table, pairs perfectly with just about anything, and brings people together. My abuelita's arroz? Magic. Fluffy and flavorful. She never used recipes, though. "Measure with your heart," she'd say, like it was the easiest thing in the world. But when I tried to re-create it, my heart didn't exactly know how much liquid or seasoning to add. I kept ending up with mushy rice or bland rice—never hers.

After nearly twenty years and countless batches, I finally nailed it. Along the way, I learned a few key things. First, rinsing the rice is nonnegotiable. If you skip this step, the rice won't be fluffy—it may even end up hard or sticky. Second, don't cook a small batch in a big pot. Rice needs a snug space to steam properly—I use a 4.8-quart caldero for the perfect pot of rice. Last, leave it alone when you cover it. No peeking—let it cook. Low and slow.

This is a recipe you'll nail on the first try—one you'll be proud to bring to family gatherings and keep coming back to. It's the kind of dish that sticks with you, measured with your heart, just like Abuelita always said.

- 4 tablespoons vegetable oil
- ½ cup cubed pork fat (like the fat from a pork chop), cut into 1-inch cubes
- ¼ cup canned tomato sauce
- ¼ cup My Famous Red Sofrito (page 236)
- 3 teaspoons Goya Sazón (culantro y achiote)
- 2 teaspoons adobo seasoning
- 1 teaspoon dried oregano
- 1 teaspoon kosher salt, or more to taste
- 1 (15-ounce) can gandules (pigeon peas), undrained
- 2½ cups low-sodium chicken broth
- 2 cups long-grain rice, rinsed (see How to Make Rice 101, page 140)
- 4 sprigs cilantro
- 1 piece banana leaf (see tip)

Render the pork fat: In a large caldero (see page 18) or Dutch oven, heat 2 tablespoons of the oil over high heat until hot and shimmering. Sauté the pork fat for 2 to 3 minutes, stirring constantly, until golden brown.

Cook the rice and beans: Stir in the tomato sauce and sofrito and cook for 2 to 3 minutes, stirring constantly, until the flavors meld. Stir in 1½ teaspoons of the Sazón, the adobo seasoning, oregano, and salt. Stir in the beans with the liquid from the can and simmer for 1 minute. Add the chicken broth and bring to a light boil, then add the rice and the remaining 2 tablespoons oil, 1½ teaspoons Sazón, and the cilantro. Stir until well combined.

Bring the rice to a boil and cook uncovered for 8 minutes, until only one-quarter of the liquid remains. Cover the rice with the banana leaf and reduce the heat to low. Cook for 30 minutes, until all the water evaporates. Remove the banana leaf and fluff the rice with a fork. Serve immediately.

Little Detail, BIG Impact: You can usually find banana leaves in the frozen section at Caribbean or Hispanic supermarkets. In this recipe, it's essential for adding that authentic flavor and helping the rice steam perfectly. Can't find any? No worries—go old-school and use a plastic bag to cover the rice before the lid goes on. It gets the job done!

Everything's Good

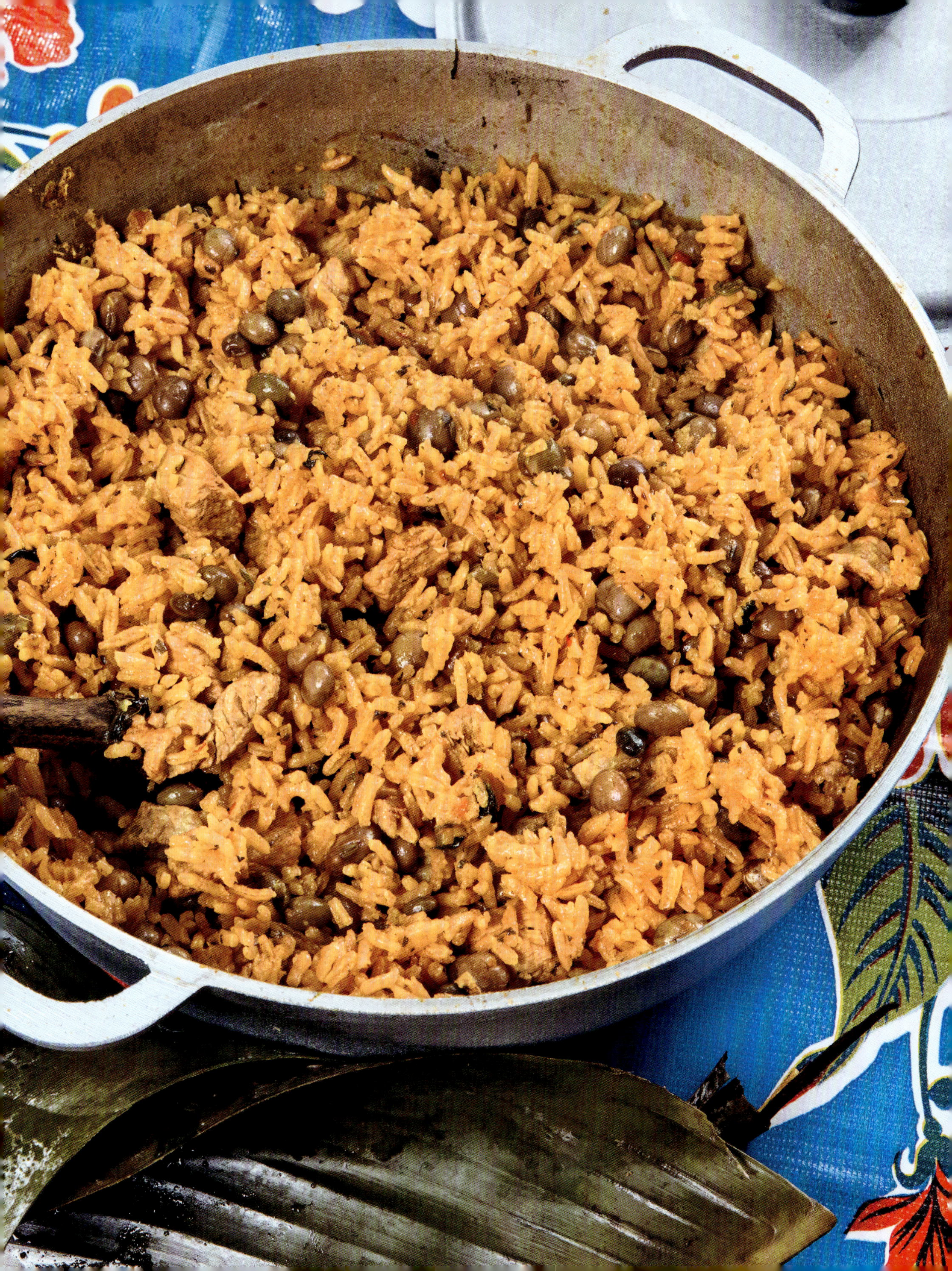

Everything's Good

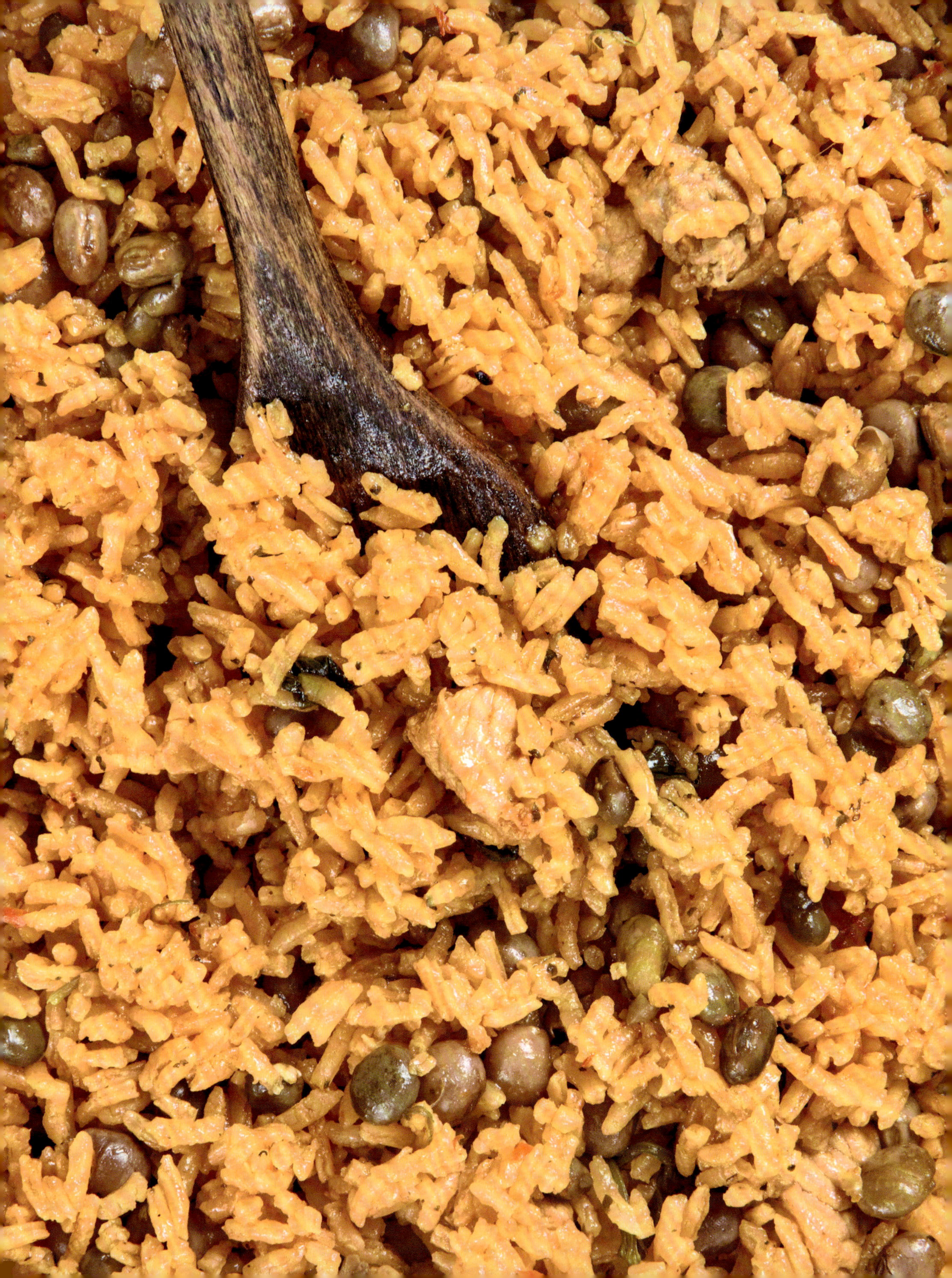

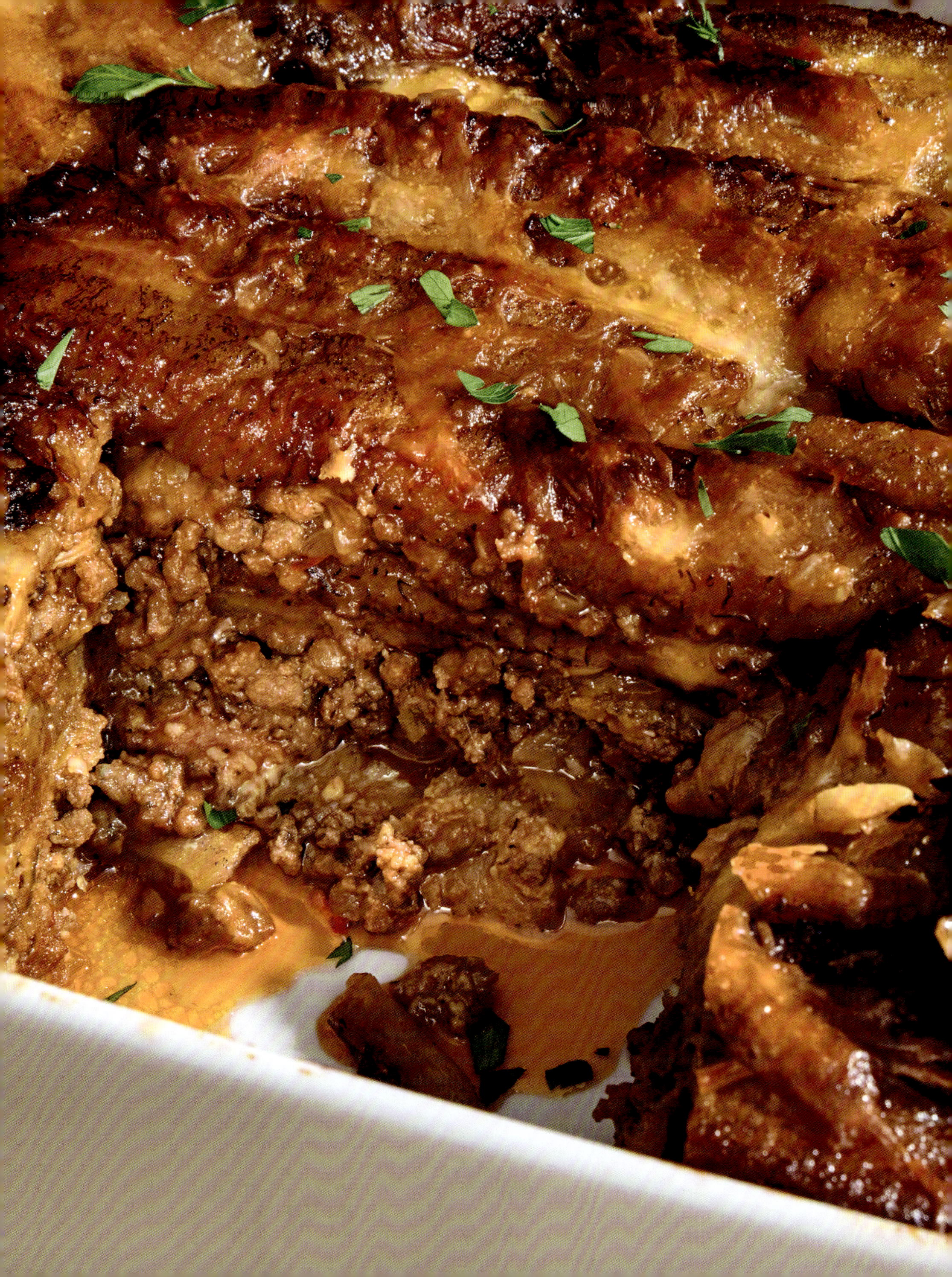

Pastelón

Serves 8

Pastelón is one of those low-key, slept-on dishes in Puerto Rican cooking, but if you know, you *know*. It's basically our version of lasagna: Think savory ground beef seasoned with sofrito, garlic, and spices and layered with melty cheese and ripe plantains instead of noodles. Hearty and comforting, it's the perfect mix of sweet and savory that hits every time. I like to serve it with some white rice to soak up all the flavors.

3 cups plus 1 tablespoon vegetable oil

10 large very ripe plantains, thinly sliced (see tip)

½ small red bell pepper, finely chopped (about ½ cup)

½ small yellow onion, finely chopped (about ¼ cup)

¼ cup finely diced jamon (Spanish cubed ham)

6 garlic cloves, minced (about 2 tablespoons)

2 pounds ground beef (85/15)

⅔ cup canned tomato sauce

¼ cup Abuela's Green Sofrito (page 233)

1 teaspoon adobo seasoning

1 teaspoon Goya Sazón (culantro y achiote)

1 teaspoon dried oregano

1 teaspoon kosher salt

¼ teaspoon ground cumin

12 ounces Colby Jack cheese, freshly shredded (3 cups)

6 large eggs, lightly beaten

Fry the plantains: Pour the 3 cups oil into a large, deep skillet and heat over high heat to 350°F. Line a plate with paper towels and have near the stove.

Working in batches to avoid overcrowding, fry the plantains for 6 to 8 minutes, until golden brown. Use tongs to remove the plantains from the oil and transfer to the paper towels to drain.

Make the beef filling: In a separate large skillet, heat the remaining 1 tablespoon oil over medium heat until hot and shimmering. Add the bell pepper, onion, jamon, and garlic and cook for 3 minutes, stirring frequently, until the jamon is seared on both sides and the vegetables are softened.

Add the ground beef and cook, stirring occasionally and breaking up the beef, for 5 to 7 minutes, until the beef is browned and no longer pink. Add the tomato sauce, sofrito, 1 tablespoon water, the adobo seasoning, Sazón, oregano, salt, and cumin. Reduce the heat to low and simmer for 5 minutes, stirring occasionally, until the sauce thickens slightly and the flavors combine.

Assemble and bake: Preheat the oven to 350°F.

Line the bottom of an 11 × 7-inch baking dish with one-third of the fried plantains. Spoon half of the beef mixture over the top. Sprinkle 1 cup of the Colby Jack over the top of the beef. Then pour half of the eggs evenly over the top of the entire dish. Repeat with another one-third of the fried plantains, the remaining beef mixture, 1 cup cheese, and the remaining eggs. Top with the remaining plantains and remaining 1 cup cheese.

Bake the pastelón for 30 to 40 minutes, until the cheese is melted and bubbling. Let it cool for 5 minutes before slicing and serving.

Little Detail, BIG Impact: The blacker the skin of the plantains, the sweeter they will be. You want very ripe plantains for pastelón so the sweetness can really shine.

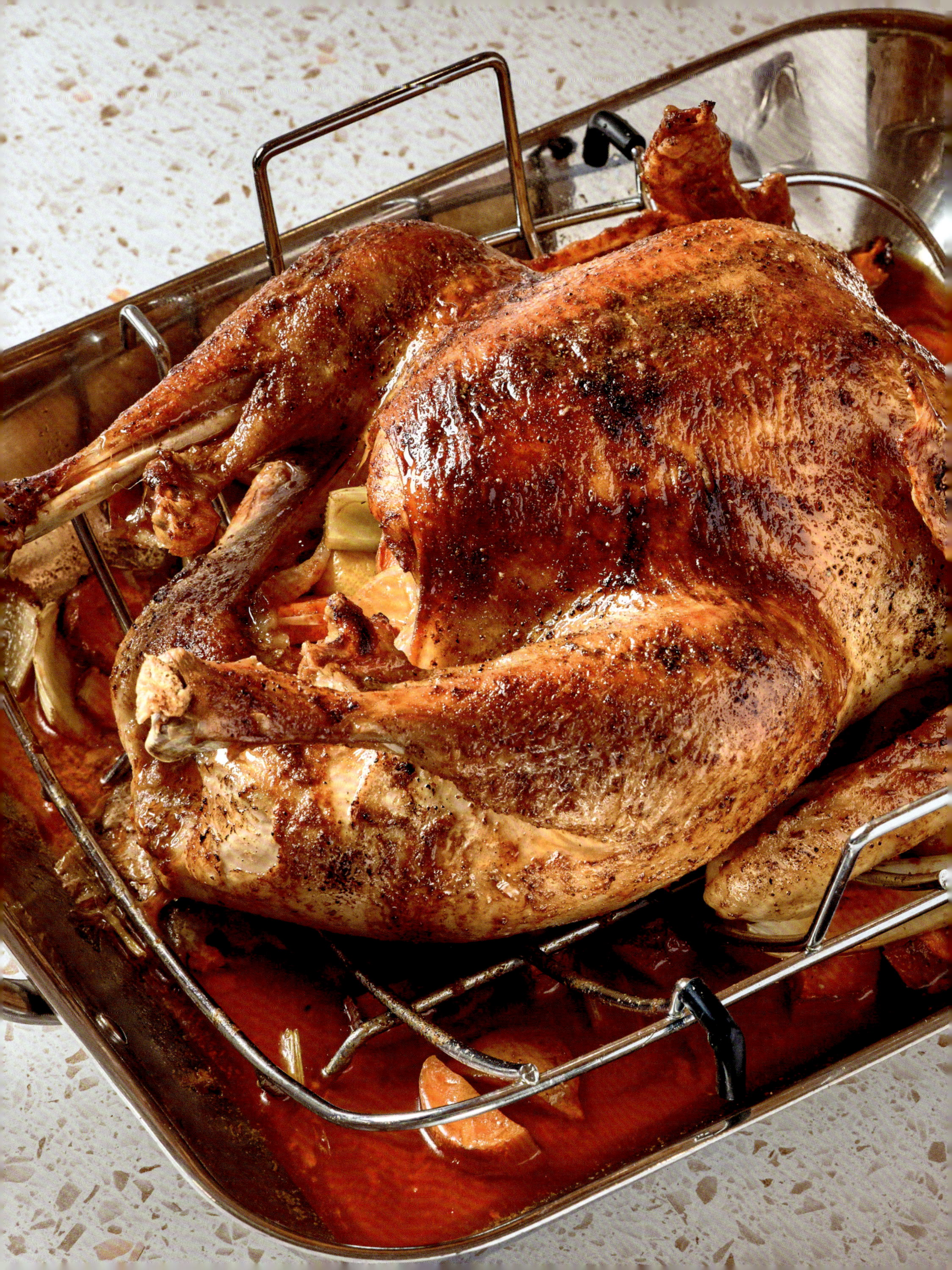

Cajun Butter Turkey

Serves 12

The women in my family are known for being "a lot." Depending on who you ask, that may be a good or bad thing, but it shaped me as a cook. We always do it *big* in the kitchen.

My mother loved to entertain. She was the sincerest woman I knew. She cared deeply about others and always wanted to make people happy. Going above and beyond was her thing. My grandmother, Edith, was a force to be reckoned with; she demanded respect in every room she walked into and was a passionate cook. Despite her larger-than-life demeanor, she was also gentle and sweet, and cooking was how she showed her love for us. She made me a home-cooked dinner every night throughout my entire childhood. When I started developing my own recipes, I had so much passion spewing out of me, and I took a little of both attitudes. I wanted to be intentional like my mother but powerful like my abuela. I wanted my recipes to be loved and celebrated and to be remarkable.

Five years ago, I was developing what would become my most popular recipe, and I said to myself, "How can I make this different?" I scanned my spice cabinet and tasted every spice for reference until I got to the Cajun, which made me cough and think, "Whew! That's A LOT!" I knew right then and there, that would be the base to turkey. Dry-brining alone wasn't enough. The herb- and spice-packed compound butter, the injections, and even the cheesecloth method weren't enough either. This turkey needed *all* of it to guarantee the juiciest bird ever. The first time I cut into this turkey, the juices poured out—rich, buttery, with a golden-red glow. I couldn't help but smile, knowing I had created magic.

Dry-Brined Turkey
1 whole turkey (12 to 15 pounds)
Kosher salt

Cajun Butter
1 pound (4 sticks) unsalted butter, at room temperature
1 tablespoon finely chopped fresh rosemary
1 tablespoon finely chopped fresh oregano
1 tablespoon finely chopped fresh thyme
1 tablespoon finely chopped fresh sage
1 tablespoon no-salt Cajun seasoning
1 tablespoon smoked paprika
1 tablespoon freshly squeezed lemon juice
1 teaspoon freshly ground black pepper

Dry-brine the turkey: Remove the neck and giblets from inside the turkey cavity. Pat the turkey dry and season generously with salt, using 1 tablespoon of kosher salt for every 5 pounds of turkey. Transfer the turkey to the fridge and let it rest for at least 6 hours and preferably overnight.

Remove the turkey from the fridge 1 hour before cooking to allow it to come to room temperature. Do not rinse the turkey. Preheat the oven to 400°F.

Make the Cajun butter: In a medium bowl, stir together the softened butter, rosemary, oregano, thyme, sage, Cajun seasoning, smoked paprika, lemon juice, and black pepper until evenly combined.

Prepare the turkey for roasting: Use your fingers or a spatula to loosen and lift the skin from the breast and legs. Rub a few tablespoons of the Cajun butter underneath the skin.

Spread half of the remaining Cajun butter on top of the turkey, coating all over, including the legs and wings. Place half of the celery, carrots, onions, and lemons in the cavity of the turkey. Use kitchen twine to tie the drumsticks together.

Arrange the remaining celery, carrots, onions, and lemons on the bottom of a roasting pan. Pour in the chicken broth and white wine. Place a roasting rack inside the roasting pan on top of the vegetables and set the turkey on top.

→

For Roasting

4 celery stalks, cut into 2-inch pieces
3 large carrots, cut into 2-inch pieces
2 medium yellow onions, quartered
2 lemons, quartered
2 cups low-sodium chicken broth or turkey stock
½ cup dry white wine, such as Chardonnay
Kitchen twine
Turkey injector
Cheesecloth

Roast the turkey: Roast for 45 minutes. Remove the turkey and reduce the oven temperature to 325°F.

Cut a piece of cheesecloth large enough to cover the turkey. In a microwave-safe medium bowl, melt the remaining Cajun butter and submerge a piece of cheesecloth in the melted butter.

Fill a turkey injector with the melted butter and inject the turkey in each thigh, breast, drumstick, and wing for a total of 8 spots, using about half of the melted butter. Lay the soaked cheesecloth snug over the top of the turkey, including the wings.

Return the turkey to the roasting rack in the oven and bake for 1 hour. Use the remaining melted butter to baste the turkey without removing the cheesecloth and bake for 2 to 3 hours longer, checking the temperature every 45 minutes, until an instant-read thermometer inserted in the breast reads 165°F.

Remove the turkey from the oven and let it rest for 1 hour before carving.

Family Style

179

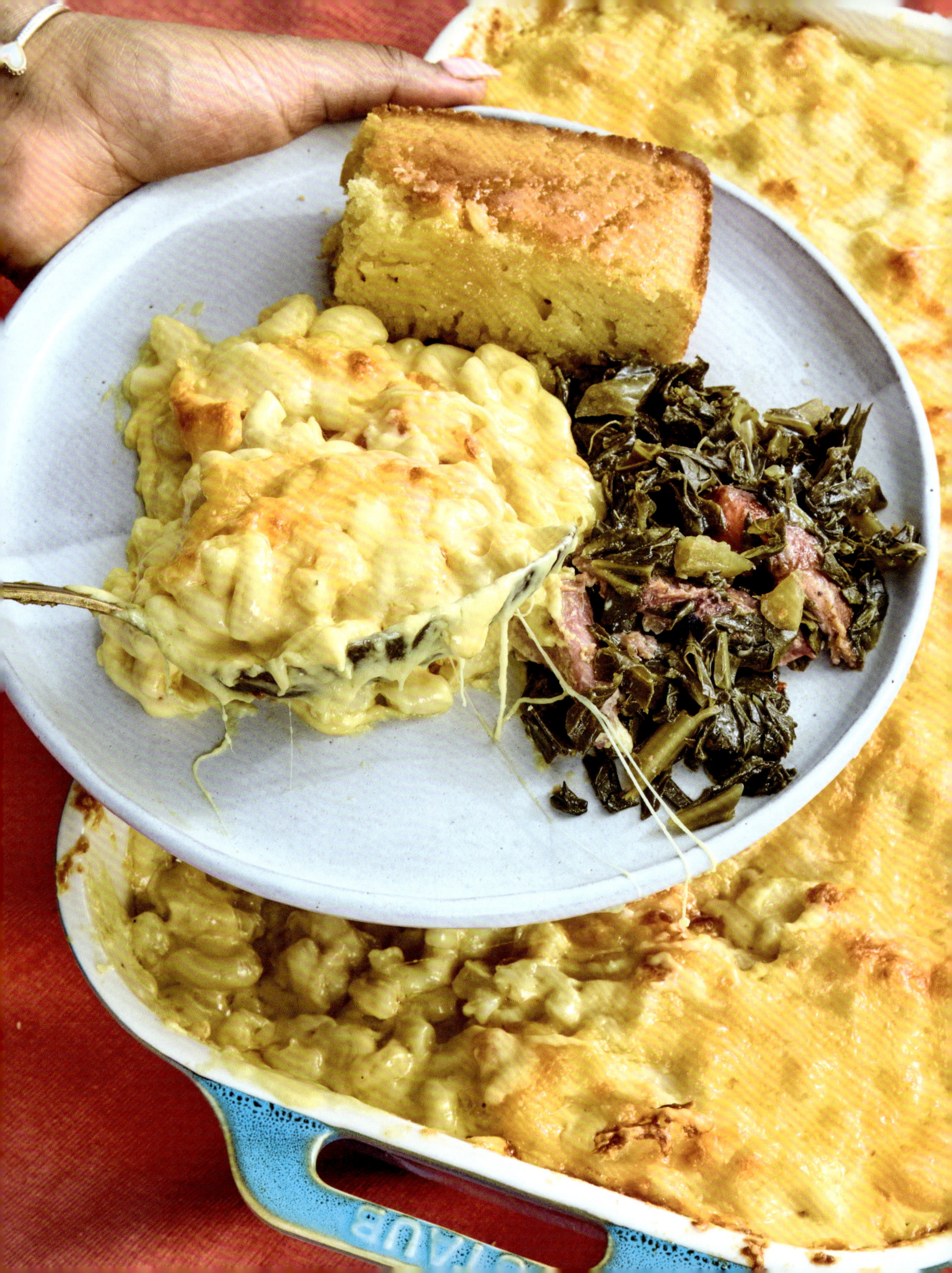

Creamy Mac and Cheese

Serves 8

There's always that one person known for bringing the mac and cheese to the party—the one everyone counts on, whose recipe is legendary. If you're reading this, you're about to become *that* person.

Mac and cheese is more than just a comfort food; it's a dish that brings everyone together, its recipe frequently passed down through generations and perfected with love. In Southern kitchens, especially in African American culture, mac and cheese is a symbol of pride, family, and celebration. It's the must-have at every holiday table, cookout, and Sunday dinner. You don't just make mac and cheese—you have to make it *right*.

When I set out to create my version, I knew it had to live up to that legacy. I spent years perfecting this recipe because I wanted it to be incredible. We skip the roux here, but we don't skip the richness. Four types of cheese weigh in at three pounds (yeah, I said three!), because this mac needs to be decadent, creamy, and bold. And for that extra layer of flavor, I add adobo (trust me), mustard powder, and white pepper. It's all about depth and balance. Broil it at the end to give you that golden, crispy crust everyone fights over.

---

1 tablespoon plus 2 teaspoons chicken bouillon powder

1½ pounds elbow macaroni (1½ boxes)

4 tablespoons (½ stick/2 ounces) salted butter

6 cups heavy cream

1 pound sharp Cheddar cheese, freshly shredded (4 cups)

1 pound Colby Jack cheese, freshly shredded (4 cups)

8 ounces Gouda cheese, freshly shredded (2 cups)

8 ounces mozzarella cheese, freshly shredded (2 cups)

4 ounces cream cheese (½ block; optional)

2 teaspoons kosher salt

1 teaspoon onion powder

1 teaspoon mustard powder

1 teaspoon adobo seasoning

1 teaspoon ground white pepper

Preheat the oven to 350°F.

Cook the macaroni: Bring a large pot of water to a boil. Add 1 tablespoon of the chicken bouillon powder to enhance the flavor of the water, then add the macaroni and cook according to the package directions. Drain and set aside.

Make the sauce: In a large pot or Dutch oven, melt the butter over low heat. Pour in the heavy cream, while whisking constantly. Stir in 2 cups of the Cheddar, 2 cups of the Colby Jack, 1 cup of the Gouda, and 1 cup of the mozzarella until well blended. Add the cream cheese (if using) and stir until melted. Simmer for 10 minutes, whisking frequently, until the sauce is creamy and all the cheese is melted. Stir in the salt, onion powder, mustard powder, adobo seasoning, white pepper and remaining 2 teaspoons chicken bouillon powder.

Assemble and bake the mac and cheese: Scoop out one-quarter of the cheese sauce from the pot and set aside. Add the macaroni to the remaining sauce in the pot and mix until smooth and well combined.

Transfer half of the macaroni mixture to a 9 × 13-inch baking dish. Pour the reserved cheese sauce over the top, then 1 cup of the Colby Jack, ½ cup of the Gouda, and the remaining 2 cups Cheddar and 1 cup mozzarella. Add the remaining macaroni mixture and top with the remaining 1 cup Colby Jack and ½ cup Gouda.

Bake for 10 minutes, until the cheese is melted and bubbling. Switch the oven to low broil and broil for 2 minutes at the end for a nice golden-brown top.

Little Detail, BIG Impact: Shredding all that cheese yourself is worth it. You can't half-do it—too much is on the line. And make sure you make the cheese sauce over low heat. If the heat is too high, your sauce can burn and come out gritty.

Chef's Kiss: Broiling at the end gives it an extra-crispy top finish. Broil on low (if that's an option on your oven) and keep your eyes on the baking dish so it doesn't burn!

Honey Butter Corn Bread

Serves 12

Corn bread was always on the table in our house. We didn't have much, but a box of Jiffy could stretch any meal. Pair it with some rice and whatever stew was bubbling on the stove and suddenly, dinner felt whole. It wasn't fancy, but it was everything—comfort, love, home in every bite. That's why I poured my heart into creating my own recipe, one that works for a regular Tuesday but feels special enough to serve at a celebration. That's the magic—no stress, no fuss, just a dish that delivers every time.

What makes this corn bread stand out is the creamed corn—it's nonnegotiable. It's the secret to a crumb so moist and tender you'll never settle for dry corn bread again. Then there's the honey butter, melting into all of the golden crevices, balancing sweetness and warmth with every bite. This isn't just corn bread—it's a recipe that embodies everything I stand for in the kitchen: flavor that's approachable but unforgettable, simple enough to make on a whim, and special enough to anchor a celebration. It's more than a dish, it's a hallmark of what I do—create food that feels like home and makes memories worth keeping.

Softened butter, for the pan
2 cups stone-ground yellow cornmeal (I like Indian Head)
2 cups all-purpose flour
1 cup sugar
2 tablespoons baking powder
1 teaspoon kosher salt
2 cups whole milk
1 (14.75-ounce) can creamed corn
⅔ cup vegetable oil
2 large eggs
8 tablespoons (1 stick/4 ounces) unsalted butter, melted and cooled
½ cup honey

Preheat the oven to 400°F. Grease a 13-inch cast-iron skillet or 9 × 13-inch baking pan with butter.

Make the corn bread: In a medium bowl, whisk together the cornmeal, flour, sugar, baking powder, and salt. In a small bowl, combine the milk, creamed corn, oil, and eggs and whisk until smooth. Make a well in the dry ingredients, then add the wet ingredients to the dry ingredients and stir until fully combined; some small lumps are okay.

Pour the batter into the prepared pan. Bake for 25 to 35 minutes, until a toothpick inserted into the center comes out clean.

Make the honey butter: In a small bowl, whisk together the melted butter and honey until combined. Drizzle over the top of the corn bread and serve warm.

Chef's Kiss: If you really want to *do it right,* melt together 2 tablespoons butter and 2 tablespoons honey, and set it aside as your secret weapon (and a little party trick). When you're serving, drizzle this additional butter on at the last minute. It's that extra touch everyone goes crazy for!

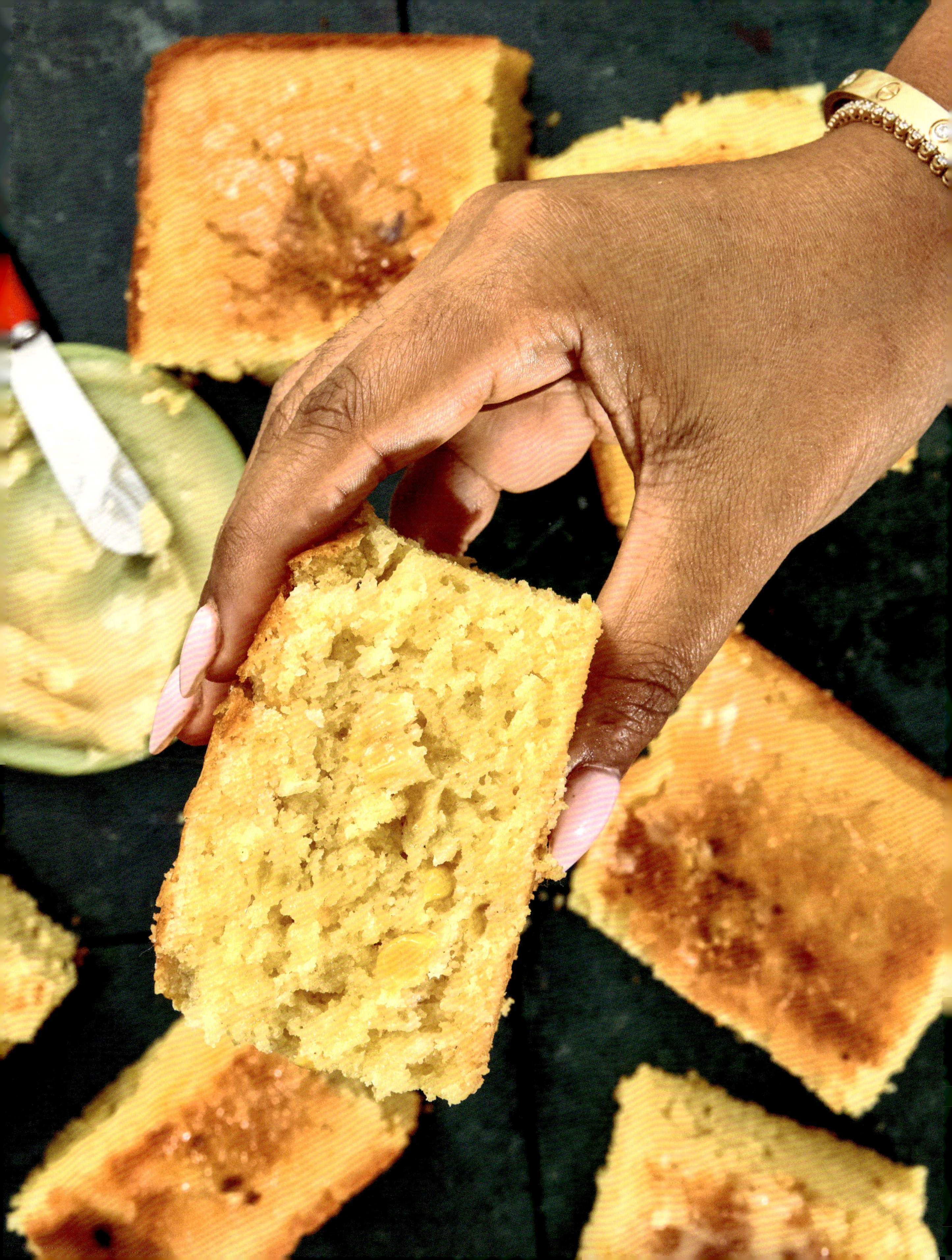

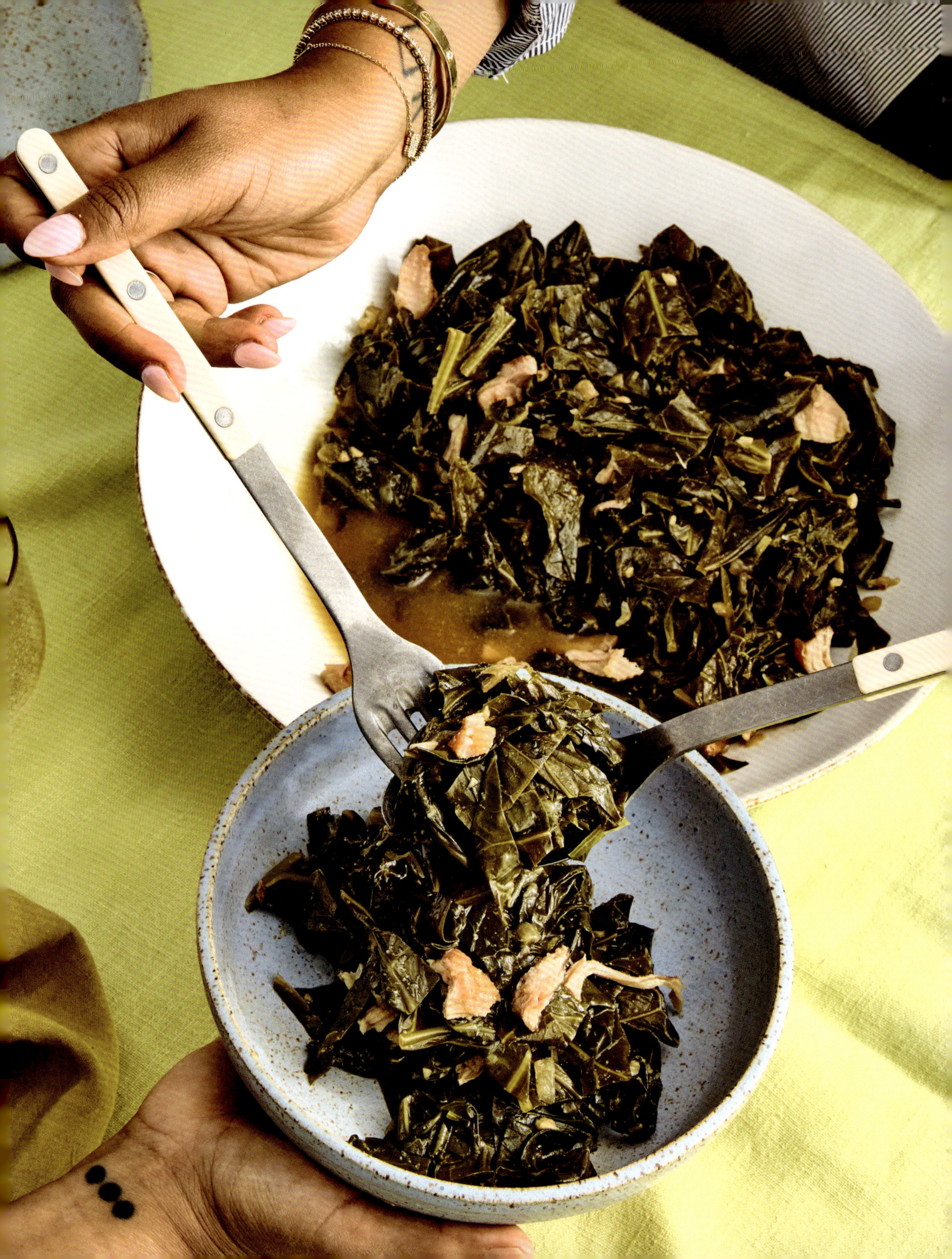

Collard Greens with Smoked Turkey

Serves 6

Collard greens got me through college. They were my go-to because they were cheap, easy to make, and just did it for me every time. I'd cook up a pot and eat them as an entrée—they were that filling and comforting. My mom was famous for her collard greens, and even though we weren't close, it feels like my love for them came from her, instinctively, like it was in my DNA. Maybe it's why collards have always been my comfort food, my way of reconnecting with that part of myself. My recipe strikes the perfect balance of a little sugar for sweetness and a splash of vinegar for that tangy bite. Let them simmer low and slow, and they come out rich, tender, and packed with flavor. The best part? You can make a big batch, freeze them, and they're just as good when you reheat them. These greens are foolproof—perfect for Sunday dinner, holidays, or whenever you want a side that feels like a warm hug on a plate.

- 3 pounds collard greens, rinsed
- 1 tablespoon vegetable oil
- 1 medium yellow onion, finely chopped (about 1 cup)
- 6 garlic cloves, minced (about 2 tablespoons)
- 1 pound bone-in smoked turkey (drumsticks, necks, or tails)
- 4 cups vegetable broth
- 1½ tablespoons sugar
- 1 tablespoon hot sauce, or more to taste
- 1 tablespoon garlic powder
- 1 tablespoon onion powder
- 2 teaspoons apple cider vinegar
- 2 teaspoons kosher salt, or more to taste

Cook the collard greens: Stack several collard green leaves together, roll them into a tight cylinder and slice them into 1-inch-wide strips.

In a large pot or Dutch oven, heat the oil over medium heat until hot and shimmering. Add the onion and sauté for 5 to 7 minutes, stirring occasionally, until translucent. Add the minced garlic and cook for 1 to 2 minutes, stirring frequently, until fragrant. Add the collard greens and cook for 5 minutes, stirring occasionally, until the greens are wilted.

Season and stew the greens: Take the turkey off the bone and shred it. Add the shredded turkey, broth, sugar, hot sauce, garlic powder, onion powder, vinegar, and salt and stir to combine. Bring the mixture to a boil. Reduce the heat to low, cover, and simmer for about 2 hours, stirring occasionally, until the greens reach your desired level of tenderness. Adjust hot sauce and salt to taste. Serve hot.

Candied Yams

Serves 6

There's something magical about that first bite of candied sweetness that hits you—warm, spiced, and buttery, like a little piece of home. The way the syrupy glaze clings to the tender yams feels like pure love, the kind you only get from a family recipe passed down through generations. These belong on every table, because no matter what else is being served, they're always the dish everyone comes back for. Serve with other sides like Collard Greens with Smoked Turkey (page 185), Creamy Mac and Cheese (page 181), and Honey Butter Corn Bread (page 182).

4 pounds sweet potatoes, peeled and cut into 1-inch cubes or rounds
1½ cups packed dark brown sugar
½ cup orange juice
2 teaspoons vanilla extract
1 teaspoon ground cinnamon
1 teaspoon ground ginger
1 teaspoon kosher salt
12 tablespoons (1½ sticks/6 ounces) unsalted butter, cubed

Preheat the oven to 350°F. Place the sweet potatoes in a 9 × 13-inch baking dish.

Make the sauce: In a medium saucepan, combine the brown sugar, orange juice, vanilla, cinnamon, ginger, and salt. Cook over medium heat for 5 minutes, stirring occasionally, until the sugar is dissolved and the mixture is well combined. Add the butter to the pan and stir until the butter is fully melted and the sauce is smooth.

Bake the yams: Pour the sauce evenly over the sweet potatoes in the baking dish. Use a spatula or spoon to gently toss the yams, coating all over. Cover the baking dish with aluminum foil. Bake for 30 minutes, then remove the foil and gently stir the yams. Continue baking uncovered for 30 minutes, until the yams are fork-tender and the sauce is thickened and bubbling.

Remove the yams from the oven and let them cool for 5 minutes before serving. The sauce will thicken further as it cools.

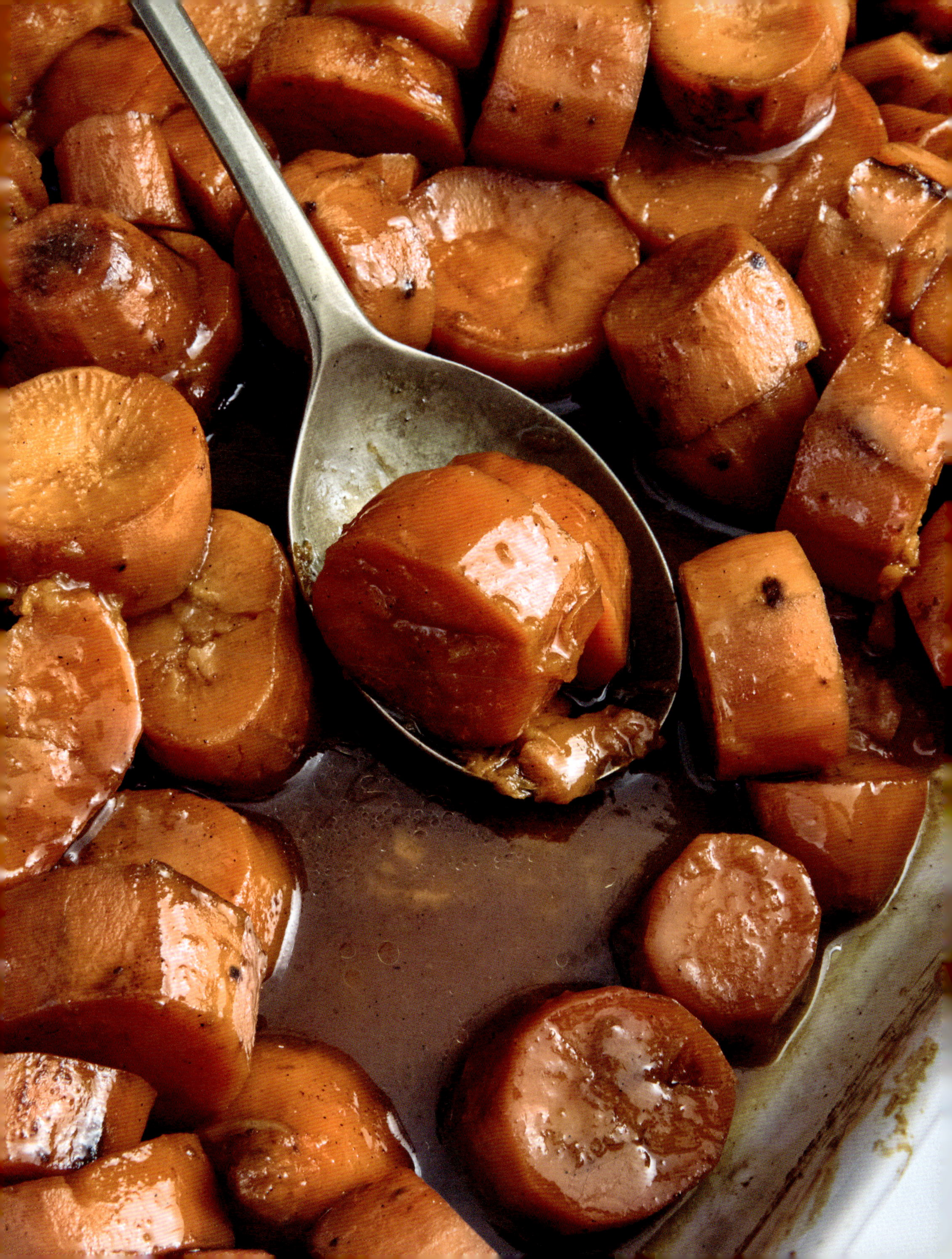

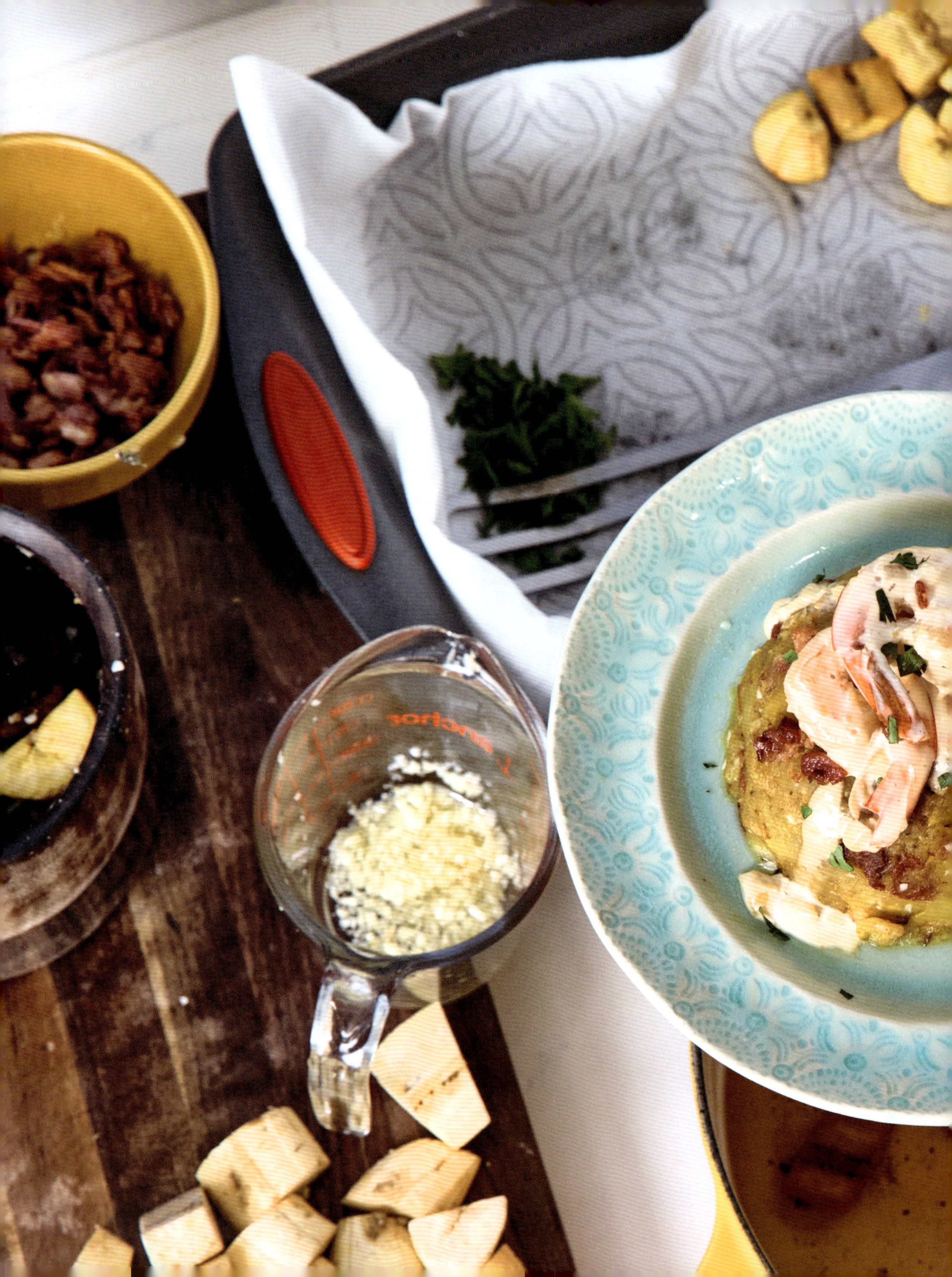

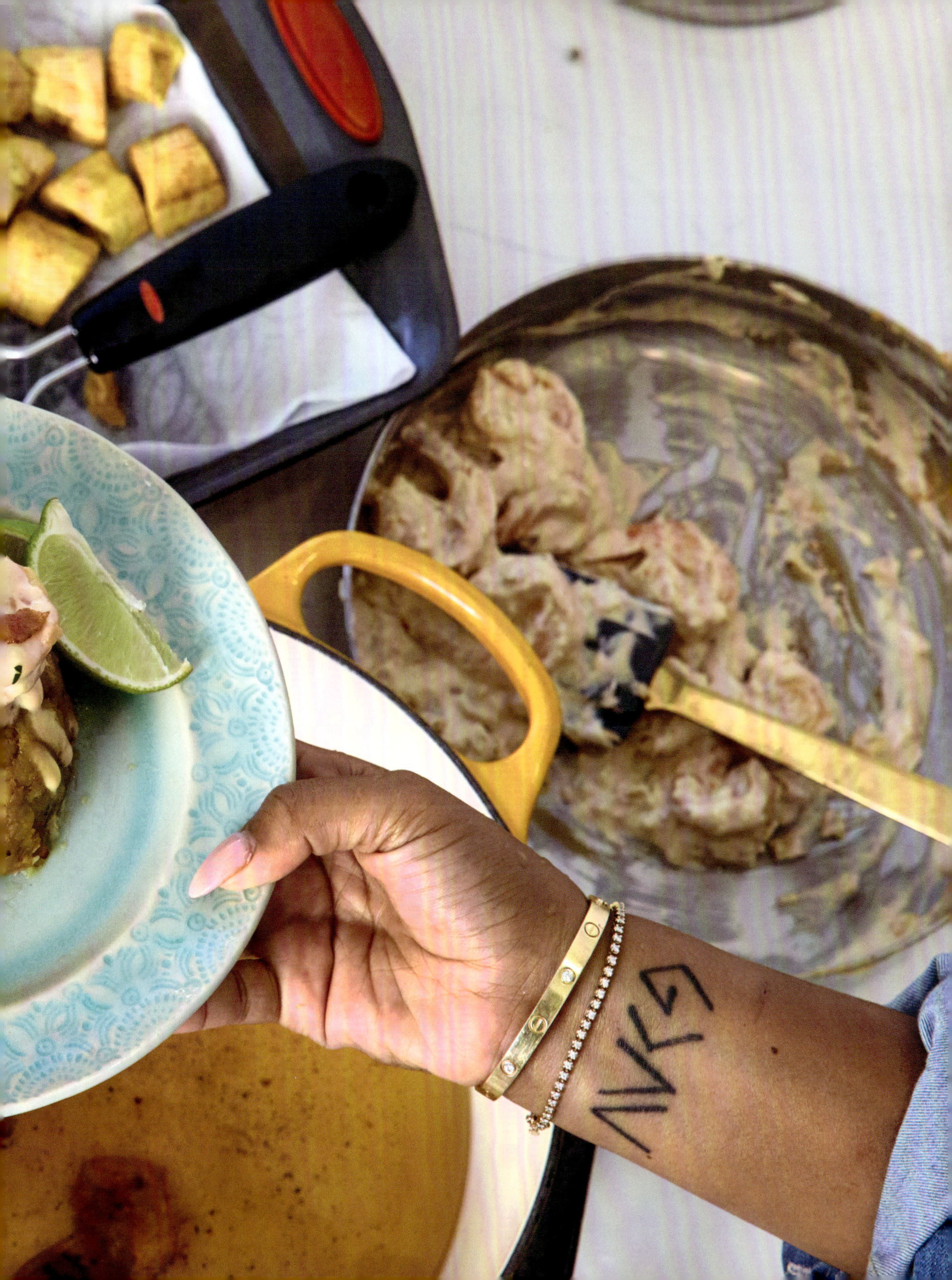

Mofongo con Camarones de Ajillo

Serves 2

When West African slaves were brought to Puerto Rico in the early 1500s, they brought their culinary traditions with them. One of which was fufu, a dish made by mashing starchy vegetables like yams or cassava. "Mofongo" comes from the Angolan Kikongo language, the word *mfwenge-mfwenge* meaning "a great amount of anything at all." While the native Taíno people were already mashing foods in wooden pilones, the influence of African cooking techniques and flavors transformed this practice into something new. Over time, these African traditions blended with Taíno techniques and Spanish ingredients to create mofongo—a dish that's now a staple of Puerto Rican kitchens. Mofongo is more than just a meal—it's a reflection of Puerto Rico's story. It speaks to resilience, adaptability, and cultural fusion, making it so much more than just food.

Mofongo is the dish that represents me the most because it ties together both sides of my heritage—Puerto Rican and African American. It's a blend of everything that's shaped who I am. But let's be real—it's not easy to make. To nail it, you've got to find that perfect balance between creamy, moist texture and bold flavor. The plantains need to be hot when you mash them in the pilón, and you've gotta hit it with that garlic, bacon, and butter combo at just the right moment. And trust me, the more fat, the better—back in the day, people were even using lard to make it extra rich. The garlicky, creamy shrimp takes mofongo from good to mind-blowing. This dish isn't just a recipe, it's a piece of history, a connection to my roots, and a celebration of the cultures that made me. It's the heart and soul of Puerto Rican cooking on a plate.

6 slices thick-cut bacon, diced

Shrimp Ajillo

⅓ cup chopped yellow onion
6 garlic cloves, minced (about 2 tablespoons)
12 extra-jumbo shrimp (16/20 count), peeled and deveined, tails on
1 teaspoon garlic powder
½ teaspoon onion powder
½ teaspoon kosher salt, plus more to taste
1 (7.5-ounce) can table cream (I use Nestlé media crema; see tip)
1 teaspoon dried oregano
½ teaspoon adobo seasoning

Cook the bacon: Line a plate with paper towels. In a large skillet, sauté the bacon over medium heat for 5 minutes, stirring occasionally, until crispy. Use a slotted spoon to remove the bacon from the fat and transfer to the paper towels. Measure out 2 tablespoons of the bacon fat and set aside. Leave the remaining bacon fat in the pan.

Make the shrimp ajillo: In the same skillet, sauté the onion and minced garlic over medium heat for 2 to 3 minutes, stirring frequently, until softened and fragrant. Add the shrimp and season with the garlic powder, onion powder, and salt. Cook for 2 to 3 minutes on each side, until the shrimp are pink and opaque. Stir in the cream, oregano, and adobo seasoning. Cook for 2 to 3 minutes, stirring occasionally, until the sauce is heated through and slightly thickened. Keep warm.

Make the mofongo: In a separate large skillet, heat the ⅓ cup oil over medium heat until hot and shimmering. Add the minced garlic and cook for 1 to 2 minutes, until fragrant. Remove the pan from the heat and set aside.

Fill a large, deep skillet or Dutch oven with 2 to 3 inches of oil and heat to 350°F. Line a plate with paper towels and have near the stove.

Fry the plantains for 5 to 7 minutes, until light golden brown and just barely crispy. Use tongs or a slotted spoon to transfer to the paper towels.

Mofongo

- ⅓ cup neutral oil, such as vegetable oil, plus more for deep-frying
- 6 garlic cloves, minced (about 2 tablespoons)
- 4 large green plantains, peeled and cut into 1-inch cubes
- 2 tablespoons (1 ounce) unsalted butter, at room temperature
- ½ teaspoon kosher salt, plus more to taste

Mash the plantains: While the plantains are still hot, put 1 tablespoon butter, 1 tablespoon of the reserved bacon fat, and 2 tablespoons of the garlic oil in a large bowl or wooden pilón (see page 18). Add half of the plantains and half the bacon and mash everything together with a potato masher or pilón club, until you reach a creamy, moist texture. Season with half of the salt and adjust to taste.

Fill a small bowl with the mofongo and then flip it over onto a plate to get a dome-like shape. Repeat with the remaining plantains, 1 tablespoon butter, 1 tablespoon reserved bacon fat, 2 tablespoons garlic oil, bacon, and salt to make a second serving of mofongo.

Top the mofongo with the shrimp ajillo and serve hot.

Little Details, BIG Impact: Table cream is a light cream with a smooth, velvety texture that's perfect for adding richness without being too heavy. It's commonly used in Latin American cooking for soups, sauces, and desserts because it blends so effortlessly. If you can't find table cream, heavy cream is a great substitute—it's slightly richer but works just as well to give you that creamy finish.

Take care not to overcook the plantains. They're ready when they are a light golden brown (so they are not too hard on the outside).

For the creamiest mofongo, be sure to mash the plantains while they're hot, and add the butter, bacon fat, and bacon as you mash, so that it's creamy and smooth.

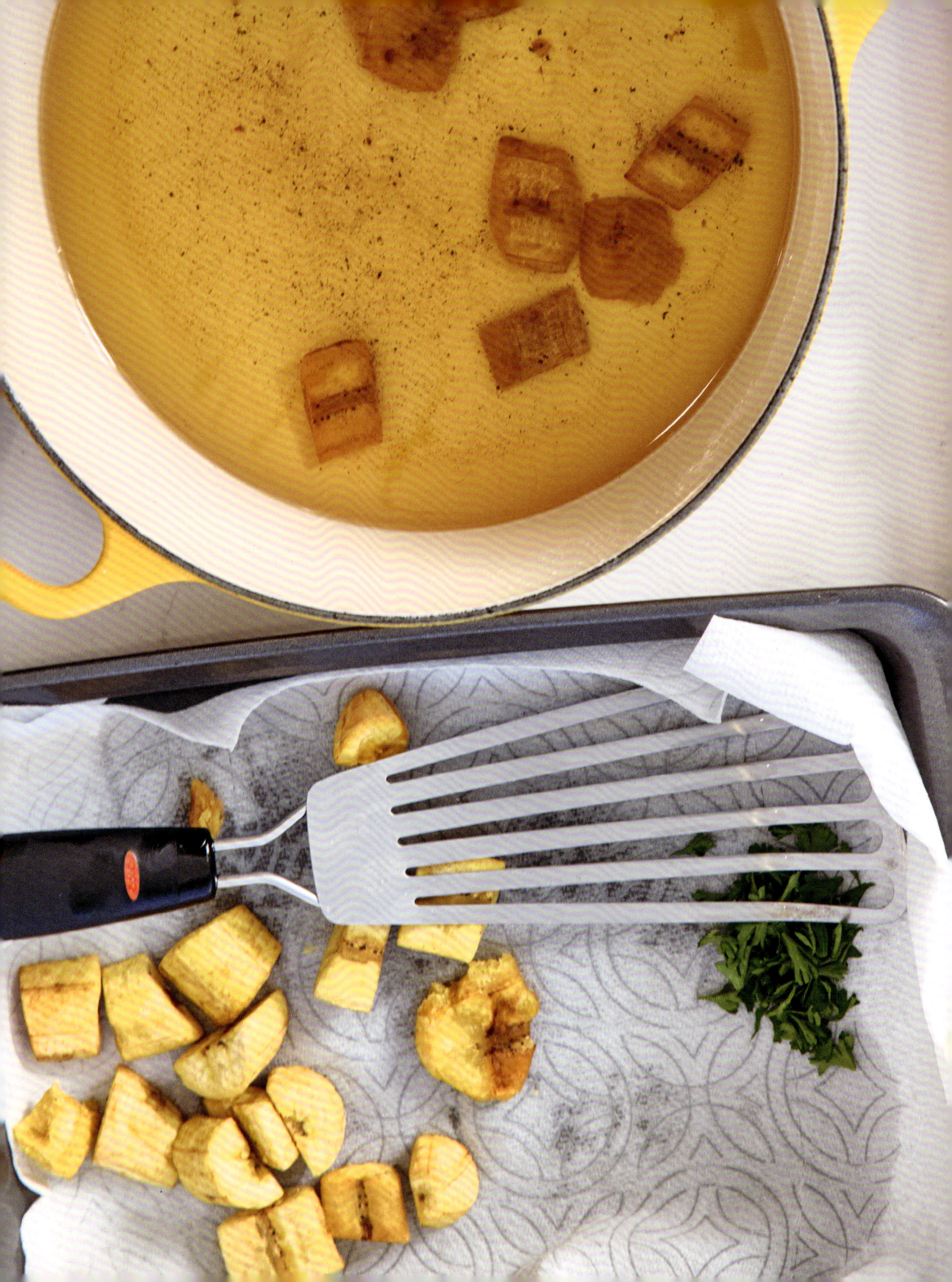

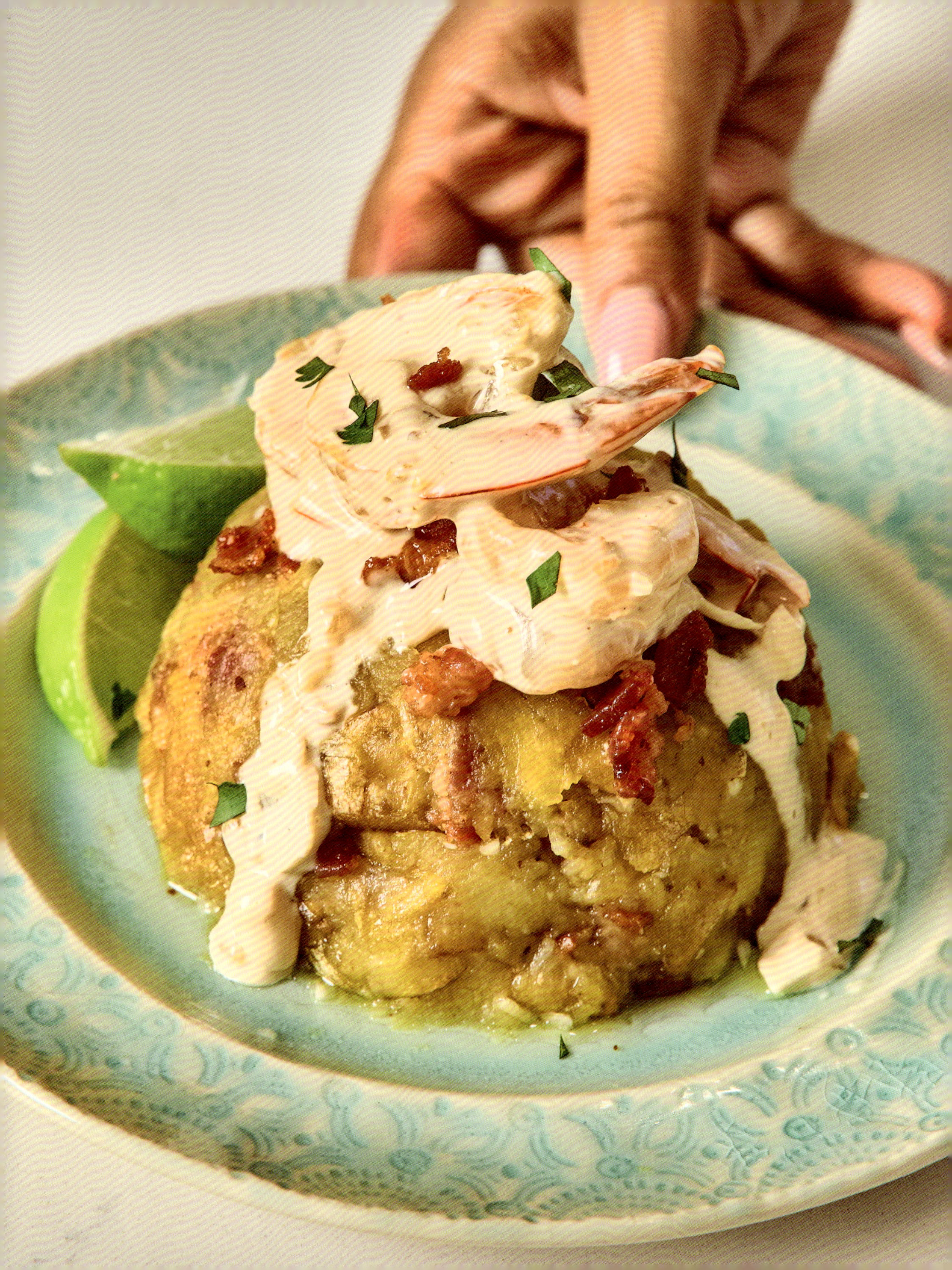

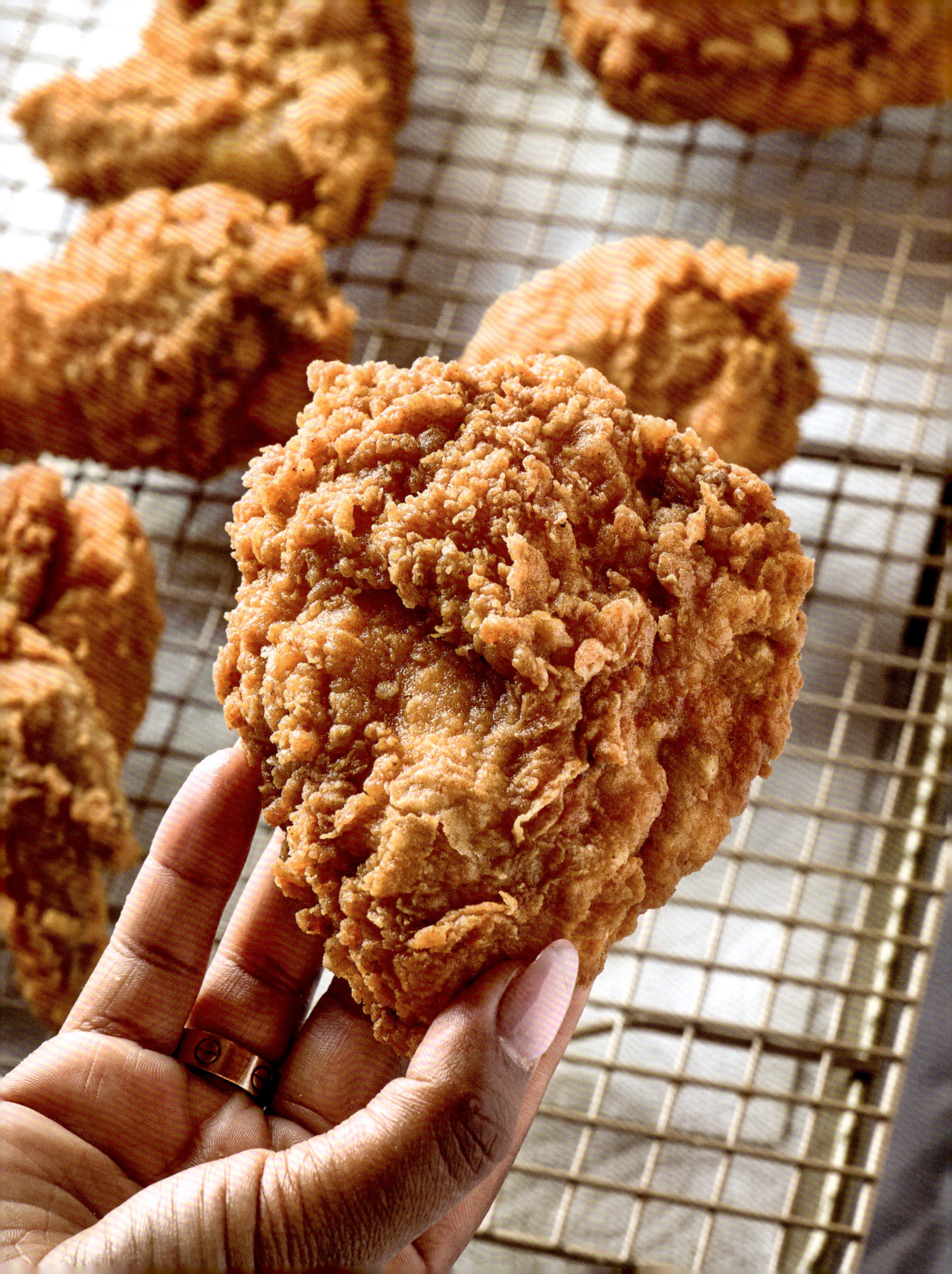

Real-Deal Fried Chicken

Serves 8

This is the fried chicken I make when the family's coming over, and for good reason—it's simple, straightforward, and tastes amazing every single time. It's that old-school fried chicken vibe—just an egg-and-flour mixture, seasoned up right. The crispy skin is perfectly golden, and the chicken stays juicy inside, with flavors that bring you right back to those classic family meals. No frills, just the real deal. It's the kind of fried chicken that never disappoints, whether you're making it for a big crowd or just craving something familiar and comforting.

6 to 8 cups vegetable oil, for deep-frying
2 cups all-purpose flour
2 tablespoons baking powder
2 teaspoons kosher salt
4 large eggs
1 tablespoon hot sauce
8 pieces bone-in chicken (4 pounds)
2 teaspoons Goya Sazón (culantro y achiote)
2 teaspoons sweet paprika
1 teaspoon chili powder
1 teaspoon garlic powder
1 teaspoon onion powder
1 teaspoon freshly ground black pepper
½ teaspoon cayenne pepper

Pour enough oil into a large, deep pot or Dutch oven to come up halfway. Clip a candy/deep-fry thermometer to the side and heat the oil over medium-high until it reaches 350°F. Line a plate with paper towels and have near the stove.

Dredge and season the chicken: Set up a dredging station in two shallow bowls. In one bowl, whisk together the flour, baking powder, and 1 teaspoon of the salt until combined. In a second bowl, whisk together the eggs, ¼ cup cold water, and the hot sauce until combined.

In a large bowl, season the chicken with the Sazón, paprika, chili powder, garlic powder, onion powder, black pepper, cayenne, and remaining 1 teaspoon salt. Toss to make sure the chicken is evenly coated.

Working with one piece at a time, remove the chicken from the bowl of seasonings and transfer to the flour mixture. Toss to coat the chicken all over, shaking off any excess. Dip the chicken in the egg mixture, letting the excess drip off, and then coat again in the flour mixture, shaking off any excess. Transfer the chicken to a plate and let it rest for 15 minutes to ensure the coating sticks well, resulting in crispy fried chicken.

Fry the chicken: Working in batches to avoid overcrowding, fry the chicken for 8 to 10 minutes, until golden brown and crispy and an instant-read thermometer reads 165°F. Place the chicken on the paper towel–lined plate to drain before serving. Serve hot.

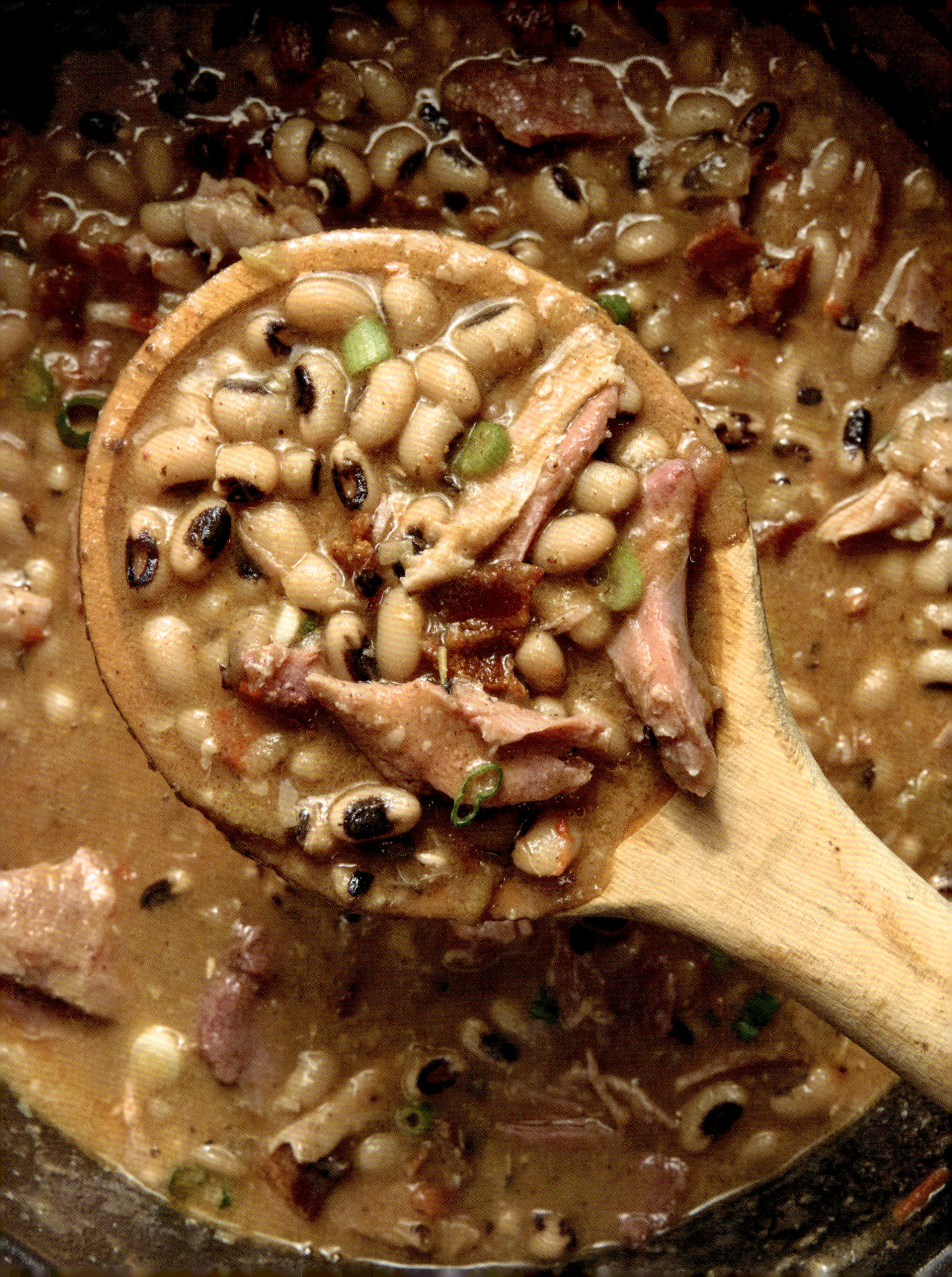

New Year's Black-Eyed Peas

Serves 6

Legend has it that making a pot of black-eyed peas on New Year's Eve or New Year's Day will bring good luck and abundance. This African American tradition holds deep significance, as it is said to be rooted in the Emancipation Proclamation that went into effect on January 1, 1863. Making and eating this deliciously soulful dish is not only a celebration of our freedom but a symbol of our bright future as a people.

This dish is so meaningful to me, connecting me to my heritage and to the people who came before me. The savory spices and smoked turkey make it rich with flavor, leaving me in awe of my ancestors' ability to turn so little into something so beautiful. I like to serve this alongside my Honey Butter Corn Bread (page 182) and Classic White Rice (page 140), or simply on its own in a big bowl with exactly five dashes of hot sauce.

1 pound bacon, roughly chopped
3 celery stalks, diced (about 1 cup)
½ small yellow onion, diced (about ½ cup)
1 small red bell pepper, diced (about ½ cup)
1 small green bell pepper, diced (about ½ cup)
6 garlic cloves, minced (about 2 tablespoons)
2 cups dried black-eyed peas (about 20 ounces), soaked overnight, drained, and rinsed
3 cups low-sodium chicken broth
2 teaspoons kosher salt, plus more to taste
1 teaspoon onion powder
1 teaspoon garlic powder
1 teaspoon adobo seasoning
1 teaspoon no-salt Cajun seasoning
1 teaspoon sweet paprika
½ teaspoon Maggi seasoning
¼ teaspoon freshly ground black pepper, plus more to taste
⅛ teaspoon red pepper flakes
2 pounds smoked turkey (drumsticks, necks, or tails)
1 turkey leg (drumstick and thigh)
Hot sauce (optional but highly recommended!)

Cook the bacon: Line a plate with paper towels and have near the stove. In a large pot or Dutch oven, sauté the bacon over medium-high heat, stirring constantly, for 5 to 7 minutes, until crisp. Use a slotted spoon or tongs to transfer the bacon to the paper towels to drain, leaving the fat in the pan.

Cook the black-eyed peas: To the bacon fat, add the celery, onion, both bell peppers, and minced garlic and sauté, stirring frequently, for about 8 minutes, until softened. Add the soaked black-eyed peas, chicken broth, and 1 cup water. Add more water, if needed, until the beans are fully covered by the liquid. Stir in the salt, onion powder, garlic powder, adobo seasoning, Cajun seasoning, paprika, Maggi seasoning, black pepper, and pepper flakes and stir to combine.

Add the smoked turkey and turkey leg to the pot. Cover and simmer for 1½ to 2 hours, until the black-eyed peas and the turkey are tender. Remove the smoked turkey and turkey leg from the pot, shred the meat and discard any bones and skin. Return the meat to the pot. Stir to combine and add more salt and pepper to taste.

Serve in bowls with the crispy bacon sprinkled on top and hot sauce, if you like (which you will).

Chef's Kiss: If you prefer a thicker bowl of beans, take out a scoop of beans and mash them with a fork before stirring them back into the pot. For a silkier texture, add more broth as needed. Remember, our ancestors measured with their hearts and eyes! You do you!

Southern-Fried Cabbage with Brussels

Serves 4

This is a classic Southern side that has been in my family for generations. My ancestors used meat and vegetable scraps to create soulful and flavorful dishes like this one, which used sausage and bacon to season the cabbage as it cooked. I swapped the bacon for prosciutto because it adds beauty and vibrancy to this dish. Additions like oregano, onions, garlic, and peppers give depth and bite. Now just because I like this as a side doesn't mean you can't eat it by itself as a meal! All you need on the side is my Honey Butter Corn Bread (page 182).

- 3 tablespoons extra-virgin olive oil
- 8 ounces sliced prosciutto, roughly chopped
- 3 andouille sausages, sliced into ¼-inch rounds (about 2 cups)
- 2 cups shredded green cabbage
- 8 ounces Brussels sprouts, thinly sliced (about 1 cup)
- 1 small red bell pepper, finely diced (about 1 cup)
- 1 tablespoon onion powder
- 1 tablespoon garlic powder
- 1½ teaspoons seasoning salt
- 1 teaspoon dried oregano
- ½ teaspoon kosher salt
- ½ teaspoon ground white pepper

Cook the prosciutto: Line a plate with paper towels and have near the stove. In a large skillet, heat 1 tablespoon of the olive oil over medium heat until hot and shimmering. Add the prosciutto and cook for 3 to 4 minutes, stirring occasionally, until crispy. Use a slotted spoon to transfer the prosciutto to the paper towels, leaving the fat in the pan.

Cook the sausage: In the same skillet, cook the sausage for 5 to 6 minutes, stirring occasionally, until browned on both sides and heated through. Transfer the sausage to the plate with the prosciutto, leaving the fat in the pan.

Cook the vegetables: Add the remaining 2 tablespoons oil to the skillet and heat until hot and shimmering. Add the cabbage, Brussels sprouts, and pepper and stir well to coat the vegetables in oil. Add the onion powder, garlic powder, seasoning salt, oregano, kosher salt, and white pepper. Sauté for 8 to 10 minutes, stirring occasionally, until the vegetables are tender but still have a bit of a bite.

Assemble: Add the cooked sausage and crispy prosciutto to the skillet with the vegetables. Stir for 2 to 3 minutes, until warmed through. Taste and adjust seasonings, if needed.

Serve warm.

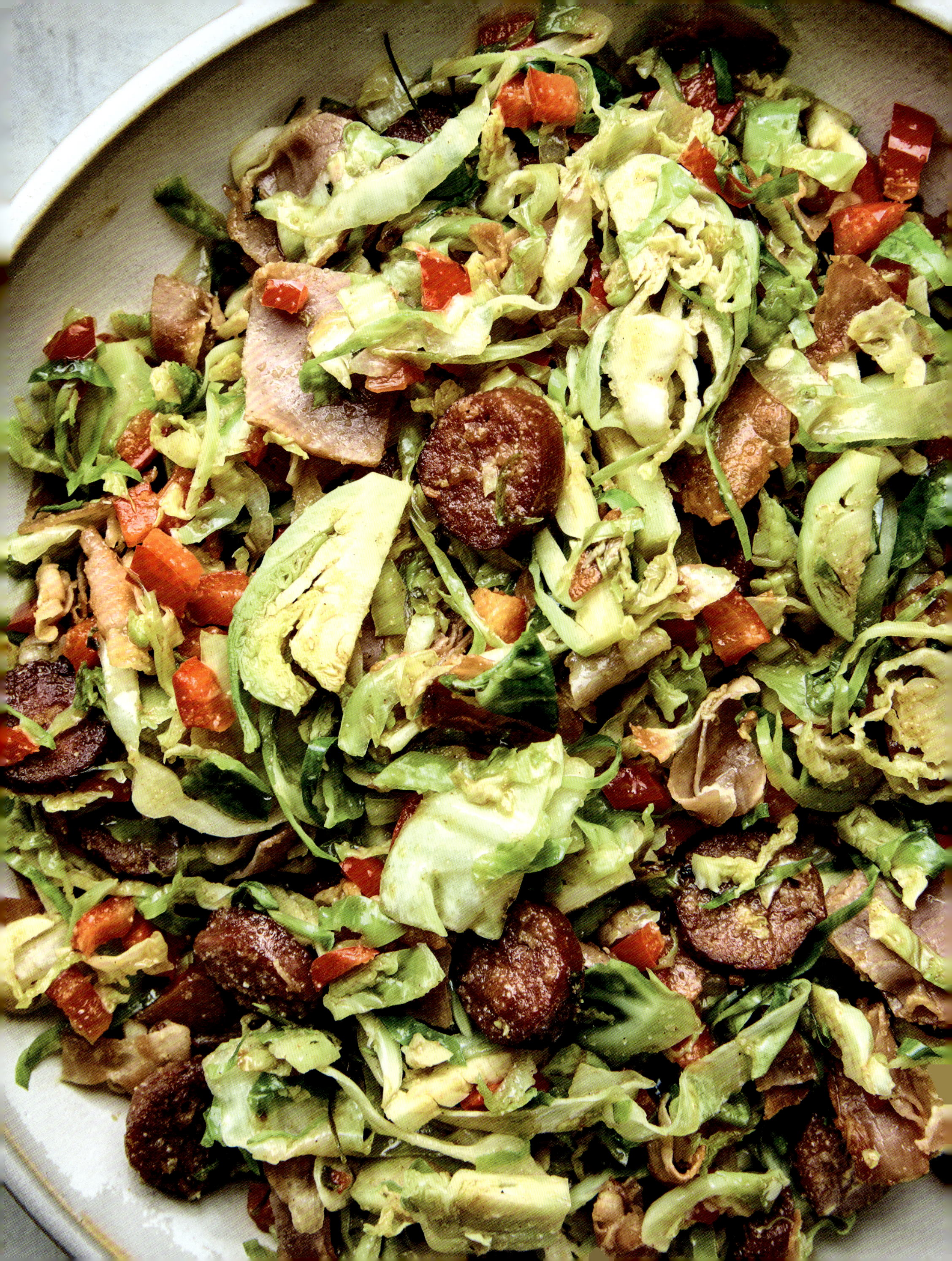

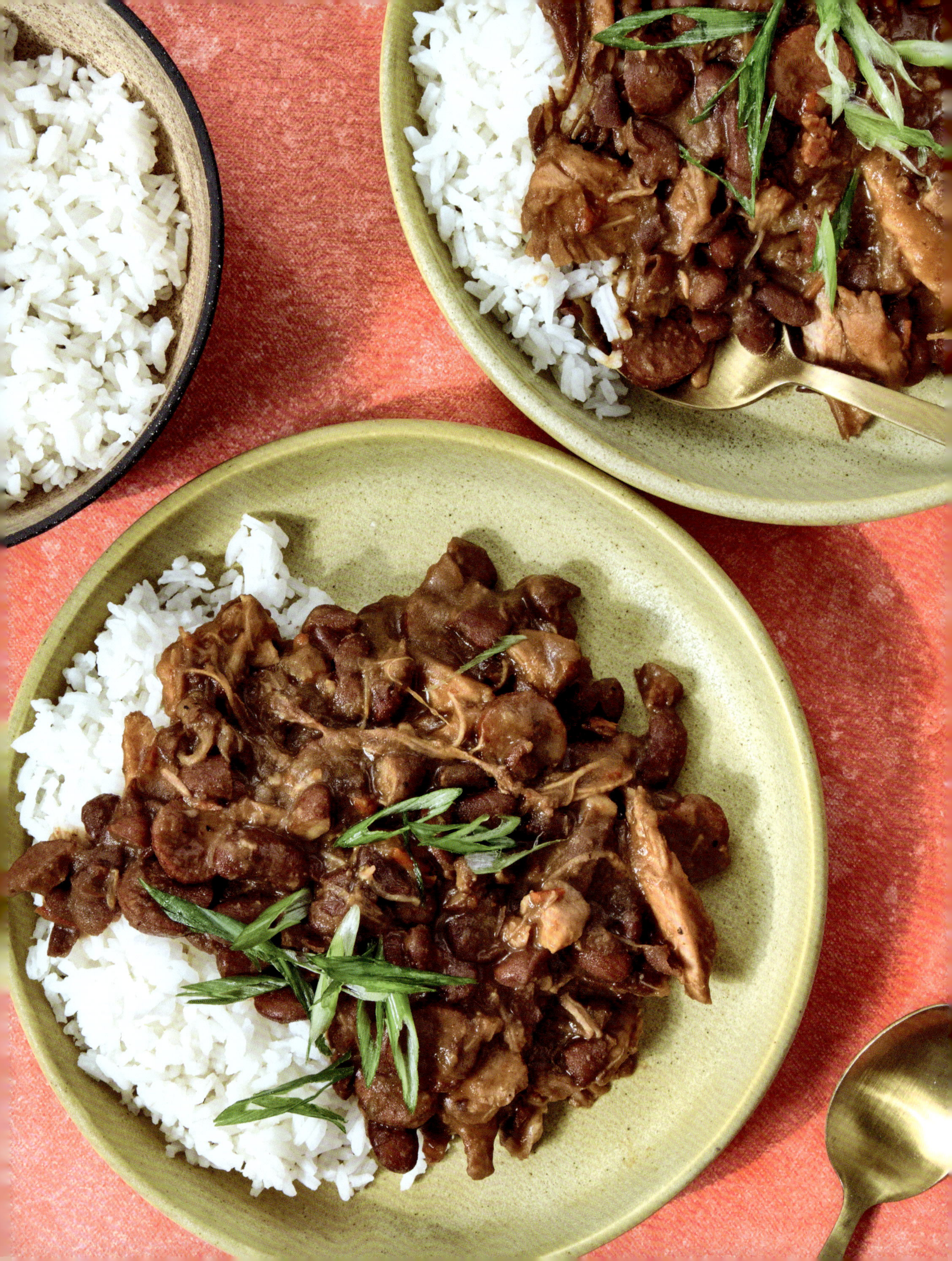

Louisiana Red Beans and Rice

Serves **6 to 8**

I've been perfecting my recipe for red beans and rice for five years. I love making it on Sundays while watching my favorite show of all time, *Insecure*. While the two main characters, Molly and Issa, had their Self-Care Sundays, red beans and rice was mine. I'd prep all my ingredients, get my rice going, and sink into the couch. The smell of the smoked ham and turkey, andouille sausage, and beans slowly cooking away made my home feel warm and cozy. All my Sunday scaries would be gone for the week—plus I ended up with dinner for the next few days. Now that's self-care.

2 tablespoons extra-virgin olive oil
12 ounces andouille sausage, sliced
3 celery stalks, diced (about 1 cup)
1 small red bell pepper, diced (about ½ cup)
1 small green bell pepper, diced (about ½ cup)
½ small yellow onion, diced (about ¼ cup)
3 garlic cloves, minced (about 1 tablespoon)
1 pound dried red kidney beans, soaked overnight, drained, and rinsed
1 pound ham hocks (about 2)
1 pound bone-in smoked turkey (drumsticks, necks, or tails)
1 cup low-sodium chicken broth
2 teaspoons lemon pepper
2 teaspoons no-salt Cajun seasoning
1 teaspoon dried basil
1 teaspoon smoked paprika
1 teaspoon garlic powder
1 teaspoon dried thyme
1 teaspoon onion powder
3 bay leaves
Classic White Rice (page 140)
1 teaspoon kosher salt
½ teaspoon freshly ground black pepper
Sliced scallions or finely chopped fresh parsley, for serving

Cook the sausage: Line a plate with paper towels and have near the stove. In a 5-quart Dutch oven or large pot, heat the olive oil over medium-high heat until hot and shimmering. Add the sausage and cook for 6 to 8 minutes, stirring frequently, until the sausage is browned on both sides. Use a slotted spoon to transfer the sausage to the paper towels, leaving the fat in the pan.

Cook the vegetables: In the same pot, combine the celery, both bell peppers, and onion and sauté for 5 minutes, stirring frequently to incorporate all of the browned bits from the bottom of the pan (this builds flavor), until the vegetables start to soften. Add the minced garlic and cook for 1 to 2 minutes, stirring frequently, until fragrant.

Cook the beans: Add the soaked beans, ham hocks, smoked turkey, chicken broth, lemon pepper, Cajun seasoning, basil, smoked paprika, garlic powder, thyme, onion powder, and bay leaves. Add 4 cups water and return the andouille to the pot. Bring the mixture to a boil. Reduce the heat to low, cover, and simmer for 2 to 3 hours, stirring occasionally, until the beans are tender and creamy. Check the pot while cooking and add more water, if needed, to keep the beans covered.

Cook the rice: About 20 minutes before the beans are done, cook the rice as directed.

Once the beans are cooked, scoop out 1 cup and place them in a large bowl. Mash the beans with a spoon until they are thick and creamy and make a paste, and then return them to the pot. Discard the bay leaves and remove the ham hocks and turkey. Shred the meat, then discard the bones and skin. Add the shredded meat to the pot and stir in the salt and black pepper.

Serve the cooked beans over the warm rice and sprinkle with sliced scallions.

Little Detail, BIG Impact: While I recommend soaking the beans overnight, you can also quick-soak your beans the day of. In a large pot, combine 6 cups water and the dried beans and bring to a rapid boil over high heat. Boil for 3 to 5 minutes, remove from the heat, and cover for 1 hour. Then drain and begin the recipe steps.

Chef's Kiss: I love using turkey, ham hock, and sausage, but use what meats you like most—I've also used bacon, Italian sausage, and even cubed-up pork chops.

Family Style

Sausage and Gravy Biscuit Bake

Serves 8

This is the kind of big family-style breakfast that everyone will devour. My take on biscuits and gravy is easier and lighter thanks to the ultimate cheat code: canned biscuits, which bake up fluffier than homemade. But let me tell you, the sauce? That's where the magic happens. It's savory, creamy, cheesy, and loaded with spices—it clings to the biscuits and soaks into every bite.

When you cut into the bake, the gravy spills over the sides, seeping into the fluffy biscuits and packing every bite with flavor. It's hearty enough to kickstart the day but still light enough to keep you feeling good. Perfect for breakfast or dinner when you need something easy and delicious but want it to taste like you went all out.

Sausage Gravy

- 2 tablespoons extra-virgin olive oil
- 24 ounces breakfast sausage links, casings removed
- 3 cups heavy cream
- 3 ounces sharp Cheddar cheese, freshly shredded (about ⅔ cup)
- 1 teaspoon sweet paprika
- 1 teaspoon ground white pepper
- 1 teaspoon dried oregano
- 1 teaspoon garlic powder
- 1 teaspoon onion powder

Biscuit Bake

- Softened butter, for the baking dish
- 8 large eggs
- ½ cup whole milk
- 1 teaspoon kosher salt
- 1 (16.3-ounce) can buttermilk biscuits
- 8 ounces sharp Cheddar cheese, freshly shredded (2 cups)
- Chopped fresh chives or fresh parsley, for serving

Preheat the oven to 375°F.

Make the sausage gravy: In a large skillet, heat the oil over medium-high heat until hot and shimmering. Crumble the sausage into the skillet and cook for 6 to 8 minutes, breaking it up with a spoon as it cooks and stirring frequently, until the sausage is browned and cooked through.

Reduce the heat to medium and add the heavy cream, Cheddar, paprika, white pepper, oregano, garlic powder, and onion powder. Cook for 3 to 4 minutes, stirring occasionally, until the sauce thickens and reaches your desired consistency. Remove from the heat and set aside.

Assemble: Grease a 9 × 13-inch baking dish with butter. In a large bowl, whisk together the eggs, milk, and salt until well combined. Set aside.

Open the can of biscuit dough and separate the biscuits. Cut each biscuit into quarters. Spread the biscuit pieces evenly across the bottom of the prepared baking dish. Pour the egg mixture over the biscuit dough. Sprinkle half of the Cheddar over the top of the eggs and biscuits. Spread half of the sausage gravy over the biscuits and eggs, then sprinkle the remaining Cheddar on top. Cover and set the remaining sausage gravy aside.

Bake the dish: Bake for 35 to 40 minutes, until the top is golden brown and the eggs are set. Remove from the oven and cool for 5 minutes. While the biscuit bake cools, heat the reserved sausage gravy over low heat until warm.

Cut the bake into squares and serve with the warmed sausage gravy and chopped chives or parsley sprinkled over the top.

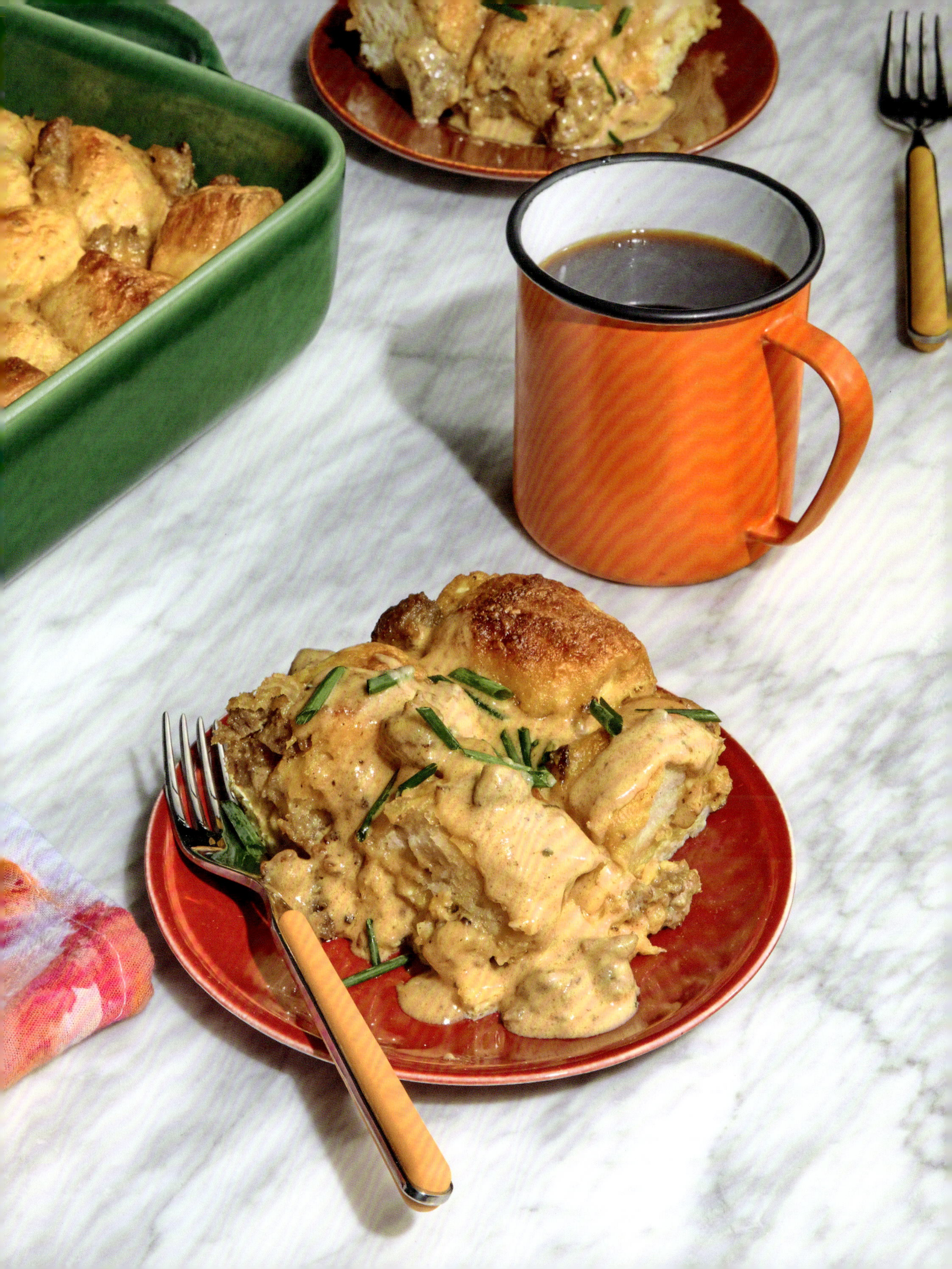

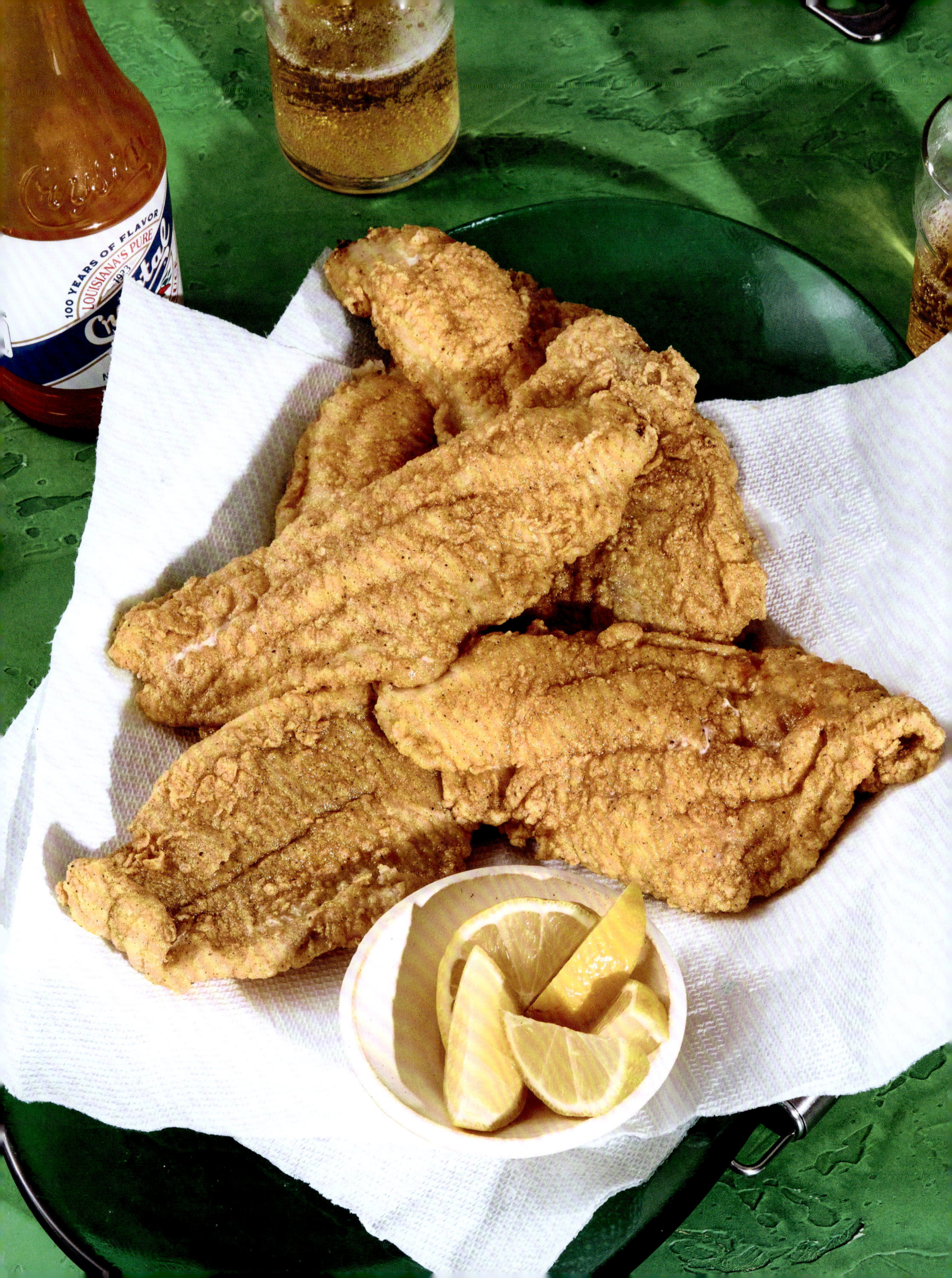
100 YEARS OF FLAVOR
LOUISIANA'S PURE

Down South–Style Fried Fish

Serves 4

When Dad got paid on Fridays, it meant one thing: We were heading to the Junction to pick up fresh fish. That fish spot was a neighborhood staple, always packed on Fridays with people shouting their orders. We'd grab our ticket, snack on crunchy fried crab sticks, and wait our turn. When it was time, we'd call out, "One pound of whiting, a pound of catfish!"—it was the highlight of my week. We'd pick up some Louisiana fish fry mix, head home, and get to work. The house would fill with the smell of crispy and crunchy fried fish, and family would come through. Those Friday nights were everything to me as a kid—family, tradition, and that end-of-week feeling that nothing could top.

6 cups vegetable oil, as needed, for frying

Catfish

3 pounds catfish fillets, cut into 8 pieces total
2 large eggs, beaten
2 tablespoons yellow mustard
1 tablespoon hot sauce
1 tablespoon Old Bay seasoning
1 teaspoon kosher salt

Dredge

1⅓ cups all-purpose flour
1 cup unseasoned fish fry mix, such as Louisiana Classic Fry
2 tablespoons cornstarch
2 teaspoons Old Bay seasoning
1 teaspoon sweet paprika
1 teaspoon kosher salt

Hot sauce, for serving (I like Crystal)
Lemon wedges, for serving

Pour 6 cups oil into a Dutch oven and heat to 350°F. Line a plate with paper towels.

Marinate the catfish: Pat the catfish dry with a paper towel. In a large bowl, combine the catfish fillets, eggs, mustard, hot sauce, Old Bay, and salt. Mix well to coat the fish all over. Marinate for 15 minutes.

Make the dredge: In a large bowl, whisk together the flour, fish fry, cornstarch, Old Bay, paprika, and salt.

Fry the fish: Dredge the marinated catfish pieces in the flour mixture, tossing to coat all over on both sides, shaking off any excess. Working in batches to avoid overcrowding, use tongs to carefully place the catfish in the hot oil and fry for 6 to 8 minutes, turning once, until golden brown and cooked through and fried hard. Use tongs to transfer to the paper towels to drain.

Serve the fried catfish hot with hot sauce and lemon wedges.

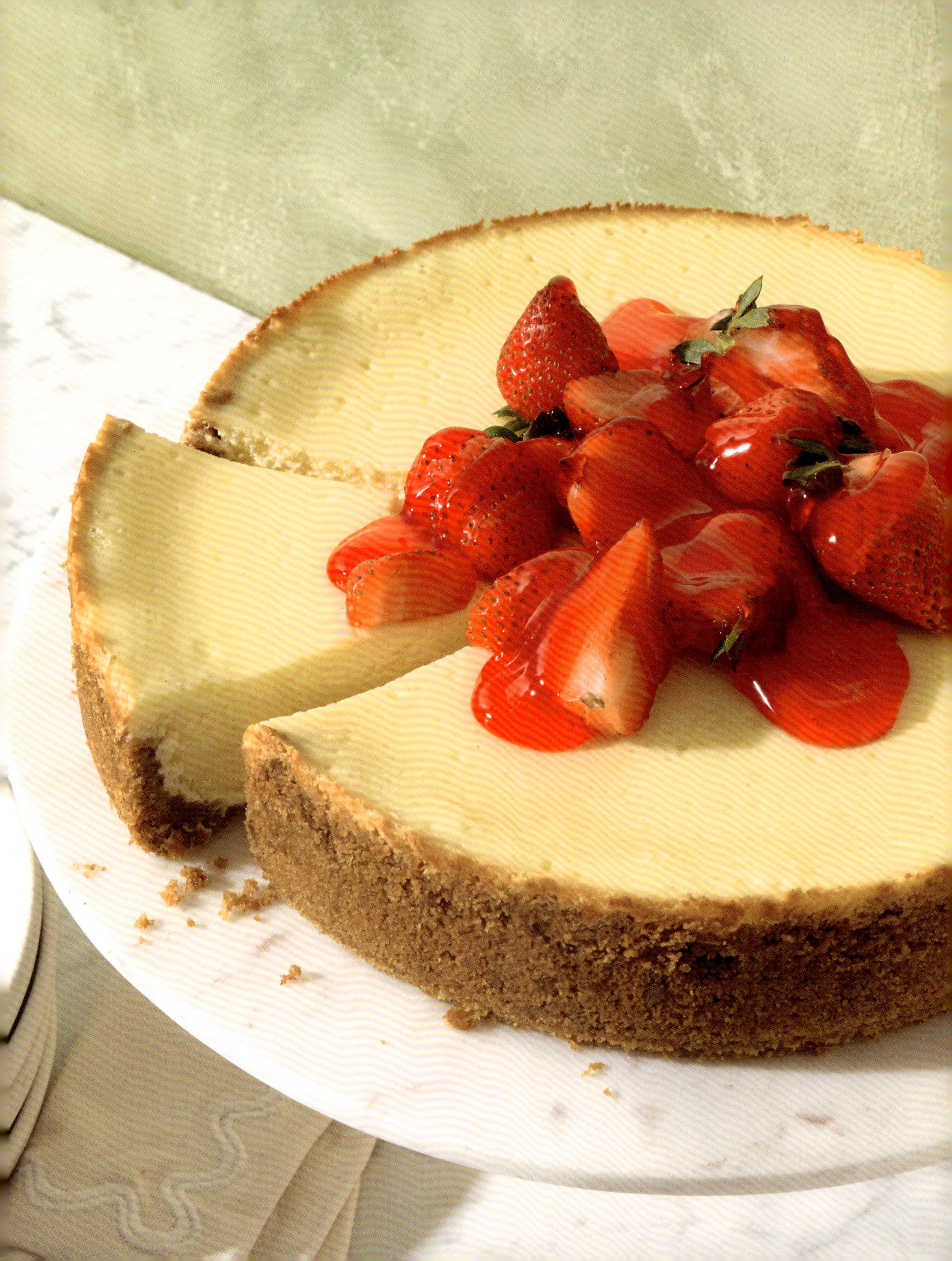

7

Life Is Sweet

Desserts of course usually come at the end of a meal, and symbolically, they remind us that there's always something sweet waiting on the other side of whatever we're going through. They're like a promise—that no matter how hard the day's been, there's a moment of joy ahead. For me, baking became that moment, especially when life got heavy.

When I was ten years old, I found out my mom had fallen into substance abuse. She had stopped coming around, so we knew something was up, but when it was confirmed, my dad and I didn't say a word. There was nothing to say. So, we baked cookies—week after week. The smell of those cookies rising in the oven filled the silence, giving us something to hold onto when everything else felt like too much. Then there was a breakup that shook me to my core. I coped by going to the farmers' market to get fresh peaches for cobbler, only to find out that using canned was easier, tasted better, and gave the perfect texture. That cobbler became my go-to comfort during that time. And when I moved to Miami, leaving everything behind, there was no furniture, no TV, just an empty house. The first thing I did was pull limes from the backyard and make a Key lime pie. Sitting on the floor, eating that pie in my new space, was a quiet reminder that "everything's good."

Baking has taught me a lot about life. You have to take your time, be intentional, and accept that not everything will come out perfect—and that's okay. The process matters just as much as the result. That's what these desserts are about: finding sweetness even in the rough moments.

The desserts in this chapter are approachable, no matter your skill level. They're simple, classic, and confidence-boosting—perfect starter recipes that anyone can master. My biscuit-topped peach cobbler is warm, buttery, and golden, while the Oreo tres leches is creamy and indulgent. The tart Key lime pie is refreshing, and my famous banana pudding is a no-fuss favorite. Every one of these desserts pairs perfectly with a scoop of vanilla ice cream, and makes enough to last a few days, so you can keep coming back to that sweetness. These aren't just recipes—they're lessons in slowing down, finding comfort, and making something beautiful from simple ingredients.

Strawberries and Cream Croissant Bake

Serves 8 to 10

It's the dishes that get the oohs and aahs for me. You know, the ones that have everyone grabbing their phones for a pic because they're just that beautiful? Yeah, this croissant bake is one of those. The secret to making it perfect is stale croissants. Those leftovers from that Costco haul are ideal. They soak up the rich, creamy custard and bake into a warm, fluffy masterpiece.

What really sets this dish off is the combo of sweet cream cheese and macerated strawberries. The cream cheese gives it this luscious, velvety texture, while the strawberries bring a bright, sweet-tart flavor that cuts through the richness. It's the perfect balance of creamy, fruity, and just a little bit crispy on the edges. This is one of those "do you" recipes—throw in your favorite berries, toss on some slivered almonds if you like, and make it your own.

Strawberries

1 pound fresh strawberries, hulled and halved if small or quartered if large
¼ cup granulated sugar
1 tablespoon orange liqueur (optional)
1 teaspoon kosher salt

Croissant Bake

Softened unsalted butter, for the pan
12 stale croissants, the older the better (I'm talking hard croissants here!)
6 large eggs
½ cup whole milk
2 tablespoons dark brown sugar
1 tablespoon granulated sugar
1 teaspoon vanilla extract
Pinch of kosher salt
8 ounces cream cheese (1 block), at room temperature
Melted unsalted butter (optional), for brushing

Macerate the strawberries: In a small bowl, combine the strawberries, granulated sugar, orange liqueur (if using), and salt. Toss to coat the strawberries all over. Let it sit at room temperature, stirring occasionally, while you preheat the oven and prepare the rest of the recipe, about 30 minutes.

Assemble and bake: Preheat the oven to 350°F. Butter a 9 × 13-inch baking dish.

Cut 8 croissants in half crosswise (cutting them into big pieces, not in half like a sandwich) and leave 4 whole. In a large bowl, whisk together the eggs, milk, brown sugar, granulated sugar, vanilla, and salt until combined. Add the croissants to the bowl a few at a time, stirring and letting them sit for about 15 seconds to absorb some of the liquid. Lift each croissant from the mixture and transfer to the prepared baking dish, arranging the whole croissants first, top-side up, and repeating until all of the croissants are soaked and in the pan, filling in the gaps with the cut croissants and squishing them to fit, if needed.

Stir the macerated strawberries and scatter them over the croissants with any juices from the bowl, tucking a few into the spaces between the croissants. Dollop the cream cheese evenly over the top and drizzle any remaining egg mixture over the croissants. Bake for 20 to 25 minutes, until the strawberries are deeply roasted and the croissants in the center of the dish feel firm to the touch.

Remove from the oven, cut into squares, and serve immediately.

Little Detail, BIG Impact: To make sure your custard gets soaked up, grab that filled baking dish and gently tilt it side to side, letting any extra custard move around and absorb into the bread. The goal is less liquid sitting at the bottom. The more it's soaked into the croissants, the better.

Chef's Kiss: For a golden glow like in this photograph, brush the tops of the croissants with melted butter, but this is optional.

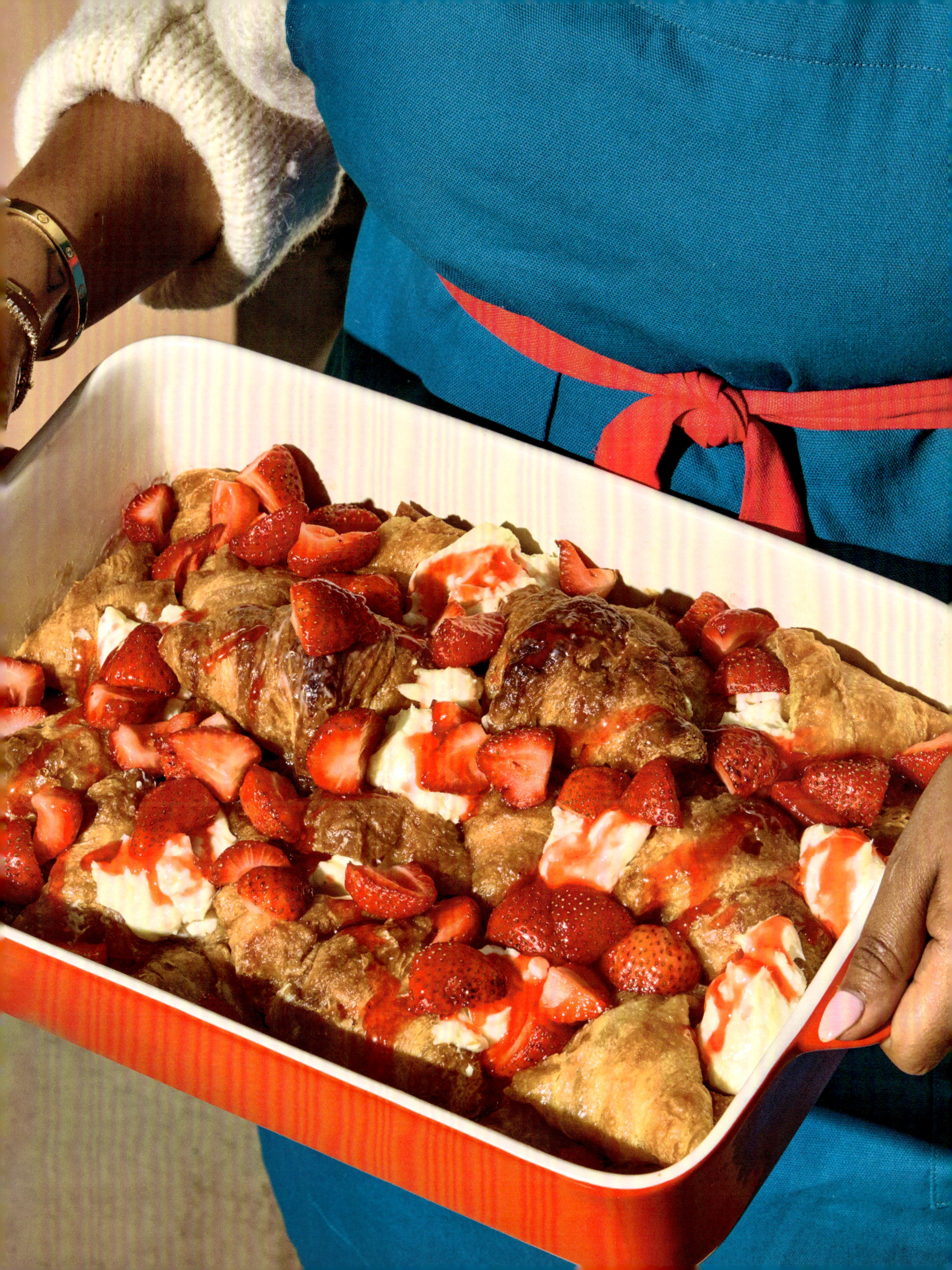

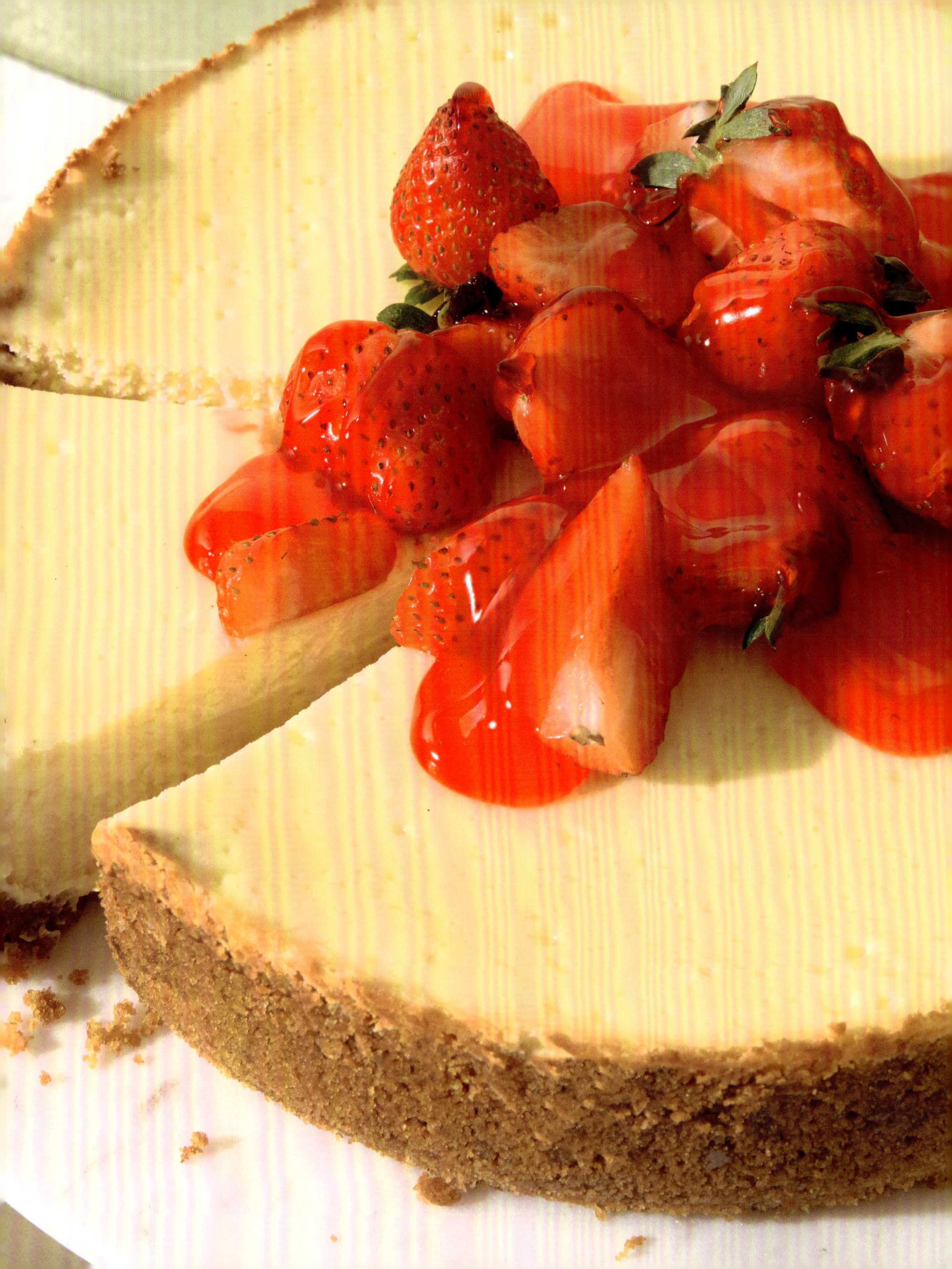

Classic New York–Style Cheesecake

Serves 8

I made it my mission to create a cheesecake recipe that anyone can pull off—from someone who's never turned on an oven to a seasoned baker. No water bath. Yep, you heard me right. Water baths are a pain, and while some claim it's the key to a creamy cheesecake, to me, it's risky. One wrong move and water leaks into the pan, leaving you with a mushy cake that just doesn't set. In this recipe, we play it safe, with a thick, creamy batter, a crust that rises up the sides, and a cake that bakes low and slow. Simple, foolproof, and still gives you that rich, dreamy cheesecake we all love.

Crust
- 9 graham cracker sheets (1 sleeve)
- ⅓ cup packed dark brown sugar
- 5 tablespoons (2½ ounces) unsalted butter, melted
- Kosher salt

Filling
- 24 ounces cream cheese (3 blocks), at room temperature
- ½ cup sour cream, at room temperature
- 2 teaspoons vanilla extract
- ¼ teaspoon kosher salt
- 1½ cups granulated sugar
- 5 large eggs, at room temperature

Chef's Kiss: For a fresh topping, macerate sliced strawberries with sugar and a splash of lemon juice until they release their juices, then spoon them over the cheesecake before serving. For a homemade strawberry filling, cook chopped strawberries with sugar and a bit of lemon juice until thick and jammy, let it cool, then swirl it into the batter before baking or layer it between the crust and filling for a rich, fruity bite.

Position a rack in the center of the oven and preheat to 400°F.

Make the crust: Place the graham crackers in a large resealable bag. Seal the bag securely, pressing out all of the air. Use a rolling pin or the bottom of a heavy glass to crush the graham crackers into fine crumbs (you should have about 1½ cups). Add them to a large bowl along with the brown sugar, melted butter, and a pinch of salt. Mix to combine, until the graham crackers are the consistency of wet sand.

Pour the mixture into the bottom of an 8-inch springform pan. Using a measuring cup or the bottom of a glass, compact the crumbs onto the bottom of the pan, pushing the crumbs 3 inches up the sides of the pan. Freeze until firm, about 15 minutes, while you prepare the filling.

Make the filling: In a large bowl using a hand mixer (or in a stand mixer fitted with the paddle attachment), beat the cream cheese, sour cream, vanilla, and salt on medium speed for 2 minutes, until fluffy. Slowly pour in the granulated sugar and mix for 2 minutes, until combined.

Reduce the speed to low and add the eggs, one by one, waiting until each egg is fully incorporated before adding the next.

Transfer the filling to the springform pan, and holding tightly with both hands, tap the pan straight down on the counter very firmly a few times to release any air bubbles in the batter.

Bake the cheesecake: Put the pan on the center rack and bake until the sides begin to puff up, about 10 minutes. Reduce the oven temperature to 225°F and bake for 1 hour 20 minutes, until set around the edges but still slightly wobbly in the center. (Yes, the temperature is correct, as this is a no-water-bath recipe, so it cooks low and slow.)

Shut off the oven and prop the door open with a wooden spoon. Let the cheesecake cool in the oven for 1 hour, then transfer to a wire rack to cool completely, about 2 more hours.

Once cool, run a knife or offset spatula along the inside edge of the pan, remove the side band from the pan, then refrigerate the cheesecake for at least 4 hours or ideally overnight.

Use a knife dipped in hot water and wiped dry to cut picture-perfect slices!

Brioche Bread Pudding

Serves 10

Every home cook needs a solid bread pudding recipe because it's a versatile dish for sharing. This one is inspired by the famous Antique Bakery in Hoboken, New Jersey—a small spot known for its brick-oven bread pudding that people literally line up for. This version is crunchy, creamy, sweet, and melts in your mouth—just like at the bakery but with two twists: rum and sweetened condensed milk. Also, instead of the usual stale bread, I use brioche and toast it until it's crouton-like so it soaks up the custard without getting soggy. The sweetened condensed milk makes the custard extra rich and thick. Baking it at a little hotter temperature than usual gives you that golden caramelized top with a soft, indulgent center. I had to include my rum sauce—but feel free to skip the rum if you're keeping it alcohol-free. This cozy, comforting bread pudding is the ultimate "cafecito" dessert, with the perfect balance of sweet and savory.

Bread Pudding

- 2 (14-ounce) loaves brioche, cut into 1½-inch cubes
- 1½ cups whole milk
- 4 large eggs
- 1 (14-ounce) can sweetened condensed milk
- 1 teaspoon vanilla extract
- ½ teaspoon ground cinnamon

Rum Sauce

- 4 tablespoons (½ stick/2 ounces) unsalted butter
- 2 cups heavy cream
- ¾ cup packed dark brown sugar
- 2 tablespoons rum (optional; I use Bacardi Gold)
- ¼ teaspoon kosher salt

Powdered sugar, for serving
Whipped cream, for serving

Preheat the oven to 375°F.

Toast the brioche for the bread pudding: Place the brioche cubes in a single layer on a baking sheet. Bake for 15 minutes, tossing once halfway through, until toasted and golden brown. Leave the oven on.

Meanwhile, make the custard: In a large bowl, whisk together the milk, eggs, sweetened condensed milk, vanilla, and cinnamon until smooth and fully combined.

Assemble: Place half of the toasted brioche cubes in a 9 × 13-inch baking dish, spreading out the pieces evenly. Slowly pour the custard over the bread, ½ cup at a time, to allow the bread to soak up the custard. Press down gently on the bread pieces to ensure they are soaked with custard. Add the remaining toasted bread cubes on top and pour the remaining custard over the bread, pressing down gently to ensure the bread is soaked. Let the mixture sit for 10 minutes, pressing down occasionally to saturate the bread.

Bake for 45 to 50 minutes, until the top is golden brown and the custard is set.

Meanwhile, make the rum sauce: In a medium saucepan, melt the butter over medium-high heat. Whisk in the heavy cream, brown sugar, rum (if using), and salt. Bring the mixture to a simmer, then reduce the heat to low and cook for 10 minutes, whisking constantly, until thickened.

Remove the bread pudding from the oven and let it cool for 10 minutes. Serve warm or at room temperature with a drizzle of the rum sauce, a dusting of powdered sugar, and a dollop of whipped cream. Store any leftover sauce in the fridge for up to 5 days and pour over pancakes or ice cream, or mix into iced coffee.

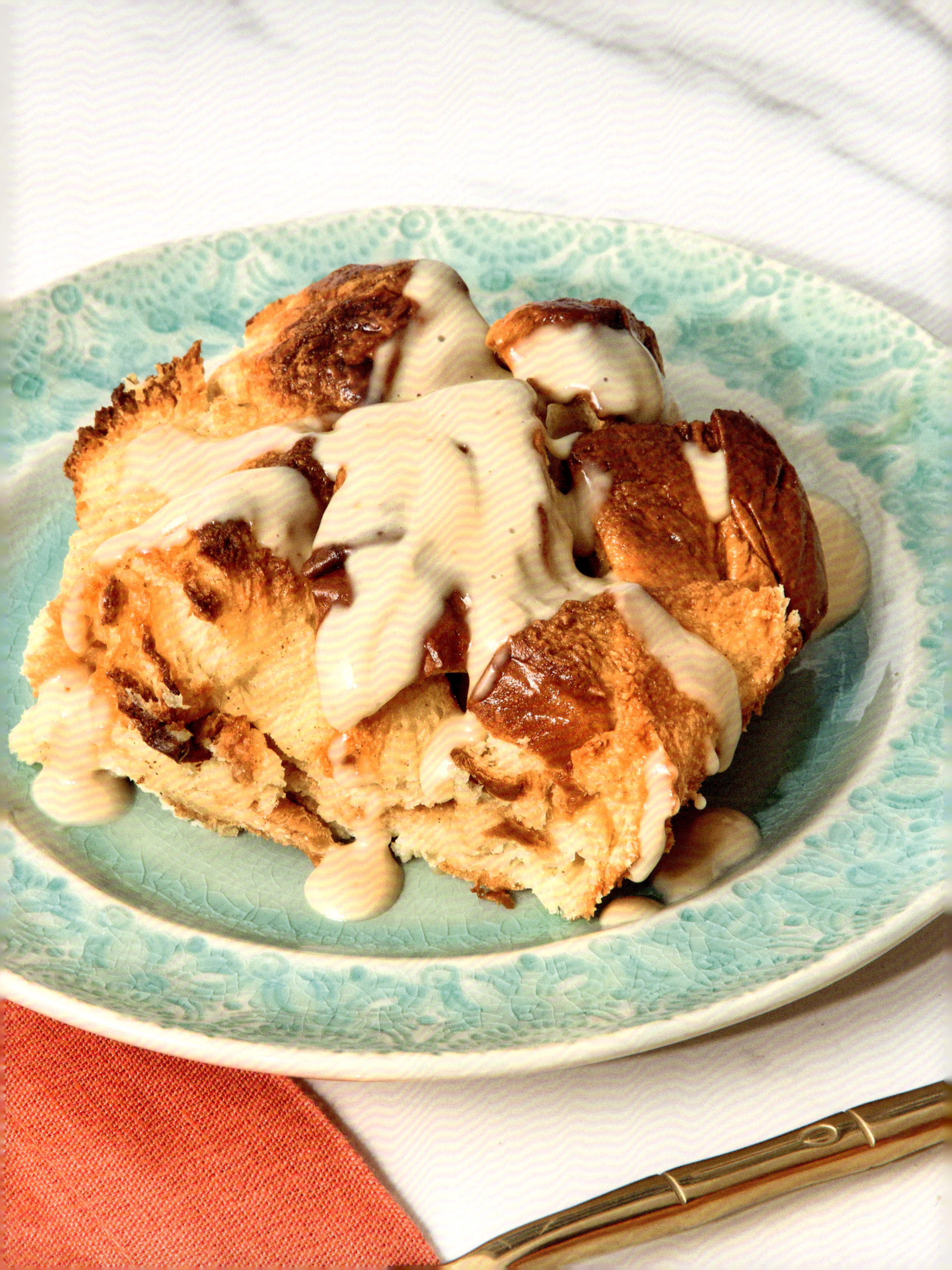

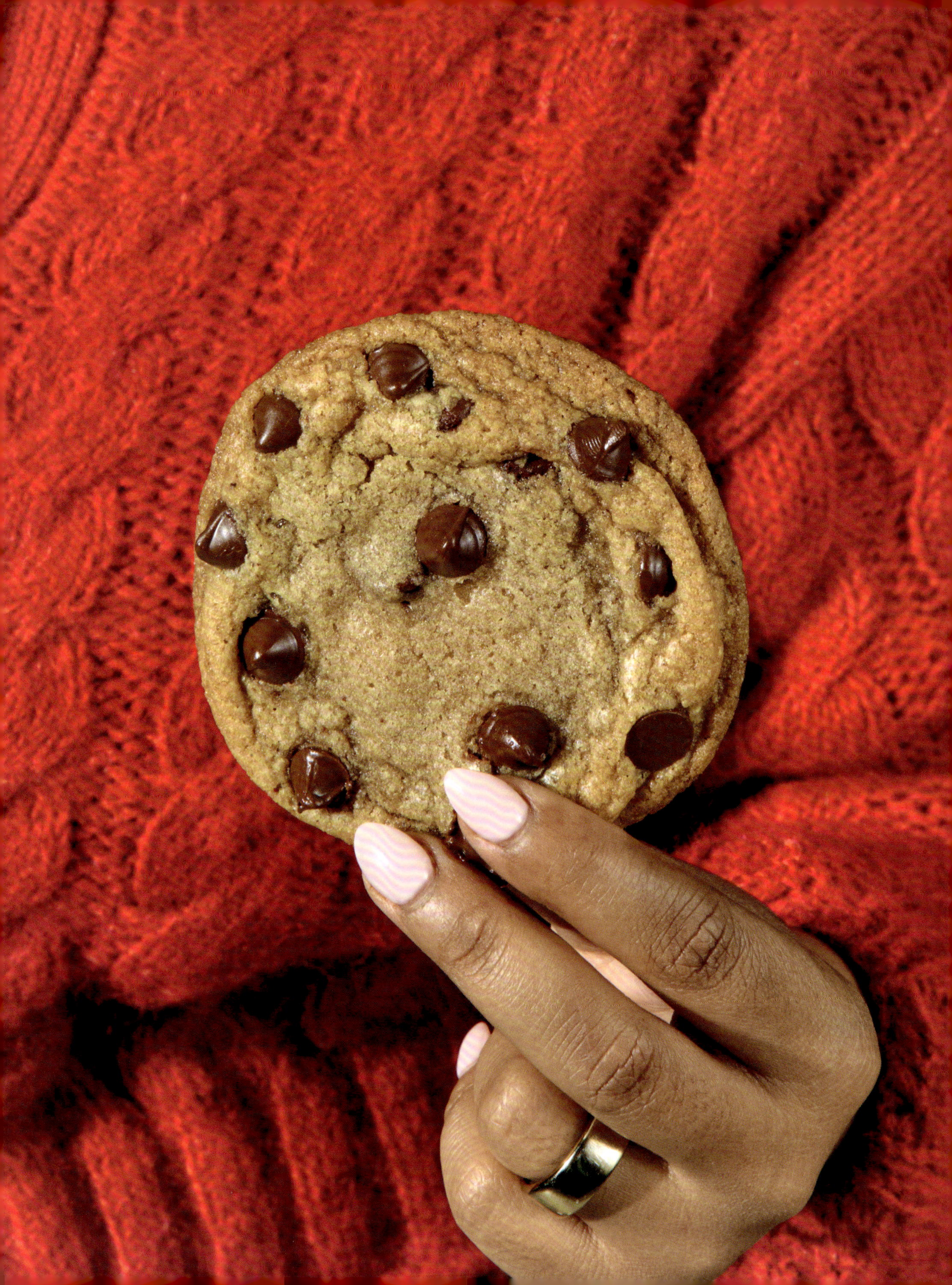

Brown Butter Chocolate Chip Cookies

Makes
24
cookies

Yes, this recipe makes two dozen cookies. Yes, they'll probably disappear faster than you can blink. And yes, they're easy to make, chocolaty, crispy, and jumbo-size! Of course, I'll share my secrets. I *had* to add brown butter because it just takes the flavor to another level. Nonnegotiable. I bake these cookies every Friday, like clockwork. It's a ritual.

8 ounces (2 sticks) unsalted butter
1 tablespoon heavy cream
2 cups all-purpose flour
1 teaspoon baking soda
¼ teaspoon kosher salt
¾ cup granulated sugar
¾ cup packed dark brown sugar
2 large eggs, at room temperature
2 teaspoons vanilla extract
1 cup semisweet chocolate chips

Brown the butter: In a medium saucepan, melt the butter over medium heat. Cook for 5 to 7 minutes, scraping the bottom of the pan occasionally with a spatula to prevent burning, until the butter begins to foam, then turns golden brown and develops a nutty aroma. Be careful not to burn the butter.

Remove the browned butter from the heat and immediately stir in the heavy cream. This prevents the butter from browning further. Transfer the mixture to a heatproof medium bowl and let it cool for 20 minutes, until it reaches room temperature.

Make the cookie dough: In a medium bowl, whisk together the flour, baking soda, and salt. Set aside.

In a large bowl using a hand mixer (or in a stand mixer fitted with the paddle attachment), combine the cooled brown butter (making sure to scrape out all of the browned bits), granulated sugar, and brown sugar. Beat on medium speed for 3 to 5 minutes, until the mixture is smooth and creamy.

Add the eggs, one at a time, beating well after each addition. Add the vanilla and mix until combined. Gradually add the flour mixture to the wet ingredients, mixing on low speed, scraping down the bowl as needed, until just combined. Fold in the chocolate chips.

Cover the bowl with plastic wrap and refrigerate the dough for at least 30 minutes and up to 1 hour. Chilling the dough helps to enhance the flavor and prevents the cookies from spreading too much when baking.

Bake the cookies: Preheat the oven to 350°F. Line a baking sheet with parchment paper.

Scoop about 1½ tablespoons of dough for each cookie and roll into balls. Place them on the prepared baking sheet, spacing them about 2 inches apart.

Bake for 10 to 12 minutes, until the edges are golden brown but the centers are still soft. The cookies will continue to cook slightly on the hot baking sheet. Cool the cookies on the baking sheet for 5 minutes, then transfer them to a wire rack to cool completely. Repeat with the remaining cookie dough.

Little Detail, BIG Impact: Once you transfer your cookies to the rack, let them cool on the rack for at least 10 minutes (even if it's tough to wait) before digging in. Crispy cookies need that time to set, and trust me, it's worth it!

Biscuit-Top Peach Cobbler

Serves 8

For the most part when it comes to my cooking, I live by the rule that "fresh is best." So when it came time to develop a peach cobbler recipe, I was adamant—the peaches *had* to be fresh. But after testing it over and over, it just wasn't giving what I thought it would. So, I decided to try canned peaches, totally against my original plan—and let me tell you, it totally turned my recipe around. Here's why: First, canned peaches are available all year round, unlike fresh ones, which can be tricky to find when it's not summer. Second, they're sweeter and soaked in syrup, making it way easier to get that thick, luscious filling. And let's be honest, they're easier; no peeling! That alone is a game changer. I also knew I wanted a biscuit topping, not a cakey one, because peach cobbler is one of those desserts I'll double up on and call "dinner" on those *whew* days. Serve it with a big scoop of ice cream, and trust me, this one's a keeper.

Peach Filling

2 (29-ounce) cans sliced peaches in light syrup, drained (reserve ½ cup of the liquid)
½ cup granulated sugar
1 teaspoon vanilla extract
1 teaspoon ground cinnamon
2 tablespoons cornstarch

Biscuit Topping

2 cups all-purpose flour
½ cup packed dark brown sugar
2½ teaspoons baking powder
½ teaspoon kosher salt
12 tablespoons (1½ sticks/6 ounces) unsalted butter, cubed
1 cup plus 2 tablespoons heavy cream
1 teaspoon vanilla extract

Vanilla ice cream, for serving

Preheat the oven to 375°F.

Make the peach filling: In a large bowl, stir together the peaches, granulated sugar, vanilla, and cinnamon. In a small bowl, whisk together the cornstarch and 2 tablespoons of the reserved peach liquid until smooth to create a slurry. Stir the slurry back into the remaining peach liquid. Stir gently to combine. Pour the liquid mixture into the peaches and stir to incorporate.

Spread the peach mixture in the bottom of a 9 × 13-inch baking dish.

Make the biscuit topping: In another large bowl, whisk together the flour, brown sugar, baking powder, and salt. Add the butter to the flour mixture. Use a pastry cutter or your fingers to cut the butter into the flour until the mixture resembles coarse crumbs.

In another large bowl, whisk together the heavy cream and vanilla. Pour this into the dry ingredients and stir until just combined. Be careful not to overmix; the dough should be slightly sticky and lumpy.

Assemble the cobbler: Drop spoonfuls of the biscuit topping evenly over the peach filling in the baking dish. The dough will spread as it bakes, so it's okay if the peaches are not completely covered.

Bake the cobbler for 40 to 45 minutes, until the biscuit topping is golden brown and the peach filling is bubbling. Cool for 5 minutes, then serve warm with a scoop of vanilla ice cream.

Chef's Kiss: Y'all know I love that extra va-va-voom and my honey butter trick? Yeah, it works here too. You know the drill—2 tablespoons honey plus 2 tablespoons melted unsalted butter, mixed and brushed on right before serving. Trust me, it's the perfect finishing touch!

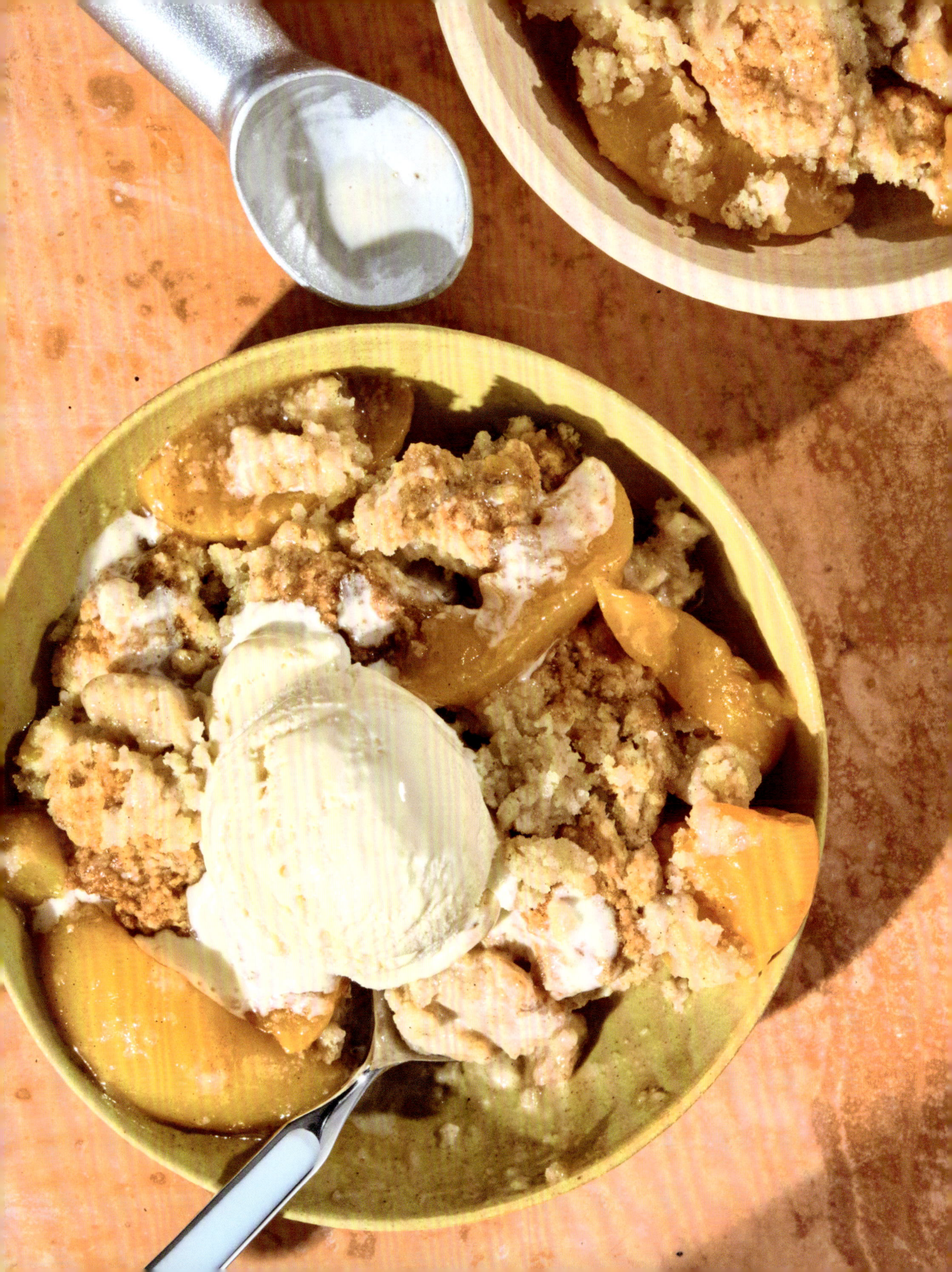

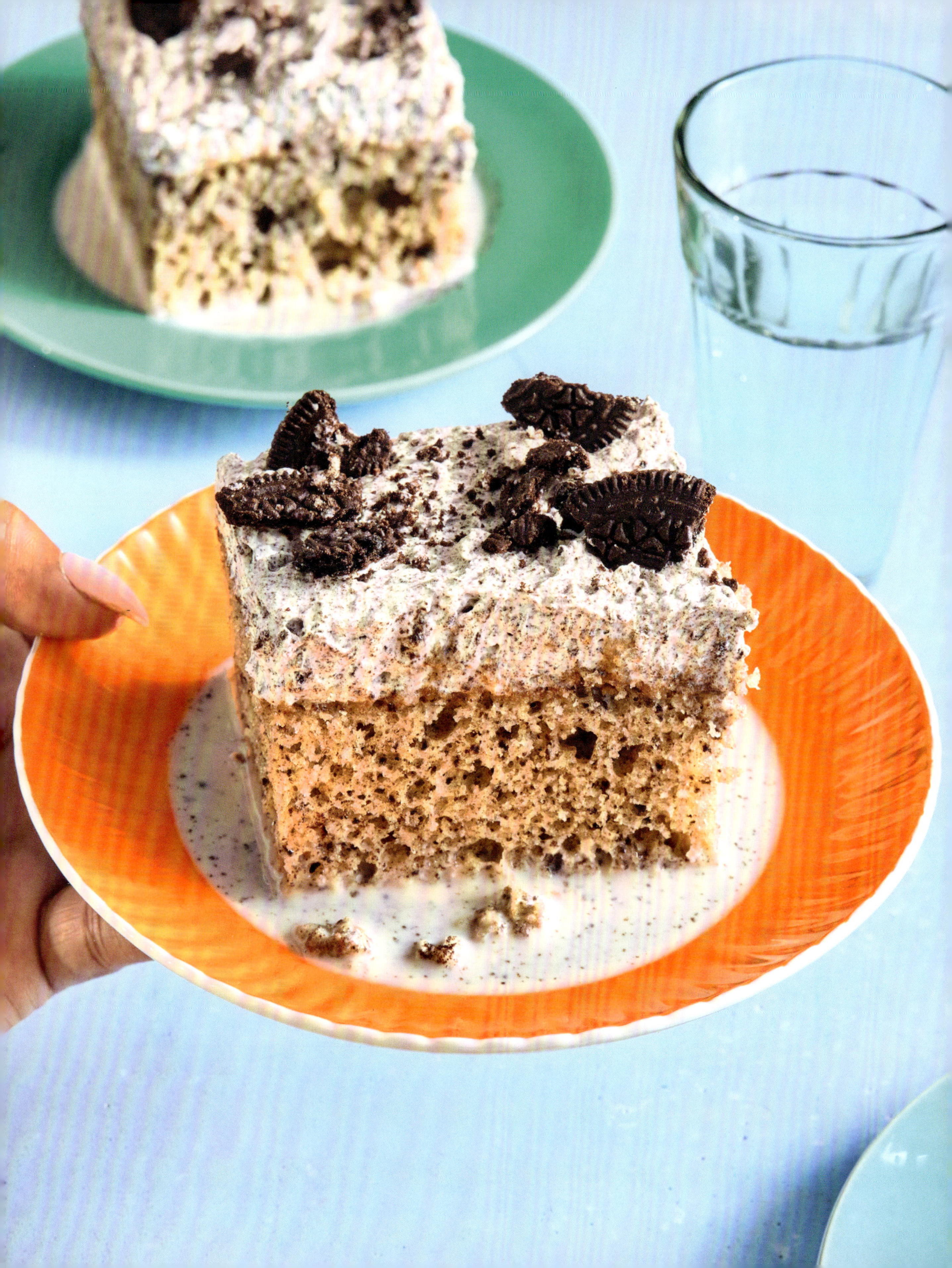

Cookies and Cream Tres Leches

Serves 12

My cooking style leans heavily on homemade because I truly believe from-scratch is usually best. But, as with any rule, there are always exceptions—and this twist on tres leches cake is one of them. Hooking up a boxed cake mix is an easy cheat code that even I couldn't resist. Plus, this comes out creamy, sweet, and insanely delicious with minimal effort. Most people have had traditional tres leches, but trust me, bring this Oreo-spiked version anywhere, and watch people's eyes pop. It's a real showstopper.

Softened butter, for the pan
30 whole Oreos, plus more broken in pieces for decorating
1 (13.25-ounce) box yellow cake mix
1¾ cups whole milk
½ cup vegetable oil
3 large eggs
1 (14-ounce) can sweetened condensed milk
1 cup evaporated milk
1 cup heavy cream
2 tablespoons powdered sugar
1 teaspoon vanilla extract

Preheat the oven to 350°F. Grease a 9 × 13-inch baking pan with butter.

Crush the Oreos: Place the Oreos in a large resealable plastic bag. Seal the bag securely, pressing out all the air. Use a rolling pin or the bottom of a heavy glass to crush the Oreos into fine crumbs. Set aside.

Bake the cake: In a large bowl, combine the yellow cake mix, ¾ cup of the milk, the oil, and eggs. Stir vigorously for 2 minutes, until well combined. Fold ½ cup of the crushed Oreos into the batter until incorporated.

Pour the cake batter into the prepared pan and bake according to the package directions, usually 28 to 30 minutes. Remove the cake from the oven and let it cool in the pan for 30 minutes.

Make the soak: In a large bowl, whisk together the remaining 1 cup milk, the sweetened condensed milk, evaporated milk, and ½ cup crushed Oreos.

Use a fork to poke holes all over the top of the cake. Slowly pour the milk mixture over the cake, allowing it to soak into the holes. Cover the cake with plastic wrap and refrigerate for at least 4 hours or up to overnight, to allow the cake to absorb the milk mixture.

Make the whipped cream: When you're ready to serve, in a large bowl, using a hand mixer (or in a stand mixer fitted with the whisk attachment), whisk the heavy cream, powdered sugar, and vanilla on medium-high speed for 2 to 3 minutes, until soft peaks form. Fold the remaining crushed Oreos into the whipped cream.

Spread the whipped cream over the top of the cake. Decorate with broken Oreos. Serve cold.

The Very Best Flan

Serves 8 to 10

This Puerto Rican–style flan is the dessert everyone fights over at the table. Silky, creamy, and perfectly sweet, it's topped with a golden caramel sauce that drips down the sides like a dream. Each spoonful melts in your mouth, with just the right balance of richness and sweetness.

The best part? It's so easy to make! Blend, bake, and flip—it's practically magic. No stress, no fancy tools, just a foolproof recipe that delivers every time. Whether it's your first flan or your family tradition, this one's a showstopper.

⅔ cup sugar
1 teaspoon dark rum (optional)
1 (14-ounce) can sweetened condensed milk
1 (12-ounce) can evaporated milk
⅔ cup heavy cream
3 large eggs
1 large egg yolk
1 teaspoon vanilla extract
½ teaspoon grated orange zest (optional)

Position a rack in the center of the oven and preheat to 350°F. Bring a large pot of water to a boil.

Make the caramel: In a small saucepan, combine the sugar and 2 tablespoons water and cook over medium-high heat for 5 to 7 minutes, swirling the saucepan occasionally but not stirring, until the sugar melts and turns a dark amber color. Remove from the heat and add the rum, if using (be careful, it'll bubble and sputter). Once the rum is calm, stir and pour the mixture into an 8-inch round cake pan, carefully tilting the pan in a circular motion until the bottom is evenly coated. Set inside in a large roasting pan.

Make the custard: In a large bowl, whisk together the condensed milk, evaporated milk, heavy cream, whole eggs, egg yolk, vanilla, and orange zest (if using) until smooth. Pour the custard into the cake pan set in the roasting pan. Transfer the roasting pan to the oven, then carefully ladle boiling water into the roasting pan to come halfway up the sides of the cake pan to create a water bath.

Bake the flan for 55 to 65 minutes, until set but still slightly jiggly in the center. Carefully remove the pan from the water bath (discard the water).

Let the flan cool on a wire rack for at least 1 hour (or up to overnight), then run a sharp knife around the edge of the pan. Invert a large plate over top of the flan, then quickly flip them together, so the pan is now on top of the plate. Tap the bottom of the pan if needed to ensure the flan has fallen.

Serve at room temperature if you just can't wait, but it's best chilled overnight.

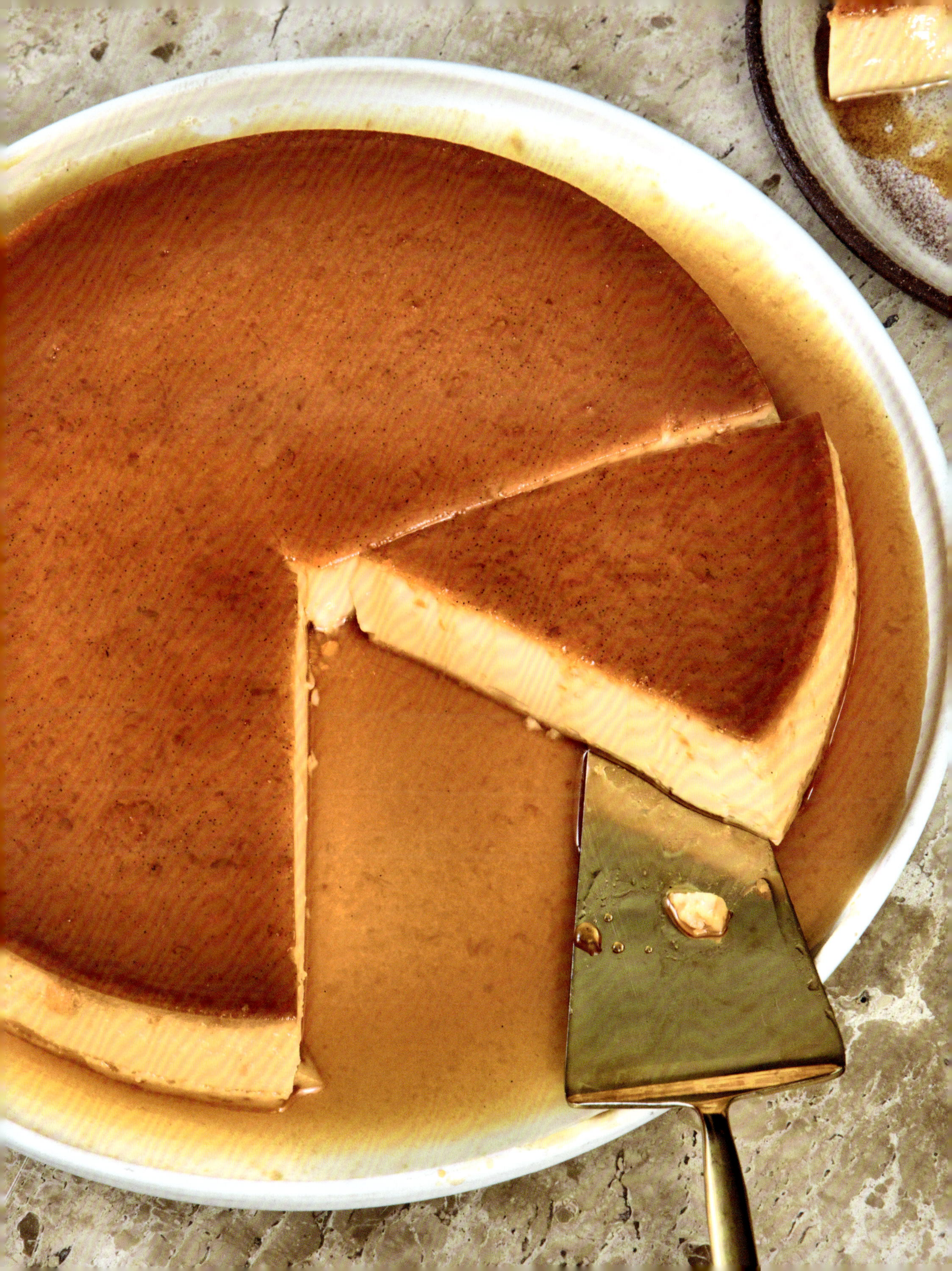

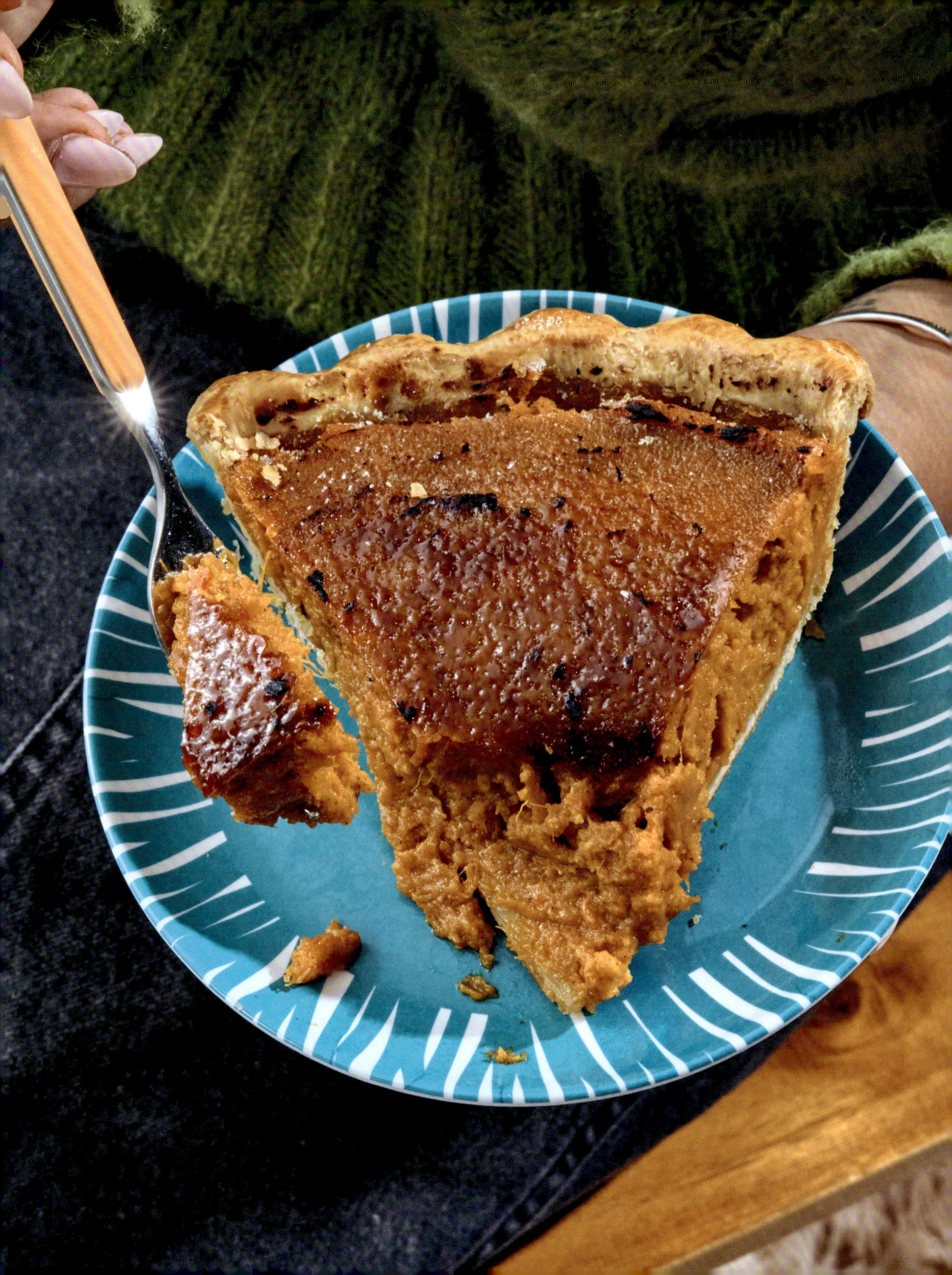

Crème Brûlée Sweet Potato Pie

Makes **1** 9-inch pie

After a while, I felt like the sweet potato pies I was trying—and even the ones I was making—lacked creativity. No wow factor, no "ooh la la." I knew the pie needed something more, something exciting. How could I hook it up? I love anything with texture, so adding a crème brûlée twist with a caramelized sugar topping was exactly what it needed. That crunchy top, paired with the creamy sweet potato filling? Now *that* is the wow factor. Plus, torching the top is a fun party trick that'll have everyone impressed—it's definitely worth the $8 kitchen torch from Amazon. But if you don't have a torch, no worries—I got you. You can still pull this off with your broiler and give your sweet potato pie that next-level shine.

3 pounds sweet potatoes, unpeeled
9 tablespoons (4½ ounces) unsalted butter, at room temperature
1¼ cups packed dark brown sugar
1½ tablespoons vanilla extract
3 large eggs, at room temperature
1 teaspoon ground cinnamon
½ teaspoon ground allspice
½ teaspoon ground ginger
¼ teaspoon ground cloves
¼ teaspoon ground nutmeg
½ cup heavy cream, at room temperature
½ cup spiced rum, such as Captain Morgan
1 (9-inch) unbaked pie shell
¼ cup raw cane sugar

Preheat the oven to 350°F.

Bake the potatoes: Place the sweet potatoes in a 9 × 13-inch baking dish. Bake for 45 minutes to 1 hour, until fork-tender. Let them cool slightly, then carefully peel them and use a fork or potato masher to mash the potatoes in a large bowl until smooth.

Make the pie filling: In another large bowl using a hand mixer (or in a stand mixer fitted with the paddle attachment), cream together the butter and 1 cup of the brown sugar on low speed for 2 to 3 minutes, until light and fluffy. Add the vanilla and mix until combined.

Add the eggs, one at a time, and mix on low speed until incorporated. Add the cinnamon, allspice, ginger, cloves, and nutmeg. Mix on medium speed for 1 minute, until well combined.

Mix in the heavy cream and spiced rum on medium speed until well combined, 1 to 2 minutes. Switch to a spatula and gently fold in the mashed sweet potatoes until just combined. If the mixture appears uneven with some curdled white spots, don't worry, it will bake just fine.

Bake the pie: Pour the sweet potato filling into the pie shell and smooth the top with a spatula. Bake for 45 minutes, until the filling is set and the crust is golden brown. Allow the pie to cool completely, 2 to 3 hours.

When the pie has cooled and you're ready to serve, sprinkle the raw sugar evenly over the top. Use a kitchen torch to caramelize the sugar until it turns dark brown and bubbles, 1 to 2 minutes, or place the pie under the broiler for 1 to 2 minutes. Slice and serve.

Backyard Banana Pudding

Serves **8**

A lot of my cooking comes from ideas I've picked up throughout my life—whether from other chefs, my own trial and error, or just inspiration from places I've eaten. My banana pudding? Same deal. I'll give credit where it's due—Paula Deen was known for adding cream cheese to hers, and I worked it into my own recipe. It's the secret to making banana pudding extra creamy, rich, and decadent. Then there's Magnolia Bakery in NYC: Their banana pudding is famous, but what stood out to me was how they presented it—layers on layers of vanilla custard, bananas, and cookies in every bite, creating the perfect mix of textures. I wanted to capture that same vibe. So, my recipe focuses on that creamy goodness, those layers, and, of course, my own decorating style to make it look as good as it tastes. This recipe is truly a masterpiece, and trust me, it's a fan favorite.

- 2 cups whole milk
- 2 (3.4-ounce) boxes vanilla instant pudding mix
- 1 (14-ounce) can sweetened condensed milk
- 8 ounces cream cheese (1 block), at room temperature
- 1 teaspoon vanilla extract
- 8 ounces Cool Whip (1 tub)
- 2 (11-ounce) boxes vanilla wafers, half left whole, half crushed
- 4 ripe bananas, sliced
- 1 (8-ounce) package Pepperidge Farm Chessmen cookies (optional)
- Caramel sauce (optional), for serving

Make the pudding: In a large bowl, whisk together the whole milk and pudding mixes until smooth. Refrigerate for 30 minutes to chill.

In a large bowl using a hand mixer (or in a stand mixer fitted with the paddle attachment), beat together the condensed milk, cream cheese, and vanilla on medium speed until well combined, 2 to 3 minutes. Switch to a spatula and fold in the Cool Whip until fully incorporated. Gently fold the cream cheese mixture into the chilled pudding until smooth and uniform.

Assemble: Spread one-third of the whole vanilla wafers in the bottom of a 9 × 13-inch baking dish. Sprinkle with half of the crushed cookies. Evenly spread one-third of the pudding mixture over the cookies. Layer half of the banana slices over the pudding mixture, then half of the remaining whole vanilla wafers. Repeat with half of the remaining pudding, then the remaining bananas, and the remaining crushed cookies. Finish with the remaining pudding on the top. Cover with plastic wrap and refrigerate overnight to let the flavors set.

Serve the pudding as is, or decorate with remaining whole wafers and Chessmen cookies and/or with caramel sauce, if desired.

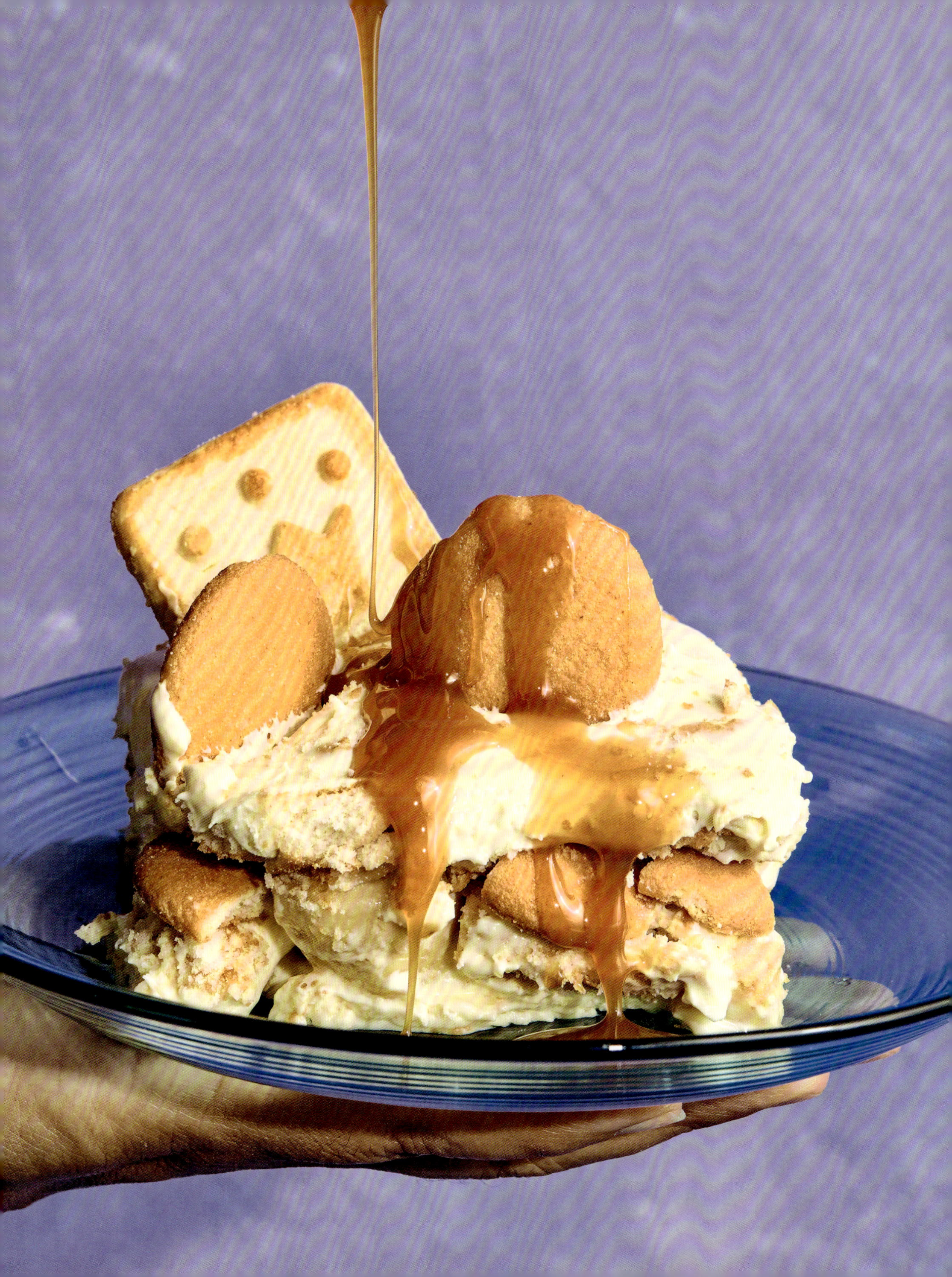

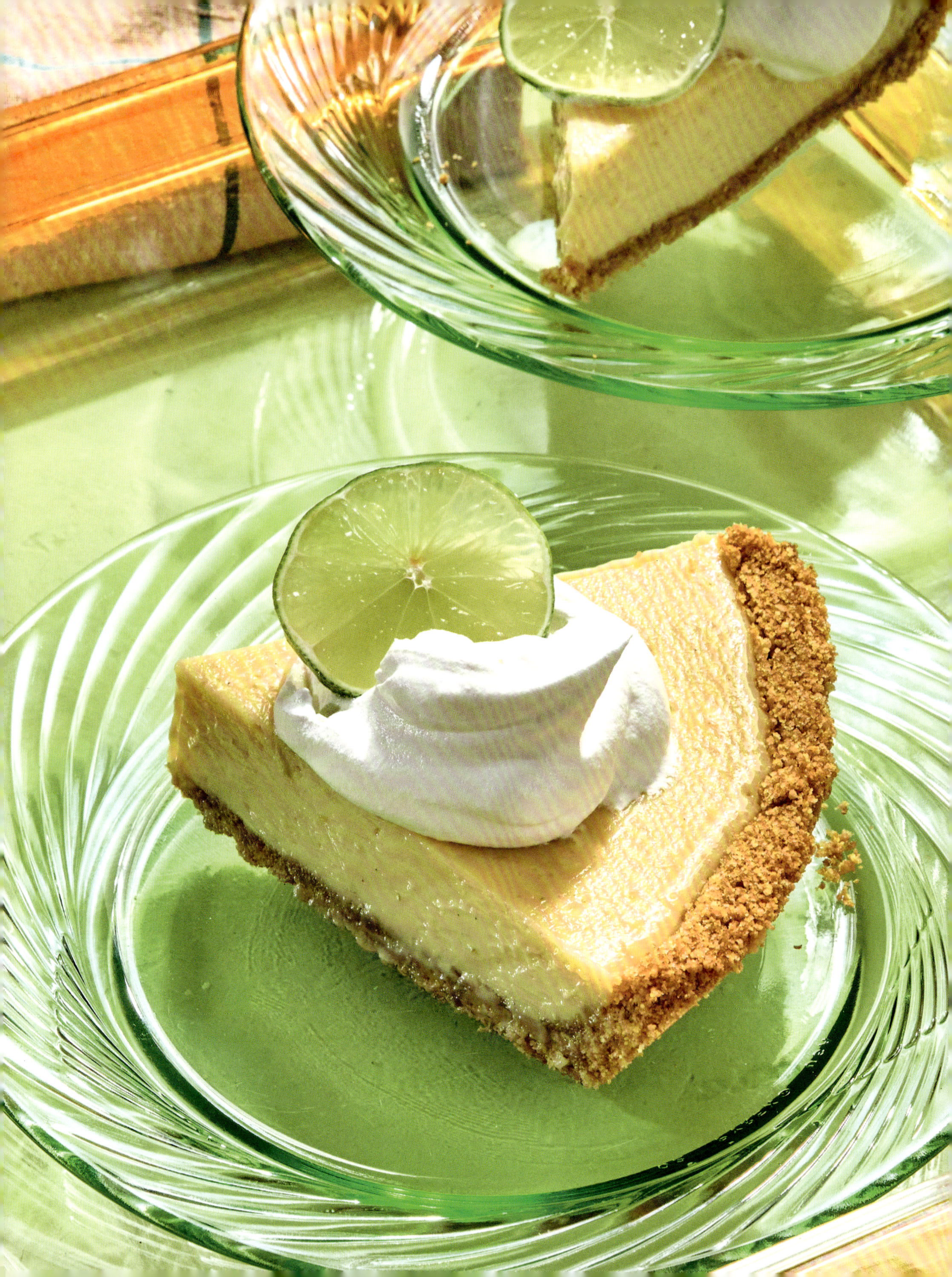

Key Lime Pie

Serves 8

Before moving to Miami, I had never had Key lime pie (I know, wild). But when I got down here, I had to transform into a true South Floridian, which meant a few things: becoming a Miami Dolphins fan, finding the best Cuban sandwich in town, and learning how to make Key lime pie, of course. Lucky for me, I had a lime tree in my backyard that produced the freshest, sweetest limes. What surprised me most was how easy the pie was to make. Aside from the limes (and no, they don't have to be Key limes, I said so!) and a banging crust, you don't need too many other ingredients. My little secret? A touch of sour cream. It adds an extra layer of tartness and creaminess that takes it to another level. I love making this pie when I need something simple to whip up for others, or even just a slice of pure deliciousness for myself—because let's be real, sometimes you need to reward yourself for making it through the week!

- 9 graham cracker sheets (1 sleeve), crushed (about 1 cup)
- 20 vanilla wafers, crushed (about 1 cup)
- ½ cup packed dark brown sugar
- 4 tablespoons (½ stick/2 ounces) unsalted butter, melted
- 5 large egg yolks
- 1 tablespoon grated lime zest, plus more (optional) for garnish
- 2 (14-ounce) cans sweetened condensed milk
- ½ cup sour cream
- ⅔ cup freshly squeezed lime juice (about 6 limes)
- 1 teaspoon vanilla extract
- Whipped cream, for serving
- Lime wheels (optional), for garnish

Preheat the oven to 350°F.

Make the crust: In a large bowl, mix together the crushed graham crackers, crushed vanilla wafers, brown sugar, and melted butter until the crumbs are evenly coated with butter. Press the mixture into the bottom and up the sides of a 9-inch pie dish to form the crust. Bake for 10 minutes, until lightly golden. Remove from the oven and cool completely.

Make the filling: In a large bowl, whisk together the egg yolks and lime zest. Gradually pour in the sweetened condensed milk and sour cream, whisking constantly, until smooth. Whisk in the lime juice and vanilla until smooth.

Bake and chill: Pour the filling into the cooled crust and spread it out evenly with a spatula. Bake for 30 minutes, or until the center is set but still jiggly. Cool to room temperature, cover with plastic wrap, and refrigerate for about 2 hours, until fully chilled and set.

Slice the pie and serve with whipped cream garnished with lime zest or a lime wheel, if desired.

On-Point Pancakes with Brown Butter Syrup

Makes **8** pancakes

These pancakes remind me of those perfect mornings—Erykah Badu playing, coffee hitting just right, and the sun pouring in. The secret to great pancakes is all about that crispy edge. People love them for a reason—there's just something about the contrast between the golden, crunchy outside and the soft, fluffy middle that makes each bite so satisfying. It's what takes an ordinary pancake and makes it unforgettable.

My recipe for perfect pancakes is foolproof, simple, and straight to the point. I can make these with my eyes closed—and honestly, on sleepy mornings, sometimes I do. The secret is my brown butter syrup. It's thick, nutty, and packed with flavor. This is a super-simple breakfast that's been elevated to the max. Sometimes the best things in life are the simple ones, and these pancakes prove that every time.

Syrup

- 8 tablespoons (1 stick/4 ounces) unsalted butter
- 1 cup granulated sugar
- 1 cup packed dark brown sugar

Pancakes

- 1½ cups whole milk
- 2 large eggs
- 1 teaspoon vanilla extract
- 2 cups all-purpose flour
- 2 tablespoons granulated sugar
- 1½ teaspoons baking soda
- 1½ teaspoons baking powder
- ½ teaspoon kosher salt
- 4 tablespoons (½ stick/2 ounces) unsalted butter, plus more as needed

Make the syrup: In a small saucepan, melt the butter over medium heat and swirl the pan constantly for 5 minutes, until the butter turns dark golden brown and smells nutty. Immediately transfer the browned butter to a small bowl, including all of the toasted flecks at the bottom of the pan.

In the same pan, stir together the granulated sugar, brown sugar, and 1 cup water. Bring to a boil over medium heat. Reduce the heat to low and simmer for 5 minutes, stirring occasionally, until it thickens to the consistency of maple syrup. Remove from the heat and stir in the browned butter, making sure to scrape up all the toasted solids—that's where the flavor is!

Pour the syrup into a pitcher with a spout to serve with the pancakes, or store in a glass jar in the refrigerator for up to 1 month.

Make the pancakes: In a medium bowl, whisk together the milk, eggs, and vanilla until smooth.

In a large bowl, whisk together the flour, granulated sugar, baking soda, baking powder, and salt. With a rubber spatula, create a well in the center of the flour mixture. Pour the wet ingredients into the flour mixture and mix well, until fully combined with no lumps.

In a large skillet, melt 2 tablespoons of the butter over medium-low heat. Add ⅓ cup of the pancake batter and cook for 2 minutes, until bubbles appear on all parts of the pancake. Flip and cook for another 2 to 3 minutes, until cooked through and golden brown. Repeat with the remaining batter, adding more butter as needed, until all of the pancakes are cooked. Serve the pancakes with a drizzle of the brown butter syrup.

Little Details, BIG Impact: Want to know why your pancakes burn so easily? Your pan's too hot! Keep the heat on medium-low to avoid that. And here's the move: After every 2 pancakes, carefully wipe the skillet with a paper towel and toss in a fresh knob of butter. This way, all your pancakes come out golden and beautiful, no burned bits in sight.

The syrup keeps for weeks in the fridge, but because of the fat in the butter, it will solidify, so leave it at room temperature for a half hour to get it to a spreadable consistency, or microwave at 10-second intervals, stirring in between, until it's liquid again.

Everything's Good

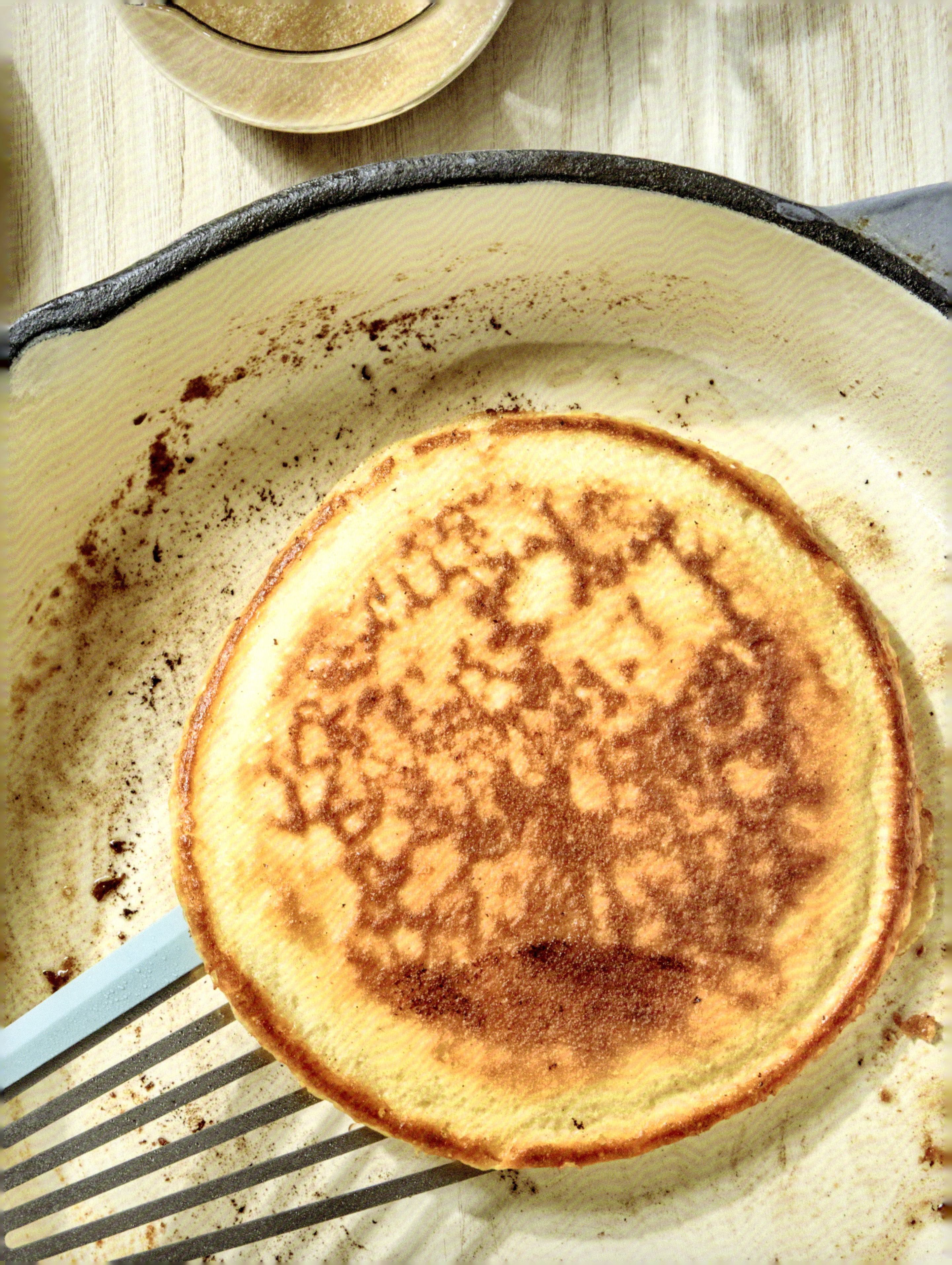

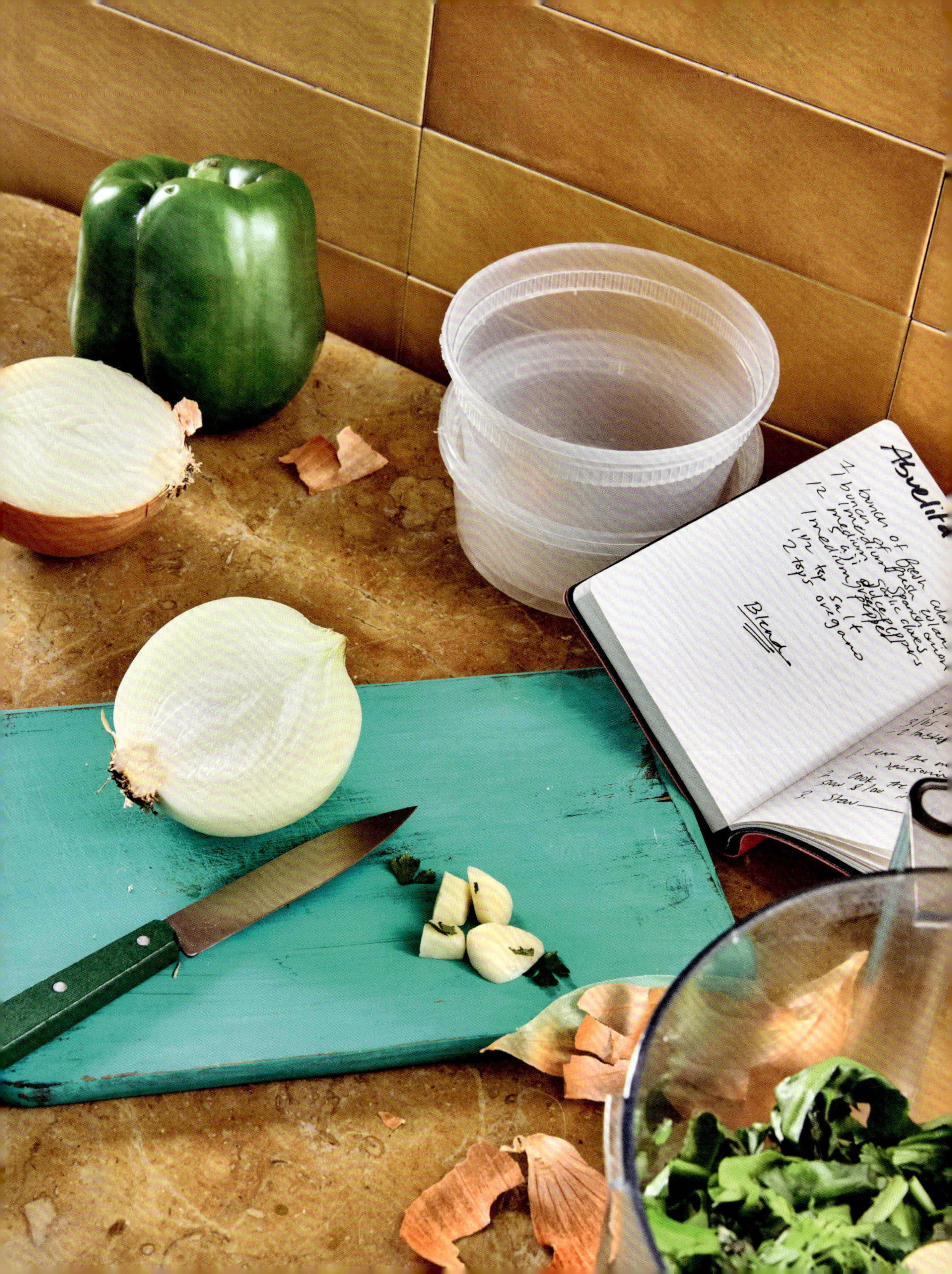

8
Sauces

The Perfect Sauce for Everything

Makes about 2 cups

No, but seriously—this really *is* the perfect sauce for everything. I'm not just talking about spreading it on a burger (though it crushes that). It's a true triple-threat: a dip, a dressing, and a marinade all in one. Picture this: I use it to marinate my chicken, then drizzle it over the finished chicken salad as a dressing. Oh, that's clutch. It's sweet, tangy, and just acidic enough to keep things bright. The light, creamy texture gives it a fresh, cooling taste, but the balance of flavors makes it unforgettable. It's versatile enough to go from tacos to salads, but good luck not eating it straight off the spoon. This sauce isn't just a sidekick—it's the star.

¾ cup Dijon mustard (I like Grey Poupon)
¼ cup honey
2 tablespoons distilled white vinegar
1 tablespoon freshly squeezed lemon juice
2 teaspoons Worcestershire sauce
1 teaspoon freshly ground black pepper
¼ teaspoon kosher salt
½ cup extra-virgin olive oil

In a medium bowl, whisk together the mustard, honey, vinegar, lemon juice, Worcestershire sauce, pepper, and salt until well combined. While whisking, slowly add the olive oil to emulsify the sauce. Taste and adjust seasonings as needed.

Serve immediately or store in a sealed container in the fridge for up to 1 week.

How to Use It

As a marinade: This marinade works on everything. Just pour about ½ cup over 1 pound of your protein of choice, toss it around with some tongs, and cover it. Let it chill in the fridge for at least 1 hour (or up to overnight) to soak up all that flavor before cooking.

As a salad dressing: Use this as you wish on your salads. It's perfect for all types!

As a dipping sauce: This is a perfect honey mustard for my Drive-Thru Chicken Nuggets (page 119) or your favorite French fries.

Abuela's Green Sofrito

Makes about
2
cups

My abuela used to say, "You're going to be someone. I can feel it." While I watched her cook, she always told me how special I was and how she knew that God would use me to change lives. I never knew that it would be the very things she was showing me that would lead to a fulfilling career that touches so many lives. She would be so proud.

Sofrito is the foundation of every Puerto Rican dish in this book. Every Puerto Rican family has their own recipe for sofrito. While some techniques are more popular than others, my grandmother, Edith, was known for her unique sofrito recipe. She was a home health aide who emigrated from Puerto Rico when she was thirteen, and cooking was how she fed her seventeen brothers and sisters. Her sofrito was so popular that she gave it to her patients as a gift on holidays and birthdays. My abuelita's sofrito gifting was a sacred ritual—everyone was elated to use her top-secret sofrito. Even today, if I close my eyes and concentrate, it's like I can hear her reciting the recipe out loud to me.

Feel free to salt this recipe to taste. Like Abuela used to say, "Trust yourself."

1 bunch of cilantro (the freshest you can find!)
1 bunch of culantro (the freshest you can find!)
1 medium Spanish onion, roughly chopped
8 green ají dulce peppers, roughly chopped
1 medium green bell pepper, roughly chopped
12 garlic cloves (about ⅔ cup)
2 teaspoons dried oregano
1½ teaspoons kosher salt

In a blender or food processor, combine the herbs, chopped vegetables, garlic, oregano, and salt and blend until smooth.

Use right away or store in a sealed container in the fridge for up to 1 week. For longer life, store it in an ice cube tray and use as needed.

How to Use It

Use in Puerto Rican Pepper Steak (page 137) or my Pastelón (page 175).

Little Detail, BIG Impact: Culantro, also known as recao, is an herb commonly used in Caribbean and Latin American cuisine. It has a long and rich history dating back to the indigenous Taíno people, who used it for its medicinal properties. If you can't find culantro, you can substitute it with more cilantro or with parsley, but keep in mind that the flavor profile will be different.

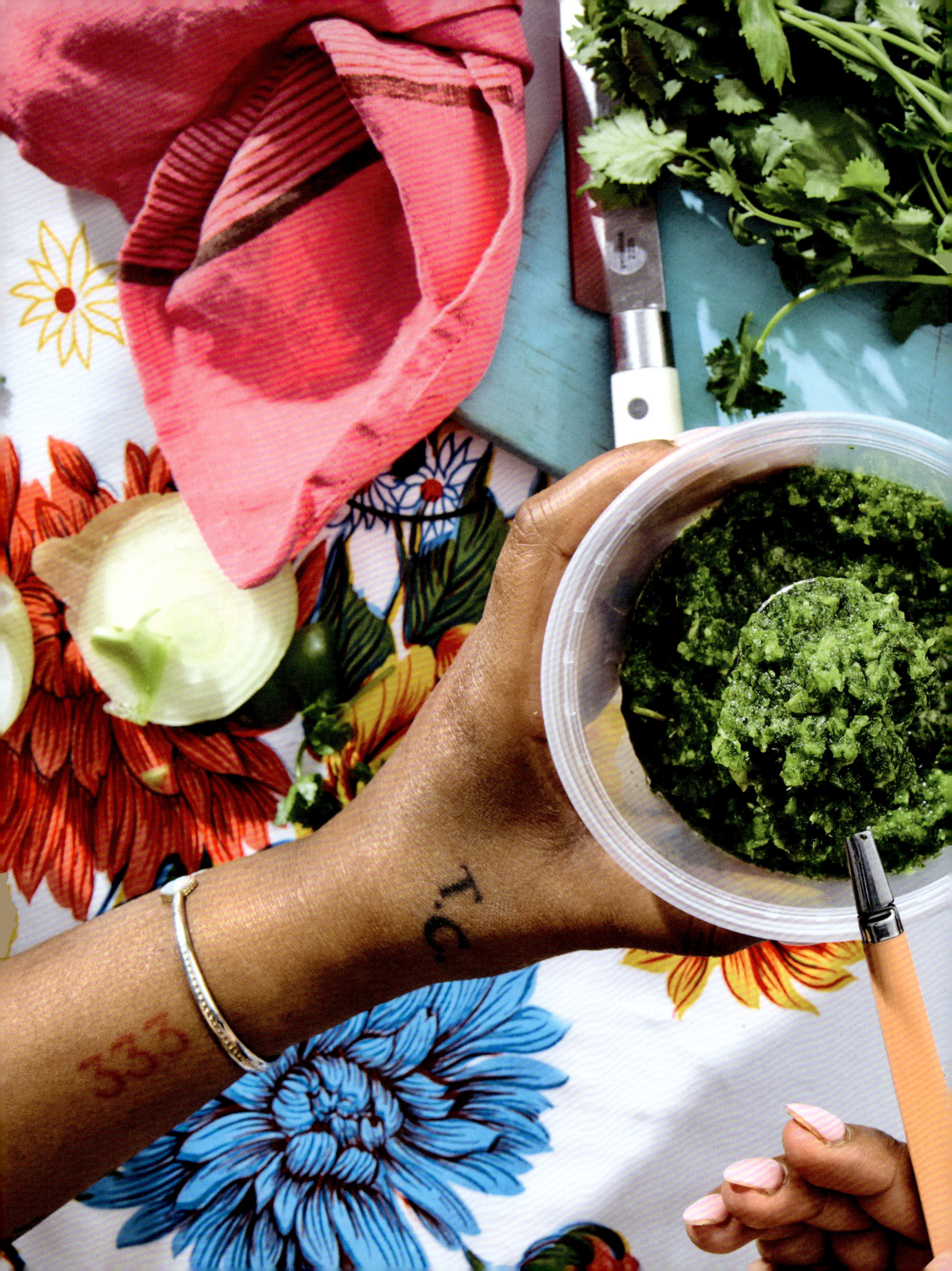
T.C.
333

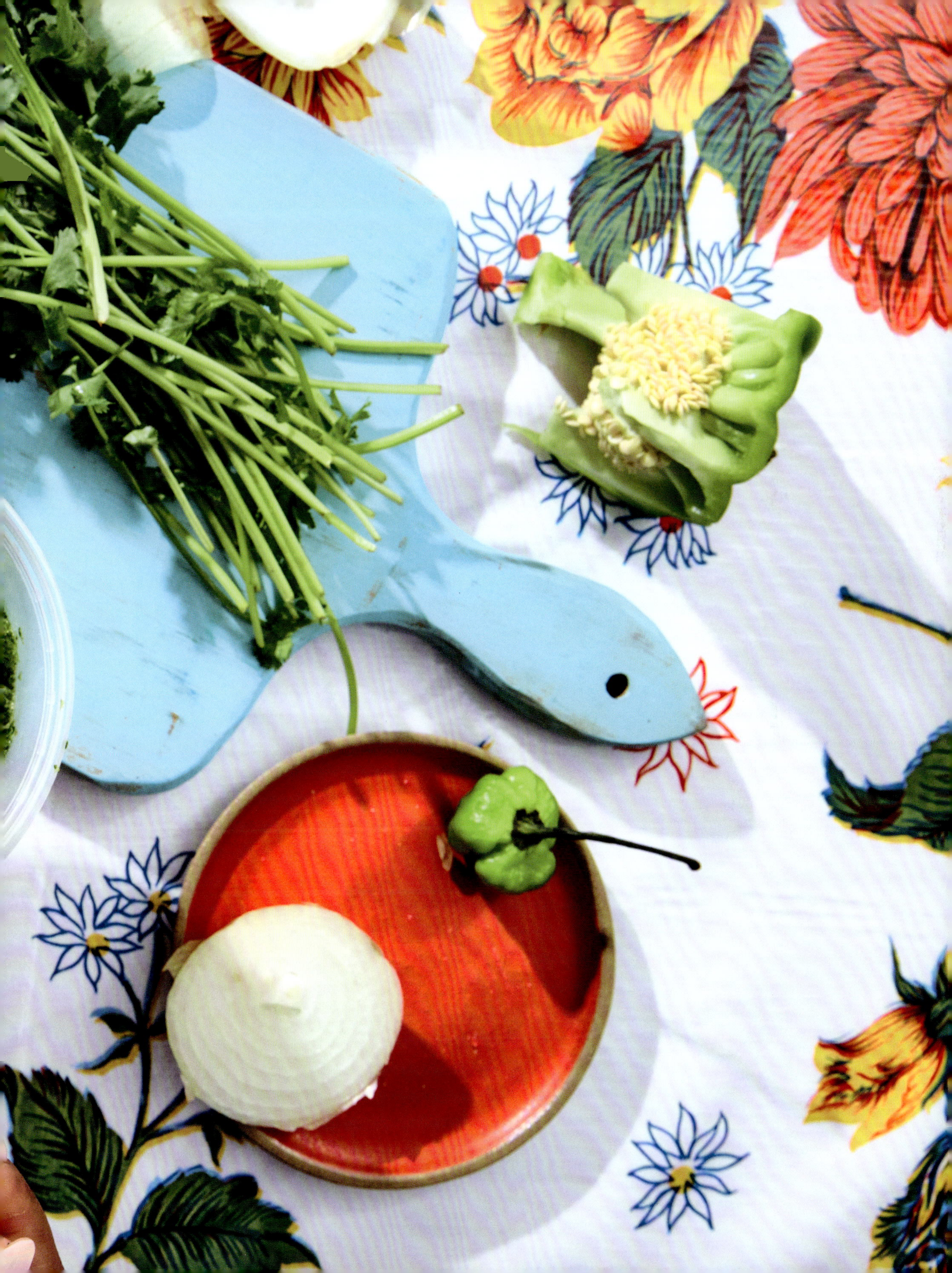

My Famous Red Sofrito

Makes about 2 cups

My grandmother only made green sofrito—she swore by it. But as I found my own rhythm in the kitchen, I started making red sofrito, too. Red sofrito is perfect for tomato-based dishes, as the tomatoes and bell peppers add that extra depth and sweetness and the annatto seasoning helps you color your food while adding a Latin flair. And yeah, you can use red and green sofritos interchangeably, but knowing how to make both is how you become a better cook. Making red sofrito is all about holding onto what my grandmother taught me while adding my own flavor to the story. It's about keeping those roots strong while creating something fresh to pass down in my *own way*.

1 bunch of cilantro (the freshest you can find!)
1 bunch of culantro (the freshest you can find!)
8 medium garlic cloves, peeled but whole
4 large Roma tomatoes, roughly chopped
1 medium red bell pepper, roughly chopped
1 small yellow onion, roughly chopped
1 tablespoon ground annatto
2 teaspoons dried oregano
1 teaspoon adobo seasoning
1 teaspoon kosher salt

In a blender or food processor, combine the cilantro, culantro, garlic, tomatoes, bell pepper, onion, annatto, oregano, adobo seasoning, and salt and pulse until smooth.

Use immediately or store in a sealed container in the fridge for up to 2 weeks. For individual portions, pour sofrito into an ice cube tray, freeze, and use as needed.

How to Use It

Use in The Perfect Pollo Guisado (page 133) or my Juicy Red Sofrito Chicken Empanadas (page 32).

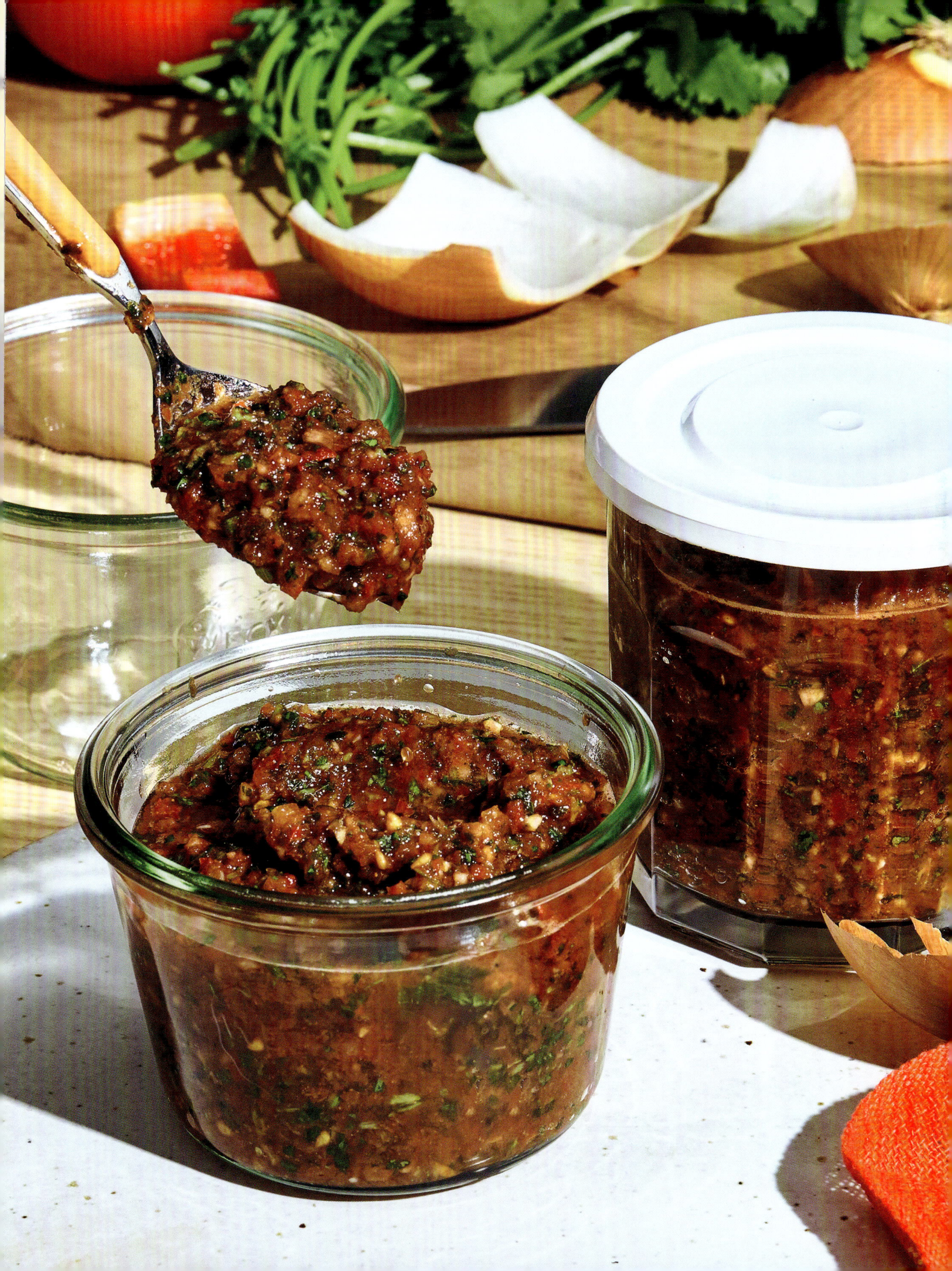

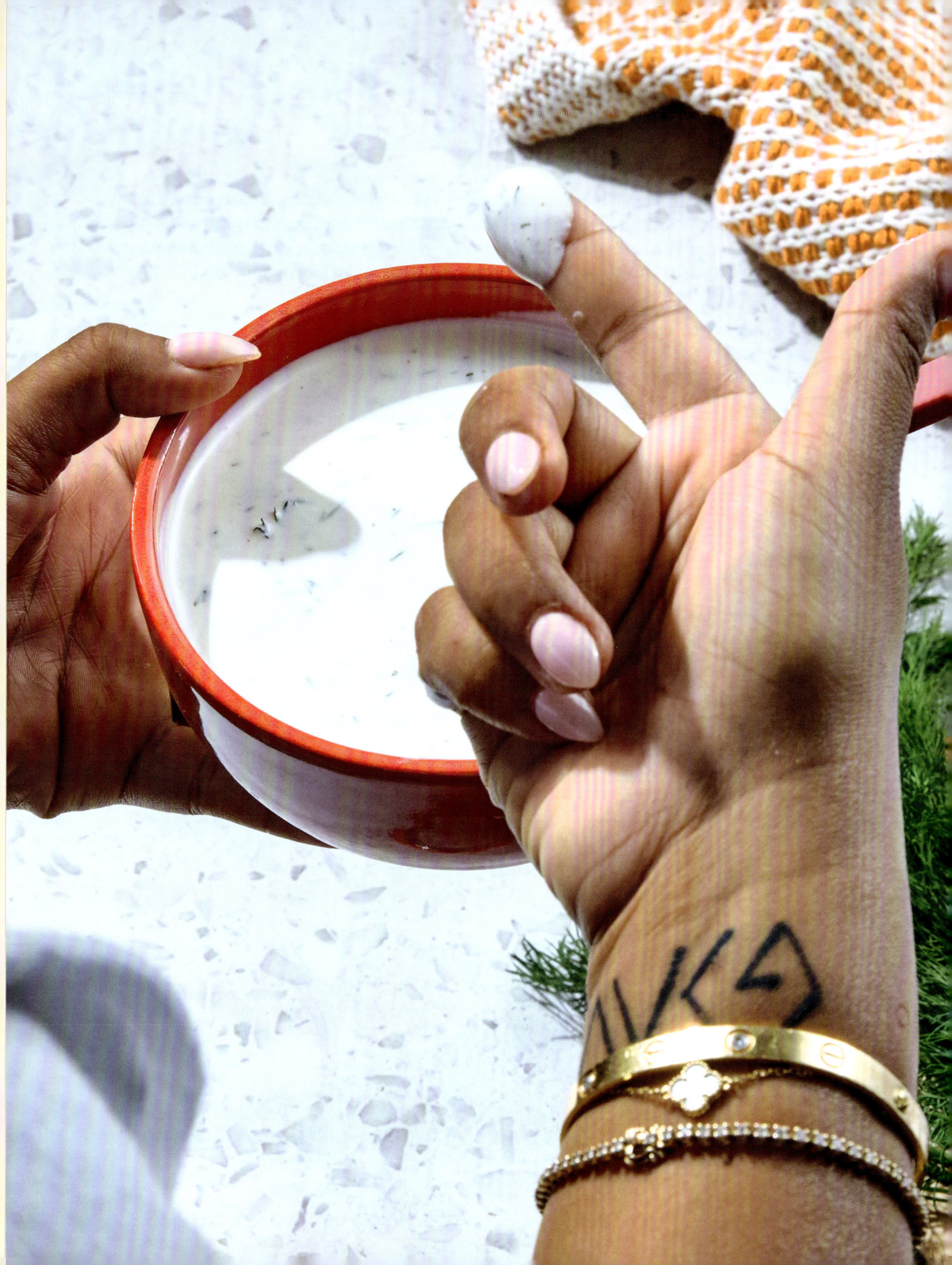

The Real MVP Ranch Dressing

Makes about **2** cups

This creamy dill-forward dressing is my ride-or-die condiment. It's tangy with just a hint of sweetness, and the fresh pop of dill makes it irresistible. Whether I'm dipping nuggets and fries, slathering it on burgers and sandwiches, or drizzling it over flatbreads and tacos, this sauce never misses. It's a universal topper in my kitchen, and I always have a jar ready to go. Some say it reminds them of Hidden Valley Ranch, but this version is fresher, brighter, and so much better. Once you taste how it transforms everything it touches, you'll see why it's a staple around here.

1 cup buttermilk
1 cup mayonnaise
½ cup sour cream
3 tablespoons finely chopped fresh dill
2 teaspoons distilled white vinegar
1½ teaspoons sugar
1 teaspoon garlic powder
1 teaspoon onion powder
1 teaspoon kosher salt

In a medium bowl, whisk together the buttermilk, mayonnaise, sour cream, dill, vinegar, sugar, garlic powder, onion powder, and salt. Transfer the dressing to an airtight glass container, like a mason jar, and refrigerate for at least 1 hour before serving.

Store leftover dressing in a sealed container in the fridge for up to 2 weeks.

How to Use It

On everything! Yes, I'm THAT person. As a dipping sauce, added to burgers and sandwiches, or as a salad dressing. Mad good.

Peruvian Ají Verde Sauce

Makes about 2 cups

Ají verde is the green sauce you didn't know you needed. Straight out of Peru, it's creamy, herby, and spicy in the best way—perfect for roasted chicken, grilled meats, fries, or honestly, by the spoonful. It's zesty and bold, with the freshness of cilantro, the heat of jalapeños, and a hit of lime that ties it all together. I love it because it turns anything into a flavor-packed masterpiece. Drizzle it, dip it, or slather it—ají verde is always the star of the plate.

- 2 bunches of cilantro
- 2 medium jalapeños, seeds removed but reserved
- 2 garlic cloves, peeled but whole
- 1 cup mayonnaise
- 2 ounces Parmesan cheese, freshly grated (about ½ cup)
- 1 tablespoon freshly squeezed lime juice (about ½ lime), plus more to taste
- 1 teaspoon kosher salt, plus more to taste
- ¼ teaspoon freshly ground black pepper

In a blender or food processor, combine the cilantro, jalapeños, and garlic and pulse until finely chopped. Add the mayonnaise, Parmesan, lime juice, salt, and pepper. Blend until smooth and creamy. If the sauce is too thick, add a splash of cold water and pulse to thin it out. Taste and adjust the seasoning if needed, adding more lime juice or salt to suit your preference. If it's not spicy enough, add a few of the reserved jalapeño seeds and blend again.

Store in a sealed container in the refrigerator for up to 2 weeks.

How to Use It

As a topping: Ají verde is delicious on chicken, shrimp, and even steak. Drench your favorite meat in it.

As a salad dressing: Stir 1 tablespoon water into ¼ cup of the ají verde and you have a bright green salad dressing.

As a pasta sauce: Yeah, you heard me! Add this to your favorite cooked noodles and it's a chef's kiss!

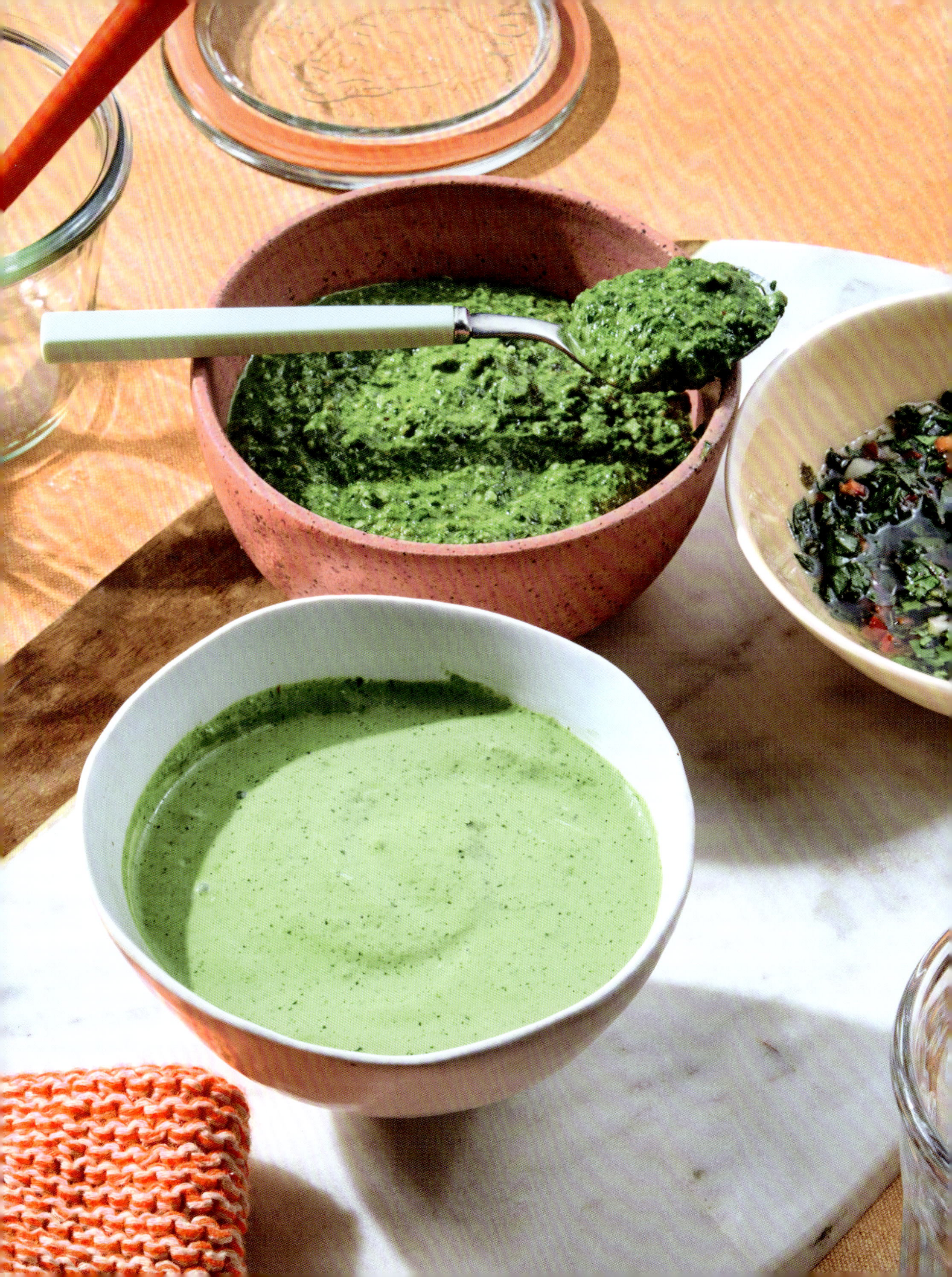

Traditional Chimichurri Sauce

Makes about **2** cups

When I first shared my chimichurri recipe online, the most common reaction was, "Wait, it's *that* easy?!" People couldn't believe that the bold, flavorful sauce you see drizzled over steaks at fancy steak houses or layered into gourmet sandwiches is totally attainable at home. But once you make it yourself, you'll understand—and you'll keep coming back for more. The secret is all in the ingredients. Fresh parsley is a must—it has an earthy, vibrant flavor that absolutely shines when it's freshly chopped. Combine that with good olive oil, tangy vinegar, and a blend of spices, and you've got a sauce that's as versatile as it is delicious. Whether you're spooning it over grilled meats or roasted veggies, chimichurri is one of those recipes you'll wonder how you ever lived without.

1 bunch of parsley, stems on, finely minced
1 or 2 small red chiles (I use Fresno or red Thai), seeded and minced
12 garlic cloves, minced (about ¼ cup)
¾ cup high-quality extra-virgin olive oil
2 tablespoons red wine vinegar
Juice of ½ lemon
1 teaspoon dried oregano
1 tablespoon kosher salt, or to taste
1 teaspoon freshly ground black pepper, or to taste

In a medium bowl, combine the parsley, chile(s), and garlic. Add the olive oil, vinegar, lemon juice, oregano, salt, and pepper. Stir until well combined. Let the chimichurri sit for at least 15 minutes before serving to allow the flavors to meld together.

Store in a sealed container in the fridge for up to 1 week.

How to Use It

In tacos: Drizzle 1 to 2 tablespoons chimichurri over your favorite grilled or shredded meat tacos for a fresh, herbaceous kick. It adds a bright flavor that cuts through the richness of the meat—especially killer on steak or chicken tacos.

On a grilled steak: Marinate your steak with ¼ cup chimichurri for at least 1 hour (and up to overnight). Grill to perfection. Serve with an extra 2 to 3 tablespoons fresh chimichurri on top for that perfect blend of charred meat and zesty herbs.

In a compound butter: Mix 8 tablespoons (1 stick/4 ounces) softened butter with 2 tablespoons chimichurri, roll it up in plastic wrap to make a log, and refrigerate until firm. Slice and melt it over steaks, put it on bread, or add to cooked veggies for an easy flavor bomb that brings all the herbaceous goodness.

On chicken thighs: Marinate 2 to 3 pounds bone-in chicken thighs in ½ cup chimichurri and 2 teaspoons kosher salt for at least 2 hours (and up to overnight). Grill or roast at 375°F until the skin is crispy and the meat is juicy. Serve with extra chimichurri (1 to 2 tablespoons) on the side for dipping.

Easy Peasy Pesto

Makes about 1¼ cups

Pesto is that sauce I always forget how much I love until I make it—and then I wonder why I don't keep it on hand all the time. There's something about the combination of fresh basil, garlic, Parmesan, and olive oil that's just magic. It's bright, nutty, garlicky, and perfectly balanced, with a silky texture that clings to everything it touches. What I love most is how versatile it is. Sure, it's amazing tossed with pasta, but try spreading it on sandwiches, swirling it into soups, or drizzling it over roasted veggies. It instantly transforms the simplest dishes into something special. Once you make it, you'll see why pesto is a kitchen essential.

- 6 tablespoons extra-virgin olive oil, plus more as needed
- ¼ cup pine nuts
- 3 cups loosely packed baby spinach
- 1 cup fresh basil leaves
- 1 tablespoon freshly squeezed lemon juice, plus more to taste
- 2 garlic cloves, minced (about 2 teaspoons)
- 1 teaspoon kosher salt, plus more to taste
- ¼ teaspoon red pepper flakes, plus more to taste
- 1 ounce Parmesan cheese, freshly grated (about ¼ cup)

In a small skillet, heat 2 tablespoons of the olive oil over medium heat until hot and shimmering. Add the pine nuts and sauté for 2 to 3 minutes, stirring frequently, until golden brown and fragrant. Be careful not to burn them. Remove from the heat and set aside to cool slightly.

In a heavy-duty food processor or blender, combine the toasted pine nuts, spinach, basil, lemon juice, garlic, salt, and pepper flakes and pulse 3 to 4 times, until the leaves and nuts start to break down.

While the food processor is running, slowly drizzle in the remaining 4 tablespoons olive oil, until smooth and creamy. If the pesto is too thick, add more olive oil or a splash of water and pulse to combine. Taste and adjust the lemon juice, salt, or pepper flakes to taste. Transfer to a bowl and stir in the Parmesan until smooth.

Store the pesto in an airtight container in the refrigerator for up to 5 days. Freeze the pesto in an ice cube tray or small freezer-safe container for up to 3 months. Thaw in the refrigerator before using.

How to Use It

On toast: Spread a generous layer of pesto on toasted bread and top with a sprinkle of flaky salt or a poached egg. It's a simple, flavorful way to elevate your breakfast or snack.

As a sauce for pasta (hot or cold): Toss 1 cup freshly cooked pasta with a few spoonfuls of pesto and a generous handful of Parmesan. Serve it hot for a quick, comforting meal, or cold as a refreshing pasta salad that's perfect for meal prep or picnics.

For Pesto Chicken with Mozzarella: Marinate 1 to 2 pounds of bone-in or boneless chicken breasts with a few tablespoons pesto, 2 teaspoons kosher salt, and 1 teaspoon paprika for 20 minutes. Bake at 350°F or grill the chicken for 15 to 20 minutes, until fully cooked. In the last few minutes, top with slices of fresh mozzarella and halved cherry tomatoes, then broil until the cheese is melted and bubbling. Serve with a fresh salad or some Crunchy Garlic Toast (page 31) for a complete, flavorful meal.

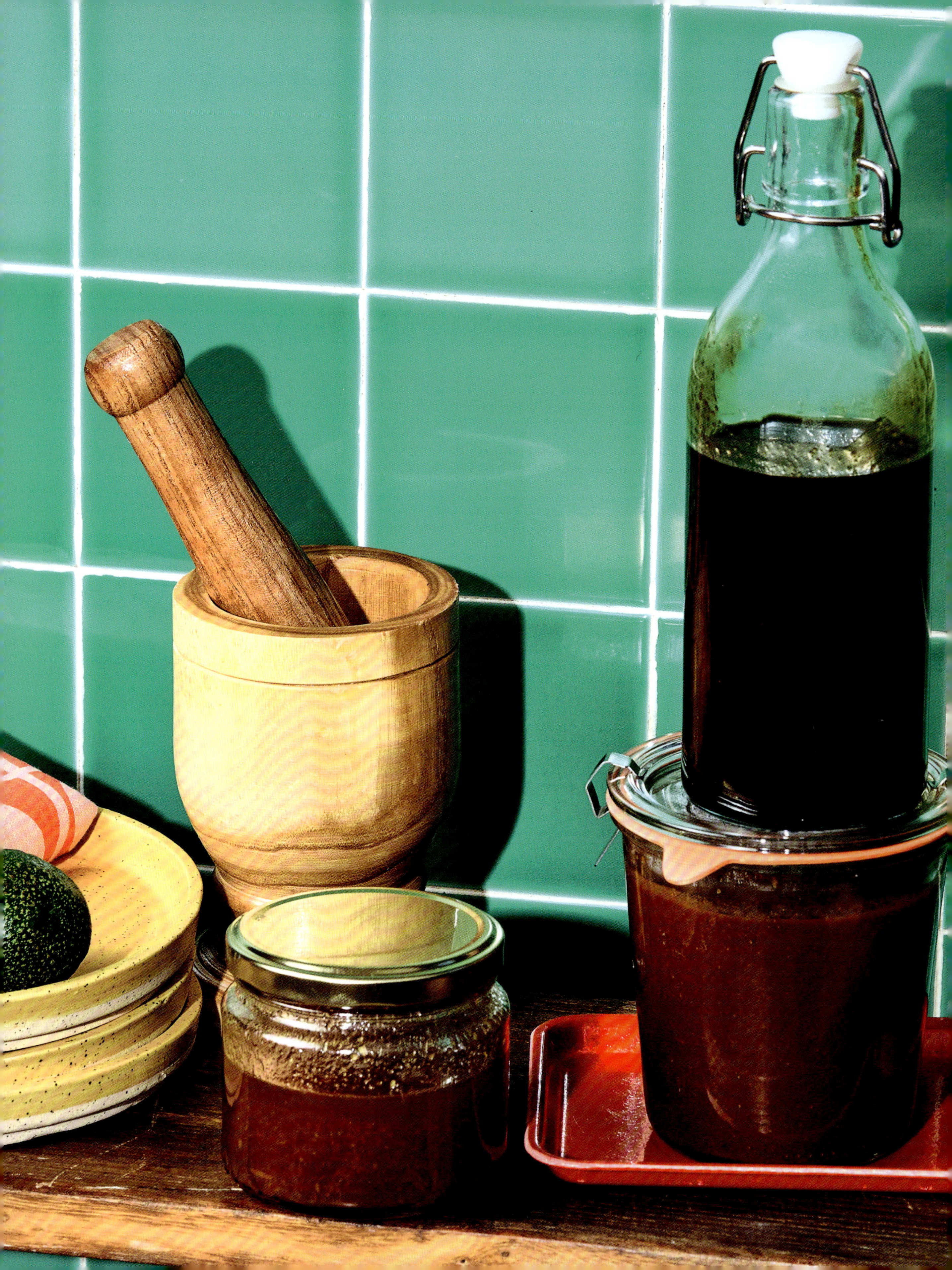

All-in-One Teriyaki Sauce

Makes about **2** cups

Teriyaki sauce is my go-to when I want to level up a meal with minimal effort. Sweet, savory, and sticky in the best way, it's the kind of sauce that makes everything taste like it came off a hibachi grill. I love pouring it over rice and grilled meats for a quick, flavor-packed dinner at home. What makes it even better? It's a total recipe chameleon. If you ever see soy sauce and sugar in one of my recipes—like Copycat Panda Chow Mein (page 105) or General Tso's Chicken (page 99)—teriyaki slides right in and brings that rich, glossy magic. It's universal, versatile, and always delivers. Keep it on hand and you'll never be far from an easy, satisfying meal.

1 tablespoon cornstarch
½ cup lower-sodium soy sauce
¼ cup packed dark brown sugar
1 teaspoon toasted sesame oil
¼ cup honey
1 teaspoon browning sauce
1 teaspoon ground ginger
1 teaspoon garlic powder
¼ teaspoon ground cinnamon
¼ teaspoon ground allspice
¼ teaspoon ground white pepper

In a small bowl, whisk together the cornstarch with 1 tablespoon water until smooth to make a slurry.

In a medium saucepan, whisk together 1½ cups water, the soy sauce, brown sugar, and sesame oil. Whisk in the honey, browning sauce, ginger, garlic powder, cinnamon, allspice, and white pepper. Bring to a simmer over medium heat, stirring frequently to dissolve the sugar.

Once the sauce is simmering, slowly add the cornstarch slurry to the saucepan, stirring constantly. Cook the sauce for 5 to 7 minutes, stirring frequently to prevent the sauce from sticking to the bottom of the pan, until it reaches your desired thickness. Remove the pan from the heat and let the sauce cool completely before using.

Store in a sealed container in the fridge for up to 2 weeks.

How to Use It

In a stir-fry: Toss it with veggies, noodles, or rice for a quick, flavorful stir-fry that's always a hit.

As a marinade: Marinate chicken, steak, shrimp—whatever you're feeling—for at least 1 hour (and up to overnight) in the fridge to let those flavors soak in.

As a sweet and umami dipping sauce: Use it as a dipping sauce for everything from spring rolls to wings.

Bold and Smoky BBQ Sauce

Makes about **2** cups

Wanna know a fun fact about me? I spent about seven years living in Texas when I was a kid, and let me tell you, that's where my love for BBQ really took root. Back then, we'd grab $2 bottles of Sweet Baby Ray's, slather it on chicken, and grill on Sundays—it was everything. But as I grew into my own as a home cook, I decided it was time to level up and make my own sauce. This version keeps that same sweetness we all love, but it's deeper, smokier, and has a richness that comes from apple cider vinegar and Worcestershire sauce. It's bold, sticky, and perfect for everything from ribs to burgers. One taste, and you'll see why I traded the bottle for this homemade magic.

- 2 tablespoons extra-virgin olive oil
- ½ medium yellow onion, finely diced (about ½ cup)
- 3 garlic cloves, minced (about 1 tablespoon)
- 1 cup tomato paste
- ½ cup packed dark brown sugar
- ¾ cup apple cider vinegar
- ¼ cup Dijon mustard
- 1 tablespoon browning sauce (optional)
- 3 tablespoons Worcestershire sauce
- 1 teaspoon garlic powder
- 1 teaspoon onion powder
- 1 teaspoon ground ginger
- 1 teaspoon smoked paprika
- 1 teaspoon kosher salt
- ¼ teaspoon freshly ground black pepper
- ⅛ teaspoon liquid smoke

In a medium saucepan, heat the oil over medium heat until hot and shimmering. Add the onion and sauté for 3 to 4 minutes, stirring occasionally, until translucent. Stir in the minced garlic and cook for 1 minute, stirring frequently, until fragrant. Stir in the tomato paste and brown sugar until smooth. Mix in the vinegar and let the sauce reduce by half, about 2 minutes.

Stir in 1 cup water, the mustard, browning sauce (if using), Worcestershire sauce, garlic powder, onion powder, ginger, smoked paprika, salt, pepper, and liquid smoke. Reduce the heat to low and simmer for 10 to 15 minutes, stirring occasionally, until it reaches your desired thickness. Remove from the heat and let it cool before serving.

Store in a sealed container in the refrigerator for up to 2 weeks.

How to Use It

For BBQ Ribs: Rub a rack of ribs with your favorite dry rub and then slather ½ cup BBQ sauce all over. Wrap the ribs in foil and slow-cook in a 350°F oven for 2 to 3 hours, until the ribs are falling off the bone. During the last 15 minutes, uncover and brush on an extra ¼ cup sauce for that sticky, caramelized finish.

As a dipping sauce for nuggets: Use ¼ cup BBQ sauce as a dipping sauce for chicken nuggets. You can serve it straight up or mix it with a little honey for a sweet and tangy twist.

For BBQ Baked Chicken: Season 2 to 3 pounds bone-in chicken pieces with 2 tablespoons BBQ sauce, 1 teaspoon paprika, and a sprinkle of all-purpose seasoning. Bake at 350°F for 35 to 40 minutes. During the last 20 minutes, baste the chicken with an additional 2 tablespoons BBQ sauce for that extra BBQ coating.

Duck Sauce

Makes about 1½ cups

Duck sauce takes me straight back to those late nights at the Chinese takeout spot, yelling "EXTRA DUCK SAUCE!" over the counter while grabbing my chicken wings and pork fried rice. It was the perfect balance of sweet and tangy, and I'd hoard those little packets like treasure.

When I left the East Coast, finding good duck sauce was impossible, so I had to figure out how to make it myself. Who knew it was so simple? A little apricot preserves, some soy sauce, and a handful of pantry staples later, and I had a sauce that brought all those nostalgic flavors right back. It's sweet, tangy, and just the right amount of sticky—perfect for dipping, drizzling, or just dunking everything in sight.

1 cup apricot preserves
2 tablespoons lower-sodium soy sauce
2 teaspoons rice vinegar
2 teaspoons sugar
1 garlic clove, minced (1 teaspoon)
1 teaspoon Shaoxing wine

In a small bowl, whisk together the apricot preserves, soy sauce, vinegar, sugar, garlic, and Shaoxing wine.

Store in a sealed container in the refrigerator for up to 1 week.

How to Use It

It's the OG dipping sauce, especially for my Takeout Classics chapter (page 93). This sauce is perfect for dipping my Chinese Takeout Wings (page 102) or Shrimp Egg Rolls (page 96).

Serve the duck sauce as a condiment for other takeout classics like Copycat Panda Chow Mein (page 105) or General Tso's Chicken (page 99).

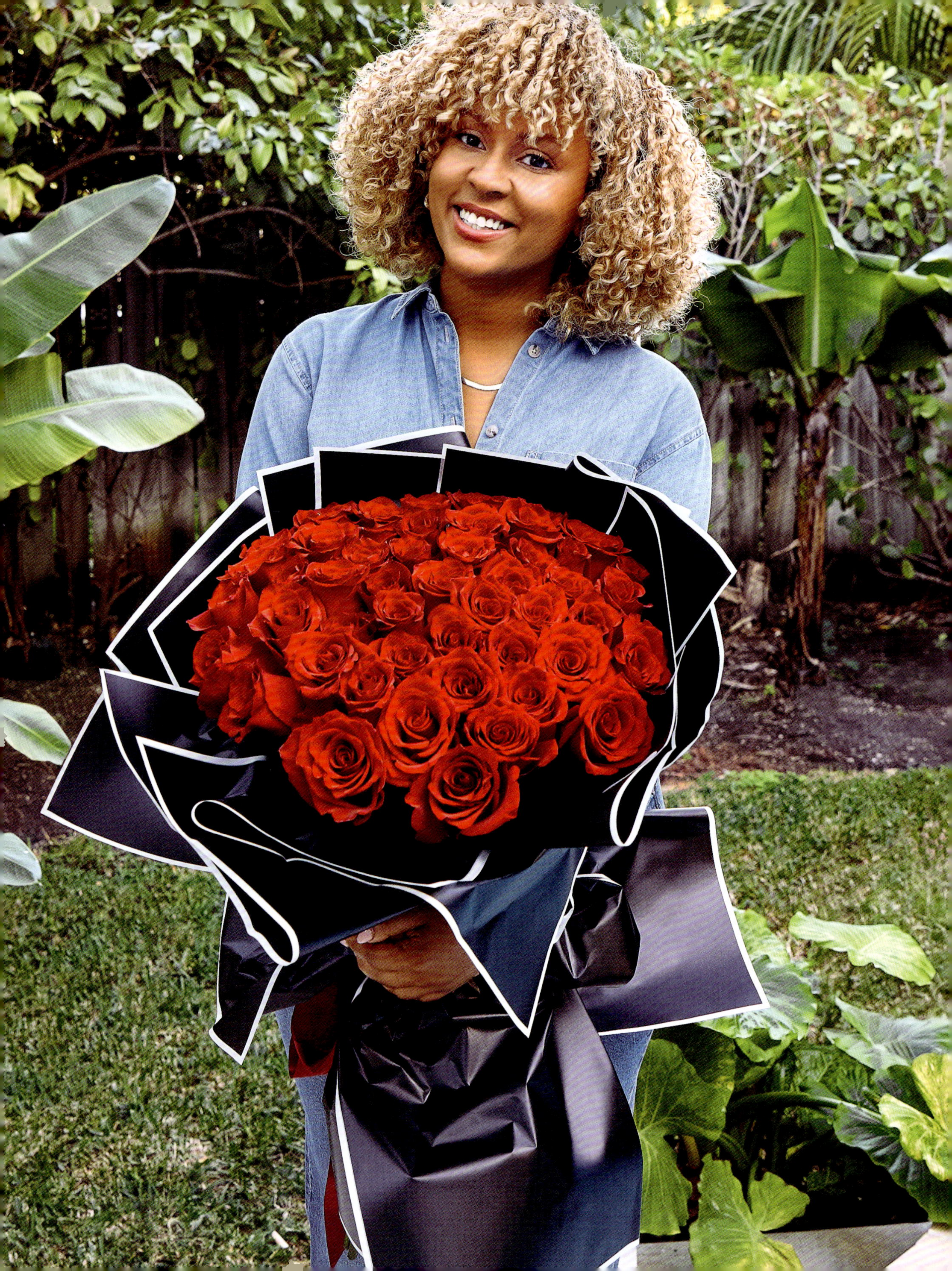

Acknowledgments

It takes a village to write a cookbook, and I am beyond grateful for mine.

Without God, none of this would be possible. Thank you, Jesus, for placing the right people in my life at the right time to make this dream a reality.

To my fans—you inspire me every single day. You fuel my fire and motivate me to pour my heart into everything I do. Thank you for buying, streaming, supporting, engaging, and loving me. Your kindness, loyalty, and patience as I wrote this book meant everything. Thank you for cooking my recipes, loving them, and sharing them. I'm grateful for you every day.

To Tara Hall, my soul sister, recipe tester, and developer—meeting you was the beginning of my career. You've poured so much of yourself into this brand, and your heart and soul are in so many of these recipes. You are an incredible chef, an amazing partner, and one of the best women I know. It's been a joy working and growing with you. Here's to a lifetime of more success—I love you dearly.

To Ashley Cote—without you, *Everything's Good* wouldn't be. Thank you for jumping on the plane as it was taking off and seeing this through. For holding my hand when I needed it, squeezing it when it mattered, demanding excellence, and making sure it happened. You managed this project with class and grace. You are brilliant.

To my co-editor, Raquel Pelzel—it has been an honor to work with you. Your soulful and intentional editing melted my heart. You shaped me into a better writer. Thank you for believing in me.

To Jennifer Sit—thank you for your refined approach to cookbook writing. Your attention to detail and thoughtful guidance helped turn this from a creative vision into a beautifully cohesive cookbook. I am grateful for you.

To Brittany Conerly—thank you for capturing such stunning photos and for your patience, strength, and positivity even when it was super hard to get *the* shot. You always got it done. You pushed through every challenge, and the results are breathtaking.

To my design team, Evi & Evi Studio—thank you for bringing my vision to life. You created something beyond what I could have imagined. Evi, working with you was an absolute joy. You're a light, and this book feels like me because of you.

To the Clarkson Potter team, Robert, Elaine, and Stephanie—thank you for your meticulous editing, planning, and dedication. We did it!

To Noah Swimmer—thank you for holding down the business side while I poured everything into this book. I appreciate you more than you know.

To the photo team, Mariana Diaz, Alexander de Pina, and Jewel—thank you for your hard work and dedication. Shooting 100 soulful comfort food recipes wasn't easy, but you made it happen.

To my agents, Mia and Sarah of Park & Fine—thank you for your professionalism, support, and belief in me. You pushed for me, and for that I'm grateful.

To Elisa Ung—thank you for writing in my voice and telling my stories so beautifully. I still can't believe how perfectly you captured it all. You're incredibly talented and a joy to work with.

To my incredible assistants, Raquel Pereira, Jhazmyn Sandifer, and Charmaine Mukurazhizha—thank you for your dedication and support throughout this process.

To my best friend, Chanel—thank you for being by my side through it all. For letting me cry, vent, and feel everything it took to make this happen. You've been my rock since the beginning.

To my close friends, Amber, Rhaelynn, Shenice, Rouxx, Karolina, Adrianna, Lyana, Will, Charlotte, Rebecca, Morgan Alexander, and Stephanie—thank you for listening to me talk about this nonstop and for always supporting me. I love you.

To my dad and stepmom, Kylie—thank you for helping take care of my puppy, Willow, so I could focus on this project. I love you!

Index

Note: Page references in *italics* indicate photographs.

A
Al dente, defined, 19
Apricots
  Duck Sauce, 249
Artichoke, Spinach, and Crab–Stuffed Shrimp, *38*, 39

B
Bacon
  Island Pasta Soup, 60, *61*
  Marry Me Chicken Soup, *58*, 59
  Mofongo con Camarones de Ajillo, *189*, 190–91, *192*
  New Year's Black-Eyed Peas, *196*, 197
  Pizza Supreme Dip, *26*, 27
  The Ultimate Loaded Baked Potato Soup, *62*, 63
Banana Pudding, Backyard, *224*, 225
Basil
  Easy Peasy Pesto, 245
Beans
  Arroz con Gandules, 170–72, *171*
  Classic Chili, *134*, 135
  Jamaican-Style Oxtail with Rice and Peas, 110–11, *112*
  New Year's Black-Eyed Peas, *196*, 197
  One-Pot Dirty Rice with Chicken and Sausage, *160*, 161
  Puerto Rican (Habichuelas Guisadas), *146*, 147
  Red, and Rice, Louisiana, *200*, 201
Beef
  Chopped Cheese Sliders, *46*, 47
  Classic Chili, *134*, 135
  Cola-Braised Short Ribs, *144*, 145
  Freezer Door Breakfast Sandos, 120, *121*
  Hooked-Up Hamburger Pasta, 158, *159*
  Jamaican-Style Oxtail with Rice and Peas, 110–11, *112*
  One-Pot Dirty Rice with Chicken and Sausage, *160*, 161
  Pastelón, *174*, 175
  Puerto Rican Pepper Steak, *136*, 137
  Straight-Fire Smash Burgers, 116, *117*
  Tacos, Crunchy, *86*, 87
Biscuit Bake, Sausage and Gravy, 202, *203*
Bread. *See also* Tortillas
  Cheesy Chicken Alfredo, *34*, 35
  Crunchy Garlic Toast, *30*, 31
  Honey Butter Corn, 182, *183*
  Honey Butter Hawaiian Rolls, 24, *25*
  Parmesan Garlic Breadsticks, 64
  Pudding, Brioche, 212, *213*
Broil, defined, 19
Brussels, Southern-Fried Cabbage with, 198, *199*
Buffalo Chicken Taquitos, 36, *37*
Burgers, Straight-Fire Smash, 116, *117*

C
Cabbage
  Copycat Panda Chow Mein, *104*, 105
  Shrimp Egg Rolls, 96, *97*
  Southern-Fried, with Brussels, 198, *199*
Cakes
  Classic New York–Style Cheesecake, *210*, 211
  Cookies and Cream Tres Leches, *218*, 219
Ceviche, Shrimp and Mango, *74*, 75
Champagne Sauce, Mussels with, *30*, 31
Cheese. *See also* Cream Cheese
  Blackened Fish and Grits, 162, *163*
  Buffalo Chicken Taquitos, 36, *37*
  Cajun Crab-Stuffed Oysters, *44*, 45
  Cheesy Chicken Alfredo Bread, *34*, 35
  Cheesy Chipotle Chicken Quesadillas, *128*, 129
  Creamy Mac and, *180*, 181
  Creamy Roasted Garlic Dip with Italian Sausage, *40*, 41
  Creamy Shrimp and Crab–Stuffed Shells, 138, *139*
  Creamy White Chicken Enchiladas with Salsa Verde, 124, *125*
  Easy Peasy Pesto, 245
  Freezer Door Breakfast Sandos, 120, *121*
  Garlic Parmesan Chicken Thighs and Potatoes, *142*, 143
  Garlic Parmesan French Fries, *114*, 115
  Goes-with-Everything Salad, 68, *69*
  Hooked-Up Hamburger Pasta, 158, *159*
  Marry Me Chicken Soup, *58*, 59
  Parmesan Garlic Breadsticks, 64
  Pastelón, *174*, 175
  Pizza Supreme Dip, *26*, 27
  Sausage and Gravy Biscuit Bake, 202, *203*
  Secret Ingredient Chicken Parmesan, *156*, 157
  Sliders, Chopped, *46*, 47
  Spicy Lasagna Soup, *50*, 51
  Spinach, Crab, and Artichoke–Stuffed Shrimp, *38*, 39
  Straight-Fire Smash Burgers, 116, *117*
  Tuscan Chicken Meatballs with Sun-Dried Tomatoes and Spinach, 148, *149*
  The Ultimate Loaded Baked Potato Soup, *62*, 63
Cheesecake, Classic New York–Style, *210*, 211
Chicken
  Alfredo Bread, Cheesy, *34*, 35
  Buffalo, Taquitos, 36, *37*
  and Dumplings, Creamy, 56, *57*
  Empanadas, Juicy Red Sofrito, 32, *33*
  Enchiladas, Creamy White, with Salsa Verde, 124, *125*
  Fried, Real-Deal, *194*, 195
  General Tso's, *98*, 99
  Indian-Style, *122*, 123
  Jerk, Caribbean-Style, 80, *81*
  Meatballs, Tuscan, with Sun-Dried Tomatoes and Spinach, 148, *149*
  Nuggets, Drive-Thru, *118*, 119
  Parmesan, Secret Ingredient, *156*, 157
  The Perfect Pollo Guisado, *132*, 133
  Quesadillas, Cheesy Chipotle, *128*, 129
  and Rice Bowls, Halal Cart, with Tzatziki Sauce, *108*, 109
  Rum and Cola Wings, *42*, 43
  and Sausage, One-Pot Dirty Rice with, *160*, 161

Soup, Abuelita's (aka Kick the Cold Soup), 52, *53*
Soup, Marry Me, *58*, 59
Thighs and Potatoes, Garlic Parmesan, *142*, 143
Wings, New York City–Style (aka Chinese Takeout Wings), 102, *103*
Chili, Classic, 134, *135*
Chimichurri Sauce, Traditional, *243*, 244
Chocolate Chip Cookies, Brown Butter, *214*, 215
Cilantro
  Abuela's Green Sofrito, 233, *234*
  -Lime Rice, 140, *141*
  My Famous Red Sofrito, *235*, 236
  Peruvian Ají Verde Sauce, 242, *243*
  Pico de Gallo, 88
  Salsa Verde, 55, 238
Cobbler, Biscuit-Top Peach, 216, *217*
Coconut
  Coquito, *168*, 169
Cod, Lemon-Butter, *78*, 79
Cola
  -Braised Short Ribs, 144, *145*
  and Rum Wings, *42*, 43
Collard Greens with Smoked Turkey, *184*, 185
Cookies, Brown Butter Chocolate Chip, *214*, 215
Cookies and Cream Tres Leches, *218*, 219
Cooking
  blending flavors, 16
  equipment and tools, 18
  glossary of terms, 19
  six important elements, 17
  six steps to joy, 20–21
Coquito, *168*, 169
Corn
  Bread, Honey Butter, 182, *183*
  Cajun Lemon Pepper, *72*, 73
Crab
  GAH DAMN Gumbo, *150*, 151–53
  Papi's Seafood Pasta Salad, *82*, 83
  and Shrimp–Stuffed Shells, Creamy, *138*, 139
  Spinach, and Artichoke–Stuffed Shrimp, *38*, 39
  -Stuffed Oysters, Cajun, *44*, 45
Cream Cheese
  Classic New York–Style Cheesecake, *210*, 211
  Pizza Supreme Dip, *26*, 27
  and Plantain–Stuffed Pork Chops with Guava Sauce, *84*, 85

Strawberries and Cream Croissant Bake, 208, *209*
Crème Brûlée Sweet Potato Pie, *222*, 223
Croissant Bake, Strawberries and Cream, 208, *209*
Cucumbers
  Goes-with-Everything Salad, *68*, 69
  Shrimp and Mango Ceviche, *74*, 75
  Tzatziki Sauce, *108*, 109
Culantro
  Abuela's Green Sofrito, 233, *234*
  My Famous Red Sofrito, *235*, 236

D
Deglaze, defined, 19
Desserts, list of, 7
Dips
  Pizza Supreme, *26*, 27
  Roasted Garlic, Creamy, with Italian Sausage, *40*, 41
Dressing, The Real MVP Ranch, *240*, 241
Drinks
  Coquito, *168*, 169
  Good Vibes Rum Punch, *76*, 77
  Mango House Margarita, *70*, 71
  Sip Slow Sangria, *90*, 91
Duck Sauce, 249

E
Egg Rolls, Shrimp, *96*, 97
Eggs
  Freezer Door Breakfast Sandos, 120, *121*
  Empanadas, Juicy Red Sofrito Chicken, *32*, 33
  Enchiladas, Creamy White Chicken, with Salsa Verde, 124, *125*
Equipment and tools, 18

F
Fish
  Blackened, and Grits, 162, *163*
  Fried, Down South–Style, *204*, 205
  GAH DAMN Gumbo, *150*, 151–53
  Lemon-Butter Cod, *78*, 79
  Seared Salmon with Creamy Lemon Orzo and Spinach, 130, *131*
Flan, The Very Best, 220, *221*
French Fries, Garlic Parmesan, *114*, 115
Fruit. *See also specific fruits*
  Sip Slow Sangria, *90*, 91
Fry (deep and shallow), defined, 19

G
Garlic
  Abuela's Green Sofrito, 233, *234*
  Easy Peasy Pesto, 245
  Jerk Marinade, 239
  Mofongo con Camarones de Ajillo, *189*, 190–91, *192*
  My Famous Red Sofrito, *235*, 236
  Parmesan Breadsticks, 64
  Parmesan Chicken Thighs and Potatoes, *142*, 143
  Parmesan French Fries, *114*, 115
  Roasted, Dip, Creamy, with Italian Sausage, *40*, 41
  Toast, Crunchy, *30*, 31
  Traditional Chimichurri Sauce, *243*, 244
Grits, Blackened Fish and, 162, *163*
Guava Sauce, Plantain and Cream Cheese–Stuffed Pork Chops with, *84*, 85
Gumbo, GAH DAMN, *150*, 151–53

H
Habichuelas Guisadas (Puerto Rican Beans), *146*, 147
Ham
  Habichuelas Guisadas (Puerto Rican Beans), *146*, 147
  Louisiana Red Beans and Rice, *200*, 201
  Southern-Fried Cabbage with Brussels, 198, *199*
Herbs. *See also* Cilantro
  Abuela's Green Sofrito, 233, *234*
  Easy Peasy Pesto, 245
  My Famous Red Sofrito, *235*, 236
  Traditional Chimichurri Sauce, *243*, 244
Hominy
  The Very Best Pozole Verde, *54*, 55
Honey
  Butter Corn Bread, 182, *183*
  Butter Hawaiian Rolls, *24*, 25
  Cajun Lemon Pepper Corn, *72*, 73
  Hot, Fried Shrimp, *28*, 29
  The Perfect Sauce for Everything, 232
Hot sauce
  Buffalo Chicken Taquitos, *36*, 37
  Hot Honey Fried Shrimp, *28*, 29

J
Jerk Chicken, Caribbean-Style, 80, *81*
Jerk Marinade, 239

Index

K

Key Lime Pie, *226*, 227
Knives, 18

L

Lemon
 -Butter Cod, *78*, 79
 Orzo and Spinach, Creamy, Seared Salmon with, 130, *131*
 Pepper Corn, Cajun, 72, *73*
Lime
 -Cilantro Rice, 140, *141*
 Key, Pie, *226*, 227
 Mango House Margarita, *70*, 71
 Shrimp and Mango Ceviche, *74*, 75

M

Mango
 Mango House Margarita, *70*, 71
 and Shrimp Ceviche, *74*, 75
Margarita, Mango House, *70*, 71
Marinade, Jerk, 239
Marinara sauce
 Pizza Supreme Dip, *26*, 27
 Secret Ingredient Chicken Parmesan, *156*, 157
Marinate, defined, 19
Meatballs, Tuscan Chicken, with Sun-Dried Tomatoes and Spinach, 148, *149*
Mofongo con Camarones de Ajillo, *189*, 190–91, *192*
Mussels with Champagne Sauce, *30*, 31
Mustard
 The Perfect Sauce for Everything, 232

N

Noodles
 Abuelita's Chicken Soup (aka Kick the Cold Soup), 52, *53*
 Copycat Panda Chow Mein, *104*, 105

O

Oranges
 Good Vibes Rum Punch, 76, *77*
 Sip Slow Sangria, *90*, 91
Oysters, Cajun Crab-Stuffed, 44, *45*

P

Pancakes, On-Point, with Brown Butter Syrup, 228, *229*
Panda Chow Mein, Copycat, *104*, 105
Parsley
 Traditional Chimichurri Sauce, *243*, 244

Pasta. *See also* Noodles
 Copycat Panda Chow Mein, *104*, 105
 Creamy Mac and Cheese, *180*, 181
 Creamy Shrimp and Crab–Stuffed Shells, 138, *139*
 Hooked-Up Hamburger, 158, *159*
 Seafood Salad, Papi's, *82*, 83
 Seared Salmon with Creamy Lemon Orzo and Spinach, 130, *131*
 Soup, Island, 60, *61*
 Spicy Lasagna Soup, *50*, 51
Pastelón, *174*, 175
Peach Cobbler, Biscuit-Top, 216, *217*
Pepperoni
 Pizza Supreme Dip, *26*, 27
Pepper(s)
 Abuela's Green Sofrito, 233, *234*
 Cajun-Spiced Potatoes, 154, *155*
 Cheesy Chipotle Chicken Quesadillas, *128*, 129
 Hooked-Up Hamburger Pasta, 158, *159*
 Island Pasta Soup, 60, *61*
 Jerk Marinade, 239
 My Famous Red Sofrito, *235*, 236
 Peruvian Ají Verde Sauce, 242, *243*
 Salsa Verde, 55, 238
 Steak, Puerto Rican, *136*, 137
 Traditional Chimichurri Sauce, *243*, 244
Pernil (Puerto Rican Roast Pork), 166, *167*
Pesto, Easy Peasy, 245
Pico de Gallo, 88
Pies
 Crème Brûlée Sweet Potato, *222*, 223
 Key Lime, *226*, 227
Pineapple
 Good Vibes Rum Punch, 76, *77*
 Pizza Supreme Dip, *26*, 27
Plantain(s)
 and Cream Cheese–Stuffed Pork Chops with Guava Sauce, 84, *85*
 Mofongo con Camarones de Ajillo, *189*, 190–91, *192*
 Pastelón, *174*, 175
Pollo Guisado, The Perfect, *132*, 133
Pork. *See also* Bacon; Ham; Sausage
 Char Siu, 106, *107*
 Chops, Plantain and Cream Cheese–Stuffed, with Guava Sauce, 84, *85*
 Classic Chili, 134, *135*
 Fried Rice, *94*, 95
 Puerto Rican Roast (Pernil), 166, *167*
 The Very Best Pozole Verde, *54*, 55

Potato(es)
 Cajun-Spiced, 154, *155*
 and Chicken, Garlic Parmesan, *142*, 143
 Garlic Parmesan French Fries, *114*, 115
 Loaded Baked, Soup, The Ultimate, *62*, 63
 Marry Me Chicken Soup, *58*, 59
 The Perfect Pollo Guisado, *132*, 133
 Sweet, Pie, Crème Brûlée, *222*, 223
Pots and pans, 18
Pozole Verde, The Very Best, *54*, 55
Pudding
 Backyard Banana, 224, *225*
 Brioche Bread, 212, *213*

Q

Quesadillas, Cheesy Chipotle Chicken, *128*, 129

R

Reduce, defined, 19
Rice
 Arroz con Gandules, 170–72, *171*
 and Chicken Bowls, Halal Cart, with Tzatziki Sauce, *108*, 109
 Cilantro-Lime, 140, *141*
 cooking directions, 140
 One-Pot Dirty, with Chicken and Sausage, *160*, 161
 and Peas, Jamaican-Style Oxtail with, 110–11, *112*
 Pork Fried, *94*, 95
 and Red Beans, Louisiana, *200*, 201
 White, Classic, 140, *141*
 Yellow, Spanish-Style, 140, *141*
Rolls, Honey Butter Hawaiian, 24, *25*
Roux, defined, 19
Rum
 Brioche Bread Pudding, 212, *213*
 and Cola Wings, *42*, 43
 Coquito, *168*, 169
 Crème Brûlée Sweet Potato Pie, *222*, 223
 Punch, Good Vibes, 76, *77*
 The Very Best Flan, 220, *221*

S

Salads
 Goes-with-Everything, 68, *69*
 Seafood Pasta, Papi's, *82*, 83
Salmon, Seared, with Creamy Lemon Orzo and Spinach, 130, *131*
Salsa Verde, 55, 238
Salsa Verde, Creamy White Chicken Enchiladas with, 124, *125*

Sandwiches
  Chopped Cheese Sliders, *46*, 47
  Freezer Door Breakfast Sandos, 120, *121*
Sangria, Sip Slow, *90*, 91
Sauces
  Abuela's Green Sofrito, 233, *234*
  Bold and Smoky BBQ, 248
  Chimichurri, Traditional, *243*, 244
  Duck, 249
  Easy Peasy Pesto, 245
  for Everything, The Perfect, 232
  Jerk Marinade, 239
  My Famous Red Sofrito, *235*, 236
  Peruvian Ají Verde, 242, *243*
  The Real MVP Ranch Dressing, *240*, 241
  Salsa Verde, 55, 238
  Teriyaki, All-in-One, 247
  Tzatziki, *108*, 109
Sausage
  and Chicken, One-Pot Dirty Rice with, *160*, 161
  Classic Chili, 134, *135*
  Freezer Door Breakfast Sandos, 120, *121*
  GAH DAMN Gumbo, *150*, 151–53
  and Gravy Biscuit Bake, 202, *203*
  Island Pasta Soup, 60, *61*
  Italian, Creamy Roasted Garlic Dip with, 40, *41*
  Louisiana Red Beans and Rice, *200*, 201
  Pizza Supreme Dip, *26*, 27
  Southern-Fried Cabbage with Brussels, 198, *199*
  Spicy Lasagna Soup, *50*, 51
Sauté, defined, 19
Sear, defined, 19
Shellfish. *See also* Shrimp
  Cajun Crab-Stuffed Oysters, 44, *45*
  Creamy Shrimp and Crab–Stuffed Shells, 138, *139*
  GAH DAMN Gumbo, *150*, 151–53
  Mussels with Champagne Sauce, *30*, 31
  Papi's Seafood Pasta Salad, *82*, 83
Shrimp
  and Crab–Stuffed Shells, Creamy, 138, *139*
  Egg Rolls, 96, *97*
  Hot Honey Fried, 28, *29*
  and Mango Ceviche, *74*, 75
  Mofongo con Camarones de Ajillo, *189*, 190–91, *192*

Papi's Seafood Pasta Salad, *82*, 83
Spinach, Crab, and Artichoke–Stuffed, *38*, 39
Simmer, defined, 19
Sliders, Chopped Cheese, *46*, 47
Sofrito
  Green, Abuela's, 233, *234*
  Red, My Famous, *235*, 236
Soups
  Chicken, Abuelita's (aka Kick the Cold Soup), 52, *53*
  Chicken, Marry Me, *58*, 59
  Creamy Chicken and Dumplings, 56, *57*
  Island Pasta, 60, *61*
  Loaded Baked Potato, The Ultimate, *62*, 63
  Spicy Lasagna, *50*, 51
  The Very Best Pozole Verde, *54*, 55
Spinach
  Cajun Crab-Stuffed Oysters, 44, *45*
  Crab, and Artichoke–Stuffed Shrimp, *38*, 39
  Easy Peasy Pesto, 245
  and Lemon Orzo, Creamy, Seared Salmon with, 130, *131*
  and Sun-Dried Tomatoes, Tuscan Chicken Meatballs with, 148, *149*
Squash
  Habichuelas Guisadas (Puerto Rican Beans), *146*, 147
Stews
  Cola-Braised Short Ribs, 144, *145*
  GAH DAMN Gumbo, *150*, 151–53
  Jamaican-Style Oxtail with Rice and Peas, 110–11, *112*
  New Year's Black-Eyed Peas, *196*, 197
  The Perfect Pollo Guisado, *132*, 133
Strawberries and Cream Croissant Bake, 208, *209*
Sweet Potato Pie, Crème Brûlée, *222*, 223

T
Tacos, Crunchy Beef, *86*, 87
Taquitos, Buffalo Chicken, 36, *37*
Tequila
  Mango House Margarita, *70*, 71
Teriyaki Sauce, All-in-One, 247
Toast, Crunchy Garlic, *30*, 31
Tomatillos
  Salsa Verde, 55, 238
Tomatoes. *See also* Marinara sauce
  Bold and Smoky BBQ Sauce, 248
  Classic Chili, 134, *135*

Goes-with-Everything Salad, 68, *69*
Indian-Style Chicken, *122*, 123
Marry Me Chicken Soup, *58*, 59
My Famous Red Sofrito, *235*, 236
Pastelón, *174*, 175
Pico de Gallo, 88
Shrimp and Mango Ceviche, *74*, 75
Spicy Lasagna Soup, *50*, 51
Sun-Dried, and Spinach, Tuscan Chicken Meatballs with, 148, *149*
Tortillas
  Buffalo Chicken Taquitos, 36, *37*
  Cheesy Chipotle Chicken Quesadillas, *128*, 129
  Creamy White Chicken Enchiladas with Salsa Verde, 124, *125*
  Crunchy Beef Tacos, *86*, 87
Tres Leches, Cookies and Cream, *218*, 219
Turkey
  Cajun Butter, *176*, 177–79
  Louisiana Red Beans and Rice, *200*, 201
  New Year's Black-Eyed Peas, *196*, 197
  Smoked, Collard Greens with, *184*, 185
Tzatziki Sauce, *108*, 109

W
Wine
  Sip Slow Sangria, *90*, 91

Y
Yams, Candied, 186, *187*
Yogurt
  Tzatziki Sauce, *108*, 109

Index 255

Clarkson Potter/Publishers
An imprint of the Crown Publishing Group
A division of Penguin Random House LLC
1745 Broadway
New York, NY 10019
clarksonpotter.com
penguinrandomhouse.com

Copyright © 2025 by Zaria Chapman
Photographs copyright © 2025 by Brittany Conerly
Penguin Random House values and supports copyright. Copyright fuels creativity, encourages diverse voices, promotes free speech, and creates a vibrant culture. Thank you for buying an authorized edition of this book and for complying with copyright laws by not reproducing, scanning, or distributing any part of it in any form without permission. You are supporting writers and allowing Penguin Random House to continue to publish books for every reader. Please note that no part of this book may be used or reproduced in any manner for the purpose of training artificial intelligence technologies or systems.

Clarkson Potter is a trademark and Potter with colophon is a registered trademark of Penguin Random House LLC.

Library of Congress Cataloging-in-Publication Data
Names: Chapman, Toni, author. | Conerly, Brittany, photographer.
Title: Everything's good: cozy classics you'll cook always & forever / Toni Chapman; photographs by Brittany Conerly.
Description: New York: Clarkson Potter/Publishers, [2025] | Includes index.
Identifiers: LCCN 2024056733 (print) | LCCN 2024056734 (ebook) | ISBN 9780593800782 (hardcover) | ISBN 9780593800799 (ebook)
Subjects: LCSH: International cooking. | Cooking, Latin American. | Comfort food. | LCGFT: Cookbooks.
Classification: LCC TX725.A1 C5236 2025 (print) | LCC TX725.A1 (ebook) | DDC 641.59—dc23/eng/20241205
LC record available at https://lccn.loc.gov/2024056733
LC ebook record available at https://lccn.loc.gov/2024056734

ISBN 978-0-593-80078-2
Ebook ISBN 978-0-593-80079-9

Editors: Jennifer Sit and Raquel Pelzel
Editorial assistant: Elaine Hennig
Designer: Evi-O.Studio
Design manager: Robert Diaz
Production designer: Christina Self
Production editor: Liana Faughnan
Production: Jessica Heim
Color manager: Phil Leung
Compositors: Merri Ann Morrell and Hannah Hunt
Food stylist assistants: Jessica Darakjian and Daniela Swamp
Prop stylist assistant: Caitlin Dinneen
Photo retoucher: Andrew Grune
Copy editor: Kate Slate
Proofreaders: Rachel Markowitz and Eldes Tran
Indexer: Elizabeth Parson
Publicists: Felix Cruz and David Hawk
Marketers: Monica Stanton and Joey Lozada

Manufactured in China

10 9 8 7 6 5 4 3 2 1

First Edition

The authorized representative in the EU for product safety and compliance is Penguin Random House Ireland, Morrison Chambers, 32 Nassau Street, Dublin D02 YH68, Ireland, https://eu-contact.penguin.ie.

Toni Chapman is a passionate home cook, a recipe developer, and the creator of *Toni's Recipes* (tonisrecipes.com) and *The Moody Foody*, where she shares bold, comforting dishes made for real life. Her flavor-packed, approachable cooking has landed her on *Good Morning America*, *Live with Kelly and Mark*, and *CBS Mornings*. Inspired by childhood favorites, takeout classics, and family traditions, she designed her recipes to impress, without the stress. Based in Miami, Toni loves cooking, entertaining, and traveling.

Cover design: Evi-O.Studio
Cover photographs: Brittany Conerly

Clarkson Potter/Publishers
New York
clarksonpotter.com